Culture of the Future

Studies on the History of Society and Culture
Victoria E. Bonnell and Lynn Hunt, Editors

Culture of the Future

*The Proletkult Movement in
Revolutionary Russia*

Lynn Mally

UNIVERSITY OF CALIFORNIA PRESS
BERKELEY LOS ANGELES OXFORD

University of California Press
Berkeley and Los Angeles, California

University of California Press, Ltd.
Oxford, England

© 1990 by
The Regents of the University of California

Library of Congress Cataloging-in-Publication Data
Mally, Lynn.
  Culture of the future: the Proletkult movement in revolutionary Russia /
Lynn Mally.
    p.   cm.—(Studies on the history of society and culture)
  Bibliography: p.
  Includes index.
  ISBN 0–520–06577–8 (alk. paper)
  1. Communism and culture—Soviet Union. 2. Soviet Union—Cultural
policy. 3. Labor and laboring classes—Soviet Union—Intellectual life.
  4. Socialism and the arts—Soviet Union. 5. Soviet Union—Politics and
government—1917–1936. I. Title. II. Series.
HX523.M3635   1990
306'.345'0947—dc19   89-30765
                                                                            CIP

Printed in the United States of America

1 2 3 4 5 6 7 8 9

The paper used in this publication meets the minimum requirements of
American National Standard for Information Sciences—Permanence of
Paper for Printed Library Materials, ANSI Z39.48-1984.

To my mother

Contents

Illustrations

Acknowledgments

Many friends and colleagues have helped to make this book better. Lidiia Alekseevna Pinegina, my academic adviser in the Soviet Union, shared her ideas and research with me; her scholarly generosity was a model of *glasnost'* before its time. Jutta Scherrer's continuing interest in my work inspired me to see this book to its conclusion. Kendall Bailes, Jeffrey Brooks, and Richard Stites carefully read the dissertation from which this book emerged; their encouragement and criticism led me to rethink many parts of the manuscript. Peter Kenez and Richard Sakwa gave incisive responses to several chapters. I was very fortunate to have a wonderful dissertation committee whose assistance continued long after I received my degree. Nicholas Riasanovsky offered many useful suggestions for turning the thesis into a book. Victoria Bonnell approached both the dissertation and the manuscript with a keen critical eye; her comments have greatly improved the final product. Most of all, I would like to thank Reginald Zelnik for his friendship and tireless commitment to his former students. His meticulous reading of the manuscript enriched this book in both form and substance.

I am indebted to the following institutions: the International Research Exchanges Board, which funded a research trip to Moscow; Temple University, for providing me with a summer stipend; and the American Philosophical Society, for research funding. I was fortunate to receive permission to work in Soviet archives when that was still an unusual occurrence, and the staff of the Central State Archive of Literature and Art deserves credit for its cheerful assistance. Both Edward Kasinec, of the New York Public Library, and Hilja Kukk, of the Hoover Institution for War, Revolution, and Peace, went far out of their way to help me.

Sheila Levine of the University of California Press has been a model editor, and I wish to thank her for her constant enthusiasm for this project. The Indiana University Press has kindly allowed me to reprint parts of my article "Intellectuals in the Proletkult: Problems of Authority and Expertise," forthcoming in *Party, State, and Society in the Russian Civil War*, edited by Diane Koenker, William G. Rosenberg, and Ronald Grigor Suny.

At every step along the way my large extended family—siblings, cousins, aunts, and uncles—provided emotional support and comic relief. Special thanks go to my parents, Helen and Samuel Urton, who encouraged me to pursue what was for them an unusual career. In the last stages of revisions my daughter Nora was born and did much to keep my work in perspective by showing only an occasional interest in the flashing lights on the computer screen. Robert Moeller was part of this project from beginning to end and read more drafts of this book than either of us can recall. His contributions as a historian, critic, and cook were considerable; as a friend, they were even greater.

Note on Dates
and Transliteration

Because this book spans the pre- and postrevolutionary years, I have employed two dating systems. All dates before February 1918 are given according to the Old Style (Julian) calendar. After that time they follow the New Style (Gregorian) calendar.

I have used a modified Library of Congress transliteration system, with two exceptions. Well-known names, such as Eisenstein, appear here in their generally accepted Anglicized forms. In the text, but not in Russian references in the notes, I have also omitted the soft sign: thus Proletkul't becomes Proletkult.

In archival references I have used standard abbreviations for Russian terms: op. for *opis'*, d. for *delo*, l. for *list*, and ob. for *oborot*.

Introduction

In October 1919 Petrograd, home of the Russian Revolution, was a devastated city. Severe food shortages had prompted the exodus of large parts of the population. To make a difficult situation even worse, the White Army general N. N. Iudenich began an assault on the city, bringing his armies almost to the suburbs. Yet this emergency did not stop a respected theater director from holding a lecture series on the history of art in an organization called the Proletkult, even though the audience changed constantly because of military mobilizations. At the same time, the Proletkult theater was preparing a performance for the second anniversary of the revolution, a play written by a Red Army soldier who had helped to storm the Winter Palace.[1]

This dramatic mix of political insecurity, physical privation, and cultural creation was not unusual in revolutionary Russia. Similar episodes can easily be found in contemporary journals and newspapers and in the memoirs of cultural activists. They illustrate quite graphically that the proponents of revolution were not willing to limit their goals to the establishment of a new political and economic order. They hoped to create a new cultural order as well.

1. "Nasha kul'tura: Petrogradskii Proletkul't," *Griadushchee*, no. 7/8 (1919), p. 31. The lecturer was E. P. Karpov, former director of the Aleksandrinskii Theater. The play, *Za krasnye sovety*, was written by Pavel Arskii, one of the leaders of the Petrograd Proletkult.

Of course culture is an ambiguous term with many different meanings, ranging from the shared values and assumptions of an entire society to a simple synonym for fine art. Bolsheviks held no common definition, and Lenin himself used the word in strikingly different ways. Sometimes he meant the accumulated knowledge of educated elites, other times the civilized accomplishments of modern industrial societies, such as cleanliness and punctuality.[2] Together with his Bolshevik colleagues, he realized that cultural transformation was an integral part of the revolutionary process, but precisely what this meant for the new government was not immediately apparent. The blueprints for building a socialist culture were no clearer than those for a socialist polity.

Revolutions invariably challenge the cultural foundations of society, whether the participants consciously acknowledge this or not. Russian revolutionaries, like their Jacobin predecessors, welcomed the challenge. The transformation of Russian culture was the topic of wide-ranging debates in the early Soviet years. All the key elements were open to dispute—the meaning of culture, the revolutionaries' power to change culture, and the consequences that such change would have for the new regime.[3]

In these discussions there was very little common ground. Politicians, educators, and artists all concurred that cultural reform in their vast country, with its large illiterate population, was an enormous task. They also rejected a tradition that sharply divided the culture of the privileged elite from that of

2. For Lenin's views on culture see V. V. Gorbunov, *Lenin i sotsialisticheskaia kul'tura* (Moscow, 1972); Zenovia A. Sochor, *Revolution and Culture: The Bogdanov-Lenin Controversy* (Ithaca, 1988), esp. chap. 5; and V. I. Lenin, *V. I. Lenin o literature i iskusstve*, 7th ed., ed. N. Krutikov (Moscow, 1986).

3. The broad range of early Soviet views on cultural transformation is presented in Abbott Gleason, Peter Kenez, and Richard Stites, eds., *Bolshevik Culture: Experiment and Order in the Russian Revolution* (Bloomington, 1985); and William G. Rosenberg, ed., *Bolshevik Visions: First Phase of the Cultural Revolution in Soviet Russia* (Ann Arbor, 1984).

the lower classes. But unanimity ended here. State leaders could not even agree on the pace of change. While Anatolii Lunacharskii, the head of the People's Commissariat of Enlightenment, constantly lobbied for more funds and supplies, Leon Trotsky, Commissar of Defense, questioned the wisdom of devoting too many resources to cultural problems as long as the state was not politically and militarily secure.[4]

Indeed, cultural activists did not even share a common vision of the old culture they wished to leave behind, let alone of the new one they hoped to found. For the most cautious the heritage of the prerevolutionary intelligentsia was a positive and inspiring force. It was enough to pass on select aspects of art and learning to the masses in order to lay the foundations for the new society. The most radical rejected this conservative course of dissemination. They perceived the revolution as a clean break, a chance to discover new artistic images and new patterns of social interaction befitting the revolutionary age.

The passion and turmoil of these cultural debates are missing from most Soviet scholarship of the revolution. Soviet works portray the early years of the regime as the first stage of the Soviet Union's "cultural revolution," a long process through which the masses finally gained the education and cultural sophistication denied them by the old regime.[5] According to the standard scheme the Bolsheviks easily defeated their cultural enemies, defined as the intellectual foes of egalitarianism, on the one hand, and, on the other, extreme radicals who rejected the value of all inherited knowledge. The

4. See James C. McClelland, "Utopianism versus Revolutionary Heroism in Bolshevik Policy: The Proletarian Culture Debate," *Slavic Review*, vol. 39, no. 3 (1980), pp. 403–25.

5. For an overview of this scholarship see S. A. Andronov, ed., *KPSS vo glave kul'turnoi revoliutsii v SSSR* (Moscow, 1972); G. G. Karpov, *O sovetskoi kul'ture i kul'turnoi revoliutsii SSSR* (Moscow, 1954); M. P. Kim, ed., *Kul'turnaia revoliutsiia v SSSR, 1917–1965 gg.* (Moscow, 1967); and M. P. Kim, *Velikii Oktiabr' i kul'turnaia revoliutsiia v SSSR* (Moscow, 1967).

state then went on to establish the basis for a literate, culturally unified society, one in which the benefits of art and learning were equally available to all. This interpretation, with its basic theme of continuous progress, obscures the many conflicts among supporters of the new regime, conflicts over such important matters as the kind of education and entertainment that were best suited for the population. It also glosses over the more profound question of whether state-sponsored enlightenment allowed any active, creative role for the people themselves.

A major argument of this book is that the struggle to found a new cultural order was just as contentious as the efforts to change the political and economic foundations of Soviet society. I aim to show this by examining a mass movement that stood in the midst of cultural debates in the early Soviet years. The Proletkult, an acronym for "Proletarian cultural-educational organizations" (*proletarskie kul'turno-prosvetitel'nye organizatsii*), first took shape in Petrograd in 1917, just a few days before the October Revolution. It began as a loose coalition of clubs, factory committees, workers' theaters, and educational societies devoted to the cultural needs of the working class. By 1918 it had expanded into a national movement with a much more ambitious purpose: to define a unique proletarian culture that would inform and inspire the new society.

The Proletkult was controversial first of all because its participants believed that rapid and radical cultural transformation was crucial to the survival of the revolution, a position they presented in loud and insistent terms. The organization's national leaders, and many of its local followers, demanded that culture, however defined, be given the same weight as politics and economics. Despite the military insecurity of the new regime, its political instability, and the rapid economic disintegration caused by the revolution and Civil War, the Proletkult's leaders wanted the state to place considerable resources at their disposal. Without due attention to culture, they warned, the state's political and economic accomplishments would be built on very shaky ground.

The movement's participants not only underscored the importance of culture but also insisted on the primacy of a new culture that would express the values and principles of the victorious working class. Proletarian culture was an amorphous concept that signified many different things at once: the artistic creations and aspirations of workers; the expression of a revolutionary spirit; and, most broadly, the emergent ideology of the proletarian ruling class. Proletkultists themselves could not agree on common definitions, and the altercations in society at large over the value of prerevolutionary models in a revolutionary age also occurred within the movement. Meanwhile, the very notion of a specific class culture raised the ire of many critics, who questioned what such an adamantly proletarian organization could contribute to the creation of a classless society.

The expansive nature of the movement also placed it at the center of cultural debates. At its peak in 1920 the national leadership claimed some four hundred thousand members organized in three hundred branches distributed all over Soviet territory. Despite lack of funds and basic supplies, Proletkult participants founded a wide network of clubs, schools, workshops, choirs, theaters, and agitational troupes that performed on the fronts of the Civil War. The organization's ambitions were as broad as its following. Proletkultists were not just interested in proletarian artistic forms. They also wanted to create a proletarian morality and ethics. Child-rearing, family relations, and scientific education were all within their purview. Because of its far-reaching interests, the Proletkult inspired both admiration and animosity among other groups seeking cultural change, including the state's own educational agencies.

Perhaps most important, the Proletkult engendered controversy because it embodied a politically charged vision of the newly empowered Soviet proletariat. The most committed members took the idea of the "dictatorship of the proletariat" quite literally and accorded all proletarian institutions a privileged position in the new society. They saw the working class as an autonomous, creative force that should be given free rein to express and develop its ideas. In the opinion of Proletkult leaders the Soviet government could not operate as a single-minded advocate for the proletariat because it had to consider the needs of other classes. Therefore, they wanted the Proletkult to be completely independent from state cultural institutions. By making this demand they were challenging the state's authority to stand above and mediate between social classes. Indeed, Proletkultists insisted on independence from the Communist Party as well, claiming that their movement, as the representative of the proletariat's *cultural* interests, was just as important as the party, the representative of its political concerns. These bold demands for autonomy finally led to confrontation. By the end of the Civil War the Communist Party had taken away the Proletkult's independence and placed the organization under the tutelage of the state's cultural bureaucracy.

The Proletkult's clashes with the Communist Party have dominated historical scholarship both in the West and in the Soviet Union, earning it a reputation as an oppositional movement. This idea is reinforced by the fact that the Proletkult's most polemical principles—the primacy of culture and proletarian hegemony—can be traced to a group of left Bolsheviks who questioned Lenin's control of the party faction in the years between the Revolution of 1905 and the First World War. The most important of these leftists was Aleksandr Bogdanov, who produced a dazzling range of work on politics, economics, culture, and science before his death in 1928. Bogdanov believed that in order for a proletarian revolution to be successful, the working class needed cultural preparation. It had to devise its own class ideology and its own proletarian intelligentsia in order to take and wield power. Bogdanov's ideas on these matters outlined a distinct approach to revolutionary politics and tactics that was boldly at odds with Lenin's own.

Soviet scholarship highlights the conflicts between Lenin and Bogdanov over the proper course of political and cultural change. Basing themselves on Lenin's generally harsh criticisms of the movement, Soviet researchers have been overwhelmingly negative. V. V. Gorbunov, the most important Soviet specialist in this area, has deemed the Proletkult a separatist, sectarian, nihilistic, and revisionist organization.[6] His highly influential work presents the Proletkult as a dangerous challenge to the political power of the Communist Party and a threat to the social and intellectual foundations of the regime.

In recent years this negative view has been tempered as scholars have attempted to reclaim at least part of this mass movement as a positive force in Soviet cultural history.[7] For example, Soviet authors are willing to concede that local or-

6. V. V. Gorbunov, "Bor'ba V. I. Lenina s separatistskimi ustremleniiami Proletkul'ta," *Voprosy istorii KPSS*, no. 1 (1958), pp. 29–40; idem, "Iz istorii bor'by Kommunisticheskoi partii s sektanstvom Proletkul'ta," in *Ocherki po istorii sovetskoi nauki i kul'tury*, ed. L. V. Koshman (Moscow, 1968), pp. 29–68; idem, "Iz istorii kul'turno-prosvetitel'noi deiatel'nosti Petrogradskikh bol'shevikov v period podgotovki Oktiabria," *Voprosy istorii KPSS*, no. 2 (1967), pp. 25–35; idem, "Kritika V. I. Leninym teorii Proletkul'ta ob otnoshenii k kul'turnomu naslediiu," *Voprosy istorii KPSS*, no. 5 (1968), pp. 83–93; and idem, *V. I. Lenin i Proletkul't* (Moscow, 1974).

7. See M. P. Kim, "Istoricheskii opyt kul'turnoi revoliutsii v SSSR," *Voprosy istorii*, no. 1 (1968), pp. 109–22, esp. pp. 116–17; V. T. Ermakov, "Ideinaia bor'ba na kul'turnom fronte v pervye gody sovetskoi vlasti," *Voprosy istorii*, no. 11 (1971), pp. 16–31, esp. pp. 27–31; V. A. Razumov, "Rol' rabochego klassa v stroitel'stve sotsialisticheskoi kul'tury v nachale revoliutsii i v gody grazhdanskoi voiny, 1917–1920," in *Rol' rabochego klassa v razvitii sotsialisticheskoi kul'tury*, ed. M. P. Kim and V. P. Naumov (Moscow, 1967), pp. 8–70, esp. pp. 15–25; and I. S. Smirnov, "Leninskaia kontseptsiia kul'turnoi revoliutsii i kritika Proletkul'ta," in *Istoricheskaia nauka i nekotorye problemy sovremennosti*, ed. M. Ia. Gefter (Moscow, 1969), pp. 63–85. Even Gorbunov participates in this revisionism to some extent; see his "Oktiabr' i nachalo kul'turnoi revoliutsii na mestakh," in *Velikii Oktiabr': Istoriia, istoriografiia, istochnovedenie*, ed. Iu. A. Poliakov (Moscow, 1978), pp. 63–74.

ganizations sometimes served a positive role, especially when they ignored the narrow restrictions of proletarian culture and devoted themselves to basic educational work.[8] In one of the latest Soviet works, L. A. Pinegina goes even further in this revision. She insists that Lenin himself favored proletarian culture when it was defined as the cultural empowerment of the working class. In her view—still the exception rather than the rule—much of the Proletkult's activity was inspired by Lenin's vision, not Bogdanov's.[9]

Although differing in many ways from Soviet scholarship, Western studies of the Proletkult have also concentrated primarily on the conflict between Lenin and Bogdanov. The earliest works looked mainly at the implementation of proletarian culture in the arts, especially literature.[10] However, an increasing number of Western scholars have begun to study Bogdanov's voluminous writings in order to find an alternative to Lenin's vision of socialist transformation.[11] When the Proletkult has appeared in these works, it has been presented

8. See, for example, T. A. Khavina, "Bor'ba Kommunisticheskoi partii za Proletkul't i rukovodstvo ego deiatel'nost'iu, 1917–1932 gg." (Candidate Dissertation, Leningrad State University, 1978), which covers the Petrograd/Leningrad Proletkult; N. A. Milonov, "O deiatel'nosti Tul'skogo Proletkul'ta," in *Aktual'nye voprosy istorii literatury*, ed. Z. I. Levinson, N. A. Milonov, and A. F. Sergeicheva (Tula, 1969), pp. 140–63; V. G. Puzyrev, "'Proletkul't' na Dal'nem Vostoke," in *Iz istorii russkoi i zarubezhnoi literatury*, ed. V. N. Kasatkina, T. T. Napolona, and P. A. Shchekotov (Saratov, 1968), vol. 2, pp. 89–105; and V. L. Soskin and V. P. Butorin, "Proletkul't v Sibiri," in *Problemy istorii sovetskoi Sibiri: Sbornik nauchnykh trudov*, ed. A. S. Moskovskii (Novosibirsk, 1973), pp. 133–46.

9. See L. A. Pinegina, "Organizatsii proletarskoi kul'tury 1920-kh godov i kul'turnoe nasledie," *Voprosy istorii*, no. 7 (1981), pp. 84–94; and idem, *Sovetskii rabochii klass i khudozhestvennaia kul'tura, 1917–1932* (Moscow, 1984).

10. See Edward J. Brown, *The Proletarian Episode in Russian Literature, 1928–1932* (New York, 1953); and Herman Ermolaev, *Soviet Literary Theories, 1917–1934: The Genesis of Socialist Realism* (Berkeley, 1963).

11. For a sampling of this scholarship see Karl G. Ballestrem, "Lenin and Bogdanov," *Studies in Soviet Thought*, no. 9 (1969), pp.

as "Bogdanov's" organization, the social consequence of his complex ideas about culture and society. The Proletkult thus becomes a symbol for Bogdanov; its size is used to show the popularity of his ideas and the possibility for a different outcome to the revolution. Even those works that focus directly on the Proletkult have made the interaction of Bogdanov's theory and the Proletkult's practice their central theme.[12]

One cannot omit the altercations between Lenin and Bogdanov from a serious history of the Proletkult. Their philosophical and political disputes informed its inception and prefigured its demise. But in my view those scholars who reduce the Proletkult organization to Bogdanov's movement give it a coherence and simplicity that it did not have. They

---

283–310; John Biggart, "'Anti-Leninist Bolshevism': The *Forward* Group of the RSDRP," *Canadian Slavonic Papers*, vol. 23, no. 2 (1981), pp. 134–53; Loren R. Graham, "Bogdanov's Inner Message," in *Red Star: The First Bolshevik Utopia*, by Alexander Bogdanov, ed. Loren R. Graham and Richard Stites (Bloomington, 1984); Dietrich Grille, *Lenins Rivale: Bogdanov und seine Philosophie* (Cologne, 1966); Kenneth M. Jensen, *Beyond Marx and Mach: Alexander Bogdanov's Philosophy of Living Experience* (Dordrecht, 1978); Peter Scheibert, "Lenin, Bogdanov and the Concept of Proletarian Culture," in *Lenin and Leninism*, ed. Bernard Eissenstaat (Lexington, Mass., 1971); Jutta Scherrer, "Les écoles du parti de Capri et de Bologne: La formation de l'intelligentsia du parti," *Cahiers du monde russe et soviétique*, vol. 19 (1978), pp. 259–84; Sochor, *Revolution and Culture*; S. V. Utechin, "Philosophy and Society: Alexander Bogdanov," in *Revisionism: Essays on the History of Marxist Ideas*, ed. Leopold Labedz (London, 1962); and Robert C. Williams, *The Other Bolsheviks: Lenin and his Critics, 1904–1914* (Bloomington, 1985).

12. The best of these works are by West German scholars. See Gabriele Gorzka, *A. Bogdanov und der russische Proletkult: Theorie und Praxis einer sozialistischen Kulturrevolution* (Frankfurt am Main, 1980); Peter Gorsen and Eberhard Knödler-Bunte, *Proletkult: System einer proletarischen Kultur* (Stuttgart, 1974), vol. 1, pp. 13–122; and Klaus-Dieter Seemann, "Der Versuch einer proletarischen Kulturrevolution in Russland, 1917–1922," *Jahrbücher für Geschichte Osteuropas*, vol. 9 (1961), pp. 179–222. One exception is Sheila Fitzpatrick's *The Commissariat of Enlightenment: Soviet Organization of Education and the Arts under Lunacharsky, 1917–1921* (Cambridge, Eng., 1970), which examines the Proletkult's conflicts with the state bureaucracy.

also place it too easily within the broader framework of an anti-Leninist opposition, a generalization that seriously distorts many participants' intentions.

In this book I examine the Proletkult as a complicated social and cultural movement with many conflicting programs. Rather than focusing primarily on the ideas of the leadership, I investigate its heterogeneous social composition and its varied cultural practices. Using the archival records and publications of both local and central organizations, I try to show the complex interaction between official pronouncements and their implementation.[13] Such an approach illuminates the diversity of this organization and shows what it shared with many other early Soviet institutions. It also reveals what the Proletkult's successes and failures can tell about the revolutionary process in general.

As an independent mass cultural movement the Proletkult was a unique phenomenon in the early history of Soviet Russia. Many of the problems it faced, however, were not unusual. Like other groups claiming a proletarian identity, it struggled to discover how to gain predominance in a country where workers were a rather small minority. The official solutions the organization devised, such as trying to limit its membership to the most experienced workers or excluding nonproletarians from its ranks, were ultimately not very successful. The Proletkult was "proletarian" only in the broadest sense of the word; it drew its major support from the laboring population at large, from industrial workers and their children, from white-collar employees and artisans, and even from the peasantry.

Proletkult participants had enormous problems articulating a role for experts and intellectuals in the new society, another common dilemma. If one judged from its most radical pronouncements alone, the movement seemed to ad-

13. This study makes extensive use of the archival holdings of the Proletkult, housed in the Central State Archive of Literature and Art in Moscow. The archive contains the records of the central organization as well as those of local circles, including membership rules,

vocate an extreme form of workers' control. Insofar as intellectuals were needed, they should be drawn from the working class. Some members went even further, opposing any form of social hierarchy whatever. As all Soviet institutions quickly discovered, however, the creation of a new intelligentsia inevitably required the participation of the old one. The Proletkult devised ingenious methods to limit nonproletarian artists, teachers, and experts to minor roles. But in the final analysis the influence of these class-alien elements was not so easy to curtail. Although the Proletkult gained a reputation for anti-intellectualism, intellectuals were in fact key actors who helped to define the form and content of proletarian culture.

Like the leaders of all other Soviet institutions, central Proletkult planners fought hard to weld their many local branches into a cohesive national structure. Their plaintive calls for more information and more compliance from provincial chapters were echoed in countless other organizations, from the Communist Party to the government's cultural bureaucracy. The Proletkult's cardinal principles, autonomy and independent action (*samostoiatel'nost'* and *samodeiatel'nost'*), encouraged local creativity. And yet the central organization struggled constantly and often unsuccessfully to implement its decisions at the local level. Despite its most valiant efforts, resolutions made at the center never dictated the practice of the organization as a whole.

In this study I try to avoid the simple dichotomy of theory versus practice, which pits the ideas of leaders like Bogdanov against the day-to-day work of local circles. Certainly there were fundamental beliefs that tied the Proletkult together. Members shared a commitment to proletarian hegemony, institutional autonomy, and the centrality of cultural change. But all these ideas were open to myriad interpretations. National leaders themselves did not always agree on the best way to nurture a new intelligentsia or to create a cohesive

---

minutes of organizational meetings, and questionnaires about social composition and cultural practices.

movement. The malleability of the Proletkult's principles helped it to attract a large following.

Proletkultists passionately asserted the proletariat's central position in the new social order, but they did not agree on just what the proletariat was. For some it was synonymous with the industrial working class. They hoped the movement would find a following among the most culturally and politically advanced representatives of the factory labor force. For many others, not unlike the Populists and Socialist Revolutionaries of years gone by, the proletariat included all of the long-suffering Russian people, the *narod*. These advocates welcomed typists, house painters, and peasants without any sense of social contradiction. The broad appeal of the Proletkult's class-based language reveals the flexibility of social categories during this period of rapid social change.

Although institutional autonomy was highly valued by Proletkult members, it too was an ambiguous concept. At its most extreme, autonomy implied that such class institutions as the Proletkult would dominate government organs, an idea that certainly posed a challenge to the authority of the party and the state. But autonomy could just as easily be read as an affirmation of local control. Provincial circles insisted on their right to find their own solutions to local problems, solutions that sometimes meant forming close alliances with party and state organs. The Proletkult's endorsement of independence did not cement its institutional integrity; instead it encouraged heterogeneity.

The most basic principle of all was a shared belief in the centrality of cultural change. But what kind of culture and what kind of change? Proletkultists' answers to these questions were as varied and contradictory as those that were circulating in society at large. The organization attracted educators who hoped to reorganize universities on the basis of a vaguely defined proletarian science. It also gained the services of music teachers who wanted to share the work of the masters with the masses. Within its confines peasant children learned Tchaikovsky's operas, workers performed Chekhov on factory stages, and urban youths discovered the principles of production art taught by the avant-garde. For many participants proletarian culture meant simply that the proletarian revolution would bring culture to them. The content of that culture, its audience, and its transmitters were all open to interpretation.

Proletkultists were inspired by a utopian vision of the society of the future. This vision is apparent in the titles of their local journals—Petrograd's *The Future* (*Griadushchee*), Kharkov's *Dawn of the Future* (*Zori griadushchego*), Tambov's *Culture of the Future* (*Griadushchaia kul'tura*), from which this book takes its title. To be sure, utopianism in itself does not constitute a unified worldview, and Proletkultists put forward many conflicting plans for the ideal culture.[14] Not surprisingly, most of the organization's work never measured up to the visionaries' expansive claims, and one of the most frequent criticisms directed against the movement was that its accomplishments were much more modest than its grandiose predictions. Although this is certainly true, I still hope to capture the utopian spirit that encouraged Proletkult members, however briefly, to view piano lessons and literacy classes as major steps toward the creation of a new society. Their sincerity and enthusiasm need to be appreciated before we can begin to assess their failures.

My focus is on the period from 1917 to 1922. In these years the Proletkult was able to gain a national following and a major voice in cultural debates. Then, as a result of its changed status and funding cutbacks at the end of the Civil War, it rapidly declined to a small and restricted core of members. The final chapter outlines the organization's fate

14. On the many varieties of early Soviet utopianism see Richard Stites, "Utopias in the Air and on the Ground: Futuristic Dreams in the Russian Revolution," *Russian History*, vol. 11, no. 2/3 (1984), pp. 236–57; and idem, *Revolutionary Dreams: Utopian Visions and Experimental Life in the Russian Revolution* (New York, 1989).

from 1923 until it was finally disbanded in 1932. In this period we are in a very altered cultural landscape, one in which the Proletkult was at best a minor player.

The period of the movement's greatest influence, 1918–1920, coincides exactly with the years of the Russian Civil War. With its peculiar combination of hardship and utopia, devastation and creation, the war helped to further enthusiastic revolutionary goals. This was, in the words of an early Soviet scholar, the "heroic phase" of the Russian Revolution.[15] All social and economic institutions appeared to be malleable and open to the most radical change. The Proletkult's euphoric promises of a new culture captured this combative, optimistic spirit.

The Proletkult's marked decline starting in the first year of the New Economic Policy can be explained in part by the Communist Party's opposition to the movement and its subordination to state organs. Faced with severe funding cutbacks and sharp restrictions on its activities, it lost most of its local network and the majority of its followers. In most Western scholarship the Proletkult's collapse is treated as the inevitable result of the Bolshevik consolidation of power.[16] The party leadership under Lenin was not willing to tolerate a large and independent workers' movement, especially one associated with the politically suspect Bogdanov. Like other groups that advocated proletarian autonomy—such as factory committees, unions, and workers' groups within the party—the Proletkult did not survive the Civil War without radical alterations.

However, government hostility alone cannot explain the Proletkult's demise. Its participants themselves were at odds over how best to realize a proletarian culture, and much of

15. L. Kritsman, *Geroicheskii period Velikoi russkoi revoliutsii*, 2d ed. (Moscow and Leningrad, 1926).

16. See, for example, Williams, *The Other Bolsheviks*, pp. 185–87. For a more differentiated view see Gorsen and Knödler-Bunte, *Proletkult*, vol. 1, pp. 114–15.

their energies were devoted to internal disputes. The central leadership intervened in the work of local affiliates, denying them resources and even closing them down when it did not approve of their activities. Although the organization constantly criticized state programs, it still relied on the government for almost all its support, making it an easy target for cutbacks. Moreover, Proletkultists' vision of a utopian future, which inspired and united the movement, was itself a fragile construct. It depended on the heroic spirit fostered by the Civil War and on an expansive interpretation of proletarian power. The realities of NEP Russia, with its fiscal restraints and commitment to class compromise, could not sustain the same enthusiasm.

Proletkultists often overstated the importance of their institution and its powers. Nonetheless the popularity of this organization shows that cultural aspirations were also part of the reason that intellectuals, workers, and peasants went to the barricades and battlefields. Participants in the Proletkult sought not only new political and economic institutions but also a fundamental reorganization of the cultural foundations of society. Indeed, they believed that without such changes the revolution would be incomplete. "The Proletkult is a spiritual [*dukhovnaia*] revolution," proclaimed the worker-poet Ilia Sadofev in 1919. "For the old, dark, capitalist world, it is more terrifying, more dangerous than any bomb. . . . They know very well that a physical revolution is only a quarter of the Bolshevik-Soviet victory. But a spiritual revolution—that is the whole victory."[17]

17. Il'ia Sadof'ev, "Chto takoe Proletkul't," *Mir i chelovek*, no. 1 (1919), p. 12. All translations are mine unless otherwise identified.

1

Proletarian Culture and the Russian Revolution

The Origins of the Proletkult Movement

The movement for proletarian culture that spread across Soviet Russia in the early years of the revolution had a complex social and intellectual heritage. It was most directly inspired by the theories of the left Bolshevik intellectual Aleksandr Bogdanov, who believed that the proletariat had to found a new cultural system, that is, a new morality, a new politics, and a new art, in order to succeed against the old elite. But proletarian culture proved to be an expansive slogan that easily bore many other meanings. It appealed to workers who were eager to break all ties with intellectuals and to cultural radicals who wanted nothing to do with Russia's past. It also inspired liberal reformers who hoped to share their knowledge of classic Russian culture with the masses.

Russian socialism, in its varied manifestations, was simultaneously a political and an educational movement. Intellectual socialist leaders keenly felt the rift between themselves, as representatives of privileged and cultured society, and the Russian masses, who were essential for a successful political upheaval. They hoped to transcend this divide by educating the masses to perceive their true interests. By doing so they believed that they were preparing the masses for radical political change. The educators had laudable goals. They tried to convey some knowledge of Russian high culture to their students, while at the same time convincing them of the need for revolution. Yet despite these good intentions, there were strains between the teachers, who conceived of themselves as the bearers of culture (*kul'turtreger*), and their students, cast in the role of willing and grateful recipients.[1]

Aleksandr Bogdanov's theory of proletarian culture was conceived as a way to transcend this tension. Inspired by his own experiences in populist circles, Bogdanov believed that it was possible to enlighten workers without dominating them.[2] His purpose was not primarily to transmit political theory or high culture. Rather he hoped to encourage workers to take control of the socialist movement themselves. This unique didactic process would allow the proletariat to formulate its own class ideology and morality, which was eventually to serve as the basis for the socialist society of the future.

Moved by their own desire to reach the people, many intellectuals devised popular educational projects in the late nineteenth and early twentieth centuries. Philanthropists, liberals, populists, and socialists of all persuasions turned in increasing numbers to become teachers in evening classes, Sunday schools, open universities, and clubs. Their efforts also encouraged a popular educational press that aimed to bring scientific knowledge, contemporary literature, and a sense of cultural community to the laboring population at large. Proletarian culture also loosely described these endeavors. The intelligentsia was bringing culture, the finest artistic and scientific accomplishment of their society, to the working

1. See Norman M. Naimark, *Terrorists and Social Democrats: The Russian Revolutionary Movement under Alexander III* (Cambridge, Mass., 1983), pp. 154–86; Allan K. Wildman, *The Making of a Workers' Revolution* (Chicago, 1967), pp. 89–117; and Reginald E. Zelnik, "Russian Bebels: An Introduction to the Memoirs of Semen Kanatchikov and Matvei Fisher," *Russian Review*, vol. 35 (1976), pp. 249–89, 417–47. The Russian word *kul'turtreger* is taken from the German *Kulturträger*.

2. See James D. White, "Bogdanov in Tula," *Studies in Soviet Thought*, vol. 22 (1981), pp. 33–58.

classes. They hoped to share this precious heritage and imbue the people with a sense of political and social responsibility.

For aspiring worker-intellectuals educated in study groups and, after 1905, in institutions affiliated with the labor movement, proletarian culture was an expression of their aim to challenge the cultural predominance of the intellectual elite. Some workers openly rejected the intelligentsia's aid and claimed that self-education was their goal. Although the members of these circles usually aspired to the fruits of high culture, they also encouraged their fellow workers to express their own artistic views and to criticize "bourgeois culture" and the class that sustained it.

When the Proletkult emerged in 1917 all these unlikely collaborators could claim some responsibility for its formation. Bogdanov and his allies molded Proletkult ideology to reflect their commitment to proletarian cultural leadership. The movement incorporated the participants in union clubs, people's universities, and self-education circles and reflected the ambivalent attitudes of these participants toward bourgeois culture and the intellectuals who possessed it. It also attracted part of the staff and the clientele of the liberal adult education movement, with its inclusive, democratic approach to education. These diverse understandings of culture, politics, and the proletariat would both shape and limit what the Proletkult could become.

Left Bolshevism and Proletarian Culture

The intellectual foundations for the Proletkult movement were laid in the years after the failure of the Revolution of 1905. The defeat of the revolutionary forces marked a severe crisis for the Russian socialist movement and for the Bolsheviks in particular. When the government disbanded the Second Duma in 1907 and the police began to restrict the activities of political parties and legalized worker groups, Social Democrats had to decide whether to participate in parliamentary elections or to continue the revolutionary struggle through underground agitation. This dilemma split the Bolshevik faction in two. Lenin argued that it made no sense to eschew legal channels because a new revolutionary upsurge lay far off in the future. He was opposed by a group known as the "left Bolsheviks," led by Aleksandr Bogdanov, who believed that the revolution would soon continue and that the Bolsheviks should not be lulled into quiescent parliamentarianism.

The left Bolsheviks, who included Bogdanov, Anatolii Lunacharskii, Maxim Gorky, and Pavel Lebedev-Polianskii, challenged Lenin's claims to leadership and his vision of party politics. They attacked him on three different fronts: political strategy, party organization, and, most fundamentally, socialist theory.[3] Lenin's authoritarian methods of party organization received special criticism. Because the ranks of intellectual leaders had been depleted through arrests, disaffection, and exile, the left Bolsheviks feared that workers in Russia had been left without guidance. They argued that the Bolsheviks needed to encourage more collective and inclusive organizational tactics and to devote more resources to the training of worker-leaders who could assume positions of power.

Most important, the left Bolsheviks were deeply committed to a reinterpretation of Marxist theory that would give ideology and culture a more creative and central role. Opposed to the rigid materialism of Lenin and Plekhanov, they believed that the ideological superstructure was more than a reflection of society's economic base. Lunacharskii had long been fasci-

3. There is a large and growing literature on left Bolshevism. For the most recent works see John Biggart, "'Anti-Leninist Bolshevism': The *Forward* Group of the RSDRP," *Canadian Slavonic Papers*, vol. 23, no. 2 (1981), pp. 134–53; Robert C. Williams, "Collective Immortality: The Syndicalist Origins of Proletarian Culture, 1905–1910," *Slavic Review*, vol. 39, no. 3 (1980), pp. 389–402; idem, *The Other Bolsheviks* (Bloomington, 1985); and Avraham Yassour, "Lenin and Bogdanov: Protagonists in the 'Bolshevik Center,'" *Studies in Soviet Thought*, vol. 22 (1981), pp. 1–32.

nated by the power of art to inspire political action. Both he and Gorky were convinced that socialism could convey the force of a "human religion" and inspire individuals to look beyond themselves to a higher good, one that encompassed the fate of all humanity. Taken together, their ideas came to be known as "god-building" (*bogostroitel'stvo*).[4] At the same time, Bogdanov was engaged in a massive project to integrate the process of cognition into Marxism in order to develop a more sophisticated understanding of ideology.

From 1907 to 1911 the leftists were serious contenders for control of the Bolshevik center. Initially, their activist political tactics were very appealing to the rank and file.[5] They spread their ideas about ideology and society in socialist journals; Bogdanov even published a popular science fiction novel, *Red Star*, which depicted the results of a successful socialist revolution on Mars.[6] Bogdanov also reached out to a scholarly socialist audience. In his book *Empiriomonism*, made famous by Lenin's violent objections to it, he employed the ideas of contemporary Western European thinkers such as Ernst Mach and Richard Avenarius.[7] In Bogdanov's view the socialist polity of the future would demand a new awareness of the relationship between the individual and society and would require a different approach to ethics, science, human values, and art.

4. Jutta Scherrer, " 'Ein gelber und ein blauer Teufel': Zur Entstehung der Begriffe 'bogostroitel'stvo' und 'bogoiskatel'stvo,' " *Forschungen zur osteuropäischen Geschichte*, vol. 25 (1978), pp. 322–23; A. V. Lunacharskii, *Velikii perevorot* (Petrograd, 1919), pp. 14–22; and idem, "Ateisti," in *Ocherki po filosofii marksizma* (St. Petersburg, 1908), pp. 107–61.

5. Geoffrey Swain, *Russian Social Democracy and the Legal Labour Movement* (London, 1983), pp. 41–43.

6. See Loren R. Graham, "Bogdanov's Inner Message," in *Red Star: The First Bolshevik Utopia*, by Alexander Bogdanov, ed. Loren R. Graham and Richard Stites (Bloomington, 1984).

7. Dietrich Grille, *Lenins Rivale* (Cologne, 1966), pp. 110–19; Kenneth M. Jensen, *Beyond Marx and Mach* (Dordrecht, 1978), pp. 67–86; and Zenovia A. Sochor, *Revolution and Culture* (Ithaca, 1988), pp. 42–45.

The leftists attempted to put their ideas about party organization and tactics into practice by starting two exile schools for worker-cadres in Capri and Bologna between 1909–1911.[8] Because training and education were a central part of their program, the leftists attached great significance to these schools. The first opened at Gorky's villa on the island of Capri in the summer of 1909 with thirteen worker-students elected from Russian party committees sympathetic to the left Bolsheviks' political stance. The teachers were prominent intellectuals, including Gorky, Bogdanov, Lunacharskii, and the historian Mikhail Pokrovskii. They devised an ambitious curriculum that included classes on the history of the socialist movement, literature, and the visual arts. In addition, the school offered practical courses on agitational techniques, newspaper writing, and propaganda.[9]

Capri school leaders also tried to give life to their ideas about party organization. To elaborate their critique of the Bolshevik center, the instructors gave lectures on socialist party organization with titles such as "On Party Authoritarianism." They tried to put party democracy into action on a small scale. Both students and teachers were elected to a school council that oversaw day-to-day affairs. When the council concluded that the lectures were too long and did not leave students enough time for questions, the teaching sched-

8. On the background of the Capri school see Jutta Scherrer, "Les écoles du parti de Capri et de Bologne," *Cahiers du monde russe et soviétique*, no. 19 (1978), pp. 259–84. On the schools in general, see S. Livshits, "Kapriiskaia partiinaia shkola, 1909 g.," *Proletarskaia revoliutsiia*, no. 6 (1924), pp. 33–73; idem, "Partiinaia shkola v Bolon'e, 1910–1911 gg.," *Proletarskaia revoliutsiia*, no. 3 (1926), pp. 109–44; N. Semashko, "O dvukh zagranichnykh partiinykh shkolakh," *Proletarskaia revoliutsiia*, no. 3 (1923), pp. 142–51; Heinz Fenner, *Die Propaganda-Schulen der Bolschewisten: Ein Beitrag zur Vorgeschichte der Proletkultbewegung* (Berlin, 1920); Williams, *The Other Bolsheviks*, pp. 151–59; and the memoirs of one participant, V. Kosarev, "Partiinaia shkola na ostrove Kapri," *Sibirskie ogni*, no. 2 (1922), pp. 63–75.

9. On the Capri students see Livshits, "Kapriiskaia shkola," pp. 51–53; on classes see Kosarev, "Partiinaia shkola," pp. 70–73; and Scherrer, "Les écoles du parti," pp. 270–77.

ule was restructured and questions were integrated into the teaching format.[10]

This first experiment did not fulfill the organizers' high hopes. The teachers fought among themselves, and Gorky eventually broke with Lunacharskii and Bogdanov. Five of the Capri students deserted the program to join Lenin. Only one worker-participant, Fedor Kalinin, would go on to distinguish himself as an important party leader. Nor did the school succeed in consolidating the left Bolsheviks' political position. Already in 1908, Lenin denounced their reinterpretation of Marxism in a weighty tome entitled *Materialism and Empiriocriticism.*[11] He ousted Bogdanov from the Bolshevik faction before the first classes in Capri began.[12] He even tried to co-opt some of the leftists' ideas by starting a party school of his own near Paris.[13]

Despite these setbacks, the Capri experiment was a formative experience for many left Bolsheviks, Bogdanov in particular. At the conclusion of the school, a group of students and teachers came together and gave themselves a new name: the Vpered (Forward) circle.[14] The Vperedists, who gained recog-

10. Kosarev, "Partiinaia shkola," pp. 66–67.

11. On Lenin and Bogdanov's philosophical disputes see David Joravsky, *Soviet Marxism and Natural Science* (New York, 1961), pp. 27–44. On the publication of this book see Nikolay Valentinov, *Encounters with Lenin,* trans. Paul Rosta and Brian Pearce (London, 1968), pp. 233–39.

12. See Georges Haupt and Jutta Scherrer, "Gor'kij, Bogdanov, Lenin: Neue Quellen zur ideologischen Krise in der bolschewistischen Fraktion, 1908–1910," *Cahiers du monde russe et soviétique,* vol. 19 (1978), p. 329.

13. Ralph Carter Elwood, "Lenin and the Social Democratic Schools for Underground Party Workers, 1909–11," *Political Science Quarterly,* vol. 81, no. 3 (1966), pp. 370–91.

14. On Vpered in general see Krisztina Mänicke-Gyöngyösi, *"Proletarische Wissenschaft" und "Sozialistische Menschheitsreligion" als Modelle proletarischer Kultur* (Berlin, 1982), pp. 25–67; K. A. Ostroukhova, "Gruppa 'Vpered,' 1909–1917 gg.," *Proletarskaia revoliutsiia,* no. 1 (1925), pp. 198–219; "Vpered," in *Bol'shaia sovetskaia entsiklopediia* (Moscow, 1926–1947), vol. 13, columns 386–89; and N. Voitinskii, "O gruppe 'Vpered,' 1907–1917 gg.," *Proletarskaia revoliutsiia,* no. 12 (1929), pp. 59–119.

nition from the Bolshevik faction only as a literary group, included a new element in their critique of Lenin and his politics: proletarian culture. In the Vpered platform, written by Bogdanov, they argued that the party had to look beyond narrow political and economic interests to prepare ideologically for the coming revolution.

There is only one conclusion. Using the old bourgeois culture, create a new proletarian one opposed to the old and spread it to the masses. Develop a proletarian science, strengthen authentic comradely relations in the proletarian milieu, devise a proletarian philosophy, and turn art in the direction of proletarian aspirations and experience.[15]

From this point on, proletarian culture became a major theme in Bogdanov's political writings. He made it clear that he did not mean art, science, or philosophy alone. Rather for Bogdanov proletarian culture meant a distinctive class ideology. It was the spirit of socialism already apparent in embryonic form within capitalist society and expressed through the proletariat's comradely collective working habits and organizational structures.[16] In his expansive use of the term, culture had the function of organizing human perception and hence shaping action in the world. Because of the existence of social classes, there could be no unified, common basis to human perception. It was the proletariat's task to create its own ideology, its own way to structure human experience. Because the working class was organized collectively through a labor process that enhanced comradely social relations, proletarian culture would contain a more unified, harmonious view of the world than the class cultures that preceded it.

Bogdanov's ideas on proletarian culture paralleled those of Marx on proletarian class rule. The proletariat was the "uni-

15. "Platforma gruppy 'Vpered': Sovremennoe polozhenie i zadachi partii," reprinted in *Sochineniia,* by V. I. Lenin, 3d. ed. (Moscow, 1936), vol. 14, pp. 452–69, quotation p. 455.

16. A. A. Bogdanov [Maksimov, pseud.], "Sotsializm v nastoiashchem," *Vpered,* no. 2 (1911), columns 59–71, esp. 70–71.

versal class"; it alone embodied the values of the classless society. Proletarian culture, Bogdanov argued, would be the most universal and inclusive of all class cultures. It would provide a fundamental preparatory step toward the creation of a truly human, classless culture in the future.[17] He insisted that cultural transformation was not a frivolous enterprise; on the contrary, it was an essential prerequisite for a successful socialist revolution. Until the proletariat devised its own collective class ideology it would forever depend on the values of the bourgeoisie. Proletarian culture was the only way to insure the victory of socialism. It had to be nurtured and developed before the proletarian revolution in order for socialism to flourish.

To implement his ambitious ideas, Bogdanov looked to institutions like the Capri school. Such programs, which he called "proletarian universities," would be open to the most sophisticated representatives of the working class. They, in turn, were to form the basis of the new proletarian intelligentsia, which would then begin the task of organizing the broad mass of workers.[18] Thus Bogdanov's program was essentially an exclusive one; he was not proposing methods for mass education. Rather than abandoning the vanguardist principles of Bolshevism, he reassessed them to insure that the vanguard came from the proletariat itself.

Vpered was not a successful political group. The Capri school had only one brief sequel, in the socialist city of Bologna during the winter of 1910–1911. By then it had no official ties to the Bolshevik center. Vperedists fell victim to émigré infighting, and Bogdanov left the circle entirely by 1911.[19] His

17. See A. A. Bogdanov, *Kul'turnye zadachi nashego vremeni* (Moscow, 1911), pp. 23, 54.

18. Ibid., pp. 69–70.

19. Bogdanov's exodus from Vpered is usually explained by his disagreements with other members over the definition and importance of proletarian culture. See Voitinskii, "O gruppe 'Vpered,'" pp. 109–10. However, Dietrich Grille speculates that he might have abandoned his political contacts in order to qualify for a general political amnesty in 1913. See Grille, *Lenins Rivale*, p. 33.

political challenge to Lenin's control of the Bolshevik faction was over.

But the left Bolsheviks did not give up their commitment to proletarian culture. Even after he left Vpered, Bogdanov continued to elaborate his theories. Lunacharskii pursued his interest in fine art and ideology by founding a circle for proletarian literature in Paris. There he trained exiled worker-writers, including Aleksei Gastev, Fedor Kalinin, and Mikhail Gerasimov, all influential figures in the early history of the Proletkult.[20]

With the start of the First World War Vpered was reconstituted in Geneva by Pavel Lebedev-Polianskii, who would later serve as the Proletkult's first president. With Lunacharskii's aid, he used the concept of proletarian culture to explain why most European socialists had given their support to the war effort. Their patriotism revealed that socialists' ideological development was weak. The only way to end workers' dependence on the bourgeoisie was to develop proletarian culture and make scientific and socialist education the central task of social democracy.[21]

The need to educate the working class for revolution was the Vperedists' central message. Culture, art, science, literature, and philosophy—these were the weapons needed to prepare a proletarian victory. If the working class devoted itself to education, if it shaped its own revolutionary leadership and class ideology, then it would not stand helpless and divided as it had in the years of reaction following 1905. But even as the Vperedists wrote about the proper preparations for revolution, the revolution itself overtook them.

20. On Lunacharskii's circle see Robert C. Williams, *Artists in Revolution: Portraits of the Russian Avant-garde, 1905–1925* (Bloomington, 1977), pp. 52–53; Lunacharskii, *Velikii perevorot*, p. 51; and Kurt Johansson, *Aleksej Gastev: Proletarian Bard of the Machine Age* (Stockholm, 1983), pp. 40–42.
21. "Ot redaktsii," and V. Polianskii, "Russkie sotsial'shovanisty i zadacha revoliutsionnoi sotsial'demokratii," *Vpered*, no. 1 (1915), pp. 1–3, 7–8.

Culture for the Proletariat: Adult Education

Vperedists arrived at their cultural platform in part because they believed that the Russian intelligentsia was not a reliable partner for the working class. Suspicions between the workers and the intelligentsia, indeed between educated society and the lower classes in general, were deeply rooted in Russia, and the failure of the Revolution of 1905 only increased this tension. Many intellectuals were leaving politics altogether. Some began to attack the ethos of the old intelligentsia, including its traditional sense of moral responsibility for the lower classes.[22] Artists and writers who had once been concerned with social and political problems in their work began to pursue new aesthetic approaches, such as modernist writing and abstract painting, which were much less accessible to popular audiences.[23] The intelligentsia seemed confused and divided over what, if any, its social role should be.

Workers' organizations and left-wing political parties interpreted these changes in the simplest way: bourgeois intellectuals, frightened by the revolution, had abandoned the lower classes.[24] This generalization was not entirely unjustified. Many intellectuals did indeed give up illegal underground activity in the years of repression, a shift felt keenly by the workers in these movements.[25] Nonetheless, not all intellectuals lost their sense of social obligation. Instead many turned away from revolution and embraced legal activity, both cultural and educational. Members of the intelligentsia

22. Jane Burbank, *Intelligentsia and Revolution: Russian Views of Bolshevism, 1917–1922* (New York, 1986), pp. 8–10.

23. For the debate on modernism see Jeffrey Brooks, "Popular Philistinism and the Course of Russian Modernism," in *Literature and History: Theoretical Problems and Russian Case Studies*, ed. Gary Saul Morson (Stanford, 1986), pp. 90–110.

24. See, for example, the complaints of workers in the Bolshevik press, reprinted in S. Breitenburg, ed., *Dooktiabr'skaia Pravda ob iskusstve i literature* (Moscow, 1937), pp. 31–32.

25. See the comments of the Bolshevik worker and Proletkult organizer Aleksandr Samobytnik-Mashirov in A. Mashirov, "Zadachi proletarskoi kul'tury," *Griadushchee*, no. 2 (1918), pp. 9–10.

organized and staffed the numerous adult education courses, people's universities, educational societies, libraries, and theaters that multiplied in cities and villages between 1906 and 1914. Through their work they created a much richer and more complex network of educational experiences for the lower classes than had existed before the Revolution of 1905.

The intelligentsia's involvement in workers' educational programs had begun in the mid-nineteenth century with the Sunday school movement. Inspired by the writings of a Kievan educator, university students and other intellectuals had opened Sunday and evening schools for the urban lower classes in St. Petersburg, Moscow, and several other Russian cities. These programs were staffed by sympathetic intellectuals who frequently devised their own curricula. The study plans varied greatly from place to place, ranging from simple literacy programs to rather elaborate training in the social and natural sciences. From these first experiments a whole complex of evening classes and weekend schools emerged.[26]

In the late nineteenth century more comprehensive educational programs began to take shape, modeled on some of the longer running Sunday and evening schools and inspired in part by English experiments in workers' adult education.[27] The Revolution of 1905 gave an enormous boost to these efforts, and new schools opened in St. Petersburg and Moscow in 1906 and soon thereafter in over twenty cities, including Ufa, Baku, Warsaw, and Tomsk. These institutions, called "people's universities," were sponsored by a variety of local groups and relied on the services of the local intelligentsia. For example, the Kuban People's University in Ekaterinodar was staffed by local doctors, lawyers, and gymnasium teachers.[28]

26. On the Sunday school movement in St. Petersburg see Reginald E. Zelnik, *Labor and Society in Tsarist Russia: The Factory Workers of St. Petersburg, 1855–1870* (Stanford, 1971), pp. 160–99.

27. See Ia. V. Abramov, *Nashi voskresnye shkoly: Ikh proshloe i nastoiashchee* (St. Petersburg, 1900); and E. N. Medynskii, *Vneshkol'noe obrazovanie: Ego znachenie, organizatsiia i tekhnika* (Moscow, 1918).

28. V. M. Riabkov, "Iz istorii razvitiia narodnykh universitetov v

Along with the popular universities there were also new art and music schools open to the general population. The People's Conservatory in Moscow, founded in 1906, was richly endowed with an excellent musical staff. Among the teachers were Aleksandr Kastalskii and Arsenii Avraamov, who would become important organizers of Proletkult musical training.[29] People's theaters, first begun in the late nineteenth century, also mushroomed in the years after 1905. These drama circles aimed to acquaint the lower classes with the best of Russian playwrights, including Gogol, Tolstoy, and especially Ostrovsky.[30] Although these programs made some concessions to popular tastes, such as incorporating folk music into conservatory curricula, inevitably the intellectual organizers conveyed their own standards of excellence.

Another educational forum were "people's houses" (*narodnye doma*). Before the Revolution of 1905 the houses were largely used as organizational centers for cultural activities in city districts and towns. After 1905 they began to take on a more independent educational function. Like people's universities, they were sustained by many different local groups. Zemstva and cooperative organizations were by far the most common sponsors, and the government contributed money from its Trusteeship of the People's Temperance, founded with funds from the liquor monopoly.[31] Organizers hoped that the friendly and comfortable clublike atmosphere of the houses would make education more appealing to the local population. The most famous of these institutions was the

gody sotsialisticheskogo stroitel'stva v SSSR," in *Klub i problemy razvitiia sotsialisticheskoi kul'tury* (Cheliabinsk, 1974), pp. 35–36; and Medynskii, *Vneshkol'noe obrazovanie*, pp. 266–70.

29. N. Briusova, "Massovaia muzykal'no-prosvetitel'naia rabota v pervye gody posle Oktiabria," *Sovetskaia muzyka*, no. 6 (1947), pp. 46–47; and Boris Schwarz, *Music and Musical Life in Soviet Russia*, rev. ed. (Bloomington, 1983), p. 5.

30. Gary Thurston, "The Impact of Russian Popular Theatre, 1886–1915," *Journal of Modern History*, vol. 55, no. 2 (1983), pp. 237–67.

31. Jeffrey Brooks, *When Russia Learned to Read: Literacy and Popular Literature, 1861–1917* (Princeton, 1985), pp. 313–14.

Ligovskii People's House, run by the Countess Panina in St. Petersburg. Opened in 1891 as a cafeteria for students, it was taken over by the Imperial Technical Society and transformed into a night school. In 1903, when Countess Panina took control, the center greatly expanded its activities, adding a theater, art classes, and much more extensive educational programs.[32] Several worker activists involved in the Petrograd Proletkult had had some contact with this cultural center.

The public served by these varied cultural institutions was diverse, reflecting the organizers' desire to reach "the people." It included workers, peasants, and the poorer townspeople. Fees were kept as low as possible, and some events were free. Although the regime hoped cultural offerings would divert the lower classes from political action, it was not always confident they would do so. Despite close government scrutiny, it proved difficult to separate politics from cultural work. Socialist teachers found opportunities to convey Marxist and other critical ideas in their classes, and working-class pupils learned to use cultural centers as a shield for clandestine political work.[33]

A popular educational press, which took root in Russia between 1905 and 1917, also propagated the cause of adult education. Publications such as *Herald of Knowledge* (*Vestnik znaniia*) and *New Journal for Everyone* (*Novyi zhurnal dlia vsekh*) gained large followings, especially among culturally ambitious white-collar employees.[34] The editors, who were themselves intellectuals, aimed to provide a general overview of the most pressing scientific, social, and cultural issues of the day in an easily accessible format. Thus these journals served as guides for those interested in self-education. Although they attracted a readership among clerks, skilled

32. Medynskii, *Vneshkol'noe obrazovanie*, pp. 102–3.
33. See the memoirs of socialist teachers in one of Moscow's best-known schools for workers, E. M. Chemodanova, ed., *Prechistenskie rabochie kursy: Pervyi rabochii universitet v Moskve* (Moscow, 1948), pp. 13–140.
34. Brooks, "Popular Philistinism."

workers, and primary school teachers, their simplified approach to complex issues earned them the scorn of many intellectuals, who believed their offerings were at the level of "third-rate people's universities."[35]

The intellectuals involved in these varied programs had many different motives. Some, especially after the experience of 1905, were frightened by the specter of a revolution by the "dark," uneducated Russian masses. Others hoped to combat the danger of a rising popular culture of adventure novels and tabloid newspapers, which offended many intellectuals' cultural values.[36] Political activists believed they could divert legal programs to further the revolutionary cause. But no matter what their immediate motivation or their political persuasion, they were all continuing an intelligentsia tradition of enlightenment and propaganda that had begun much earlier in the nineteenth century. These new institutions were a forum where the "culture bearers" could pass their burden on to the people and in the process help to shape the people's cultural heritage.

Clearly, most of these intellectuals had different goals than the Vperedists. They understood "culture" as the finest products of Russian and European civilization, not as a class ideology. They wanted to enlighten all of the laboring masses, not the industrial proletariat alone. Regardless of their political beliefs, they felt that the transmission of high culture was the single most important step toward positive social change. Yet despite these fundamental disagreements, both Vperedists and the reform-minded intelligentsia shared common ground. Both were convinced that education was essential for emancipation and that intellectuals had a role to play in the process of enlightenment. Although their emphasis was very different, both found value in Russia's cultural heritage. Thus it is not surprising that many of those who took part in adult educational projects offered their services to the Proletkult

35. Ibid., p. 99.
36. Brooks, *When Russia Learned to Read*, especially pp. 295–352.

after the October Revolution. There they continued the task of bringing culture to the masses, now rechristened as the proletariat.

Culture by the Proletariat: Workers' Institutions

The Revolution of 1905 spurred yet another cultural network, one that was controlled by the laboring classes themselves. The organizational laws of 1906, which allowed the legal formation of unions, encouraged the creation of workers' clubs and educational societies closely tied to the labor movement. With names such as "Enlightenment," "Education," and "Knowledge," these groups gained great popularity among both unionized and nonunionized workers.[37] The intended membership was the urban proletariat, which, although not always easy to define, was surely a narrower public than the people earmarked for general adult education. The programs were also more limited, largely because of restricted resources.

The rapid growth of cultural circles showed the workers' desire for education and entertainment. It was also an expression of their profound distrust of the intelligentsia. Many believed that the liberals had betrayed them in the revolution and were appalled by the socialist intellectuals' waning interest in the political struggle.[38] The new institutions were a way to educate a proletarian leadership through channels workers themselves controlled. Participants hoped that these circles would encourage an independent working-class intelligentsia, thus insuring that the proletariat would never have to

37. Victoria E. Bonnell, *Roots of Rebellion: Workers' Politics and Organizations in St. Petersburg and Moscow, 1900–1914* (Berkeley, 1983), pp. 328–34.

38. See David Mandel, "The Intelligentsia and the Working Class in 1917," *Critique*, no. 14 (1981), pp. 68–70; and A. Mashirov, "Zadachi proletarskoi kul'tury," *Griadushchee*, no. 2 (1918), pp. 9–10.

depend on unreliable intellectual allies, as it had during the Revolution of 1905.[39]

Unions and clubs had an uneasy relationship with people's universities and related groups associated with the highly suspect liberal intelligentsia.[40] Although workers attended these institutions, many believed that their own clubs and societies should replace them and become, in the words of one union publication, "the center of [workers'] entire intellectual lives."[41] They aspired to self-education (*samoobrazovanie*) and aimed to exclude the intelligentsia entirely. Yet despite these optimistic hopes for autonomy, cultural circles still solicited the help of intellectuals as teachers and lecturers. These contradictory sentiments of need and resentment further strained relations between workers and educated society.[42]

The offerings in workers' clubs and theaters revealed the dominant influence of the prevailing high culture. Along with classes on the history of the socialist movement were events very similar to those offered in people's universities and people's houses. Tchaikovsky and Rimskii-Korsakov were performed at musical evenings and the repertoire of proletarian drama circles was not markedly different from that of people's theaters. In its first season the theater at the Petrograd workers' society "Source of Knowledge and Light" performed Pushkin, Tolstoy, and Shakespeare. Russian classics were by far the favorites in club libraries.[43] Although the proletariat

39. See I. N. Kubikov, "Rabochie kluby v Petrograde," *Vestnik kul'tury i svobody*, no. 1 (1918), pp. 28–29; Leopold Haimson, "The Problem of Social Stability in Urban Russia, 1905–1917," in *The Structure of Russian History*, ed. Michael Cherniavsky (New York, 1970), p. 346; and Swain, *Russian Social Democracy*, pp. 34–35.

40. Swain, *Russian Social Democracy*, pp. 36–37.

41. *Nadezhda*, no. 2 (1908), p. 8, cited in Bonnell, *Roots of Rebellion*, p. 332. Bonnell's translation.

42. Bonnell, *Roots of Rebellion*, pp. 332–34.

43. I. N. Kubikov, "Literaturno-muzykal'nye vechera v rabochikh klubakh," *Vestnik kul'tury i svobody*, no. 2 (1918), pp. 32–34; idem, "Uchastie zhenshchin-rabotnits v klubakh," *Vestnik kul'tury i svobody*, no. 2 (1918), pp. 34–37; I. D. Levin, *Rabochie kluby v dorevoliu-*

was certainly not immune to the attractions of the tabloid press and popular adventure stories, these societies tried to encourage more "refined" cultural tastes.[44]

Not all workers were content to accept the Russian classics as their own, however. While participants in proletarian clubs debated the value of bourgeois culture, creative literature by workers began to appear in the socialist press. Inspired in part by the example of Maxim Gorky, proletarian authors began to describe their lives of labor and political struggle in stories, poems, and plays. The worker-poet Egor Nechaev made a name for himself at the end of the nineteenth century with his evocations of political freedom, socialism, and factory life. By the first decades of the twentieth century socialist newspapers and journals published more and more literature by authors with direct experience in the factory. The best known writers associated with the Proletkult, including Mikhail Gerasimov, Vladimir Kirillov, and Aleksei Samobytnik-Mashirov, all began publishing in leftist journals and newspapers before 1917.[45] Sympathetic workers and intellectuals pointed to this new literature as evidence that the proletariat could create a significant artistic culture of its own.

The results did not please everyone. A prominent Menshevik, Aleksandr Potresov, gave a very somber assessment of workers' creative accomplishments. Because of their time-consuming economic and political struggles, he believed that workers did not have the leisure to turn to culture. The art

---

tsionnom Peterburge (Moscow, 1926), pp. 108–10; Medynskii, *Vneshkol'noe obrazovanie*, p. 293; and Breitenburg, *Dooktiabr'skaia Pravda*, pp. 50–51.

44. On the attraction of popular culture see Semen Kanatchikov, *A Radical Worker in Tsarist Russia: The Autobiography of Semen Ivanovich Kanatchikov*, trans. and ed. Reginald E. Zelnik (Stanford, 1986), pp. 19, 401; and Swain, *Russian Social Democracy*, p. 60.

45. For an overview of this literature see V. L. L'vov-Rogachevskii, *Ocherki proletarskoi literatury* (Moscow, 1927), pp. 32–44; L. N. Kleinbort, *Ocherki narodnoi literatury, 1880–1923 gg.* (Leningrad, 1924), pp. 108–28; and A. M. Bikhter, "U istokov russkoi proletarskoi poezii," in *U istokov russkoi proletarskoi poezii*, ed. R. A. Shatseva and O. E. Afonina (Moscow, 1965), pp. 5–30.

they engendered was modest and unoriginal, and revealed the overwhelming dominance of bourgeois culture over their creative lives. The proletarian community, organized around struggle, was a Sparta, not an Athens. Workers should not delude themselves into thinking that they could create a proletarian culture under capitalism; instead they should alleviate the conditions that caused their subjugation.[46]

Many people, including Gorky himself, stood up to defend the quality of proletarian literature against such charges.[47] But the most passionate responses came from those who insisted that Potresov did not understand how culture and politics were intertwined. Valerian Pletnev, a Menshevik worker-intellectual who would eventually become president of the Proletkult, argued that the proletariat was creating a culture through its clubs, evening schools, and theaters. Workers should be encouraged in these pursuits; they should not be told that their efforts were of little value, for the proletariat could only be victorious if it challenged the power of the bourgeoisie with its own proletarian culture.[48]

Writing in an exile journal, the Vperedist Lunacharskii insisted that Potresov minimized the importance of art in workers' lives and in the working-class movement as a whole. Potresov's depressing predictions about the dominance of capitalist culture were irrelevant. Workers should learn from the art of the past, but they would also learn how to apply that knowledge for their own ends.[49] Rather than turning their

46. A. Potresov, "Tragediia proletarskoi kul'tury," *Nasha zaria,* no. 6 (1913), pp. 65–75. See also idem, "Otvet V. Valerianu," *Nasha zaria,* no. 10/11 (1914), pp. 41–48.

47. See M. Gor'kii, "Predislovie k 'Sbornik proletarskikh pisatelei,' " in *Sobranie sochinenii v tridtsati tomakh,* by M. Gor'kii (Moscow, 1953), vol. 24, p. 170.

48. V. F. Pletnev [V. Valerianov, pseud.], "K voprosu o proletarskoi kul'ture," *Nasha zaria,* no. 10/11 (1913), pp. 35–41.

49. A. V. Lunacharskii, "Chto takoe proletarskaia literatura i vozmozhna li ona?" *Bor'ba,* no. 1 (1914), reprinted in *Sobranie sochinenii v vos'mi tomakh,* by A. V. Lunacharskii, ed. I. I. Anisimov (Moscow, 1967), vol. 7, pp. 167–73.

backs on culture for politics, they should discover how to use art as a weapon in the struggle for socialism.

The links between culture and politics were illustrated very graphically when the revolutionary movement began to regain its momentum in the turbulent years from 1912–1914. Workers' clubs and educational societies became increasingly politicized, as many participants moved from the more cautious Menshevism to Bolshevism.[50] Because unions were under close surveillance, clubs became centers for underground organization. The St. Petersburg educational society "Science and Life," dominated by Bolsheviks, was a planning center for the strike activity that swept the city in July 1914.[51]

The outbreak of the First World War abruptly halted the expansion of workers' cultural groups. Fear of worker unrest led the government to repress independent workers' organizations. However, people's universities and people's houses did not suffer the same fate. Associated mainly with the liberal intelligentsia, the government did not view them as a substantial threat. The network of people's houses even expanded during the war as its two main sponsors, cooperatives and the zemstva, increased their power and responsibilities. Enterprising workers intent on continuing illegal activities learned to conduct their propaganda within this moderately neutral setting.[52] This avenue for workers' cultural activities survived even during the repressive war years.

Workers' circles offered no consensus on the meaning of proletarian culture. United by their distrust of the old intelligentsia, the collaborators in this network had a complicated

50. See Haimson, "The Problem of Social Stability," pp. 355–59; and Bonnell, *Roots of Rebellion*, pp. 400–403.

51. Haimson, "The Problem of Social Stability," p. 358.

52. On the repression of workers' organizations during the war see John L. H. Keep, *The Russian Revolution: A Study in Mass Mobilization* (New York, 1976), pp. 42–45; on people's houses and universities see Medynskii, *Vneshkol'noe obrazovanie*, pp. 99–100, 269–70; on illegal political activities in the Ligovskii People's House see "Podpol'naia rabota v gody imperialisticheskoi voiny v Petrograde," *Krasnaia letopis'*, no. 2/3 (1922), pp. 129–30.

link to the cultural world that intellectuals represented. The elite's definitions of refinement and learning held many workers in their sway. But by 1917 some were ready to sweep away this old cultural edifice along with the political and economic institutions that sustained it.

The Founding of the Proletkult

The broad array of cultural programs that flourished before 1917 shared one common purpose: they were preparatory courses for political change. The activists in these diverse projects disagreed about the most fundamental issues, but they all agreed that cultural training was necessary for a lasting and meaningful transformation of Russian society. The February Revolution of 1917, which came as a surprise to organized political parties and labor groups, immediately changed the context of further political discussion and altered the assumptions of cultural activists. Programs for enlightenment now became a way to continue the revolution, to shape its outcome, and to determine the purity of its goals.

The February Revolution inspired a multitude of new organizations, from factory committees to soviets, that from the outset challenged the efforts by the Provisional Government to consolidate its power.[53] The precarious new government, formed from the defunct Duma, took charge until elections could be held. It was overseen by a popularly controlled system of soviets that put forward its own agenda for political change. This complex arrangement, known as "dual power," was not limited to politics. In the economic sphere capitalists faced recalcitrant factory committees and unions, and landowners were opposed by the land-hungry peasantry. There

---

53. For a discussion of these new institutions see Keep, *The Russian Revolution*, pp. 65–152; Marc Ferro, *The Russian Revolution of February 1917*, trans. J. L. Richards (Englewood Cliffs, N.J., 1972), pp. 93–96; and Diane Koenker, *Moscow Workers and the 1917 Revolution* (Princeton, 1981), pp. 142–86.

was also a cultural divide. The government's authority was undercut by a plethora of organizations at the grass roots that tried to impose their own visions of cultural transformation.

The Provisional Government inadvertently contributed to the growth of new cultural programs by its inactivity. The new Ministry of Education, headed by the Moscow University professor A. A. Manuilov, was not eager to begin major educational reforms until the revolution became more secure. Manuilov believed that the government's major responsibility was to remove the many strictures on education developed under tsarism. The new regime of course supported the democratization of education and the expansion of institutions open to the lower classes. Significantly, Countess Panina, whose people's house had played such an important role in the lives of many Petersburg workers, was named assistant Minister of Education under Kerensky. However, the government had neither the time nor the inclination to develop bold educational policies that promised significant change or a new approach to cultural affairs.[54]

While the government hesitated, alternative cultural programs were springing up everywhere. Unions and factory committees founded their own educational sectors, as did political parties and soviets. In Petrograd alone, workers' groups claimed some 150 clubs with one hundred thousand members.[55] Participants in these programs condemned the new government for its lack of concern for public education, and the state's inaction invested them with political and moral authority. It appeared that they, not the government,

54. Daniel T. Orlovsky, "The Provisional Government and its Cultural Work," in *Bolshevik Culture*, ed. Abbott Gleason, Peter Kenez, and Richard Stites (Bloomington, 1985), pp. 39–56; William G. Rosenberg, *Liberals in the Russian Revolution* (Princeton, 1974), pp. 82–83, 97, 279; and Oskar Anweiler, *Geschichte der Schule und Pädagogik in Russland vom Ende des Zarenreichs bis zum Beginn der Stalin Ära* (Berlin, 1964), pp. 70–72.

55. G. E. Bylin, "Iz istorii kul'turno-prosvetitel'noi deiatel'nosti profsoiuzov i fabzavkomov Petrograda v period podgotovki Oktiabr'skogo vooruzhennogo vosstaniia," *Uchenye zapiski VPSh VTsSPS*, vol. 1 (1969), p. 115.

had the cultural interests of the workers at heart. Cultural policy became yet another contested arena between the Provisional Government and the opposition.

Despite their numbers, the hastily formed cultural circles were very unstable. They lacked staff and supplies, and often had very shallow roots. Many competing groups laid claims to the same scarce resources, and there were no generally recognized institutions to oversee and manage affairs. Some participants believed that the best solution would be to create some centralized coordinating body, but this posed additional problems. In the polarized political atmosphere between February and October, it was difficult to decide just who should take control. If the Provisional Government was not to be in charge, then who was?

The most obvious candidates were the soviets. In some parts of Russia local soviets moved quickly to establish influential cultural and educational divisions.[56] The national Congress of Soviets also tried to devise a cultural agenda. Faced with an inactive government, it proposed to start a national commission that would arrogate to itself the tasks of a state ministry, overseeing education from the elementary school to the university level. But with such broad duties, the specific needs of the adult working-class population were a relatively minor issue.[57] Accordingly, proletarian groups began to question whether the soviets could meet their needs.

Trade unions, as long-standing supporters of workers' enlightenment, were the first to propose a new institution to sustain specifically proletarian cultural projects. At the national union conference in June 1917 the Menshevik Ivan Maiskii argued eloquently for unions to assume responsibility for cultural training. "The workers' movement is, among other things, also a cultural movement. Only a worker who is

56. On soviet programs in Moscow and Petrograd see V. P. Lapshin, *Khudozhestvennaia zhizn' Moskvy i Petrograda v 1917 godu* (Moscow, 1983), pp. 127–35.

57. See the discussion on education at the first national soviet in June 1917, *Pervyi Vserossiiskii s"ezd sovetov rabochikh i soldatskikh deputatov* (Moscow, 1930), vol. 2, pp. 277–97, esp. pp. 291–94.

consciously concerned with his surroundings can be a convinced socialist and an active participant in the union movement."[58] He proposed that unions form a broad national apparatus, with its central committee in Petrograd, to coordinate workers' cultural-educational activities. This new structure would include representatives from unions, soviets, cooperatives, and Social Democratic parties.[59] But the union bureaucracy faced pressing political and economic problems that left it little time for education. Maiskii's entire presentation had a somewhat plaintive tone; he seemed to beg his colleagues to give more time to culture. Not surprisingly, union efforts brought few results.[60]

It was the most militant workers' organizations, the factory committees, that succeeded in founding a proletarian cultural network. These bodies, intended first as defensive mechanisms to insure jobs when the Russian economy began its long spiral downward, expanded rapidly after the February Revolution.[61] Many factory committees formed cultural commissions devoted to education, leisure activities, and agitational work at the factory site. These cultural circles were particularly active in Petrograd.[62] When the Petrograd factory com-

58. *Tret'ia Vserossiiskaia konferentsiia professional'nykh soiuzov, 3–11 iiulia (20–28 iiunia staryi stil') 1917 goda: Stenograficheskii otchet* (Moscow, 1927), reprint, ed. Diane Koenker (Millwood, N.Y., 1982), p. 405.

59. Ibid., pp. 407, 412–13, 464–65.

60. Knizhnik, Karl Ozol'–Prednek, and A. M., "God bor'by za proletarskuiu kul'turu," *Griadushchee*, no. 8 (1918), pp. 13–14.

61. There is a growing literature on factory committees. For works that focus on the pre-October period see Paul Avrich, "The Bolshevik Revolution and Workers' Control in Russian Industry," *Slavic Review*, vol. 22, no. 1 (1963), pp. 47–63; David Mandel, *The Petrograd Workers and the Fall of the Old Regime: From the February Revolution to the July Days 1917* (New York, 1983); idem, *The Petrograd Workers and the Soviet Seizure of Power: From the July Days 1917 to July 1918* (New York, 1984); and S. A. Smith, *Red Petrograd: The Revolution in the Factories, 1917–1918* (Cambridge, Eng., 1983).

62. See Smith, *Red Petrograd*, pp. 84–85, 94–98; I. A. Baklanova, *Rabochie Petrograda v period mirnogo razvitiia revoliutsii* (Leningrad, 1978), pp. 142–43; and I. I. Mints et al., eds., *Fabrichno-zavodskie*

mittees gathered in a citywide meeting in August 1917, the delegates proposed to create a new body to unify and direct the proletariat's cultural work.

That factory committees succeeded in this endeavor was in large part because of the efforts of cultural activists from the Vpered circle. In 1917 they returned from exile and, except for Bogdanov, rejoined the Bolshevik Party. Lunacharskii, who followed Lenin from Switzerland in a second sealed train, was the most important figure.[63] It was he who united the theoretical positions of Vpered with the growing network of proletarian cultural groups and thus created the basis for the Proletkult.

When he arrived in Petrograd, Lunacharskii started work on Gorky's newspaper, *New Life* (*Novaia zhizn'*), using this platform to popularize his views on cultural transformation.[64] He proclaimed that cultural organization should be the "fourth form" of the working-class movement alongside political parties, unions, and cooperatives.[65] The creation of a central structure for workers' cultural societies was more than an administrative convenience. It was a way to start a new proletarian movement that alone could insure that culture became a central focus of revolutionary change.

Lunacharskii made his points forcefully at the August 1917 gathering of factory committees. He argued against those who seemed to think that culture was some sort of dessert, a treat to be enjoyed when the political situation had stabilized. "Cultural-educational work is just as essential as the other forms of the workers' movement. In our understanding of it, this does not mean just adult education and literacy classes. It

---

komitety Petrograda v 1917 godu: Protokoly (Moscow, 1982), pp. 60, 142, 145–47, 157.

63. On Lunacharskii in 1917 see Timothy O'Connor, *The Politics of Soviet Culture: Anatolii Lunacharskii* (Ann Arbor, 1983), pp. 13–14.

64. N. N. Sukhanov, *The Russian Revolution: A Personal Record*, ed. and trans. Joel Carmichael (Princeton, 1984), pp. 374–76.

65. A. V. Lunacharskii, "Kul'tura sotsializma torzhestvuiushchego i sotsializma boriushchegosia," *Novaia zhizn'*, June 21, 1917; and idem, "Politika i kul'tura," *Novaia zhizn'*, July 30, 1917.

is the development of a sensible, harmonious world view."[66] To insure an institutional structure suited to their demands, workers had to form their own cultural administration. Because the soviets and the city duma were not class-exclusive institutions, they could not represent workers alone. Unions, which were class-exclusive, were mainly interested in technical education. Thus the proletariat had no choice but to create a new center of its own.[67] Convinced by Lunacharskii's arguments, delegates passed a resolution confirming culture's dominant position in the labor movement. To realize these ideas, the conference proposed to found a centralized cultural institution that would assume control of all cultural activities among workers, first in Petrograd and then throughout Russia.[68]

The first step in this ambitious program was to call a conference of all the city's proletarian cultural-educational organizations. Lunacharskii was at the center of these preparations, aided by his old friends from exile, Lebedev-Polianskii, Kalinin, and Pavel Bessalko. Members of the newly formed Society of Proletarian Writers, especially I. I. Nikitin and Aleksei Samobytnik-Mashirov, also took part in the planning. Other organizers included the avant-garde writer Osip Brik, the Bolshevik art and theater expert Platon Kerzhentsev, and a proletarian actor named Vasilii Ignatov.[69] Except for Brik, all of these men were to become important figures in the early history of the Proletkult.

Conference preparations were very thorough. Planners drew up questionnaires soliciting information about the range and content of cultural work in the capital. In the hope that the conference would represent all circles serving the working class, they invited factory committees, unions, army

66. P. N. Amosov et al., eds., *Oktiabr'skaia revoliutsiia i fabzav-komy: Materialy po istorii fabrichno-zavodskikh komitetov* (Moscow, 1927), vol. 1, p. 234.
67. Ibid., p. 235.
68. Ibid., pp. 236–37.
69. A. V. Lunacharskii, "Ideologiia nakanune Oktiabria," in

groups, socialist parties, and soviets to take part. The socialist press printed impassioned appeals explaining the significance of cultural organization. To quote one:

The proletariat believes that true art ennobles and elevates the individual, making him capable of great emotions and deeds. Unlike any other force, [art] organizes the masses into a unified collective. Knowledge and beauty cultivate the individual and the class. . . . Education and creation in science and art are an integral part of every powerful social movement, every revolution.[70]

Although conference planning was technically in the hands of the factory committees, the Bolsheviks, who by now controlled most of these committees, were crucially important.[71] The main organizers were party members, although many were recent converts from the Vpered faction, and the Bolshevik press was the most active in publicizing the event. However, other socialist parties did not view the conference as a strictly partisan affair. Both the Menshevik Internationalist paper *New Life* and the Menshevik *Worker's Paper* (*Rabochaia gazeta*) greeted the preparations and gave the conference good coverage.[72] Discussions about aesthetics and education did not break down neatly along party lines.

In mid-October, just one week before the storming of the Winter Palace, the first conference of proletarian cultural-

Vospominaniia i vpechatleniia, by A. V. Lunacharskii (Moscow, 1968), pp. 166–67.

70. "Vozzvanie," *Novaia zhizn'*, September 15, 1917.

71. Soviet scholarship gives the Bolsheviks full credit. See Bylin, "Iz istorii kul'turno-prosvetitel'noi deiatel'nosti," pp. 114–23; T. A. Khavina, "Bor'ba Kommunisticheskoi partii za Proletkul't i rukovodstvo ego deiatel'nost'iu, 1917–1932 gg." (Candidate dissertation, Leningrad State University, 1978), pp. 21–30; and V. V. Gorbunov, "Iz istorii kul'turno-prosvetitel'noi deiatel'nosti Petrogradskikh bol'shevikov v period podgotovki Oktiabria," *Voprosy istorii KPSS*, no. 2 (1967), pp. 25–35.

72. See *Novaia zhizn'*, September 15, October 17, October 19, October 20, 1917; and *Rabochaia gazeta*, October 15, October 17, October 20, 1917.

educational organizations opened in the Petrograd city duma. The Bolsheviks had already begun preparations for an armed uprising; the first national conference of factory committees was meeting in Petrograd at the same time; and there was also a gathering of garrison committees. All of Petrograd's political parties were preparing for the upcoming Congress of Soviets.[73] In this politically charged atmosphere, some two hundred workers and intellectuals met to discuss the role of fine arts and education in the working-class movement.[74]

Lunacharskii presided over the conference, aided by Fedor Kalinin (representing unions), the Bolshevik organizers Konkordiia Samoilova and Iurii Steklov, as well as Vasilii Ignatov.[75] In the opening address Lunacharskii asked delegates to confirm the importance of culture in the struggle for socialism. Despite some objections from the floor, his position carried the day: "The cultural-educational movement must be part of the general working-class movement together with political, economic, and cooperative organizational forms."[76]

Most of the lectures on artistic practice were given by intellectuals. Lunacharskii addressed problems of literature, the futurist Osip Brik spoke on the arts as a whole, and the folk music expert Arsenii Avraamov lectured on music.[77] Both Brik and Avraamov reflected the values of the prerevolutionary adult education movement. They hoped the new organization would help to bring art to the masses. Brik in particular used the vocabulary of liberal and leftist intellectual educa-

73. For a detailed account of the days preceding the revolution see Alexander Rabinowitch, *The Bolsheviks Come to Power: The Revolution of 1917 in Petrograd* (New York, 1976), pp. 209–44.
74. According to Lunacharskii there were 208 delegates. A. V. Lunacharskii, "Pervaia proletarskaia prosvetitel'naia konferentsiia," in I. S. Smirnov, comp., "K istorii Proletkul'ta," *Voprosy literatury*, no. 1 (1968), pp. 118–19. The most detailed newspaper report lists 189 representatives, mainly from factories, unions, and clubs. See also *Rabochaia gazeta*, October 19, 1917.
75. *Rabochii put'*, October 17, 1917.
76. *Rabochaia gazeta*, October 17, 1917.
77. *Rabochii put'*, October 17, October 26, 1917.

tors. Avoiding any references to proletarian culture, he insisted on the need to democratize the arts.[78]

The prominent role of intellectuals irritated some workers, who raised the same objections that participants in workers' clubs and educational societies had voiced since 1905. Intellectuals, particularly those who were not socialists, were fickle allies. Lunacharskii tried unsuccessfully to get delegates to agree that they should accept the help of all sympathetic intellectuals, regardless of their political views. One worker, B. D. Mandelbaum, objected so violently that he swayed the assembly to override the proposal. Delegates determined that nonparty intellectuals would only be accepted to teach in the natural sciences, presumably the area where they could do the least harm.[79]

The February Revolution created a new problem that cultural activists before 1917 had not seriously considered. What relationship would this new cultural organization have to the existing state? The delegates agreed with the Bolshevik intellectual D. I. Leshchenko that the structure they were founding had to be completely independent from the government, reflecting the general dissatisfaction with the Kerensky regime. Only workers themselves could guarantee that their education had a revolutionary, Marxist content.[80] At the same time, however, conference participants insisted that the groups they represented had to retain their own integrity. The new organization would not be able to dictate the practices of the clubs and circles gathered within it. The center would be an exchange (*birzha*) for supplies and staff, but it would in no way limit local control.[81]

Defining proletarian culture proved to be the most difficult problem of all. Whereas Osip Brik did not even address the issue of class culture, Vasilii Ignatov took a militant position.

78. *Rabochii put'*, October 17, 1917.
79. *Rabochii put'*, October 26, 1917; and *Rabochaia gazeta*, October 17, 1917.
80. *Rabochaia gazeta*, October 19, 1917.
81. *Novaia zhizn'*, October 20, 1917.

He argued that proletarian theater should use only proletarian actors and a proletarian repertoire, resorting to plays written by intellectuals only when they specifically met the needs of the working class. The audience was also split. Some delegates insisted that workers should first absorb the cultural classics, but others denied that "bourgeois" culture had anything to teach them.[82]

Lunacharskii emerged somewhere in the middle. He endorsed the idea of proletarian culture wholeheartedly but reminded workers that they had much to learn from the culture of the past. His position eventually prevailed, and the final resolution was worded so that both sides could support it:

> In both science and art the proletariat will develop its own independent forms, but it should also make use of all the cultural achievements of the past and present in this task. . . . Nonetheless, [the proletariat] must have a critical approach to the fruits of the old culture. It accepts them not as a student, but rather as a builder who is called to erect bright, new structures using the bricks from the old ones.[83]

Although all the preparations were completed at the October conference, it was only in mid-November, after the Bolsheviks took power, that the organizing committee had a chance to meet. It set up an office within the state's educational commission and began plans to start a theater and a library.[84] At this point the group's secretary, Ignatov, suggested an abbreviation for their cumbersome title. The amalgam of proletarian cultural-educational organizations would henceforth be known as the Proletkult.[85]

82. *Novaia zhizn'*, October 19, 1917; and *Rabochii put'*, October 17, 1917. See also Lunacharskii, *Vospominaniia i vpechatleniia*, pp. 166–68.

83. *Rabochii put'*, October 17, 1917.

84. *Izvestiia TsIK*, November 27, December 1, 6, 22, and 29, 1917.

85. P. I. Lebedev-Polianskii, "Kak nachinal rabotat' Narodnyi Komissariat Prosveshcheniia: Lichnye vospominaniia," *Proletarskaia revoliutsiia*, no. 2 (1926), p. 51.

The Proletkult inherited many persistent controversies from its precursors. Long-standing debates about the meaning of proletarian culture, from the transmission of elite learning to the discovery of working-class art, resurfaced at the founding conference. The Proletkult's planners did not move far past the old disputes about intellectuals' place in proletarian movements. The heated discussions about workers' need for a grounding in the culture of the past could have been taken directly from the pages of labor journals in the years after 1905.

However, the organization that took shape in 1917 was more than the sum of its prerevolutionary parts. The political struggle fought in the name of the proletariat unavoidably enhanced its goals. Lunacharskii's vision of a cultural movement parallel to unions, socialist parties, and cooperatives was much more ambitious than the elite training schools Bogdanov had proposed. It was also less cohesive. Individual circles' demands for autonomy foreshadowed future tensions between the advocates of local control and those who hoped to forge a centralized national movement.

The revolutionary origins of the Proletkult also complicated its relationship to the state and to the party that would play such an important role in state affairs. Many times during conference preparations, Lunacharskii stressed that governmental institutions could never represent the needs of the working class alone. Only a consciously proletarian organization could be an effective advocate for the workers' educational and cultural demands. This stance was formulated in opposition to the Provisional Government. But for many involved in the planning of the Proletkult, their strong commitment to class institutions did not end when the Bolsheviks heralded the beginning of the new Soviet state.

2

Institution Building

The Proletkult's Place in Early Soviet Culture

The Proletkult was conceived in the revolution and took root during the Russian Civil War. Its transformation from a local workers' organization into an important national institution was both enriched and complicated by the tumultuous political environment in which it grew. An ally of the new order, it expanded with the government's aid. At the same time, its outspoken demands for independence and power brought it into conflict with many other institutions, including the Communist Party and the state's cultural bureaucracy.

During the first years of the Soviet regime, all new institutions were in flux and in potential competition. In order to build a social base and justify their organization's existence, Proletkult leaders laid claims to a distinct constituency and a special role within society. In their view the Proletkult was to be the industrial proletariat's independent advocate in the field of culture, an agenda that was partially determined by the movement's prerevolutionary predecessors. However, the precise meaning of Proletkult autonomy and the limits to its authority were structured gradually through dissension and dialogue with its many cultural rivals. Its identity was also shaped by clashes between the national organization and its provincial affiliates, which were only too eager to interpret autonomy as an endorsement of local control.

Organizing Soviet Culture

The October Revolution led to an explosion in the number of new cultural groups and organizations. Independent clubs and societies sprang up, as did cultural sections for unions, soviets, factories, Komsomol groups, cooperatives, and the Red Army.[1] The state's educational apparatus financed theaters, meeting halls, and schools. Open lectures abounded on themes from religion to Esperanto. New festivals honoring revolutionary holidays, such as May Day, brought enthusiasts into the streets and the public squares. This remarkable expansion gave early Soviet culture a great vitality, although critics wondered if quantity was not completely eclipsing quality. To the theater director Prince Sergei Volkonskii, the population seemed to be gripped with some kind of organizational fever. Amazed by the mushrooming of new theaters, Volkonskii wrote: "Yes, if art consisted in numbers, it would be possible to say that the dramatic art flourished in Russia."[2]

The Soviet government recognized immediately that education and artistic creation were powerful channels through which to establish a new social and political ethos.[3] As soon as they took power, the Bolsheviks began a structural reorganization of national cultural life. Despite the precarious position of the regime, the state offered funds, physical resources, and food rations to a broad array of revolutionary cultural circles. At the same time, it denied support to institutions whose sympathies were suspect, even intervening to close them down.

The People's Commissariat of Enlightenment, known by its

1. See E. N. Gorodetskii, "Bor'ba narodnykh mass za sozdanie sovetskoi kul'tury, 1917–1920 gg.," *Voprosy istorii*, no. 4 (1954), pp. 18–37; and V. V. Gorbunov, "Oktiabr' i nachalo kul'turnoi revoliutsii na mestakh," in *Velikii Oktiabr'*, ed. Iu. A. Poliakov (Moscow, 1978).

2. Serge Wolkonsky, *My Reminiscences*, trans. A. E. Chamot (London, 1924), vol. 2, p. 220.

3. See Peter Kenez, *The Birth of the Propaganda State: Soviet Methods of Mass Mobilization* (Cambridge, Eng., 1985).

Russian acronym Narkompros, burgeoned into a complex bureaucratic structure with seventeen different divisions. It
sought to control state schools and universities as well as
concert halls, theaters, and museums. The Red Army sponsored theaters, reading rooms, and literacy programs. The
Central Economic Council (Vesenkha) hoped to control technical education, and the trade unions devised their own cultural divisions. City soviets financed and influenced local
schools and artistic centers. In addition, a whole complex of
educational societies and circles flourished under the loose
collective control of several state bureaucracies.[4] Because the
responsibilities of these new groups were not clearly defined,
they quickly came into conflict.

All early Soviet institutions struggled against what was
called "parallelism," the duplication of services by competing
bureaucratic systems. The revolution raised difficult questions about governmental organization that were only slowly
answered during the first years of the regime. Political activists disputed the authority of the central state, the role of the
Communist Party within it, and the influence national agencies should wield over local groups. Altercations over scarce
resources and institutional authority were intertwined with
theoretical debates over the ideal structure of the new polity.

Cultural agencies competed for funds, staff, and control of
a clearly defined constituency. Who, for example, would be
responsible for the cultural life of trade unionists? Individual
factories often had their own educational circles, some with
long histories, which were separate from union programs.

4. For a description of these new cultural bureaucracies see
Sheila Fitzpatrick, *The Commissariat of Enlightenment* (Cambridge,
Eng., 1970); A. I. Fomin, "Stanovlenie tsentral'nogo sovetskogo ap-
parata gosudarstvennogo rukovodstva narodnym prosveshcheniem," *Voprosy istorii*, no. 12 (1976), pp. 17–29; Kenez, *Birth of the
Propaganda State*; S. S. Tarasova, "Kul'turnoe stroitel'stvo v pervyi
god sovetskoi vlasti," in *Pobeda Velikoi Oktiabr'skoi sotsialisticheskoi
revoliutsii*, ed. G. N. Golikov (Moscow, 1957); and Mark von Hagen,
*The Red Army and the Revolution: Soldiers' Politics and State-Building
in Soviet Russia, 1917–1930* (forthcoming), chaps. 2 and 3.

Narkompros had an Adult Education Division (*Vneshkol'nyi Otdel*) with special activities for workers.[5] The Central Economic Council wanted to direct workers' technical education, and the Proletkult hoped to gain them as candidates for its artistic and pedagogical projects.

Some disputes, such as the long-running battle between Narkompros, the trade unions, and the Central Economic Council over the purpose of workers' education, were political and philosophical. Narkompros, and particularly its leader, Lunacharskii, wanted school curricula to be broad and well-balanced enough to educate accomplished citizens. Trade unions and Vesenkha, however, were more interested in vocational training that would provide a competent labor force.[6] Other disputes were simply bureaucratic rivalries over power. Disturbed by these wranglings, Nadezhda Krupskaia, head of the Adult Education Division, continually warned cultural workers to avoid the waste and confusion engendered by competing parallel programs.[7] Yet even her solution—to have all other institutions, including the army, unions, and the Proletkult, remove themselves from the field of adult education altogether and give exclusive control to her division— was part of the problem.

These entangled agendas were further confused because national institutions exercised little authority over their local affiliates. Factory workers ignored the careful arrangements devised by central trade unions. Teachers rejected the de-

5. "*Vneshkol'nyi otdel*" is usually translated as the "Extra-Mural Educational Division," but I think that Adult Education Division better conveys a sense of its programs. It oversaw libraries, clubs, evening schools, and museum programs aimed primarily at the adult population. On its structure see T. A. Remizova, *Kul'turno-prosvetitel'naia rabota v RSFSR, 1917–1925* (Moscow, 1968), p. 6.

6. On these disputes see Fitzpatrick, *Commissariat*, esp. pp. 26–88, 210–55; and idem, *Education and Social Mobility in the Soviet Union, 1921–1934* (Cambridge, Eng., 1979), pp. 41–63.

7. See, for example, N. K. Krupskaia, "Organizatsiia komissariatov," from *Pravda*, 1919, reprinted in *Pedagogicheskie sochineniia v desiati tomakh*, by N. K. Krupskaia (Moscow, 1957), vol. 2, pp. 99–100.

tailed curriculum proposals worked out by Narkompros. Complex deals dividing the responsibilities of national bureaucracies, such as those that were eventually arranged between Narkompros and the Proletkult, were disregarded by lower-level organizations. The revolution was initially a centrifugal force that challenged the traditional overcentralization of the old regime. In the postrevolutionary process of state construction central institutions increasingly attempted to reverse the trend, asserting more and more power over their affiliates. Nonetheless, there was still much room for local intransigence, if not local control.

In this contest for cultural influence the Proletkult started in a strong position. The regime needed allies, and Proletkultists were partisans of the new order. For this they were rewarded with funds, physical resources, and the benevolent protection of the cultural commissar, Lunacharskii. Yet as soon as the organization began to act, this early alliance was threatened because the Proletkult laid claim to areas of responsibility that other cultural organizations wanted for themselves.

Autonomy and Identity:
Proletkult, Narkompros, and the Communist Party

Although the workers and intellectuals who met in Petrograd in October 1917 to lay the foundations for the Proletkult were preparing for revolution, they did not envision the consequences the impending upheaval would have on the structure they were creating. The Petrograd Proletkult had been shaped in opposition to the Kerensky regime's perceived cultural inadequacies. Now, when the Bolsheviks came to power, the Proletkult refused to give up its autonomy, much to the surprise of many advocates of the Soviet state. Its partisans insisted that an independent Proletkult would enhance the proletariat's position in the new political order.

Lunacharskii had already provided a justification for this

position when he insisted that there were four organizational forms of the workers' movement—political parties, trade unions, cooperatives, and cultural circles—and that the last was no less important than the others. In the same spirit Proletkultists—combining unions and cooperatives under the rubric of "economic organizations"—began to write about the three paths to workers' power through economics, politics, and culture.[8] In institutional terms this meant that unions, the Communist Party, and the Proletkult should pursue their own agendas, free from state intervention. Implicitly, it also denied the party any special power over Proletkult or union affairs.

The Proletkult's claims to autonomy (*samostoiatel'nost'*) and its slogan of "three paths to workers' power" quickly became controversial. When the Proletkult lost favor with the Communist Party at the end of the Civil War, critics chose to interpret its initial demand for independence as an anti-Soviet, anticommunist posture. This negative or oppositional explanation has colored subsequent scholarship to such an extent that it is difficult to recapture what autonomy meant to Proletkult members. Because the organization's best known leader, Aleksandr Bogdanov, never rejoined the party after his ouster before the revolution, many commentators have assumed that the Proletkult's claim to independence was an implicit critique of the Communist Party's role.[9]

However, if we examine the Proletkult's demands for autonomy more closely, it becomes apparent that they were directed much more against the state than against the party. Proletkult theorists did not equate state and party power. For

8. In "Ot redaktsii," *Proletarskaia kul'tura*, no. 1 (1918), pp. 1–3, Bogdanov discusses the importance of cultural, political, union, and cooperative organizational forms and then combines the latter two. On the authorship of this unsigned article see A. A. Bogdanov, *O proletarskoi kul'ture, 1904–1924* (Moscow, 1924), p. 100.

9. This is a common theme in Soviet scholarship. See, for example, V. V. Gorbunov, *V. I. Lenin i Proletkul't* (Moscow, 1974), esp. pp. 5–7. For a Western assessment that makes a similar point see Zenovia A. Sochor, *Revolution and Culture* (Ithaca, 1988), pp. 140–42.

them the Communist Party, like their own organization and trade unions, was an expression of proletarian class interests. The government, by contrast, had to take the needs of non-proletarian classes into account, and this necessity made it a suspect partner for workers' groups. In the minds of Prolet-kult theorists only pure working-class institutions could usher in the dictatorship of the proletariat. "In questions of culture we are *immediate socialists*," proclaimed the editorial board of the central Proletkult journal *Proletarian Culture* (*Proletarskaia kul'tura*). "We demand that the proletariat start right now, immediately, to create its own *socialist forms of thought, feeling, and daily life*, independent of alliances or com-binations of political forces. And in this creation, *political allies*—the rural and urban poor—cannot and must not con-trol [the proletariat's] work."[10]

Proletkultists were not the only ones to draw a sharp dis-tinction between state and party authority as the new system took shape. The function of the Communist Party within the state was not predetermined in 1917.[11] As party members gained dominant positions in the central government, some revolutionaries, including Evgenii Preobrazhenskii, sug-gested that the party be disbanded altogether because it du-plicated the structure of the state.[12] These ideas also found favor at the local level, where many activists initially as-sumed that the soviets would take precedence over the party bureaucracy.[13]

10. "Ot redaktsii," *Proletarskaia kul'tura*, no. 3 (1918), p. 36. Em-phasis in the original.

11. See Edward Hallett Carr, *The Bolshevik Revolution, 1917–1923* (New York, 1952), vol. 2, pp. 214–32; and T. H. Rigby, *Lenin's Government: Sovnarkom, 1917–1922* (Cambridge, Eng., 1979), esp. pp. 160–89.

12. Richard Sakwa, "The Commune State in Moscow in 1918," *Slavic Review*, vol. 46, no. 3/4 (1987), p. 444; and Rigby, *Lenin's Government*, p. 178.

13. Alexander Rabinowitch, "The Evolution of Local Soviets in Petrograd, November 1917–June 1918: The Case of the First City District Soviet," *Slavic Review*, vol. 46, no. 1 (1987), pp. 20–37, esp. pp. 27–28.

To be sure, some leaders envisioned the Proletkult as the Communist Party's equal, which lent a peculiar bravado to their statements. In this regard the most extreme was Pavel Lebedev-Polianskii, the first Proletkult national president. He insisted on a kind of symmetry between the Proletkult and the Communist Party; if no one questioned the party's need for independence, they should not question his organization's autonomy either. "If a proletarian political organization is necessary and its existence does not contradict the institution of Soviet power, then the Proletkult is also necessary as an independent workers' organization. Like the party, it will not contradict the basis of Soviet power, but rather will strengthen it."[14] There might come a time when the Proletkult was no longer necessary, but by then the Communist Party would not be needed either.

Not all of the organization's members defined their relationship to the party in such provocative terms. Instead they felt that the Proletkult could aid the Bolsheviks' cause. "Of course Communists play a leading role in the Proletkult," wrote one activist in Tambov. "But the Communist Party's hegemony is in essence a political dictatorship; its performance in the field of cultural construction leaves much to be desired. Therefore the Proletkult remains the pure dictatorship of the proletariat in the creation of socialist values."[15]

Proletkultists did not present themselves as opponents of the Communist Party. Indeed, the national organization had a high percentage of Bolsheviks among its leaders, including Lebedev-Polianskii. At the first national conference in 1918 over half the delegates were party members. By the 1920 conference the share had risen to two-thirds, and the only person on the national presidium who was not a Bolshevik was Bogdanov.[16] Prominent leaders included people with impeccable party credentials, such as the old Bolsheviks Anna

14. P. I. Lebedev-Polianskii [V. Polianskii, pseud.], "Zlobodnevnye voprosy," *Griadushchee*, no. 2 (1918), pp. 1–3, quotation p. 3.
15. L. B-a, "K gubernskomu s"ezdu Proletkul'tov," *Griadushchaia kul'tura*, no. 2 (1918), pp. 15–16.
16. *Izvestiia VTsIK*, September 26, 1918; *Griadushchee*, no. 12/13

Dodonova and Fedor Blagonravov, who had helped to insti-
gate the revolution in Moscow, and the union activist Vladimir Kossior, whose brother would later join Stalin's central
committee.[17] Some participants, such as Karl Ozol-Prednek, a
leader in both the Petrograd and the national organizations,
even asserted that only party members should be allowed to
join the movement.[18]

The Proletkult's first serious clashes over its autonomous
status were with representatives of the state's cultural bureaucracy, not with the Communist Party. In fact, in these
early altercations Lebedev-Polianskii suggested that the Proletkult would more willingly accept subordination to the
party than to Narkompros.[19] Only as the distinction between
party and state power became increasingly blurred was the
Proletkult's opposition to state control increasingly interpreted as opposition to the Soviet system itself.[20]

Conflicts between the Proletkult and Narkompros began
soon after the organization started operation. Already early in
1918 leaders of the Petrograd Proletkult refused to cooperate
with efforts to create a citywide theater consortium, insisting
that they would not align themselves with nonproletarian
groups.[21] At the founding conference for the Moscow Proletkult in February 1918 delegates laid claim to vast areas of
competence that extended far beyond any narrowly defined

(1920), p. 22; and "Neobkhodimoe ob"iasnenie," *Tsentral'nyi Gosudarstvennyi Arkhiv Literatury i Iskusstva* [henceforth cited as TsGALI]
f. 1230 (Proletkul't), op. 1, d. 51, l. 6.

17. For more on the background of Proletkult leaders see Chapter 4.

18. *Protokoly pervoi Vserossiiskoi konferentsii proletarskikh kul'-
turno-prosvetitel'nykh organizatsii, 15–20 sentiabria, 1918 g.*, ed. P. I.
Lebedev-Polianskii (Moscow, 1918), p. 24.

19. The protocols from the April 8, 1918, meeting of the government educational commission are reprinted in I. S. Smirnov, comp.,
"K istorii Proletkul'ta," *Voprosy literatury*, no. 1 (1968), p. 121.

20. See Chapter 7.

21. Fitzpatrick, *Commissariat*, pp. 92–93. For similar struggles in
Moscow see "Proletarskaia kul'tura," *Izvestiia VTsIK*, August 13,
1918, and "Ot redaktsii," *Proletarskaia kul'tura*, no. 3 (1918), pp.
35–36.

cultural sphere. Speakers considered ways to improve workers' hygiene and expand the city's cafeteria system. Lecturers
on educational issues endorsed measures to start labor
schools, technical education courses, and to create a proletarian university for the city's workers. They also proposed plans
to direct the education of all proletarian children.[22] The broad
range of topics raised a host of organizational questions. Just
where would the Proletkult's responsibilities end and the government's begin? Did it intend to satisfy all of the proletariat's cultural and educational needs? What would the role of
Narkompros be?

State cultural workers were clearly alarmed by the Proletkult's ambitions. In the spring of 1918 Lunacharskii called a
series of meetings to discuss relations between the government and the Proletkult.[23] State representatives argued that
Proletkultists did not understand how the revolution had
changed the political landscape. The new state was the expression of proletarian rule, even if it did have to consider the
needs of other classes. Krupskaia worried that the Proletkult
would detract workers from the important task of state construction and, because of its autonomy, turn into a haven for
anti-Soviet forces. Dora Elkina was convinced that an independent Proletkult would duplicate the Adult Education Division's work. Even the sympathetic Lunacharskii wondered
whether the Proletkult was really the proper organ to create a
proletarian culture, as it had already attracted nonproletarians to its ranks.[24]

In these discussions the Proletkult was represented by
Fedor Kalinin, head of the government's Division of Proletar-

22. For conference delegates see *Pervaia Moskovskaia obshchegorodskaia konferentsiia proletarskikh kul'turno-prosvetitel'nykh organizatsii, 23–28 fevralia 1918 goda: Tezisy, rezoliutsii* (Moscow, 1918), p.
1. For the full range of speeches see pp. 62–63.
23. Minutes of the March and April 1918 meetings of the Government Commission of Education, *Tsentral'nyi Gosudarstvennyi Arkhiv
RSFSR* [henceforth cited as TsGA RSFSR] f. 2306 (Narkompros), op.
1, d. 35, ll. 14–79. The protocols for the April 8 and April 13 meetings
are reprinted in Smirnov, "K istorii Proletkul'ta."
24. Smirnov, "K istorii Proletkul'ta," pp. 120, 124.

ian Culture, which had been created by Lunacharskii in 1917.[25] Pavel Lebedev-Polianskii, chair of the organizing bureau for the national Proletkult, was also on hand to defend the organization.[26] They both contended that the government had no right to tell them what to do. Because the Proletkult and Narkompros had different purposes, they should be allowed to maintain separate institutional identities. If no one demanded that unions become part of the Commissariat of Labor, or that the Communist Party itself cease to exist because there was now a Soviet government, Lebedev-Polianskii argued, then no one should question the separate identity of the Proletkult from that of Narkompros.[27] Their forceful arguments, combined with disagreements among Narkompros representatives, won the advocates of autonomy an initial victory.

Yet despite their abrasive tone, Kalinin and Lebedev-Polianskii took government fears of parallelism seriously. Working together with other Proletkultists associated with the new journal *Proletarian Culture*, they sought to define a separate sphere of cultural activity that would not duplicate Narkompros work. Already in the first issue of the journal in March 1918, Lebedev-Polianskii wrote that purely educational programs could be left to other groups. The proletariat obviously had to assimilate the accomplishments of past culture, but that was not the Proletkult's task. Its role was to awaken independent creative activity (*samodeiatel'nost'*) within the working class.[28]

Proletarian Culture's editorial board, which included Alek-

25. "Dekret ob uchrezhdenii gosudarstvennoi komissii po prosveshcheniiu," November 22, 1917, *Dekrety sovetskoi vlasti* (Moscow, 1957), vol. 1, pp. 60–62.

26. On the organizational bureau see *Proletarskaia kul'tura*, no. 2 (1918), p. 25.

27. Smirnov, "K istorii Proletkul'ta," p. 121; see also Lebedev-Polianskii's speech at the first national conference, "Revoliutsiia i kul'turnye zadachi proletariata," *Protokoly pervoi konferentsii*, pp. 27–29.

28. P. I. Lebedev-Polianskii [V. Polianskii, pseud.], "Pod znamia Proletkul'ta," *Proletarskaia kul'tura*, no. 1 (1918), p. 6.

sandr Bogdanov, defined the Proletkult as a laboratory and compared its functions to those of the Communist Party. The party was a laboratory for political affairs where the direction of government policies could be planned. "The proletariat's cultural-educational organizations are also laboratories to realize the revolutionary-cultural program of the proletariat on a national level and then, of course, in the world."[29] By choosing this particular description, Proletkult leaders implied that the organization would be a controlled environment that served a restricted following and that studied carefully selected projects. By definition a laboratory was not open to everyone.

There are clear links to the Vperedist platform in this formulation of the Proletkult's mission. This is not surprising because key veterans of that prewar movement—Bogdanov, Lebedev-Polianskii, and Kalinin—all helped to shape it. Rejecting the idea that the Proletkult should educate the entire proletarian population, they hoped to capture the interest of a working-class vanguard particularly suited for their cultural laboratory. Let Narkompros take control of mundane educational concerns; the Proletkult would take charge of cultural creation.

However, this division of cultural terrain was not simply the result of prerevolutionary conceptions. It was reached through dialogue and conflict with Narkompros. The Proletkult's central planners were intelligent enough to realize that if the organization's independence was going to be respected, they would have to limit its power. Thus they backed away from expansive claims, directly contradicting the ideas of many local followers. Participants in Moscow and Petrograd advanced very ambitious schemes, with some members even demanding that the Proletkult become the "ideological leader of all public education and enlightenment."[30] The conception

29. "K sozyvu Vserossiiskoi kul'turno-prosvetitel'noi konferentsii rabochikh organizatsii," *Proletarskaia kul'tura*, no. 1 (1918), p. 27.

30. Vasilii Ignatov, "Tvorchestvo revoliutsii," *Griadushchee*, no. 4 (1918), p. 15.

of the Proletkult as a laboratory, with all the restrictions that this idea implied, tempered these demands and thus marked an astute trade-off with the government. The grandiose vision of the Proletkult as a rival to Narkompros was renounced in return for greater independence from the state.

Forging the National Agenda

The Proletkult was initially well supplied by the new government. In the first half of 1918 Narkompros gave it a budget of over 9,200,000 rubles, compared with 32,500,000 for the entire Adult Education Division.[31] The Petrograd organization received a large and luxurious building, located on a street off Nevsky Prospect, that had formerly been a club for nobles. It was soon rechristened the "Palace of Proletarian Culture," and the street renamed "Proletkult Street" (*Ulitsa Proletkul'ta*), a name that remained long after the organization's demise.[32] This pattern was repeated in many other cities and towns. In Moscow the Proletkult took over the mansion of the industrialist Savva Morozov, located on one of the city's major thoroughfares.[33] In the area near Kologriv, Kostroma province, Proletkult groups moved into the manor houses of local nobles. The new Tambov organization occupied the elegant building of the Land Bank.[34]

The state also facilitated the creation of the national or-

31. Gorbunov, *Lenin i Proletkul't*, p. 59; N. K. Krupskaia, "God raboty Narodnogo Komissariata Prosveshcheniia," 1918, reprinted in *Pedagicheskie sochineniia v desiati tomakh*, by N. K. Krupskaia (Moscow, 1957), vol. 2, p. 93.

32. "Dekret o natsionalizatsii doma kluba prinadlezhashchego 'Blagorodnomu sobraniiu' v Petrograde i peredache ego Proletkul'tu," February 2, 1918, *Dekrety sovetskoi vlasti*, vol. 1, pp. 380–81; and D. Zolotnitskii, "Teatral'nye studii Proletkul'ta," *Teatr i dramaturgiia: Trudy Leningradskogo gosudarstvennogo instituta teatra, muzyki i kinematografii*, vol. 3 (1971), pp. 135–36.

33. *Proletarskaia kul'tura*, no. 2 (1918), p. 25 lists the Morosov mansion, Vozdvizhenka 16, as Proletkult headquarters. This building, located near the Lenin Library, is now the House of Friendship.

34. *Zhizn' iskusstv*, no. 4 (1918), p. 15; and Dmitrii Vasil'ev-Buglai, "Na fronte v 1918 godu," *Sovetskaia muzyka*, no. 2 (1940), p. 13.

ganization. The Division for Proletarian Culture in Narkompros, headed by Kalinin, became a major planning center.
When the government moved from Petrograd to Moscow in
March 1918, the new capital became the center for Proletkult
activity. Five representatives from the Moscow group, including Bogdanov and the cooperative activist Stefan Krivtsov,
joined the Petrograd leaders Lebedev-Polianskii, Kalinin, Platon Kerzhentsev, and others to plan the organization's first
national conference.[35] They drew up the conference agenda,
decided which groups should be represented, and sent agitators to the provinces to drum up local support. Through the
Proletkult's expanding press, especially *Proletarian Culture*,
they tried to popularize their vision of the Proletkult as an
independent cultural institution designed to represent a distinct and limited constituency.

The preparations for the first national conference were
elaborate. Soviet newspapers and Proletkult journals announced the agenda and guidelines for participation.[36] Kalinin's Narkompros division distributed mass mailings to provincial cultural circles, along with detailed instructions for
propagandists who were sent out to solicit local support.[37]
Vasilii Ignatov, the proletarian actor from Petrograd, turned
up in Tula in August 1918 to get an endorsement from the
provincial Communist Party.[38] In Ivanovo-Voznesensk a
member of the organizing committee, E. P. Khersonskaia,
appealed to local factory workers to elect delegates for the
upcoming meeting.[39]

With much fanfare 330 delegates and 234 guests convened

35. The other members were N. M. Lukin, E. P. Khersonskaia,
and N. M. Vasilevskii, according to the published proceedings of the
first national Proletkult conference. See *Protokoly pervoi konferentsii*.
36. See *Proletarskaia kul'tura*, no. 1 (1918), pp. 28–29.
37. "Vsem sovdepam," TsGALI f. 1230, op. 1, d. 137, ll. 7–8; "In-
struktsiia dlia tov. instruktorov po sozyvu Vserossiiskoi konferentsii," ibid., ll. 9–9 ob.
38. "Vypiska iz protokola Tul'skogo komiteta RKP, 1-ogo avgusta, 1918 g.," TsGALI f. 1230, op. 1, d. 1536, l. 8.
39. This untitled report was written by a delegate to the first
conference, TsGALI f. 1230, op. 1, d. 1245, ll. 4–5.

in Moscow in September 1918, one of the most difficult stages of the Civil War. Two weeks earlier, a Socialist Revolutionary had tried to assassinate Lenin. Siberia, the Ukraine, and South Russia were in the hands of anti-Soviet forces, and the British had begun their occupation of Archangel. The Red Army had only started to make headway in its campaign along the Volga. Yet these national emergencies did little to mar the festive spirit of the gathering. Delegates enjoyed folk music and revolutionary songs performed by the Moscow organization's new orchestra and heard dramatic readings by the Petrograd Proletkult theater. *Pravda* reported that the auditorium of the Women's Higher Courses, where the conference was held, was filled to overflowing.[40] Although there is no extant list of conference delegates or the groups they represented, the conference proceedings indicate that they came mainly from working-class organizations—unions, factory circles, clubs, and cooperatives.[41]

The organizational issues that had preoccupied conference planners were among the first items on the program. Lebedev-Polianskii used the opening address to outline his conception of the Proletkult's relationship to the state. He argued in favor of an autonomous Proletkult that would pursue carefully circumscribed cultural tasks.[42] His proposal, which had already been elaborated at length in *Proletarian Culture*, was opposed from two different sides. On the one hand were those whom one participant called the "maximalists," who believed that the planners' vision was much too modest.[43] On the other

40. *Pravda*, September 17, 1918. On the theater performances see A. A. Mgebrov, *Zhizn' v teatre* (Moscow, 1933), vol. 2, pp. 394–403.

41. *Protokoly pervoi konferentsii* identifies forty-seven delegates by name and organization. Eight were from the organizing committee, nine came from the Moscow or Petrograd Proletkults and thirty others came from a variety of groups, including unions, soviets, factories, and clubs. For the delegates' party affiliation see *Izvestiia VTsIK*, September 26, 1918; and *Proletarskaia kul'tura*, no. 5 (1918), p. 26.

42. "Revoliutsiia i kul'turnye zadachi proletariata," *Protokoly pervoi konferentsii*, pp. 17–21, esp. pp. 20–21.

43. The term is Stefan Krivtsov's, "Konferentsiia proletkul'tov," *Rabochii mir*, no. 14 (1918), p. 33.

hand were those who felt that the Proletkult should soften its claims for independence.

The maximalists objected that the lines drawn between Proletkult and Narkompros work were artificial. The Proletkult should not relinquish control over general educational programs because there could be no cultural creation without education. Some insisted that the new organization take control of all the cultural needs of the proletariat, leaving no responsibilities for Narkompros. They even proposed that the Proletkult assume responsibility for the education of all proletarian children.[44] Even more radical was the demand that the Proletkult take over Narkompros altogether. "Only the Proletkult, and no one else, can achieve a revolutionary culture," proclaimed the Petrograd art director, A. A. Andreev.[45]

Those on the other side, the "minimalists," showed little sympathy for Proletkult autonomy. Echoing the concerns of Narkompros workers, they feared that the Proletkult could ultimately weaken Soviet culture by making exaggerated demands on the new state's resources. Because there were so few cultural workers in the provinces to begin with, one delegate objected, the expansion of the Proletkult would only decrease existing groups' chances of survival. As one Moscow metalworker insisted, "We have a Commissariat of Enlightenment. We should unite around it and not create independent parallel organizations."[46] However, neither of these alternative approaches swayed the convention leaders or the majority of the delegates; resolutions worked out in advance by the planning committee were accepted with very few minor alterations.

Although Proletkult leaders had agreed to restrict the organization's powers, the cultural agenda they presented at the conference was still expansive. Bogdanov expounded on the need for a proletarian science, a topic he had already developed in his voluminous writings before the revolution. To realize this goal, he proposed to create a special proletarian

44. *Protokoly pervoi konferentsii*, pp. 51–52, 63–64.
45. Ibid., pp. 25–26, quotation p. 26.
46. Ibid., p. 26.

university where participants would fashion a proletarian encyclopedia, codifying working-class knowledge in the same
way that the eighteenth-century French encyclopedia had
done for the bourgeoisie. Cultural workers discussed ways to
shape a proletarian music, art, literature, and theater through
special artistic studios. They planned to popularize their creations through their own publications, exhibitions, and performances. Advocates of workers' clubs believed the Proletkult could create a new kind of proletarian collective where
the old habits of daily life would be transformed. The delegates envisioned special circles to discover inventive ways to
educate the young. They even hoped to found an international
organization to spread the idea of proletarian culture from
revolutionary Russia to the rest of the world.[47]

The sobering problem of funding was raised only once during the conference. Although the Proletkult was autonomous,
it still expected Narkompros to foot the bills. The government
would supply the central Proletkult with a subsidy, to be
distributed among provincial affiliates. But because financial
dependence on the state clearly contradicted the organization's claims to independence, the central leaders held out the
hope that their affiliates would soon discover their own means
of support. "All independent proletarian cultural-educational
organizations receiving monetary aid from state organs when
they start and expand their activities must strive to exist on
their own funds."[48]

One of the most important results of the meeting was the
election of a governing board for the national Proletkult. Delegates chose a central committee, an editorial board for *Proletarian Culture*, now the official journal of the national organization, and confirmed Proletkult representatives to
Narkompros. Not surprisingly, the elections reflected already

<hr>

47. On science see ibid., pp. 31–42; on art see ibid., pp. 44–47,
72–80, 110–28; on clubs see ibid., pp. 90–100; on youth see ibid., pp.
66–72; on the International Proletkult see ibid., p. 14.

48. Ibid., p. 54.

existing power relations. Lebedev-Polianskii, who had served as both the chair of the conference organizing committee and the chair of the conference itself, was elected the first national president. The other officers, Fedor Kalinin and Aleksei Samobytnik-Mashirov as vice presidents and Vasilii Ignatov as secretary, had been involved in the Proletkult from the start. Aleksandr Bogdanov was chosen for the central committee and the editorial board of *Proletarian Culture*. The rest of the central committee members came largely from Moscow and Petrograd.[49]

The shape of the national organization was elaborated in discussions and resolutions. At its head was to be a central committee, chosen from an elected national council. More precise descriptions of the Proletkult hierarchy were approved at the first meeting of the national council in January 1919.[50] The basic Proletkult cell was to be the factory, where all workers interested in culture would congregate. Factory circles would unite to form a district (*raionnyi*) Proletkult, and these would combine into a city organization. City groups would then unite at the provincial level, and from this broadly based pyramid the national organization would emerge.[51] At each stage Proletkult operations would be governed by a democratically elected council. This plan owed something to both party and union organizational structures and in fact proposed that the territorial divisions for the Proletkult be the same as those for unions. Although Proletkultists may have renounced their claims to control all of Soviet culture, they clearly had very ambitious plans; they envisioned a base in every factory in Soviet Russia.

The national structure now seemed secure. By building up

49. Ibid., pp. 7, 55.
50. "Plan organizatsii Proletkul'ta," from TsGALI f. 1230, op. 1, d. 138, ll. 1–3; reprinted in *Proletarskaia kul'tura*, no. 6 (1919), pp. 26–29.
51. Ibid. This structure is graphically represented in Peter Gorsen and Eberhard Knödler-Bunte, *Proletkult: System einer proletarischen Kultur* (Stuttgart, 1974), vol. 1, pp. 62–63.

from factory organizations, the Proletkult meant to guarantee a proletarian following. Its autonomous standing was intended to protect the organization's unique class identity. Finally, the hierarchical framework outlined in the national charter aimed to give the central leadership enough power to set the standards and guidelines for local networks. But this elegant scheme failed at every level. As the Proletkult began its rapid expansion throughout Soviet-held territory, central leaders began to face some very disquieting circumstances. The careful arrangements they had made with Narkompros were ignored or misunderstood. The Proletkult's highly valued autonomy often proved difficult to realize, and local groups shaped their own agendas with little concern for national programs. The careful plans of Proletkult theorists were quickly rent asunder as the needs and desires of local followers began to assert themselves.

The Local Reception

"We are entering the beginning of a new Renaissance," pronounced one orator in Perm at a celebration to mark the opening of the local Proletkult in the summer of 1918.[52] His hyperbole conveys some of the enthusiasm that greeted the Proletkult in the first years of Soviet power. The popularity of this cultural movement astounded even its most optimistic supporters. New organizations sprang up "like mushrooms after a spring rain," to quote the cliché advocates used to describe its proliferation. Proletkult expansion was so rapid and chaotic that the central organization could not control or even successfully monitor it. New groups opened and closed in waves, victims of the Civil War, financial problems, or local struggles over cultural resources. To make things even more confusing, some circles called themselves Proletkults without having any ties to the center at all.

52. Cited in *Proletarskaia kul'tura*, no. 3 (1918), p. 31.

During the spring and summer of 1918 a few groups started operation in provincial cities and towns, inspired by press reports and the efforts of propagandists sent from Moscow and Petrograd.[53] But the real organizational upsurge began after the September conference, which received extensive coverage in the national press.[54] "The national conference opened up a new world of thought for us," wrote one participant from Ivanovo-Voznesensk. He and others returned home laden with masses of material and set to work to found local chapters.[55] A representative from the Tver province tailors' union became a strong booster back in his hometown. A performance by the Petrograd Proletkult theater troupe convinced him that the organization could make a difference in Tver's cultural life.[56]

The Proletkult quickly captured the imagination of many cultural activists, and the center already listed 147 local affiliates by the end of 1918.[57] Although this is not a completely reliable estimate, it still shows a remarkable increase in just a few months. As one participant remarked, the organization seemed to be growing by the hour, not by the day.[58] By the fall

53. See reports in *Proletarskaia kul'tura*, no. 1, p. 32; no. 2, p. 34; no. 3, p. 31; no. 4, p. 34.

54. *Pravda*, for example, printed reports almost every day from September 17 to 25, 1918, including verbatim texts of numerous resolutions.

55. Unsigned report from 1922, TsGALI f. 1230, op. 1, d. 1245, l. 5.

56. "Kak sozdalsia Tverskoi Proletkul't," *Proletkul't: Tverskoi vestnik proletarskoi kul'tury*, no. 1/2 (1919), p. 41.

57. "Proletkul'ty, zaregistrirovannye v 1918 godu," TsGALI f. 1230, op. 1, d. 117, ll. 40–41. There is some cause to be skeptical about this list. It includes, for example, the Krasnodar regional Proletkult at a time when Ekaterinodar, not yet renamed, was the center for the White Army in the South. Similarly, it includes cities in Siberia that were not yet under Soviet control. Nonetheless, the central Proletkult consistently used this figure in its estimates of organizational expansion and decline. See "Sostav Proletkul'tov i rukovodiashchikh organov Proletkul'ta," TsGALI f. 1230, op. 1, d. 121, l. 51; and "Piat' let bor'by za proletarskuiu kul'turu," TsGA RSFSR f. 2313 (Glavpolitprosvet), op. 1, d. 19, l. 48.

58. "Vserossiiskaia konferentsiia predstavitelei sovetov Proletkul'ta," *Griadushchee*, no. 1 (1919), p. 19.

of 1920 the national organization determined that there were some three hundred Proletkults in Soviet Russia.[59] The Petrograd journal *The Future* (*Griadushchee*) claimed an even more impressive network, with 1,384 organizations in all.[60] These vastly different totals show the frustrating inaccuracy of Proletkult records, but the lower figure is a better estimate because it is the one that the national organization repeatedly used.

Provincial branches were not shaped according to a standard pattern. Ideally, they were founded at organizing conferences, such as the ones held in Petrograd and Moscow. However, some began operation without much public participation. On the peripheries of Russia or in the battle zones of the Civil War, new groups opened and closed depending on the success of the Red Armies. In Kiev there were three separate efforts to start a Proletkult from 1918 to 1920.[61] Central organizers sent out from Moscow helped to found a handful of provincial groups, but most were the result of local initiative. Workers who had been mobilized from one town to the next

59. P. I. Lebedev-Polianskii [V. Kunavin, pseud.], "Vserossiiskii s"ezd Proletkul'ta," *Proletarskaia kul'tura*, no. 17/19 (1920), p. 74. On Lebedev-Polianskii's many pseudonyms see "Bibliografiia literaturnykh rabot P. I. Lebedeva-Polianskogo," *Literaturnoe nasledstvo*, vol. 55 (1947), p. 612.

60. "Pervyi Vserossiiskii s"ezd Proletkul'tov," *Griadushchee*, no. 12/13 (1920), p. 21. The main difference is in the number of factory Proletkults; the *Griadushchee* report includes over eight hundred. Zenovia Sochor suggests that the low figure of three hundred simply excludes factory organizations, thus accounting for the difference. See Sochor, *Revolution and Culture*, p. 129. However, central lists include factory organizations, and their figures are never as high. Perhaps the larger figure included workers' clubs, which were part of the Proletkult apparatus but not considered independent organizations.

61. See *Proletarskii den' kul'tury: V den' prazdnika kul'tury, 6. avgusta, 1919* (Kiev, 1919), columns 17–19, 22, 26–27; *Biulleten' pervoi Kavkazsko-Donskoi konferentsii proletarskikh kul'turno-prosvetitel'-nykh organizatsii, 25–28 sentiabria 1920 goda* (Armavir, 1920), no. 2, p. 5; and the meeting of the central Proletkult presidium, October 24, 1920, TsGALI f. 1230, op. 1, d. 6, l. 92.

during the Civil War also helped to familiarize the populace with the new organization, and Proletkult agitational troupes performing at the front sometimes inspired local audiences to start circles of their own.[62]

Local unions, factory committees, soviets, Communist Party sectors, and Narkompros divisions all helped to make the Proletkult popular.[63] In various combinations they contributed funding and supplies to help support new organizations. The Tula province soviet gave a small stipend from its budget in 1918 and early 1919.[64] The organization at the Lenin State Sugar Factory in Kursk province got part of its support from the Sugar Workers' Union.[65] The Tambov Proletkult received a modest 2,000 ruble donation from the city's party sector.[66] In the process of expansion local circles also made their own enemies. The Izhevsk Proletkult in Viatka province ran up against opposition from the local party committee, even though many of the leaders were party members.[67] In the Tver province town of Kashin trade union activists insisted that the Proletkult be subordinated to their cultural apparatus.[68]

A dazzling variety of motivations was at work in Proletkult formation. For some groups opening a Proletkult was a way to get funds for preexisting projects, but for others it was an expression of their wholehearted endorsement of the aims of

62. See the reports of the local response to the Moscow Proletkult's Workers' Theatrical Troupe touring the front lines in 1920, TsGALI f. 1230, op. 1, d. 393.

63. For a short list of the groups and individuals responsible for starting twenty-three Proletkult organizations see Gorbunov, "Oktiabr' i nachalo kul'turnoi revoliutsii," p. 66.

64. *Tretii s"ezd sovetov rabochikh, krest'ianskikh i krasnoarmeiskikh deputatov Tul'skoi gubernii* (Tula, 1919), pp. 79, 81.

65. General meeting of the factory organization, May 29, 1919, TsGALI f. 1230, op. 1, d. 1280, l. 6.

66. *Zarevo zavodov*, no. 2 (1919), p. 70.

67. Report of the Izhevsk Proletkult president Kozochkin, 1920, TsGALI f. 1230, op. 1, d. 1221, l. 10 ob.

68. "Protokol konferentsii Proletkul'ta goroda Kashina," December 9, 1920, TsGALI f. 1230, op. 1, d. 531, l. 8 ob.

the central planners. As a result, an institution calling itself a Proletkult could have many functions—an entertainment center, a surrogate Narkompros division, a village club offering literacy classes, or a tightly organized and exclusive factory cell. The flexibility of the Proletkult's identity partially explains its popularity.

It is difficult to determine precisely why people chose to join the Proletkult rather than one of the many other cultural circles available, but proximity surely must have been a factor. In some areas Proletkult organizations began work before state educational agencies and offered the most comprehensive local programs.[69] In large cities like Moscow and Petrograd the Proletkult sponsored a broad network of neighborhood clubs in working-class districts. When the Moscow organization tried to consolidate its clubs into larger and more effective units, participation sank dramatically.[70] Some people may have become members by default. The leadership of the Tula Armament Factory's cultural commission, begun before the October Revolution, petitioned to become a Proletkult organization in 1919 in order to gain additional funds for its theater.[71] As a result, factory theater enthusiasts were transformed into Proletkultists, perhaps without much personal commitment.

The Proletkult's organizational principles clearly inspired local participants. Some embraced Proletkult autonomy and enthusiastically endorsed the movement's independent stance toward the state.[72] The presidium of the Kostroma Proletkult proclaimed that the Narkompros Adult Education Division, as a government organ staffed mainly with intellec-

69. See the case of Vladikavkaz later in this chapter.

70. *Gorn*, no. 2/3 (1919), pp. 126–27; no. 5 (1920), pp. 71–87.

71. "Poiasnitel'naia zapiska k smete kul'turno-prosvetitel'nogo komiteta Tul'skogo oruzheinogo zavoda," TsGALI f. 1230, op. 1, d. 1536, ll. 45–46.

72. See, for example, reports from Penza, cited in *Proletarskaia kul'tura*, no. 5 (1918), p. 40 and from an organizing conference for the Iurevsk Proletkult, Ivanovo-Voznesensk, March 1919, TsGALI f. 1230, op. 1, d. 1271, l. 4.

tuals, could not represent the proletariat's needs as well as a working-class organization.[73] According to one commentator small rural towns opened up Proletkults alongside Narkompros divisions because the organizers hoped the Proletkult would offer something better suited to local needs than public education alone.[74] Even Krupskaia, no friend of the Proletkult, conceded in early 1919 that the rival institution held great popular appeal. "It is characteristic that the public turns to the Proletkult and not the Commissariat because we are not tied to the masses."[75]

Despite the center's elaborate organizational goals, it exercised little control over the Proletkult's rapid growth. Requests for money, materials and, most of all, for leaders and staff members came from all kinds of cultural groups. The overwhelmed central committee responded by sending out copies of *Proletarian Culture*, the Proletkult's organizational plan, and the printed protocols of the first conference. But the committee did not have enough staff to assign to local organizations. Indeed, key leaders were frequently mobilized to the front, including Lebedev-Polianskii himself.[76] Even if the new circles requested help, in most cases they would at best receive a stipend and a packet of materials that they were left to decipher and implement themselves.

With or without central guidance, local enthusiasts devised their own interpretations of the Proletkult's mission. Some clearly saw it as a continuation of the adult education circles that had begun well before the October Revolution. A Kaluga

73. "Organizatsiia Kostromskogo Proletkul'ta," *Sbornik Kostromskogo Proletkul'ta*, no. 1 (1919), p. 107.

74. Rainin, "Rost Proletkul'ta," *Proletarskaia kul'tura*, no. 9/10 (1919), p. 31.

75. See the excerpts from Krupskaia's speech at a meeting for leaders of provincial Adult Education Divisions, January 24–28, 1919, cited in *Vneshkol'noe obrazovanie* (Moscow), no. 2/3 (1919), column 73.

76. See the minutes of Proletkult central committee meetings for the first part of 1919, TsGALI f. 1230, op. 1, d. 3, ll. 1–30. On Lebedev-Polianskii see d. 230, l. 71 ob.

educational and self-help society that had been established in 1914 now applied to the central Proletkult for aid. The society's chairman insisted that he had worked for the Proletkult's aims since his group had started, even though it was obvious that his circle did not cater exclusively to the working class.[77]

The educational division in the small town of Novosil, in Tula province, believed that the Proletkult continued the tradition of people's houses, local cultural centers with long prerevolutionary histories. The division president forwarded reports to Narkompros explaining that the low cultural level of the population in his district could be remedied if they started an active cultural center. The local population had nowhere to go and nothing to do with its free time. The solution was to build a Proletkult center. In fact the town really needed two centers, a small wooden Proletkult right away and a large brick one for future activities.[78]

Even under the best of circumstances, the careful distinctions between Proletkult and Narkompros work were difficult to implement. Some organizers refused to give up their maximalist claims to cultural control. Vasilii Ignatov, national leader and head of the Tula organization, was a particularly brazen offender. He had helped to formulate very ambitious programs for both the Petrograd and the Moscow organizations. When he moved on to Tula in early 1919, he insisted that the Proletkult take control of all city and provincial theaters and cinemas and even seize all available photographic equipment for its projects.[79] To solve potential disputes with Narkompros, he proposed to take charge of the Proletkult and

77. Questionnaire dated 1919, TsGALI f. 1230, op. 1, d. 117, ll. 30–30 ob. See also the questionnaire from the cultural-educational circle in the village of Karchum, Viatka province, December 24, 1918, ibid., l. 27.

78. "Doklad uezdnomu Ispolkomu o postroike v g. Novosile uezdnogo Proletkul'ta," May 23 [1919], TsGA RSFSR f. 2306, op. 3, d. 317, ll. 17–18.

79. January 1919 meetings of the Tula Proletkult, TsGALI f. 1230, op. 1, d. 1537, ll. 1, 6.

the local Adult Education Division simultaneously, a suggestion that was categorically rejected by the national organization.[80]

In other cases Narkompros workers were guilty of violating Proletkult autonomy. In Izhevsk the Proletkult was started by the head of the local Adult Education Division, who ran it as the artistic subsection of her own department. She formed a choir and a small theater group, both of which were open to the population at large. Participants included workers, teachers, and white-collar employees.[81] Dissatisfied with this arrangement, several local workers sent a representative to Moscow to gather information about how the organization should be structured. When the representative returned, armed with issues of *Proletarian Culture*, the dissatisfied workers decided to establish the Proletkult on an independent footing. They held a local conference and elected the metalworker and party member Andrei Kozochkin, one of the critics of the first organization, as their president.[82]

When local Proletkults started work before Narkompros divisions were formed, they were tempted to take charge of comprehensive educational programs far exceeding the limitations set by the central leaders. In Vladikavkaz, a major battle zone of the Civil War, a Proletkult opened in 1918 before Soviet power was firmly established in the area. The new organization was composed of representatives from the local soviet, Socialist Revolutionary and Communist parties, the teachers' union, the theater workers' union, and the central bureau of labor unions. It operated an art school and a workers' club, but the most lively sections were those for agitation and preschool education. The Proletkult sent organizers out into the surrounding mountains to gather support for Soviet power. It opened literacy classes for the local population and

80. Discussed at the July 4, 1919, meeting of the Proletkult central committee, TsGALI f. 1230, op. 1, d. 3, l. 49 ob.
81. "Doklad o deiatel'nosti Izhevskogo Proletkul'ta s 15-ogo avgusta 1919 g. do 1920 g.," TsGALI f. 1230, op. 1, d. 1221, l. 1.
82. Ibid.

sponsored very successful courses for children.[83] In this instance the Proletkult functioned as the local pro-Soviet educational institution.

In distant Vladivostok the Proletkult also served a very broad educational function. It was founded in 1920 by the proletarian writer Aleksandr Alekseevich Bogdanov (no relation to the central leader), who had gone to Siberia as a Proletkult organizer.[84] Bogdanov was driven further east by Kolchak's forces and ended up in Vladivostok in early 1920. With the help of unions, the Communist Party, and the leftist intelligentsia, he quickly organized a Proletkult. The zemstvo government in power gave its qualified support, and the new organization assumed a similar role to the one the Petrograd Proletkult had claimed in 1917, serving as an educational and cultural base for the city's working-class population. It sponsored lecture series, classes, festivals, and artistic workshops. Local teachers gave their services, as did two well-known futurist poets residing in the city, David Burliuk and Nikolai Chuzhak. Because Vladivostok was entirely cut off from Moscow by the war, this circle existed without the aid or even the knowledge of the central organization.[85]

The pyramidlike structure envisioned by central planners—where factory Proletkults banded together to form citywide groups, and these combined into provincial Proletkults—never materialized. Many factory organizations operated independently, without any ties to city or provincial bodies; city-level Proletkults were formed in areas with no factories; and there were even some provincial organizations with no infrastructure at all. This chaotic situation enormously complicated the center's efforts to transmit funding

83. *Proletkul't* (Vladikavkaz), no. 1 (1919), esp. pp. 10–17.
84. See his personnel file in TsGALI f. 1230, op. 1, d. 715, ll. 19–23.
85. V. G. Puzyrev, " 'Proletkul't' na Dal'nem Vostoke," in *Iz istorii russkoi i zarubezhnoi literatury*, ed. V. N. Kasatkina, T. T. Napolona, and P. A. Shchekotov (Saratov, 1968), vol. 2, pp. 90–93, 115; on the zemstvo government's aid see Canfield F. Smith, *Vladivostok under Red and White Rule* (Seattle, 1975), p. 20.

and information and of course to establish control over the rapidly growing enterprise. Indeed, much of the central committee's time was spent trying to discover just what was going on in the provinces. Although the Proletkult's expansion was an impressive accomplishment, it was not clear just what was being created—a loose cultural alliance or a self-conscious and purposeful force in the new state.

In the first years of the Soviet regime Proletkult advocates struggled to define a coherent identity and a secure national structure. Most of their problems were not unique. All early Soviet institutions confronted the confusion of parallelism, learning to defend their constituencies from rival groups. Similarly, all new central bureaucracies found it hard to shape a smoothly working national network, and the dislocations of revolution and war greatly complicated the task. We can add to this list the familiar complaints of poor staffing, funding, and communication, grievances that fill the protocols of all institutions from village soviets to national commissariats.

In some respects the Proletkult was in a very fortunate position. Because of Lunacharskii's intervention, its independence, however limited, was protected by its closest competitor, Narkompros. Thus national leaders could quickly lay claims to a distinct place within the confusing array of cultural institutions. The deals they struck with Narkompros were intelligent ones. The Proletkult would not be just another cultural organization; instead it would be a creative "laboratory," with all the exclusivity that this implied. It would cater to a specialized proletarian audience involved in cultural creation and leave standard educational duties to groups that served the general population. And yet the potential for confusion, misunderstanding, and resentment in these arrangements was enormous. Although the Proletkult was formally autonomous, at the local level it depended on the goodwill and support of potential rivals to secure a stable base. Many of the conflicts supposedly resolved at the national level were played out again and again in the provinces.

The Proletkult also faced peculiar difficulties raised by its ambitious cultural agenda. Demands for autonomy and independent action (*samostoiatel'nost'* and *samodeiatel'nost'*) evoked a sympathetic local response. But such beliefs necessarily fed centrifugal forces, taking power away from national organs. These principles not only legitimated the national Proletkult's challenges to the state's cultural bureaucracy; they also encouraged participants to shape their own institutions to serve local needs.

New Proletkults were formed for many reasons—to continue educational projects conceived long before the revolution or to agitate for a Soviet victory in the Civil War. In the process participants devised an impressive array of cultural programs, from traveling theatrical studios to literacy classes, and they also opened their doors to a very broad audience. Proletkult theorists' commitment to creative independence unwittingly sanctioned this diversity and undercut all efforts to create a cohesive national movement.

3

Proletkult Membership

The Problem of Class in a Mass Organization

The Bolsheviks promised to create a proletarian dictatorship in a largely peasant country, a formidable undertaking. For the Proletkult, even founding a proletarian institution posed insurmountable problems. The Communist Party and trade unions, the Proletkultists' closest reference points, had easier tasks. Although the party presented itself as the vanguard of the proletariat, it never claimed that its ranks would be composed of workers alone. Trade unions, with their roots in the factory, were guaranteed a working-class composition. Proletkult leaders saw their organization as a hybrid of these two forms—a vanguard that would be truly proletarian. But this proved to be a very difficult species to breed in the uncertain social climate of the Civil War.

Proletkult ideology demanded a worker following. According to the Proletkult's national leaders, only the industrial proletariat could express the collective spirit of socialism. These leaders had important organizational concerns as well: Proletkult autonomy was justified as a way to shield the movement's pure proletarian essence from the encroachments of the state. Because a proletarian identity was so important, central leaders devised a whole series of rules and restrictions to keep out socially undesirable elements. Yet despite their best efforts, the Proletkult attracted a very mixed membership drawn from the laboring classes as a whole.

The reasons were partly demographic. Factory workers were never a large social group in Russia, and their numbers diminished during the Civil War. But more important was the fact that the national Proletkult lacked the power to impose its vision of the organization on the provincial affiliates that rejected its narrow social rules. Local circles opened the organization to a broad alliance of the underprivileged, including artisans, white-collar workers, and sometimes even peasants. Thus as it grew, the Proletkult lost its pure class identity. In the process, however, it gained a mass following.

Defining the Proletkult's Constituency

In a rudimentary sense the Proletkult's intended membership was already apparent in its name—it was to be a cultural organization for the proletariat. But the issue was not resolved with the Proletkult's title because "proletariat" was a term open to many interpretations. Did it mean everyone who labored for a living without owning the means of production? Did it include artisanal workers who themselves might hire and supervise other employees? Did it encompass the entire breadth of Russia's half-urbanized, half-ruralized labor force? These definitional problems were particularly complex for the Russian proletariat because the lines between the working class and the peasantry had always been very hard to draw.[1] Processes set in motion by the revolution and Civil War

1. There is a vast literature on the problems of defining the Russian proletariat, particularly in relationship to the peasantry. See Victoria E. Bonnell, *Roots of Rebellion* (Berkeley, 1983); Laura Engelstein, *Moscow, 1905: Working Class Organization and Political Conflict* (Stanford, 1982); L. M. Ivanov, ed., *Istoriia rabochego klassa Rossii, 1861–1900 gg.* (Moscow, 1972); Leopold Haimson, "The Problem of Social Stability in Urban Russia, 1905–1917," in *The Structure of Russian History*, ed. Michael Cherniavsky (New York, 1970); Robert E. Johnson, *Peasant and Proletarian: The Working Class of Moscow in the Late Nineteenth Century* (New Brunswick, N.J., 1979); and

made it even more difficult to set clear limits.[2] This was a time of rapid social change, as workers left factories for the countryside, the army, or the state bureaucracy, and new groups took up industrial jobs.

Before the revolution Russian Marxists, and Bolsheviks in particular, addressed the complexities of the Russian working class by stressing hierarchies within it. Although the Bolsheviks realized that it was very hard to separate the industrial proletariat from the peasantry, for them the workers who really mattered, those who were most inclined to develop a revolutionary consciousness, were the ones who had completely severed their rural ties.[3] The Bolsheviks not only defined the proletariat narrowly, reducing it to the industrial working class alone, but also insisted that only an elite within this group would develop a keen political awareness. This proletarian vanguard would be led by the political vanguard of the Bolshevik Party.

Proletkult national leaders, who were themselves Bolsheviks (or in Bogdanov's case a former Bolshevik), shared many of these assumptions.[4] If anything, the workers they cared about formed an even smaller vanguard. They searched for a political *and* cultural elite within the industrial proletariat. Those positive values that were to form the foundation for the culture of the future were nurtured by the industrial labor process. The factory taught workers the need for cooperation, group action, and collective solutions to shared problems. Working-class neighborhoods and families could also help to mold a proletarian worldview, but those who had not studied long and hard at the school of factory labor could not hope to

Reginald E. Zelnik, *Labor and Society in Tsarist Russia* (Stanford, 1971).

2. See Leopold H. Haimson, "The Problem of Social Identities in Early Twentieth Century Russia," *Slavic Review*, vol. 47, no. 1 (1988), pp. 1–28.

3. These ideas are generally accepted in Soviet scholarship, but they have been disputed by many Western researchers. See Haimson, "The Problem of Social Stability," for the classic rebuttal of these views.

4. See Chapter 4 for an analysis of the national leadership.

develop the values necessary to shape a proletarian culture.[5]

After October the Bolshevik Party began to stress the need for cross-class alliances, particularly with poor peasants and those intellectuals who were willing to cooperate with the new regime. Although Proletkult leaders understood the reasons for these conciliatory programs, most still insisted on class purity within their organization. Proletarian culture could not be created by representatives from the peasantry, the army, the Cossacks, or the narrow-minded urban poor proclaimed the editorial staff of *Proletarian Culture* in 1918.[6]

For Proletkult leaders the most serious threat to proletarian consciousness lay within the laboring masses themselves because workers could easily be led astray by petty-bourgeois influences. Lebedev-Polianskii, the Proletkult's first president, was particularly sensitive to these dangers. He felt the organization had to be free of all unskilled and unemployed workers, as well as artisanal laborers and the urban poor. Proletarians who had not broken their ties to the countryside were also questionable allies because they might be too sympathetic to the peasantry.[7] Those who had no factory experience at all had no business in the Proletkult. Lebedev-Polianskii lumped professionals, shop workers, and salaried employees together with the petty bourgeoisie and categorically denied them all the right to participate in the movement.[8]

The peasantry posed a particular danger to proletarian consciousness. In the opinion of Aleksandr Bogdanov, the

5. See A. A. Bogdanov, "O tendentsiakh proletarskoi kul'tury: Otvet A. Gastevu," *Proletarskaia kul'tura*, no. 9/10 (1919), pp. 46–52, esp. p. 46.

6. "Ot redaktsii," *Proletarskaia kul'tura*, no. 3 (1918), p. 36.

7. P. I. Lebedev-Polianskii [V. Polianskii, pseud.], "Pod znamia Proletkul'ta," *Proletarskaia kul'tura*, no. 1 (1918), pp. 3–7; idem, "Revoliutsiia i kul'turnye zadachi proletariata," *Protokoly pervoi Vserossiiskoi konferentsii proletarskikh kul'turno-prosvetitel'nykh organizatsii, 15–20 sentiabria, 1918 g.,* ed. P. I. Lebedev-Polianskii (Moscow, 1918), p. 20; idem, "Nashi zadachi i puti," *Proletarskaia kul'tura*, no. 7/8, (1919), p. 7; and idem, "Poeziia sovetskoi provintsii," *Proletarskaia kul'tura* no. 7/8 (1919), pp. 44, 49–50.

8. P. I. Lebedev-Polianskii [V. Polianskii, pseud.], "Pod znamia

most articulate spokesman on this subject, it did not matter that both the working class and the peasantry had been exploited under capitalism. They still engaged in very different labor processes that engendered two different worldviews, two opposing class ideologies. Through the process of factory labor, the proletariat had developed a collectivist consciousness. The peasantry, however, was individualistic, patriarchal, and religious. Therefore it was emotionally and psychologically closer to the bourgeoisie than to the working class.[9]

At times the proponents of class purity assumed a shrill and frightened tone. They seemed to fear that workers' psyches were much too fragile and their class ideologies too uncertain to ward off the temptations posed by other social groups. The only solution, then, was isolation. Mikhail Gerasimov, a popular proletarian poet and a founding member of the organization, gave an impassioned exposition of these views at the national Proletkult conference in 1918, using the industrial imagery so common to Proletkult writers:

We know that the psychology of the peasantry is petty-bourgeois. [Peasants] hide their grain and won't hand it over to urban workers. If there are many petty-bourgeois attitudes among workers now, what can we say about the peasantry? . . . We must found a workers' palace where workers' interests will always be central. We cannot abandon the Proletkult. It is an oasis where our class will (*volia*) can crystallize. If we want our furnace to blaze, we must throw coal and oil into the fire, and not the peasants' salt or chips from the intellectuals. Nothing but smoke can come from these.[10]

The national organization's membership rules reflected these restrictive understandings of class and class consciousness. They stated in no uncertain terms that only the most

Proletkul'ta," *Proletarskaia kul'tura*, no. 1 (1918), p. 6; see also "Plan organizatsii Proletkul'ta," *Proletarskaia kul'tura*, no. 6 (1919), p. 27.

9. A. A. Bogdanov, "Nasha kritika," *Proletarskaia kul'tura*, no. 3 (1918), p. 13; see also P. Bessal'ko, "O poezii krest'ianskoi i proletarskoi," *Griadushchee*, no. 7 (1918), pp. 12–14.

10. *Protokoly pervoi konferentsii*, pp. 26–27.

conscious and culturally advanced *industrial* workers belonged in the Proletkult. The argument was made by comparing the Proletkult to the Communist Party. Clearly, the party could not let its political line be determined by the least conscious workers because that would not be the best expression of proletarian class interests. If the party descended to the level of the majority, it would forfeit its leadership role. Similarly, the Proletkult could not let its cultural line be determined by the least conscious mass of workers, because it would lose its claim to leadership in the field of culture. It was intended for the cultural vanguard of the working class.[11]

This vision of the Proletkult's constituency proved to be very difficult to put into practice because its rigid social categories contradicted local "languages of class."[12] Membership rules drawn up by provincial organizations illustrate this contradiction quite clearly. In the Parfenev Proletkult, Kostroma province, the local charter allowed the participation of all "toilers" (*trudiashchiesia*), a word often used by Socialist Revolutionaries to apply to workers and peasants alike. Tver Proletkultists rejected a suggestion to limit their organization to industrial workers alone and instead extended an invitation to all "laboring and exploited people."[13] Numerous groups offered their services to local "citizens," an expansive social term made popular after the February Revolution. Still others avoided class definitions altogether and linked Proletkult participation to social needs. One factory circle in Ekaterinburg was open to all who wanted to improve their knowledge.[14]

At issue were fundamentally different understandings of

11. "Plan organizatsii Proletkul'ta," *Proletarskaia kul'tura*, no. 6 (1919), pp. 26–29.
12. This term is from Gareth Stedman Jones, *Languages of Class: Studies in English Working Class History, 1832–1982* (Cambridge, Eng., 1983). See especially pp. 7–8.
13. *Pervaia Tverskaia gubernskaia konferentsiia kul'turno-prosvetitel'nykh organizatsii: Protokoly zasedanii* (Tver, 1919), p. 56.
14. From a speech by the organization's leader at a general meet-

what the proletariat was. Local groups that welcomed toilers defined the working class broadly, including all the laboring masses in its ranks. They did not share the strict Marxist understanding of the industrial proletariat as a class distinct from and more conscious than other laborers. In fact, many used the word "proletariat" as a synonym for "the people" (*narod*), something particularly common in provincial Proletkult poetry.[15] According to this conception of the working class, laborers were united against their common enemies above them. Intellectuals, the bourgeoisie, and the supporters of the old regime might be the villains, but certainly not "petty-bourgeois influences" within the laboring classes themselves. Local groups simply ignored strictures against artisans, office workers, unskilled workers, and the urban poor. Some openly contradicted official statements about the peasantry.

Such divergent perceptions of class insured the Proletkult a large and diverse following. Lebedev-Polianskii was fond of comparing his organization to the Communist Party, but in fact it was a very poor analogy.[16] It implied that the Proletkult was much more cohesive and better organized than was in fact the case. Although the party had methods of supervising who its members were (even though these methods were often ineffective), the central Proletkult had very little authority over its affiliates. There were no centrally approved "Proletkult cards,"[17] no candidate membership periods, nor any secure methods to eliminate undesirable elements. The national

ing, October 27, 1920, *Tsentral'nyi Gosudarstvennyi Arkhiv Literatury i Iskusstva* [henceforth cited as TsGALI] f. 1230, op. 1, d. 1240, l. 18.

15. See, for example, Il'ia Il'in, "Proch byloe," *Molot*, no. 1 (1920), p. 10.

16. This comparison is also made by contemporary Western scholars. See Zenovia A. Sochor, *Revolution and Culture* (Ithaca, 1988), pp. 128–29.

17. Some local organizations had cards that they administered themselves. See the records of the Lenin State Sugar Factory organization in Kursk province, July 7, 1920, TsGALI f. 1230, op. 1, d. 1280, l. 12.

leadership had to depend on local groups to understand and implement its wishes.

In fact, the central Proletkult was not a very competent collector of data about its rapidly expanding network. It is even difficult to make definitive statements about the organization's size. In the fall of 1920 the center claimed between four hundred thousand and five hundred thousand members, eighty thousand of those in elite artistic studios.[18] These figures, the only aggregate totals available, are very problematic. On the one hand, they are necessarily incomplete because there were many registered organizations that did not provide information about their participants.[19] On the other hand, the central leadership never gave any sources for these estimates, nor did it clarify exactly what it meant by membership, allowing ample room for exaggeration. To take one example, the Petrograd Proletkult asserted that it controlled over one hundred and twenty clubs with approximately five hundred participants in each in 1919.[20] Of these estimated sixty thousand "members," how many were casual auditors of plays or lectures, and how many actively identified with the organization's goals?

Whether they were accurate or not, these substantial membership figures were readily exploited by the movement. They gave the Proletkult visibility and power and also lent some credence to its claim to be the organizational equal of trade

18. *Proletarskaia kul'tura*, no. 17/19 (1920), pp. 2, 5, 74. There is no source given for these figures, but presumably they were generated from the periodic questionnaires sent out to local affiliates. However, these questionnaires were most reliable in determining the number of participants in studio workshops, not the various other activities the Proletkult sponsored. See, for example, those from the Viatka province and Pudemskii factory organizations, TsGALI f. 1230, op. 1, d. 117, l. 32; d. 430, l. 20 ob.

19. In 1919 the center compiled a list of nineteen organizations it would no longer support because they had not answered requests for membership figures, "Spisok ne subsidirovannykh Proletkul'tov," TsGALI f. 1230, op. 1, d. 117, ll. 7–8.

20. "Deiatel'nost' Petrogradskogo Proletkul'ta," *Vneshkol'noe obrazovanie* (Petrograd), no. 4/5 (1920), p. 70.

unions and the Communist Party. Some Proletkult advocates went so far as to argue that the membership was drawn entirely from the working class, which would have assured the movement a hold over a significant percentage of Soviet Russia's small proletariat.[21] But such boasts can be easily disproved by the records of local affiliates, which show sizable numbers of nonworkers within the ranks. They were also contradicted by the more candid comments of the central leaders themselves, who frequently bemoaned the organization's social diversity.

Despite their angry rhetoric directed at nonworkers, national leaders were at times quite willing to stretch their stiff guidelines in order to secure a broad following. Although there were strong ideological justifications for class purity, there were equally strong organizational reasons for large membership figures. The Proletkult's size and breadth made its cultural agenda very difficult to ignore. Thus both the actions of local circles and the partial complicity of national leaders ensured that many different social groups found a place under the banner of the Proletkult.

The Worker Contingent

The Proletkult expanded as the proletariat declined. It gained popularity as mobilizations, food shortages, and factory closures drastically diminished the ranks of Russian workers. Not only did the number of workers drop, but the lines between the industrial proletariat and other laboring classes—never very clear in the best of times—became more fluid as a result of wartime upheavals. This process could not help but affect an organization aimed at the working class.

21. When Lenin asked for specific information about Proletkult members in 1920, the central leaders Vladimir Faidysh and Vasilii Ignatov sent word that it united four hundred thousand proletarians. See *V. I. Lenin o literature i iskusstve*, 7th ed., ed. N. Krutikov (Moscow, 1986), p. 542.

In numerical terms the early Soviet years were a disaster for the industrial proletariat; many scholars have noted that the most immediate consequence of the workers' revolution was the decimation of the working class.[22] The process of what Lenin called the "declassing" (*deklassirovanie*) of the proletariat had already begun during the First World War.[23] Experienced workers were mobilized into the army and their places taken by the unskilled, either members of workers' families or fresh recruits to factory life from the cities and the countryside. With the outbreak of the October Revolution, which brought demobilization, the situation improved somewhat as seasoned workers reclaimed their jobs. However, the beginning of the Civil War was a renewed blow to the size and quality of the labor force. Hunger, disease, the decline of industry, and renewed mobilizations all combined to deplete workers' ranks.[24] In the first three years of Soviet power the industrial labor force was more than halved.[25]

Factory workers left the cities in search of food and were absorbed into the peasantry. They also either voluntarily joined or were drafted into the Red Army. As a result, many of those who held industrial jobs were new, inexperienced recruits. Nonproletarian city dwellers who, unlike workers, often did not have relatives in the countryside, entered urban factories. In rural areas industrial plants found new laborers among the local peasantry. Not only did the size of the working class decline, its social makeup changed as well.

22. See D. A. Baevskii, *Rabochii klass v pervye gody sovetskoi vlasti, 1917–1921 gg.* (Moscow, 1974); Edward Hallett Carr, *The Bolshevik Revolution, 1917–1923* (New York, 1952), vol. 2; E. G. Gimpel'son, *Sovetskii rabochii klass, 1918–1920 gg.* (Moscow, 1974); Diane Koenker, "Urbanization and Deurbanization in the Russian Revolution and Civil War," *Journal of Modern History*, vol. 57, no. 3 (1985), pp. 424–50; V. M. Selunskaia, ed., *Izmeneniia sotsial'noi struktury sovetskogo obshchestva, Oktiabr' 1917–1929* (Moscow, 1976); and William G. Rosenberg, "Russian Labor and Bolshevik Power after October," *Slavic Review*, vol. 44, no. 2 (1985), pp. 213–38.
23. V. I. Lenin, *Polnoe sobranie sochinenii*, 5th ed. (Moscow, 1970), vol. 43, p. 42, cited in Baevskii, *Rabochii klass*, pp. 260–61.
24. Baevskii, *Rabochii klass*, pp. 244–49.
25. Gimpel'son, *Sovetskii rabochii klass*, p. 80.

As the Proletkult spread throughout Soviet territory, it secured a following in the most industrially advanced areas of the country. During the Civil War it expanded from Petrograd, a stronghold of the metalworking industry, to the Central Industrial Region, the Urals, and even to parts of the White-controlled industrial South. Metalworkers, the traditional elite of the working class and a much sought after clientele, appeared to be very open to the organization's message.[26] Many defense-related engineering and metalworking factories had Proletkult organizations. Of the ten large private plants that were nationalized in 1918 and united to form a machine-building consortium called "GOMZ" (*Tsentral'noe pravlenie gosudarstvennykh ob"edinennykh mashinostroitel'-nykh zavodov*), at least half sponsored Proletkults.[27] Both metalworking plants in Tula opened Proletkult organizations, as did many others: the Simbirsk cartridge factory, the Kovrov machine-gun factory, the Bezhetsk armament factory, metalworking plants in Izhevsk and Podolsk, the Putilov factory in Petrograd, and the Pudemskii factory in Viatka province.[28]

Several of the Proletkult's first organizers, Fedor Kalinin, Vladimir Kossior, and Aleksei Gastev, were active in the Metalworkers' Union.[29] Perhaps because of their influence,

26. Lebedev-Polianskii singled out metalworkers as the best candidates for the Proletkult. See V. Polianskii [pseud.], "Nashi zadachi i puti," *Proletarskaia kul'tura,* no. 7/8 (1919), p. 7.
27. The Sormorskii, Brianskii, Tverskoi, Rybinskii, and Raditskii factories all had Proletkults. See *Proletarskaia kul'tura,* no. 11/12 (1919), p. 65; *Proletkul't* (Tver), no. 1/2 (1919), p. 15; and local questionnaires in TsGALI f. 1230, op. 1, d. 121, l. 58 ob.; d. 117, ll. 5, 18.
28. For the Simbirsk Proletkult see *Proletarskaia kul'tura,* no. 7/8 (1919), p. 69. For the remaining groups see the local questionnaires in TsGALI f. 1230, op. 1, d. 1540, l. 6 and d. 1538, l. 14 (Tula); d. 121, l. 56 (Kovrov); d. 121, l. 57 (Bezhetsk); d. 117, l. 58 (Izhevsk); d. 117, l. 63 (Podolsk); d. 121, l. 41 (Putilov plant); d. 430, l. 27 ob. (Pudemskii plant).
29. On Fedor Kalinin see *Sbornik pamiati F. I. Kalinina* (Rostov on Don, 1920), p. 14; on Kossior see *Protokoly pervoi konferentsii,* p. 103; on Gastev see Kendall E. Bailes, "Alexei Gastev and the Controversy over Taylorism, 1918–1924," *Soviet Studies,* vol. 29, no. 3 (1977), p. 374.

some local trade union branches became strong Proletkult backers. The organizations in Izhevsk and Rybinsk were largely financed through the union.[30] The Moscow Metalworkers' Union even came to the aid of the Proletkult in a territorial dispute with the city's educational division.[31]

Railroad workers, another elite sector of the working class, were well represented in the Proletkult, too. There were special organizations for these workers in many parts of Russia, and railroad stations were frequent sites for local circles in the provinces.[32] As in the case of the metalworkers, the Railroad Workers' Union showed a lively interest in Proletkult ideas. In mid-1918 the cultural division of the union, named "Tsekult," organized classes in Moscow for provincial cultural workers. Among the many lecturers was Aleksandr Bogdanov, who addressed the topic "Culture and Life."[33]

However, even these leading proletarian groups had suffered severely from the combined effects of war and revolution. The quick expansion of the metal industry during the First World War meant that new and unskilled workers had entered the labor force. During the Civil War parts of the industry moved away from urban centers to areas where the working class had much closer ties to the peasantry.[34] Thus just because one was a metalworker did not in itself insure a proletarian pedigree, nor did it guarantee the possession of

30. Letter from the Izhevsk leadership to P. I. Lebedev-Polianskii, TsGALI f. 1230, op. 1, d. 1222, l. 16; see also the 1919 questionnaire filed by the Rybinsk organization, d. 117, l. 5 ob.

31. "Vypiska iz protokola zasedaniia komiteta Moskovskogo raionnogo otdela soiuza metallistov," October 15, 1920, TsGALI f. 1230, op. 1, d. 3, l. 108.

32. See the list of six operating railroad Proletkults in the records for the 1921 national congress, TsGALI f. 1230, op. 1, d. 122, ll. 1–2. Moscow province's local organizations were located on the railroad lines, *Proletkul'tvorets*, no. 1 (1920), p. 4.

33. N. S. Zaichenko, ed., *Organizatsionnye kursy po kul'turno-prosvetitel'nomu delu na zheleznykh dorogakh* (Moscow, 1918), pp. 13–14, 20, 40.

34. Selunskaia, *Izmeneniia sotsial'noi struktury*, p. 144; and Gimpel'son, *Sovetskii rabochii klass*, p. 122.

any of those special traits—literacy, job experience, and a long separation from the countryside—that so appealed to Proletkult theorists.

Moreover, the Proletkult was not restricted to the most advanced segments of the working class. The movement also found a following in industries employing mainly unskilled labor. Textile workers in Ivanovo-Voznesensk were some of the first to start local organizations. By 1920 the provincial Proletkult encompassed groups in twenty-six factories along with district branches in Shuia, Kineshma, Vichuga, Rodniki, Sereda, and Teplov. The Ivanovo-Voznesensk Textile Workers' Union was an active supporter of both the city and the provincial networks.[35] In Saratov the cultural activities of the Tobacco Workers' Union were taken over by the Proletkult.[36] As in the textile industry, the labor force for tobacco factories was primarily composed of unskilled workers. The national Sugar Workers' Union tried to unite all its factory cultural circles with the Proletkult. According to the union, sugar workers had a special need for well-planned cultural activities because refineries were located in small villages far away from cultural centers.[37]

Rather than trying to isolate a cultural vanguard within the proletariat, many local groups made a special effort to reach out to the least advanced and least educated workers. The Kostroma Proletkult is an excellent case in point. In this town dominated by the textile trade a Proletkult took shape after many other attempts to organize educational projects for workers had failed. One commission, funded and organized by the local Narkompros division, determined through surveys and census data that there were over sixteen thousand illiterate or semiliterate workers in Kostroma, concen-

35. 1922 report from the Ivanovo-Voznesensk organization, TsGALI f. 1230, op. 1, d. 1245, ll. 5–13.

36. "Svedenie kasaiushchiesia deiatel'nosti Proletkul'ta," *Tsentral'nyi Gosudarstvennyi Arkhiv RSFSR* f. 2306, op. 17, d. 9, l. 8.

37. Meeting of the central committee presidium, September 25, 1920, TsGALI f. 1230, op. 1, d. 6, l. 82.

trated especially among women. It also concluded that workers' willingness to make use of cultural offerings decreased as
their educational level decreased. The commission's solution
was to start active agitation among the least educated workers. It proposed to open literacy schools right at the workplace, aimed specifically at female workers.[38] As one com-
missioner noted, it was not possible to create a proletarian
culture without sharing the rudiments of culture with the
broadest possible working-class audience.[39]

When the Kostroma Proletkult began operation, it reflected
the concerns of the educational circles that preceded it. A
founding member, V. A. Nevskii, was also the head of the local
Narkompros division. He believed that the new organization
should not abandon the masses for the quiet of isolated studios. Rather, the creation of a proletarian culture had to be
accomplished by the masses themselves.[40] To demonstrate its
commitment to these goals, the Proletkult absorbed the factory workers' literacy commission into its organizational
structure.

Together with unskilled laborers, many artisanal workers
joined in local Proletkult activities, despite repeated warn-
ings that they posed a threat to genuine proletarian values. As
recent research on the Russian working class has shown, artisans were often well integrated into the factory proletariat,
even constituting a significant percentage of those employed
in large industrial complexes.[41] Indeed, one might argue that
the most common symbol of Proletkult creation, the mighty
blacksmith wielding his hammer over an anvil, was itself an
artisanal image. It certainly did not portray a worker whose
life was regulated by the pace of the machine. The records for

38. I. P. Beliaev, "Komissiia fabrichno-zavodskikh predpriatii po
kul'turno-prosvetitel'noi rabote sredi shirokikh mass," *Sbornik Kostromskogo Proletkul'ta*, no. 1 (1919), p. 100.
39. Ibid., p. 104.
40. "Organizatsiia Kostromskogo Proletkul'ta," ibid., pp. 106–7.
41. Bonnell, *Roots of Rebellion*, pp. 25–37, especially p. 30.

organizations that compiled precise occupational data reveal all kinds of members with artisanal occupations, including tailors, seamstresses, bakers, and house painters.[42]

Unfortunately, most local organizations did not keep detailed descriptions of the occupational status of their participants; at best they distinguished between workers and nonworkers. But the category of "worker" by itself was a blunt tool for social analysis in revolutionary Russia. It conveyed political power, and local groups at times distorted their official records to make themselves appear more proletarian.[43] It also had a metaphorical meaning that extended to the "people" as a whole. It is only in this sense that we can understand why one Proletkult music teacher could survey her class, composed of the children of priests, peasants, artisans, and petty bureaucrats, and conclude that "the majority are workers."[44]

White-Collar Workers and the "Laboring Intelligentsia"

The Proletkult reached beyond the industrial working class to embrace laborers in the service sector—office workers, shop assistants, and sales personnel. Their ubiquitous presence reflected the open-door policy that many local groups pursued. However, they also found a place because many employees considered themselves, and were considered by their peers, to be legitimate members of the working class. The two shopkeeper's apprentices who founded the Proletkult theater studio in Tambov called themselves workers, and so did the

42. See Tver and Archangel membership lists, TsGALI f. 1230, op. 1, d. 1525, ll. 66–69 and d. 1209, ll. 35 ob.–36.

43. The Archangel Proletkult reported 90 percent worker participation in 1921, but a more detailed list, with members' occupations specified, revealed that less than half of the members were workers. Compare TsGALI f. 1230, op. 1, d. 54, ll. 2–5 to d. 1209, l. 48.

44. Report by Mariia Shipova, Kologriv Proletkult, TsGALI f. 1230, op. 1, d. 1278, l. 13.

young typist who was the president of the Rzhev organization.[45]

Before October the poor working conditions of many salaried employees led them to form alliances with artisanal and industrial workers.[46] Although there were frequent hostilities in factories between workers and the white-collar staff during the 1917 revolutions, there were also strong alliances formed between manual laborers and those engaged in "mental labor."[47] With the nationalization of industry and the expansion of the Soviet bureaucracy the distinction between manual and mental laborers became even less clear. Wartime conditions created new opportunities for workers to leave their factory jobs and become part of the expanding bureaucracies in the new Soviet state. Thus although a part of the proletariat was declassed, another part was reclassed and advanced into the hierarchies of trade unions, industry, and government. Those who took employment in the burgeoning bureaucratic system did not feel that they were abandoning their class. Rather, they were serving a state dedicated to the victory of the proletariat. In turn, the state showed its commitment to workers by promoting them to responsible managerial and governmental posts.[48]

At all levels of the Proletkult hierarchy, nonmanual laborers took part in cultural activities. These participants were variously described as white-collar workers (*sluzhashchie*), the "laboring intelligentsia," or "workers no longer involved in production." The inclusion of white-collar workers began already in factory Proletkults, the bottom rung of the orga-

45. For Tambov see L. Granat and N. Varzin, *Aktery-agitatory, boitsy* (Moscow, 1970), pp. 123–24; for Rzhev see the delegate list for the 1921 national congress, TsGALI f. 1230, op. 1. d. 144, ll. 117–18.

46. See Engelstein, *Moscow, 1905*, p. 16, pp. 20–25.

47. S. A. Smith, *Red Petrograd* (Cambridge, Eng., 1983), pp. 134–38.

48. See Sheila Fitzpatrick, *Education and Social Mobility in the Soviet Union, 1921–1934* (Cambridge, Eng., 1979), chapter 1; and Selunskaia, *Izmeneniia sotsial'noi struktury*, pp. 282, 298–99.

nizational ladder. Although these groups could have easily fulfilled the center's mandate to serve only the industrial proletariat, in practice many of them encompassed the entire factory community, including the office staff. The Proletkult at a textile mill in Pushkino, Moscow province, reported that its activities were attended by factory workers and white-collar employees alike. At the Staro-Gorkinskii factory, a quarter of the members were drawn from the office staff.[49]

The participation of white-collar workers did not end as one moved up the organizational hierarchy. In questionnaires sent out by the central Proletkult in 1921, most city and provincial circles reported significant percentages of white-collar employees in their ranks. Fifty percent of all studio members in the factory town of Rybinsk, site of one of the most successful Proletkults, came from the laboring intelligentsia. Only the Proletkult in Ivanovo-Voznesensk claimed an all-proletarian constituency, and this was because it had formed an elite central studio for its most advanced working-class students. In lower level workshops only half the members were workers, with the rest holding office jobs.[50]

At least some of these employees were former workers, or the children of workers, who had moved into white-collar and bureaucratic posts. At the second Proletkult congress in 1921 delegates gave detailed personal information about their class status, including their social background (*soslovie*), social position, specialty, and current occupation. Among the 141 delegates, many of whom were not workers at all, are several examples of industrial laborers who had taken jobs outside of factories. The textile worker V. F. Mozer from the Sokolovskii factory Proletkult worked in 1921 as a typist for her factory committee. L. I. Zaitsev from the Tula Proletkult

49. Local questionnaires in TsGALI f. 1230, op. 1, d. 117, ll. 33, 61 ob.
50. Reports on the activities of music, art, literature, and theater studios for provincial Proletkults at the 1921 congress, TsGALI f. 1230, op. 1, d. 54, ll. 2–5. For the provincial organization in Ivanovo-Voznesensk see d. 117, l. 83 ob.

was a weaver by trade who had left the factory to become a union organizer. Mark Grishchenko of the Iurevsk organization listed his background and social status as "worker" and had only received a primary education. In 1921 he had a job as an employee for the railroad.[51]

The presence of white-collar workers sometimes caused conflict in local circles. One disgruntled railroad worker in Samara bitterly attacked the Proletkult for allowing non-workers to take part. Tula membership rules restricted office workers to 13 percent of the total membership and only accepted those who were in favor of Soviet power. Anna Dodonova, leader of the Moscow organization, defended Proletkult autonomy in a meeting with Lenin, insisting that it was necessary to keep employees from taking over workers' clubs.[52]

Nonetheless, the confusion of social categories caused by the revolution worked in favor of white-collar employees who wanted to participate in Proletkult activities. As more and more workers gained jobs in state bureaucracies, soviets, trade unions, and the party, distinct divisions between the working class and the laboring intelligentsia became much harder to draw. This confusion made it more difficult for local groups to exclude white-collar workers from their ranks.[53] Although there were those who opposed workers leaving the factory for any reason, these purists eventually lost out in internal organizational debates.[54] By the 1920s the central

51. List of delegates at the second national Proletkult congress, November 17, 1921, TsGALI f. 1230, op. 1, d. 144, ll. 124, 117, 118. Several other delegates who gave their background and social position as workers were currently occupying white-collar jobs; see ll. 122, 125, 126.

52. D. I'lin, "Rzhavoe pero," *Zarevo zavodov*, no. 2 (1919), pp. 65–66; "Ustav," TsGALI f. 1230, op. 1, d. 1536, l. 1; A. Dodonova, "Iz vospominanii o Proletkul'te," in *V. I. Lenin o literature i iskusstve*, 7th ed., ed. N. Krutikov (Moscow, 1986), p. 501.

53. See, for example, a debate on this issue in the Moscow Proletkult in 1918, "Khronika," *Gorn*, no. 1 (1918), p. 91.

54. See the discussion of professionalization in Chapter 5.

leadership counted "workers no longer involved in production" as part of the Proletkult's proletarian contingent.[55]

Peasants in the Proletkult

Artisans and white-collar employees clearly posed a gray area for those who tried to delineate the boundaries of the working class. These groups often had close ties to the industrial proletariat and individuals within them may even once have been workers themselves. However, the case of the peasantry was less ambiguous. Although the central leaders eventually altered their perception of workers who joined the bureaucracy, their stance on the peasantry was quite unyielding. Peasants had no place in a proletarian organization. The national Proletkult central committee tabled a request by Sergei Esenin and others to open a special section for peasant literature in the Proletkult.[56] It threatened to close down organizations in areas where there was evidence of widespread peasant participation. In addition, its members warned continually of the dangers peasants posed to proletarian class consciousness.

The official Proletkult position on this issue was at odds with the Communist Party line, which advocated an alliance between the poor peasantry and the proletariat. Indeed, Bogdanov seemed to be arguing directly with the Bolshevik platform when he insisted that peasants could not share a proletarian worldview, regardless of how poor they were.[57] However, many local groups articulated a position much closer to the party line, one that reflected what appeared to be

55. See the 1922–1924 membership figures, "Sostav Proletkul'tov i rukovodiashchikh organov Proletkul'tov," TsGALI f. 1230, op. 1, d. 121, l. 51.

56. On Esenin's application see Gordon McVay, *Esenin: A Life* (Ann Arbor, 1976), p. 105. At a meeting in October 1918 the central Proletkult decided to hand the issue over to the peasant section of the national soviet, TsGALI f. 1230, op. 1, d. 2, l. 4.

57. A. A. Bogdanov, "Nasha kritika," *Proletarskaia kul'tura*, no. 3 (1918), p. 13.

an obvious truth to many participants: under capitalism, both workers and peasants, particularly poor peasants, had been oppressed and thus both were entitled to the cultural benefits of the revolution. "The proletariat is an exploited class struggling for its emancipation," wrote one Proletkultist in the small town of Klin, Moscow province. "It has its own form of comradely cooperation to a high degree. But aren't these traits also inherent in the poor peasantry? Don't they also shape the character of the future art of the peasant masses? Of course they do. Therefore it follows that the art of the future will be the same for both classes.[58]

This perception that worker and peasant interests were intertwined encouraged the proliferation of Proletkult organizations in small towns and villages with negligible working-class populations. The phenomenon was so widespread that the fate of "peasant" and "socially mixed" organizations was a recurring topic of debate for the central leaders. To take one example, a Smolensk organization petitioned to register fifty-eight new Proletkult circles in small rural centers (*volosti*) during the summer of 1919. The central Proletkult responded with a decision to turn over all groups with a peasant composition to Narkompros.[59] By the following year national leaders claimed to have closed down many nonproletarian Proletkults and reorganized others to conform to their guidelines.[60]

But if the center intended to purge all branches with strong nonproletarian followings, that process was incomplete. According to national records many rural and small town organizations survived through the 1920 congress.[61] The Prolet-

58. K. S., "Kul'tura proletariata i bedneishchago krest'ianstva," *Zori*, no. 1 (1918), p. 3.
59. Central Proletkult presidium meeting, July 18, 1919, TsGALI f. 1230, op. 1, d. 3, l. 58. See also the discussions on March 4 and 19, 1919, in ibid., ll. 26, 31.
60. P. I. Lebedev-Polianskii [V. Kunavin, pseud.], "Vserossiiskii s"ezd Proletkul'ta," *Proletarskaia kul'tura*, no. 17/19 (1920), p. 76.
61. A late 1920 Proletkult list includes the Myshkin Proletkult, Iaroslavl province, the Mglinsk Proletkult near Chernigov, and the Odeev Proletkult in Tula province, all small *volost'* organizations. See TsGALI f. 1230, op. 1, d. 56, l. 17.

kult in Kologriv, Kostroma province, is an interesting example. It was started in September 1918 by an organizer from
the Petrograd Proletkult named Chumbarov-Luchinskii.[62]
Kologriv was a very small district center; in 1917 it had a
population of only 3,350, and by 1920 it had shrunk to 2,700.
The 1923 city census showed that less than 10 percent of the
population was workers.[63] Just why the Petrograd organizer
picked this small town for his endeavors remains unclear, but
he pursued his task with vigor.

From its founding, the Kologriv Proletkult directed its activities to include the "broad masses," a notion that also encompassed the peasantry. Chumbarov-Luchinskii felt that the
Proletkult should sponsor literacy schools, peasant reading
rooms, and peasant theaters in the surrounding villages.[64] In
late 1919 the leadership was taken over by a local man who
had just completed a course at the Moscow Proletkult. With
aid from Moscow he announced his intention to reorganize
the Proletkult "more in the spirit of the central organization."[65] He hoped to put the Kologriv Proletkult on the correct
proletarian path. However, even the new leadership could not
change the social structure of the town. From the many membership lists sent from Kologriv to Moscow, it is quite clear
that the proletarian path in Kologriv was trod mainly by
nonworkers. The art studio, for example, had fifty-nine students, mainly from the peasantry and the petty bourgeoisie,
with a few from a clerical background. Workers were not
mentioned on the roster at all.[66]

Despite ample evidence showing the suspect social composition of the Kologriv circle, the central Proletkult made no

62. Questionnaire for the instructor's division of the Proletkult in
1919, TsGALI f. 1230, op. 1, d. 1278, l. 64.
63. Narodnyi Komissariat Vnutrennikh Del, RSFSR. *Goroda
soiuzov SSSR* (Moscow, 1927), p. 41.
64. *Zhizn' iskusstv*, no. 4 (1918), p. 7.
65. Correspondence from the Kologriv organization to the center,
September 13 and 23, 1919, TsGALI f. 1230, op. 1, d. 1278, ll. 41–42,
51–51 ob., quotation l. 51.
66. "Otchet o deiatel'nosti Kologrivskogo Proletkul'ta za vtoruiu
polovinu 1919-ogo goda," ibid., l. 11 ob.

effort to close it down. Its demise was the result of other causes. In March 1921 the local Narkompros division took it over, dispatching a terse telegram to inform the central Proletkult that the Kologriv Proletkult branch no longer existed. Rather than welcoming the end of this nonproletarian affiliate, the national organization protested the action.[67]

The center's reluctance to relinquish control of the Kologriv organization illuminates a real tension in its operating procedures. Should it promote a broadly based popular movement, or should it instead attempt to achieve social homogeneity? On the one hand, dedicated Proletkultists were afraid to dilute the movement's proletarian essence with peasant followers. On the other hand, it was appealing for them to watch their organization expand as "a strong young tree, budding everywhere across the boundless expanses of Soviet Russia."[68] Petrograd participants were quite proud of their role as the original supporters of the Kologriv organization. The editors of the radical Petrograd journal *The Future* (*Griadushchee*) declared that the existence of a Proletkult in such a remote corner of Russia showed the vitality of proletarian culture.[69]

Even if all village circles had closed their doors, that would not have rid the Proletkult of its peasant members. Factory organizations in rural areas drew in part on peasant labor, and some offered cultural activities for the peasant population at large. At the Lenin State Sugar Factory in Kursk province the Proletkult sponsored literacy classes together with the local labor school. Its choir was composed of factory workers and peasants alike, and the theater even decided to start evening performances for village youth in the hopes of curbing their rowdy behavior on the street.[70] Such practices be-

67. Correspondence between the Kologriv Politprosvet and the central organization, March 25 and April 16, 1921, ibid., ll. 84–84 ob.

68. "Peredovaia," *Griadushchee*, no. 7/8 (1919), p. 1.

69. *Griadushchee*, no. 10 (1918), pp. 22, 24.

70. Meeting of the factory Proletkult, November 15, 1920, TsGALI f. 1230, op. 1, d. 1280, ll. 16–16 ob., 18–18 ob.

came official policy in the Moscow Province Proletkult, which united nineteen different local groups. Delegates at a 1920 conference decided to make greater efforts to include the peasant population living near rural factories. The membership rules made this quite explicit: the organization was open to workers, poor peasants, intellectual laborers in factories, and all party members.[71]

The Proletkult's collaboration with the Red Army opened yet more doors to peasants because soldiers came overwhelmingly from the countryside. At the first Proletkult conference in 1918 the issue of peasant-soldiers was a topic of a heated debate. Some delegates demanded that soldiers be considered part of the proletariat, which was the official party position. Others wanted to exclude them because peasant soldiers' "petty-bourgeois" mentality would undermine the Proletkult's claims to be a pure proletarian movement. As a compromise, delegates voted to open special Red Army clubs, which would be kept separate from the rest of Proletkult activities.[72]

As with so many other resolutions, this one was not followed very closely. Numerous Proletkults included soldiers in their activities; in some soldiers constituted the majority of members. According to one local report, 80 percent of all men in the Archangel organization came from the military.[73] Some groups even merged parts of their operations with Red Army divisions.[74] For Tambov Proletkultists the soldier took precedence over the worker during the big mobilization of 1919. Military imagery completely eclipsed the factory metaphors so common in Proletkult pronouncements: "On the Red Front with our rifles in our hands we will continue to break a trail to the Culture of the Future."[75]

71. *Proletkul'tvorets*, no. 1 (1920), pp. 2–3.
72. *Protokoly pervoi konferentsii*, pp. 48–49.
73. Letter from Proletkult president Leonid Tsinovskii, January 24, 1921, TsGALI f. 1230, op. 1, d. 1209, l. 35 ob.
74. See the Tula Proletkult records for 1919, TsGALI f. 1230, op. 1, d. 1537, l. 44.
75. "Ot redaktsii," *Griadushchaia kul'tura*, no. 6/7 (1919), p. 1.

The movement's official stance on the peasantry reflected the vanguardist visions of the prerevolutionary Bolsheviks, who determined workers' sophistication and consciousness according to their distance from the countryside. However, the revolution and Civil War confused these preconceptions and drastically reformulated class configurations. It was a shift some committed Proletkultists saw quite clearly. Pavel Arskii, a Petrograd leader, proletarian writer, and Red Army soldier, had sympathetic words for the Russian peasantry. "I am your son," he wrote in the 1919 poem "A Worker to a Peasant." "I left my native fields for the kingdom of smoke, iron, and steel." The poem stresses the common interests of the two groups and concludes: "Together we will live as a close and happy family in the new, radiant, and mighty Russia."[76]

Youth

In descriptions of the Proletkult's variegated membership one common denominator stands out—their age. Again and again observers commented on the youthfulness of Proletkult participants. "Young people, freshly arrived in the cities and swept along by the whirlwind of events, were only too ready to accept the simplified ideas of Proletkult extremists," wrote Ilia Ehrenburg in his memoirs of the Civil War years. "I often heard remarks such as 'Why be so complicated? It's all rotten intellectual rubbish.' "[77]

Until the years of the New Economic Policy the national organization did not solicit detailed information about the age of its followers, but many local sources bore witness to the Proletkult's appeal to adolescents and young adults. In the Novotorsk artistic studios 80 percent of the participants were

76. P. Arskii, "Rabochii krest'ianinu," *Mir i chelovek*, no. 1 (1919), p. 5.
77. Ilya Ehrenburg, *First Years of Revolution, 1918–1921*, trans. Anna Bostock (London, 1962), p. 175.

under twenty. The entire acting troupe of the Proletkult theater in the Presnia district of Moscow, one of the oldest proletarian parts of the city, was young. An observer of a local art studio noted that all its members were between the ages of sixteen and twenty.[78] Lecturers and instructors continually remarked on the enthusiasm (and the ignorance) of their young charges.[79] When the central Proletkult finally published age statistics in 1925, the youthful nature of the Proletkult was made overwhelmingly clear; 65 percent of all members were under the age of nineteen.[80]

It is not surprising that the Proletkult excited youthful imaginations. Youth organizations founded in urban centers during the revolution were very interested in cultural and educational work. Urban adolescents were better educated than their parents or their rural counterparts and had both the leisure and the dedication to devote their free time to study and self-improvement. Not yet burdened by family responsibilities, young workers made educational and artistic circles part of urban youth culture.[81] The Proletkult, with its broad offerings of cultural studios, lectures, and festive evenings, gave the young ample opportunities for education, entertainment, and conviviality.

Young people also came to the Proletkult because they were welcome there. Many other proletarian organizations, such as trade unions and factory committees, limited their member-

78. "Novotorskii Proletkul't," *Proletkul't* (Tver), no. 1/2, p. 53; *Gorn*, no. 1 (1918), p. 94; and E. Lozovaia, "O raionnom Moskovskom Proletkul'te," *Vestnik zhizni*, no. 6/7 (1919), p. 141.

79. See Serge Wolkonsky, *My Reminiscences*, trans. A. E. Chamot (London, 1924), vol. 2, p. 220; and V. Mitiushin, "Tesnyi kontakt," *Gudki*, no. 6 (1919), p. 16.

80. "Sostav Proletkul'tov," *Al'manakh Proletkul'ta* (Moscow, 1925), p. 183.

81. See Diane Koenker, "Urban Families, Working Class Youth Groups and the 1917 Revolution in Moscow," in *The Family in Imperial Russia*, ed. David Ransel (Urbana, 1978), pp. 289–90, 294–97; and David Mandel, *The Petrograd Workers and the Fall of the Old Regime* (New York, 1983), pp. 40–41.

ship rules to exclude those under eighteen.[82] However, this was not the case for the Proletkult. Although central leaders clearly preferred experienced, skilled, and hence adult workers, they did not enforce age restrictions. Local groups made their own rules, but their age limits were usually low. The Novoselsk village circle took members from age fifteen on, the Tula Proletkult from age sixteen.[83]

The preference of Russian youth for the most radical and extreme solutions to social problems has been well documented. During 1917 young workers turned much more quickly to support the Bolsheviks than did their older colleagues.[84] As a result, the Bolshevik Party could claim a very youthful membership, as could the Red Guards, special units formed to defend the revolution.[85] The Proletkult's reputation as the most revolutionary and utopian cultural organization clearly won it friends in the same circles. In the words of Maksim Shtraukh, who came to the Moscow Proletkult as a teenager and eventually became a famous actor and director: "We wanted to serve the kind of art that would answer the combative spirit of the times, that would be a weapon in the revolutionary struggle. That's why we went to the Proletkult. . . . We young people chose this theater because we were burning with the desire to serve not simply art, but a new and revolutionary art."[86]

At the local level many Proletkult organizations had close ties to the Komsomol, the Communist Party's youth organization, which encouraged a young following. In the small town

82. Isabelle A. Tirado, "The Socialist Youth Movement in Petrograd," *Russian Review*, vol. 46, no. 2 (1987), pp. 139–41.
83. "Novosel'skoe Prosvetitel'noe Obshchestvo 'Proletkul't,' " TsGALI f. 1230, op. 1, d. 430, l. 73; "Ustav," d. 1536, l. 1.
84. Mandel, *Petrograd Workers and the Fall of the Old Regime*, p. 41; and Smith, *Red Petrograd*, pp. 197–200.
85. Koenker, "Urban Families," pp. 281, 300; and Rex A. Wade, *Red Guards and Workers' Militias in the Russian Revolution* (Stanford, 1984), pp. 173–75.
86. Quoted in G. A. Shakhov, *Maksim Maksimovich Shtraukh* (Moscow, 1964), p. 31.

of Lukino, in Tver province, the Proletkult president helped to start the local Komsomol division. A Proletkult club on the Moscow-Kazan railroad line catered exclusively to Komsomol members.[87] In Samara the Komsomol and the Proletkult even had overlapping leaderships.[88]

Surely another attraction was the fact that the Proletkult advanced young people into responsible positions. The records of the 1921 national congress offer many examples of teenagers in leadership roles. Iakov Smirnov, assistant head of a theater section in Ivanovo-Voznesensk in 1921, was only eighteen years old but he had already been in the Proletkult for three years. Nina Polekova, age nineteen, was president of the Rzhev organization. At twenty Pavel Karpov was part of the governing presidium in Saratov. Anatolii Stepanov, metalworker and Komsomol member from Rzhev, was on the presidium of his local organization at age seventeen. He had first joined the Proletkult when he was fourteen years old.[89]

Proletkult organizers valued young people because they were seen as the future of the revolution. Work with adolescents and children insured the survival of proletarian culture and the Proletkult as an institution.[90] Although class origins were a dominant theme in discussions about adult workers, the same standards did not apply to the young. In both local and central records Proletkultists counted the children of workers as part of the proletariat, regardless of their current occupation.[91] Unlike adults, young people were to some de-

87. *Proletarskaia kul'tura*, no. 11/12 (1919), p. 66; and the 1919 questionnaire for the Perovskii raionnyi klub, TsGALI f. 1230, op. 1, d. 430, l. 10.

88. From a local questionnaire, TsGALI f. 1230, op. 1, d. 117, l. 98 ob. See also reports for the Shchelkovo and Archangel organizations, d. 117, l. 70, d. 1209, l. 85.

89. Delegate list for the 1921 national congress, TsGALI f. 1230, op. 1, d. 144, ll. 114, 117, 124, 116.

90. For a discussion of the issue of the Proletkult and young children see Chapter 6.

91. See, for example, the records for the Novotorsk Proletkult in Tver province, *Proletkul't* (Tver), no. 1/2 (1919), p. 53.

gree "classless." At the founding national conference in 1918 the central leader E. P. Khersonskaia insisted that the Proletkult had to take dramatic steps to include adolescents; she went so far as to extend an invitation to the children of intellectuals, shopkeepers, and artisans.[92] This solicitous concern won the Proletkult youthful support. At the same time, however, it further diluted the organization's industrial proletarian identity.

Who wasn't drawn to our little light—children, young girls, youth from the barricades, graybeards in homespun coats and bast shoes from the countryside, poets no one had ever heard of who previously had scratched out their verses in a scrawl in cellars, under the eves of stone houses, at their workbench, or behind a plow. Until then I had never seen such characters and costumes in my life as those that appeared in the Proletkult.[93]

These loving memoirs by Aleksandr Mgebrov, a theater instructor in the Petrograd Proletkult, are a testament to the movement's broad social appeal. Mgebrov obviously relished this mixed following, but for those who perceived the Proletkult as a purely proletarian movement, such diversity posed a real threat to the organization's identity.

The Proletkult's popularity reveals the flexibility—and inaccuracy—of class categories in this period of rapid social change. The label "proletarian" was not a neutral class description: it conveyed political power and revolutionary sentiment. This was not the only allegedly proletarian institution faced with a crisis of class identity. In the Communist Party, supposedly the vanguard of the working class, workers were

92. E. P. Khersonskaia, "O rabote s iunoshestvom," *Protokoly pervoi konferentsii*, pp. 66–67, 72.
93. A. A. Mgebrov, *Zhizn' v teatre* (Moscow and Leningrad, 1933), vol. 2, pp. 314–15.

no longer in the majority by the end of the Civil War.[94] But the party, in contrast to the Proletkult, never professed to appeal to the proletariat alone.

One result of the Proletkult's diversity was certainly positive. Its large size helped it to win national attention and gain the backing of local cultural groups. Proletkultists' attempts to stand equal to trade unions and the party in proletarian affairs would have had no resonance at all if the organization had really limited itself to a small vanguard of industrial workers. And despite the national leaders' distress about the organization's mixed following, they were certainly in part responsible for making it into the mass organization it became.

However, the Proletkult's large and varied membership also posed real threats to the organization's continued survival. Proletkultists had initially won the support of Narkompros precisely because they were supposed to be doing something different than state educational institutions. The more socially diverse the Proletkult was, the weaker this argument became. By the end of the Civil War Narkompros educational workers asked with ever greater urgency why an organization that duplicated state programs so closely needed to maintain its autonomy. In addition, party leaders came to doubt the wisdom of sustaining a mass institution that defended its independence so fiercely.

The Proletkult's heterogeneity also complicated the internal workings of the movement. Bogdanov and his allies envisioned an experienced, literate, sophisticated following able to work on its own or with minimum aid from the intelligentsia. With such a membership they believed that they would have the human resources necessary to question prevailing scientific propositions and to create unique artistic forms.

94. Official party figures show the working-class contingent declining from 60 percent to 41 percent in the years 1917 to 1921, T. H. Rigby, *Communist Party Membership in the U.S.S.R.* (Princeton, 1968), pp. 52, 85.

However, the organization drew in a much broader constituency, thus altering the scope of all its work. Local groups offered literary circles for the uneducated, French classes for those who sought "refinement," and dance evenings for young people's entertainment. Rather than investigating the nature of working-class creativity, Proletkult circles tried to satisfy the wide-ranging cultural demands of the lower classes. This skewed the very definition of proletarian culture and undermined the national leadership's conception of the movement. The central Proletkult could not shape its constituency. It was very much the other way around; the constituency shaped the Proletkult.

4

Proletkult Leadership
The New and the Old Intelligentsia

The Russian Revolution, like all revolutions, challenged the authority of the old elites and the long-standing patterns of social hierarchy. Once in power, however, the Bolsheviks quickly discovered that if they wanted to build a stable system, they had to construct a new elite to take the place of the old one. To find the necessary human resources, the party reached out to the lower classes, a solution that best fitted the spirit of the revolution. However, this solution was not enough to sustain the state. The new leaders promoted from the proletariat and peasantry often had little training or experience for their jobs. In order for the regime to survive it employed both force and persuasion to induce intellectuals and experts trained under tsarism to serve the Soviet government.

The creation of a stable, accomplished, and loyal elite was a major preoccupation of the regime during the early Soviet years. The state's solution, to mold a hybrid leadership from representatives of both the lower and the old privileged classes, was one born of necessity. Nonetheless, it raised objections from workers' groups, which resented the status this course conferred on their old class enemies. It also dismayed revolutionary idealists, who envisioned an egalitarian society without an elite at all.

To their credit, Bogdanov and his allies in the Vpered circle had anticipated many of these difficulties long before the October uprising. They argued that in order for the coming revolution to be successful, the working class would have to generate its own elite before it attempted to take power. But the solution they had proposed, the slow and painstaking education of a working-class intelligentsia before the revolution came, was of little relevance after 1917. Proletkultists, like government leaders and party officials, had to devise new schemes to solve the problem of revolutionary leadership.

Because the movement placed such emphasis on proletarian creativity and independence, its proponents often asserted that the working class could undertake the management of revolutionary society on its own. Proletkultists were famous for their glorification of proletarian abilities, something particularly evident in the organization's artistic productions. "We are everything, we are everywhere, we are the conquering fire and light," proclaimed the poet Vladimir Kirillov. "We are our own God, Judge, and Law."[1] Such sentiments inspired denunciations of the old intelligentsia and its place in revolutionary society. No wonder, then, that many scholars see the Proletkult as one of the most extreme advocates of workers' control.[2]

Yet despite its radical reputation, the Proletkult could not avoid the problems faced by other revolutionary institutions in the early Soviet years. The Russian proletariat was too small, too overburdened, and too inexperienced to take power on its own. New state commissariats tried to induce tsarist bureaucrats to remain in their old positions. The Red Army

1. Vladimir Kirillov, "My," in *Stikhotvoreniia i poemy*, by Vladimir Kirillov (Moscow, 1970), p. 36.
2. See, for example, Kendall E. Bailes, *Technology and Society under Lenin and Stalin: Origins of the Soviet Technical Intelligentsia* (Princeton, 1978), p. 59; and S. A. Fediukin, *The Great October Revolution and the Intelligentsia*, trans. Sinclair Lourit (Moscow, 1975), p. 47.

could not fight the Civil War without the aid of tsarist generals. In Soviet factories a combination of economic hardship
and severe political pressure forced workers to accept the aid
of managers and engineers. And even the most iconoclastic
Proletkult participants discovered it was not possible to engage in cultural creation without the services of the old cultural elite—the writers, painters, and educators who had
gained their experience under the old regime.

The Ideals of Proletkult Leadership

Proletkult theorists posed challenging questions about authority, class identity, and expertise in the new revolutionary
society. They hoped to nurture an ethos of socialism that was
based on the spirit of collectivism. At the same time, they
wanted to advance new proletarian intellectuals to prove that
the working class had the skills and the resources to take
charge. Finally, they intended to make use of the talents of the
old intelligentsia in a way that would augment, not inhibit,
proletarian creativity. These were daunting and sometimes
contradictory goals.

For Proletkultists socialism meant the victory of the collective over bourgeois individualism, the victory of "we" over "I."
The principle of collectivism pervaded Proletkult organizational guidelines: power was delegated to groups rather than
to individuals. The national charter gave control to large leadership councils elected at periodic conferences.[3] There were
no written guidelines about the class makeup of the leadership, surely because Proletkult planners assumed that a
collective of worker-members would select a collective of
worker-leaders. The rules also did not describe power rela-
tionships within the leadership councils; there were no instructions about conventional offices like president, vice
president, or secretary. This same commitment to collectiv-

3. "Plan organizatsii Proletkul'ta," *Proletarskaia kul'tura*, no. 6
(1919), pp. 27–28.

ism emerged in any number of local manifestoes and guidelines. Participants in one Kolpino art section declared that they wanted "neither literary generals nor colonels." Their group would be composed of equals who might know a little more or a little less.[4]

Despite this commitment to egalitarianism, many local groups followed the organizational patterns set by the national Proletkult and common practice, choosing presidents, subordinate officers, and the leaders of artistic divisions. Ideally, these officials were elected at periodic conferences and could be recalled if they abused their position, but these democratic principles were not always realized. Some circles began work without founding conferences, and others never reconvened after the opening session.[5] Of course, even when leaders were confirmed through elections, they could exercise considerable personal influence over local cultural agendas.

This tension between group leadership and personal authority was partially implicit in the organization's goals. The foremost Proletkult theorist, Aleksandr Bogdanov, did not believe that collectivism meant the denial of individual accomplishment. Only selfish bourgeois individualism would be extinguished under socialism. Human individuality, separate but tied to the good of the collective, would flower in the new society.[6] In less abstract terms many Proletkultists were proud of the talents of individual worker-artists and organizers. When Fedor Kalinin, the best-known proletarian leader, died in early 1920, the Proletkult press abounded with moving remembrances of his exploits, and Bogdanov praised him as

4. "Ot literaturnoi sektsii Kolpinskogo Proletkul'ta," *Mir i chelovek*, no. 1 (1919), p. 10.

5. Both the Izhevsk and Pudemskii factory Proletkults began without conferences. The Archangel organization reported only one conference between its founding in early 1920 and late 1921. See local questionnaires in *Tsentral'nyi Gosudarstvennyi Arkhiv Literatury i Iskusstva* [henceforth cited as TsGALI] f. 1230, op. 1, d. 117, ll. 10, 54 ob.; d. 118, l. 39.

6. Zenovia A. Sochor, *Revolution and Culture* (Ithaca, 1988), pp. 137–38.

the best example of the new kind of worker-intellectual.[7] The achievements of this gifted individual and others like him symbolized the abilities of the entire proletariat.

Inevitably, this complex interrelationship between the individual and the collective caused confusion. Not only was there ample room for power abuses, but organizations were often torn between conflicting goals. Should they devote their resources to the education and training of the proletariat as a whole? The advocates of this radical course denounced all forms of hierarchy, including the cultivation of a worker-elite to stand at the forefront of the proletariat.[8] Or should they nurture the talents of the most promising workers? Those in favor of this position believed that it was the best way to show the accomplishments of the working class and the power of proletarian culture. Each position brought its own dangers. If the Proletkult was too egalitarian, then it could easily turn into a basic educational movement whose activities were barely distinguishable from those of Narkompros. If it catered to the most sophisticated, it could lose its ties to the masses.

The role of the old intelligentsia posed equally difficult dilemmas. Rancorous debates about intellectuals' place in a proletarian movement began at the founding conference in 1917 and continued unabated throughout the Proletkult's history. In a revolutionary world split between a plebeian "us" versus a patrician "them," the intelligentsia was easily singled out as an implacable class enemy. Proletkult publications bristled with denunciations of the educated elite. The worker-writer Aleksei Samobytnik-Mashirov insisted that the Proletkult rely on the proletarian intelligentsia alone. "Only in it can there be a guarantee of proletarian culture."[9] Fedor

7. A. A. Bogdanov, "Novyi tip rabotnika," in *Sbornik pamiati F. I. Kalinina* (Rostov on Don, 1920), pp. 33–38.

8. See the denunciation of any kind of intelligentsia in R., "Sushchnost' intelligentsii," *Griadushchaia kul'tura*, no. 1 (1918), p. 20.

9. A. Mashirov, "Zadachi proletarskoi kul'tury," *Griadushchee*, no. 2 (1918), p. 10.

Kalinin warned that intellectuals possessed a different world-view than the working class. No matter how sympathetic they were, they still would draw workers away from proletarian forms of expression.[10]

Such outbursts revealed the lower classes' longstanding distrust of the intelligentsia, but they served mainly a rhetorical function. As president of the Petrograd Proletkult, Samo-bytnik-Mashirov helped to recruit intellectuals to his programs. Kalinin shared the leadership of the central Proletkult with his friends and mentors, the intellectuals Bogdanov and Lebedev-Polianskii. Many other lower class participants welcomed intellectuals' aid without any ambivalence at all.

The national organization contributed to the confusion, sending out very mixed messages on this complex issue. Proletkult theorists worried that the intelligentsia might gain control of the creative processes in local organizations, and they warned about the dangers this posed to proletarian culture. But they also recognized that the movement could not survive without some intellectual aid. In the words of the first Proletkult president Lebedev-Polianskii, the socialist intelligentsia who came to the Proletkult had *kul'turnyi stazh*, cultural experience.[11] That was one asset a cultural organization could not forgo.

Torn between suspicion and need, the central Proletkult tried to discover ways to harness intellectuals' experience while limiting their influence. At the first national conference delegates decided that the Proletkult would make use of intellectuals' skills "as far as possible."[12] The 1919 national charter

10. Fedor Kalinin, "Proletariat i iskusstvo," *Proletarskaia kul'tura*, no. 3 (1918), p. 13. See also I. Sadof'ev, "Na solnechnyi put'," *Griadushchee*, no. 10 (1918), pp. 15–16 and S. Kluben', "S burzhuaznogo Parnasa—v Proletkul't: O 'proletarizatsii pisatelei,' " *Griadushchaia kul'tura*, no. 3 (1919), pp. 17–18.

11. "Revoliutsiia i kul'turnye zadachi proletariata," *Protokoly pervoi Vserossiiskoi konferentsii proletarskikh kul'turno-prosvetitel'nykh organizatsii, 15–20 sentiabria, 1918 g.*, ed. P. I. Lebedev-Polianskii (Moscow, 1918), p. 20.

12. Ibid., p. 29.

spelled out just how far that was. A real knowledge of proletarian spirit and character could only be achieved through long exposure to workers' lives and customs, something very difficult for nonworkers to achieve. Therefore, sympathetic nonproletarian elements would be limited to technical and auxiliary roles in Proletkult creative work.[13]

Yet this simple solution, which turned intellectuals into outside helpmates in an organization supposedly composed of and led by workers, proved to be very difficult to implement. The old intelligentsia's cultural experience granted them authority that the rules of collective management could not confine. Committed artists and educators gained considerable influence in local circles and left an indelible mark on the movement's cultural programs.

By addressing the problems of leadership and class identity, Proletkultists wrestled with the contradictions posed by the socialist revolution itself. Could egalitarianism be reconciled with skill and talent? Was it possible to nurture a new intelligentsia without conferring power on the old? In the variety of answers that participants found to these questions they inadvertently acknowledged the limits of proletarian power and redefined the language of class control.

Leaders from the Lower Classes

The Proletkult owed its existence in large part to the efforts of self-made artists and thinkers from the lower classes who had won their education with great difficulty in exile schools and adult education circles under the old regime. For these talented individuals the Proletkult was a showcase for their accomplishments and also a way to further their education in an environment designed to meet their needs. The most visible worker-leaders were those who served on the national central committee and presidium. Although proletarians always

13. "Plan organizatsii Proletkul'ta," *Proletarskaia kul'tura*, no. 6 (1919), p. 27.

shared these posts with nonworkers, they held a significant percentage of the top jobs, and their numbers grew over the years.

The first cohort of proletarian leaders, elected at the 1918 national convention, included Fedor Kalinin, Aleksei Samobytnik-Mashirov, Vasilii Ignatov, Mikhail Gerasimov, Vladimir Kossior, Vladimir Kirillov, Karl Ozol-Prednek, and Ilia Sadofev.[14] Except for the actor Ignatov and the union activist Kossior they were all writers who had tried their hands at creative work and criticism in a variety of socialist journals and newspapers. The careers of four—Kalinin, Kirillov, Gerasimov, and Samobytnik-Mashirov—will serve as examples of this accomplished generation.

Easily the most important was Fedor Kalinin, an influential contributor to *Proletarian Culture*, head of the Proletkult division in Narkompros, and admired friend of Bogdanov and Lebedev-Polianskii. He was also the brother of Mikhail Ivanovich Kalinin, the future president of the Supreme Soviet under Stalin. Born into a peasant weaver's family in 1882, Kalinin began factory work at an early age. By 1901 he already faced exile for political activity. He was released in time to take an active part in the Revolution of 1905, for which he received a three-year prison term. When his sentence was over, Kalinin began underground agitation for the Bolsheviks in Moscow. Because of his sympathies for the left Bolshevik faction, he made his way to the exile schools in Capri and Bologna, quickly distinguishing himself as a student and an organizer. He later joined Lunacharskii's circle for proletarian literature in Paris. While working at an airplane factory in France, Kalinin began to publish his thoughts on cultural creation in the journal *Struggle* (*Bor'ba*) and the main journal of the Vperedists, *Forward* (*Vpered*). His many writings on proletarian thought and culture earned him the title of "proletarian philosopher."[15]

14. *Protokoly pervoi konferentsii*, p. 7.
15. For a summary of Kalinin's life and accomplishments see

Vladimir Kirillov was one of the best-known creative writers in the movement. His panegyric to proletarian power, the poem "We," is constantly cited as the prototype of Proletkult creation. Born in Smolensk in 1890, he went to a village school and began his working life as a shoemaker's apprentice. At the age of thirteen he left to join the merchant marines, later taking part in sailors' rebellions during the Revolution of 1905. For his role in the revolution, he received three years in exile. Once freed, he left Russia and traveled around the world, including an extended stay in the United States. Kirillov began his career as a writer while abroad, although he would not start publishing until just before the First World War. On his return to Russia in 1912 Kirillov refined his literary skills in classes at Countess Panina's famous People's House in St. Petersburg.[16] His first poetry collections, including *Dawn of the Future (Zori griadushchego)* and *The Iron Messiah (Zheleznyi messiia)*, were put out by the Proletkult.

Another important organizer and writer was Mikhail Gerasimov. He was born in Samara in 1889, the son of a railroad worker. Gerasimov attended primary schools sponsored by the railroad and went to work at the age of nine. Like Kirillov and Kalinin, he quickly became involved in political activity and also faced imprisonment for his involvement in the Revolution of 1905. After his release Gerasimov resumed political agitation. Facing imminent arrest, he had to flee the country in 1907. He stayed in Europe for many years, where he continued his political work, even spending time in foreign prisons. In Paris he joined Lunacharskii's circle for proletarian literature and began to publish his work in socialist journals and newspapers. During the First World War, he volunteered to

---

Sbornik pamiati F. I. Kalinina. His most important works are reprinted in P. Bessal'ko and F. Kalinin, *Problemy proletarskoi kul'tury* (Petrograd, 1919).

16. Vladimir Timofeevich Kirillov, "Avtobiografiia," TsGALI f. 1372, op. 1, d. 1, ll. 1–5; and Z. S. Papernyi and R. A. Shatseva, eds., *Proletarskie poety pervykh let sovetskoi epokhi* (Leningrad, 1959), pp. 515–17.

serve in the French army, but was sent back to Russia for engaging in antiwar propaganda. In 1917 Gerasimov became a leading Bolshevik organizer in his native Samara, where he took charge of the city Soviet and helped to form the local Red Guard unit.[17]

Aleksei Mashirov, who gave himself the pen name "Samobytnik" (from the Russian word for "original" or "distinctive"), was born in St. Petersburg in 1884. The son of an artisan, he was sent to primary school in the city and then, at the age of twelve, to a metalworking plant. His political commitments led to arrest and exile after 1905. On returning to St. Petersburg in 1908 Samobytnik-Mashirov joined the Bolshevik faction and began to write literature, taking classes in Panina's People's House. His poetry appeared in Gorky's first collection of workers' writing and in *Pravda*. A founder of the Proletkult in 1917, Samobytnik-Mashirov became president of the Petrograd city organization.[18]

These worker-intellectuals shared many common experiences. They were all approximately the same age and had left manual labor behind to pursue political and cultural work. Their history in the revolutionary movement also followed similar paths. Bolsheviks of long standing, they had taken part in the Revolution of 1905 and served time in prison and exile. There were also strong friendship ties between them. Kalinin knew Gerasimov from the exile schools; Gerasimov was a friend of Kirillov's; and Kirillov had studied with Samobytnik-Mashirov and another proletarian author, Ilia Sadofev, at the Countess Panina's People's House.

It is difficult to overestimate the importance of these four writers in the formation of the Proletkult. Kalinin and Samobytnik-Mashirov, together with Vasilii Ignatov and two other writers, Aleksandr Pomorskii and Aleksei Gastev, were key

17. F. Levin, "Mikhail Gerasimov," in *Stikhotvoreniia*, by Mikhail Gerasimov (Moscow, 1959), pp. 7–11.

18. Papernyi and Shatseva, *Proletarskie poety*, pp. 528–29; and *Kratkaia literaturnaia entsiklopediia* (Moscow, 1962–1978).

organizers of the first Proletkult in 1917.[19] Kalinin, friend and former student of Lunacharskii's, provided the crucial links between the Proletkult and Narkompros. This circle of committed workers was also responsible for starting some of the most important local organizations. Kirillov and Pomorskii went to Tambov.[20] Gerasimov founded the Proletkult in his native Samara, where the local journal, *Glow of the Factories* (*Zarevo zavodov*), bore the name of one of his poems.[21] Ignatov opened and led the Tula Proletkult and helped to initiate new organizations in the Caucasus.[22]

This first generation of Proletkult leaders was very anxious to make its mark as serious artists and thinkers, not amateurs who pursued their vocations on the side. They wanted the Proletkult's resources to be spent on developing the skills of the best representatives of their class, not on basic educational work to benefit the masses. The organization's first responsibility was to help the most talented, wrote Kalinin; they could then serve as role models for the others.[23] Such attitudes dulled their sensitivity to the problems of aspiring cultural activists who had not yet established themselves.

However impressive the qualifications of this cohort, their resources alone were not enough to sustain the organization.

19. A. V. Lunacharskii, *Vospominaniia i vpechatleniia* (Moscow, 1968), pp. 164–66. Gastev was never elected to a position in the national organization and by 1919 had distanced himself from the Proletkult. See *Protokoly pervoi konferentsii*, p. 103; and Kendall E. Bailes, "Alexei Gastev and the Controversy over Taylorism, 1918–1924," *Soviet Studies*, vol. 29, no. 3 (1977), pp. 373–94.

20. "Soveshchanie o proletarskoi kul'ture," *Griadushchaia kul'tura*, no. 3 (1919), p. 25.

21. See the local questionnaire in TsGALI f. 1230, op. 1, d. 117, l. 6; and *Zarevo zavodov*, no. 1 (1919), pp. 8–10.

22. "Vypiska iz protokola Tul'skogo komiteta RKP," August 1, 1918, TsGALI f. 1230, op. 1, d. 1538, l. 8; and I. S. Smirnov, comp., "Tsennoe priznanie: Pis'ma proletkul'tovtsa V. V. Ignatova K. S. Stanislavskomu, S. M. Eizenshteinu, V. E. Meierkhol'du," *Teatr*, no. 12 (1976), p. 49.

23. F. Kalinin, "O professionalizme rabochikh v iskusstve," *Proletarskaia kul'tura*, no. 7/8 (1919), p. 30.

Politically experienced workers were much sought after, and the Proletkult was rarely their only responsibility. Kalinin, for example, worked for Narkompros, the Communist Party, and the Red Army in addition to his responsibilities in the Proletkult. He was killed by typhus in early 1920 while organizing a military newspaper on the Southern front. Kossior quickly put aside his Proletkult duties to assume party responsibilities in the Ukraine.[24] Others were disillusioned when the movement became too actively involved in general educational work at the expense of more specialized programs. Both Gerasimov and Kirillov left the Proletkult national leadership in 1920. Although they still kept ties to the movement, their primary energies went to two new cultural organizations, the Proletarian Writers' Union and the journal *The Foundry* (*Kuznitsa*), that aimed to improve working conditions for professional proletarian artists.[25]

It was a sign of the Proletkult's vitality that new leaders from the lower classes stepped forward to take the place of the old. The national governing council elected in 1920 included Valerian Pletnev, a worker turned playwright, Pavel Arskii, a proletarian author who helped to lead the Petrograd organization, Georgii Nazarov, a former Petrograd metalworker, and another metalworker, Andrei Kozochkin.[26] These men were part of a new generation of proletarian leaders who worked their way up into the national organization through local governing boards.

Valerian Pletnev was the most important, elected to the post of national president in late 1920. Born in 1886, Pletnev was a joiner by trade and claimed nineteen years at the bench. A Menshevik until the revolution, Pletnev was an eloquent

24. On Kossior's background see an account of his brother Stanislav's career in Georges Haupt and Jean-Jacques Marie, *Makers of the Russian Revolution: Biographies of Bolshevik Leaders*, trans. C. I. P. Ferdinand and D. M. Bellos (Ithaca, 1974), pp. 149–51.

25. See Chapter 5 on this split.

26. For a list of central Proletkult officers elected at the 1920 congress see *Proletarskaia kul'tura*, no. 17/19 (1920), pp. 78–79.

defender of workers' literature in one of the earliest disputes on proletarian culture before 1917.[27] He was a key participant in the Moscow Proletkult theater and became a member of the local executive committee in 1919. By 1920 he gained a place in the national Proletkult presidium. His numerous plays, focusing on the history of the revolutionary movement, were widely produced in workers' theaters by the end of the Civil War.[28]

Pavel Arskii, another member of this new cohort, was elected to the national governing board from the Petrograd organization. Like Pletnev, he had a few publications to his credit before 1917. Mobilized during the war, he took part in the February Revolution and had helped to storm the Winter Palace, although he did not join the Bolsheviks until 1918. An early member of the Petrograd Proletkult, Arskii contributed poetry to Proletkult journals and wrote plays for the Petrograd theater. His first literary collection, *Songs of Struggle* (*Pesni bor'by*), was published in 1919.[29]

The Petrograd worker Georgii Nazarov, elected to the central committee in 1920 and again in 1921, was another national leader who gained recognition for his work in local organizations. A machinist by trade, he was the head of the cultural commission of the Baltic factory committee in Petrograd in 1917. Although Nazarov had participated in cultural circles before the revolution, the Proletkult developed both his dramatic and his organizational talents. When the director Aleksandr Mgebrov started a theater at the Baltic factory,

27. V. F. Pletnev [V. Valerianov, pseud.], "K voprosu o proletarskoi kul'ture," *Nasha zaria*, no. 10/11 (1913), pp. 35–41; and idem, "Pervyi shag," *Bor'ba*, no. 7/8 (1914), pp. 44–46.

28. *Teatral'naia entsiklopediia* (Moscow, 1961–1967); Sheila Fitzpatrick, *The Commissariat of Enlightenment* (Cambridge, Eng., 1970), p. 315; and the delegate list for the 1921 Proletkult congress, TsGALI f. 1230, op. 1, d. 144, l. 115.

29. A. A. Mgebrov, *Zhizn' v teatre* (Moscow and Leningrad, 1933), vol. 2, p. 319; and G. I. Kopanev, ed., *Geroi Oktiabria: Biografii aktivnykh uchastnikov podgotovki i provedeniia Oktiabr'skogo vooruzhennogo vosstaniia v Petrograde* (Leningrad, 1967), vol. 1, pp. 107–8.

Nazarov was a star student. He followed Mgebrov to the Petrograd Proletkult and there came into contact with the energetic theater organizer, Vasilii Ignatov. Nazarov went to Tula
with Ignatov, where he took control of the local Proletkult
theater and joined the executive committee. In 1922 Nazarov
returned to Petrograd to assume the job of Proletkult president.[30]

The lathe operator Andrei Kozochkin from the Izhevsk organization also rose rapidly from the ranks to assume a position of responsibility. A Proletkult first opened in this factory
town under the guidance of the Narkompros division. However, workers from the local metalworking plant were dissatisfied with its nonproletarian leadership and decided to
restructure it. Kozochkin, himself the son of a metalworker,
was part of the new organizing committee. Without any special training for the job, he took charge of the theater studio.
He was soon elected president of the Izhevsk Proletkult and in
this capacity was chosen to serve in the national central committee as a candidate member in 1920 and a full member in
1921.[31]

This new generation did not come to the Proletkult with
established reputations, as Kirillov had done. Although they
were all members of the Communist Party, their credentials
were newly minted compared to someone like Samobytnik-
Mashirov, who had worked on the prerevolutionary *Pravda*.
With less revolutionary and party experience they also had
fewer commitments to other institutions. Kozochkin, for example, held no posts outside the Proletkult.[32]

These national leaders were the most visible but by no
means the only examples of Proletkultists from the lower

30. Mgebrov, *Zhizn' v teatre*, vol. 2, p. 304; the meeting of the Tula
Proletkult presidium, January 9, 1919, TsGALI f. 1230, op. 1, d. 1537,
l. 3; the local questionnaire from the Tula organization, d. 117, l. 105;
and "Lichnaia anketa," d. 118, ll. 27 ob.–28.
31. "Doklad o deiatel'nosti Izhevskogo Proletkul'ta," TsGALI f.
1230, op. 1, d. 1221, l. 1.
32. "Lichnaia anketa," 1922, TsGALI f. 1230, op. 1, d. 118, l. 43 ob.

classes who rose to high positions. Lower-level organizations rarely provided detailed biographical information on their staff. However, if the delegates to the 1921 Proletkult congress are any indication, the number of workers in leadership positions increased the further down one moved on the hierarchical ladder. Of the thirty-four delegates serving as executive officers in local organizations, only fourteen (41 percent) had working-class occupations. However, figures for presidium members, who served on the large collective governing boards, show a different picture: twenty-four of thirty-three representatives (73 percent) were from the working class.[33]

The same definitional problems that complicated debates about Proletkult membership recurred in discussions on leadership. What exactly was a proletarian leader? Judging by factory employment alone, someone like Kalinin would not qualify because his time at the bench lay far in the distant past. Nor would V. M. Blinkov, the self-educated baker who headed the Saratov literary studio, qualify nor Anton Chuvinok, an office worker who sat on the Tula Proletkult presidium.[34] But clearly for many participants lower-class origins, or evidence of proletarian sympathies, were just as important as a current factory job. This opened up the leadership to a very broadly defined proletariat. At the same time, it made it much easier for intellectuals to justify their place in this working-class movement.

Leaders from the Old Intelligentsia

Anti-intellectualism was very strong in the Proletkult movement, as indeed it was in many institutions in the early Soviet years. Whereas central leaders' criticisms of peasants and the

33. From the delegate list for the 1921 Proletkult congress, TsGALI f. 1230, op. 1, d. 144. For general statistics, not broken down according to occupational standing, see *Biulleten' vtorogo s"ezda Proletkul'tov*, no. 1 (1921), pp. 92–93.

34. From the delegate list to the 1921 national congress, TsGALI f. 1230, op. 1, d. 144, ll. 115, 124.

petty bourgeoisie were often ignored, the negative language they employed against intellectuals struck a responsive chord among the membership. It evoked the deeply rooted resentment of the laboring masses against the privileged. In the words of a delegate at the first Proletkult national congress, "I know of only two classes—the oppressed poor and the rich exploiters."[35] The old intelligentsia, as a representative of the old elite, was easily consigned to the alien and hostile world of "the *burzhui* and their lackeys."[36]

However, this Manichaean worldview proved too simple to describe the complex social realities of Soviet Russia. The angry attacks on intellectuals, so common in the Proletkult press, were not consistent in their targets. Participants separated the intellectual elite into two camps; on one side was the hostile "bourgeois" intelligentsia, on the other a potentially friendly group of "socialist" or "revolutionary" intellectuals. Political sympathies, not social origins, determined an individual's assignation. Those who doubted the revolution were the enemies, but the ones who had proven their commitment to the working class through political work or longstanding involvement in proletarian cultural projects were often exempted from criticism.[37] They escaped condemnation through a metamorphosis from outsider to insider. This redefinition of friend and foe, based on attitude and function rather than on class standing, allowed Proletkult participants to entrust intellectuals with important positions without appearing to abandon the organization's principles.

The Proletkult's most important theorists contributed to this complicated use of social categories. Lebedev-Polianskii

35. *Protokoly pervoi konferentsii*, p. 22.
36. A. P., "Kholmskii s"ezd rabotnikov po vneshkol'nomu obrazovaniiu," *Vneshkol'noe obrazovanie* (Petrograd), no. 2/3 (1919), p. 96.
37. See, for example, I. Fuks, "Intelligentsiia i kollektivnoe tvorchestvo," *Griadushchaia kul'tura*, no. 4/5 (1919), p. 20; S. Krivtsov, "Konferentsiia Proletkul'tov," *Rabochii mir*, no. 14 (1919), p. 32; and Knizhnik, Karl Ozol'–Prednek, and A. M., "God bor'by za proletarskuiu kul'turu," *Griadushchee*, no. 8 (1918), p. 18.

was one of the most outspoken advocates of class purity. Intellectuals come to us, he said, and they have skills we need, but we should place them under strict controls.[38] Despite his own privileged background, he obviously excluded himself from the role of "suspect outsider." Bogdanov, another intellectual, argued for the integrity of the proletarian worldview, unsullied and unaltered by the manipulations of class-alien elements.[39] But he certainly did not question his own ability to articulate the thoughts of the proletariat.

Despite numerous rules regulating their involvement, socialist intellectuals took part in Proletkult leadership at all levels, from membership in the national central committee to advisory roles in factory circles. The most influential were those in the central organization, where intellectuals held some of the most important positions. They all had excellent revolutionary credentials. Like their worker-counterparts, they were members of the Communist Party, with the notable exception of Aleksandr Bogdanov.[40] Many also held high posts in other Soviet institutions.

The national Proletkult president from 1918–1920, Pavel Lebedev-Polianskii, was the university-educated son of a minor tsarist official. Born in 1881, he first attended a seminary school, went to the university to study medicine, and then turned to professional political work in 1903. In 1908 he fled Russia for Switzerland, joining the left Bolshevik Vpered faction. Lebedev-Polianskii did not return to Russia until 1917, when he officially rejoined the Bolshevik Party. He took on important positions in the new state, serving on the Petro-

38. P. I. Lebedev-Polianskii, "Revoliutsiia i kul'turnye zadachi proletariata," *Protokoly pervoi konferentsii*, p. 26. See also his speech at the first meeting of the Proletarian Writers' Union in 1920, "Privet-stvie Vserossiiskomu s"ezdu proletarskikh pisatelei ot mezhdun-arodnogo biuro Proletkul'tov," in V. Volkova, comp., "Materialy Proletkul'ta v TsGALI," *Voprosy literatury*, no. 1 (1958), p. 183.

39. See, for example, A. A. Bogdanov, "Proletarskii universitet," *Proletarskaia kul'tura*, no. 5 (1918), pp. 9–13.

40. See "Neobkhodimoe ob"iasenie," TsGALI f. 1230, op. 1, d. 51, l. 6.

grad soviet, the national soviet, and heading the literary publishing division of Narkompros, where he also edited a major educational journal.[41] In his role as national president and editor of *Proletarian Culture* Lebedev-Polianskii had the power to define the Proletkult's institutional identity.

Aleksandr Bogdanov was the Proletkult's main theorist and inspirational figure. A member of the Proletkult central committee and editor of *Proletarian Culture*, his influence extended well beyond his formal institutional position. His prolific writings on the themes of culture, science, and social organization earned him a following far outside the confines of the Proletkult. Bogdanov worked as a lecturer and educator in Moscow during the early Soviet years, giving his services to many different cultural groups, including the Socialist Academy.[42]

Other important intellectuals in the national organization included Anna Dodonova, who served on all national governing boards from 1918 until the Proletkult was disbanded in 1932. Born in 1888, Dodonova joined the Bolshevik faction in 1911. She took part in the October uprising as the secretary of the Moscow Military Revolutionary Committee and joined the cultural division of the Moscow soviet.[43] Vladimir Faidysh, a Moscow party member, also served on the Moscow Military Revolutionary Committee. Elected to the national Proletkult in 1918, he became vice president in 1921.[44] Fedor Blagonravov, an old Bolshevik, was a member of the Prolet-

41. Fitzpatrick, *Commissariat*, pp. 306–7; B. Iakovlev, *Kritik-boets: O P. I. Lebedeve-Polianskom* (Moscow, 1960); and *Literaturnaia entsiklopediia* (Moscow, 1929–1936).

42. See Dietrich Grille, *Lenins Rivale* (Cologne, 1966), pp. 69–72; and S. Krivtsov, "Pamiati A. A. Bogdanova," *Pod znamenem marksizma*, no. 4 (1928), p. 185.

43. See the delegate list for the 1921 national congress, TsGALI f. 1230, op. 1, d. 144, l. 115; *V. I. Lenin o literature i iskusstve*, 7th ed., ed. N. Krutikov (Moscow, 1986), p. 709; and I. I. Mints, *Istoriia Velikogo Oktiabria* (Moscow, 1973), vol. 3, p. 70.

44. See the delegate list for the 1921 national congress, TsGALI f. 1230, op. 1, d. 144, l. 116; and Mints, *Istoriia*, vol. 3, p. 45.

kult central committee and helped to lead the Moscow organization.[45] Platon Kerzhentsev, another old Bolshevik and accomplished party intellectual, had a seat on the Moscow Proletkult executive committee and initially was one of the chief editors of *Proletarian Culture*. In addition to his work in the Proletkult, he held posts in Narkompros and the state news agency, ROSTA.[46]

Provincial organizations also placed nonworkers in very powerful positions. Ilia Trainin, a former Vperedist and friend of Lebedev-Polianskii, served on the executive committee of the Samara Proletkult in 1918. His writings are featured prominently in the Samara Proletkult journal, *Glow of the Factories*.[47] Vladislava Lie, a university-educated communist from a noble background, was the president of the Tver organization.[48] In the town of Belev, Tula province, local Proletkult members elected Valentin Nikolaitsev as their president in 1921. He was a party member, son of a school teacher and a forester, and had studied at Moscow University.[49]

These men and women from the socialist intelligentsia had long careers in cultural and political work behind them. They hardly intended to threaten the "pro-worker" stance of the organization. The Petrograd Proletkult under the leadership of the former worker Aleksei Samobytnik-Mashirov was not more sympathetic to the proletariat than the Tver Proletkult headed by the former noble Vladislava Lie. Indeed, sometimes intellectuals appeared to be the most passionate defenders of workers' interests.

Yet despite their revolutionary sympathies, these intellec-

45. "Vospominaniia P. N. Zubovoi," TsGALI f. 1230, op. 2, d. 14, l. 6; and the delegate list for the 1921 national congress, d. 144, l. 123.
46. Fitzpatrick, *Commissariat*, p. 304; P. M. Kerzhentsev, *Revoliutsiia i teatr* (Moscow, 1918), p. 12; and *Literaturnaia entsiklopediia*.
47. On Trainin's background see "Vpered," in *Bol'shaia sovetskaia entsiklopediia* (Moscow, 1926–1947); and protocols of the national Proletkult soviet, TsGALI f. 1230, op. 1, d. 138, ll. 20–21.
48. Delegate list for the 1921 national congress, TsGALI f. 1230, op. 1, d. 144, l. 128.
49. "Lichnaia anketa," 1922, TsGALI f. 1230, op. 1, d. 118, ll. 5–6.

tuals still exerted a problematic influence. Lebedev-Polianskii used the journal *Proletarian Culture* to shape the form and content of workers' writing, bemoaning the state of proletarian literature in numerous articles and reviews. He accused aspiring writers from the lower classes of lacking style, skill, and evidence of "real" class consciousness; however, he never seemed to doubt his own ability to chart the proper course for workers' poetry and prose.[50] Platon Kerzhentsev gave graphic instructions on how workers should organize their creative circles to emphasize proletarian collectivism.[51] In his job on the Proletkult central committee Bogdanov censured a division of proletarian education started by trade unionists in the Petrograd Proletkult. He argued that the division, which sponsored courses in mechanics and foreign languages, was not really pursuing proletarian culture at all.[52] Through their Proletkult offices intellectuals could articulate their own visions of proletarian culture, even though it sometimes meant telling workers what was best for them.

These influential leaders were joined by countless other artists and experts who worked as advisers and teachers in cultural sections and art studios. Although Proletkult rules permitted nonworkers in such posts, they were supposed to be limited to technical assistance and placed under the strict control of proletarian collectives. Staff members performed a variety of tasks, from occasional guest lectures to the management of cultural workshops.

Despite its abrasive anti-intellectual rhetoric, the Proletkult was in a strong position to attract a well-trained techni-

50. P. I. Lebedev-Polianskii [V. Polianskii, pseud.], "Motivy rabochei poezii," *Proletarskaia kul'tura*, no. 3 (1918), pp. 1–12; and idem, "Poeziia sovetskoi provintsii," *Proletarskaia kul'tura*, no. 7/8 (1919), pp. 43–57.
51. See P. M. Kerzhentsev [V. Kerzhentsev, pseud.], " 'Proletkul't'—organizatsiia proletarskoi samodeiatel'nosti," *Proletarskaia kul'tura*, no. 1 (1918), pp. 7–8; and idem, "Organizatsiia literaturnogo tvorchestva," *Proletarskaia kul'tura*, no. 5 (1918), pp. 23–26.
52. August 12, 1919, Proletkult central committee meeting, TsGALI f. 1230, op. 1, d. 3, l. 69.

cal staff. Some were drawn by the organization's class-based ideology and saw their own participation as a way to prove their loyalty to the victorious working class. Others perceived the Proletkult as an educational institution similar to those popular before the revolution where they could put their talents to work in order to serve the people. And finally, many came to the organization just to find employment. The Proletkult had wages and rations to offer, and that alone was a very compelling motivation during the hard years of the Civil War.

"Who didn't teach in the Proletkult!" exclaimed the actor Maksim Shtraukh. His years as a student in the Moscow Proletkult theater brought him into contact with Stanislavsky, Sergei Eisenstein, Sergei Tretiakov, and many other illustrious theatrical personages.[53] Some of Russia's finest writers taught literature courses, including Andrei Belyi, Valeryi Briusov, Nikolai Chuzhak, Nikolai Gumilev, and Vladislav Khodasevich.[54] In music the Proletkult had the services of Aleksandr Kastalskii, Reinhold Glière, and Arsenii Avraamov.[55] Art classes were led by avant-gardists like Liubov Popova and Olga Rozanova and more traditional figures like the academician Timofei Katurkin.[56]

Many of these gifted artists and teachers were enthusiastic

53. M. Shtraukh, "Dva Sergeia Mikhailovicha," *Teatr*, no. 12 (1966), pp. 69–72, quotation p. 69.

54. On Andrei Belyi see "Literaturnaia studiia," *Gudki*, no. 2 (1919), p. 30; on Valeryi Briusov see the protocols of national Proletkult presidium meetings, December 5 and 31, 1919, TsGALI f. 1230, op. 1, d. 3, ll. 92, 95; on Nikolai Chuzhak see V. G. Puzyrev, " 'Prolet-kul't' na Dal'nem Vostoke," in *Iz istorii russkoi i zarubezhnoi literatury*, ed. V. N. Kasatkin, T. T. Napolona, and P. A. Shchekotov (Saratov, 1968), vol. 2, pp. 93–96; on Nikolai Gumilev see *Griadushchee*, no. 7/8 (1919), p. 30; and on Vladislav Khodasevich see V. Khodasevich, *Literaturnye stat'i i vospominaniia* (New York, 1954), pp. 325–31.

55. *Muzykal'naia entsiklopediia* (Moscow, 1973–1981).

56. On Popova and Rozanova see Christina Lodder, *Russian Constructivism* (New Haven, 1983), pp. 255, 259; on Katurkin see N. A. Milonov, "O deiatel'nosti Tul'skogo Proletkul'ta," in *Aktual'nye voprosy istorii literatury*, ed. Z. I. Levinson, N. A. Milonov, and A. F. Sergeicheva (Tula, 1969), p. 158.

supporters of the Proletkult and came with the express purpose of serving the working class and the revolution. As a music teacher in Kologriv explained, the Proletkult gave the intelligentsia a chance to pay off a centuries-old debt to the people by opening up the doors of art to them.[57] The same tone pervades the memoirs of Aleksandr Mgebrov, who headed the Petrograd Proletkult theater with his wife, Viktoriia Chekan. For Mgebrov participation in the Proletkult ended "long ordeals and a dissatisfying separation from the masses." With romantic enthusiasm he recalled, "Once again, as in 1905 when I stood with the workers on the barricades, I found myself side by side with the working class in its grandiose struggle for the future."[58] The Proletkult offered a dual advantage to sympathetic intellectuals like Mgebrov. It allowed them to settle past accounts and also let them feel as if they were helping to build the future.

Of course not everyone was so zealous. Prince Sergei Volkonskii, a lecturer in the Moscow Proletkult, did not attempt to conceal his doubts about the theoretical premises of the organization. Volkonskii had been the director of the imperial theaters before October; he lost his post and all his property in the wake of the revolution. His lectureship in the Proletkult was just one of many small jobs he took in order to survive. In his memoirs, written after he emigrated to the West, Volkonskii admitted that he was very impressed by the eager attention of his working-class students, but he never believed that there could be anything like a uniquely proletarian art form.[59] In the opinion of the actor Igor Ilinskii, who was briefly a participant in the Moscow provincial organization, "Only a very small group of theater people went to the

57. From a Kologriv Proletkult report, TsGALI f. 1230, op. 1, d. 1278, l. 13.

58. Mgebrov, *Zhizn' v teatre*, vol. 2, p. 301. On how Mgebrov and Chekan got involved in the Proletkult see Viktoriia Chekan, "O rabochem teatre," *Griadushchee*, no. 7/8 (1918), pp. 102–3.

59. Serge Wolkonsky, *My Reminiscences*, trans. A. E. Chamot (London, 1924), vol. 2, pp. 220–23, 227.

workers, to their uncomfortable, poor, and cold clubs out of a conscious commitment. . . . The majority went there only to get rations to supplement their paltry wages, which were shrinking because of the inflation."[60]

When intellectuals conveyed their reservations about proletarian culture, they could face close scrutiny from students and organizers. Both Volkonskii and Khodasevich, who openly questioned the Proletkult's mission, complained of harassment and intervention into their classes as a result.[61] However, those who offered their unqualified support could readily work their way up the organizational bureaucracy, taking control of cultural studios and serving on leadership councils. Mgebrov was not only the head of the Petrograd theater division but also an influential member of the local governing board.[62]

Whether they assumed official leadership positions or not, intellectuals' experience earned them cultural authority. For those participants who came to learn a specific skill like drawing or singing, studio instructors could exert more influence over their work than the local leadership did. Despite the supposed restrictions placed on them by governing collectives, instructors and workshop leaders had considerable freedom to shape their offerings according to their own understanding of what proletarian culture was.

As a consequence, artistic and educational programs differed radically from one organization to the next, and even one workshop to the next. In Moscow the music department was largely controlled by Aleksandr Kastalskii and Grigorii Liubimov, who had long histories in workers' artistic programs. Both believed that folk music was the best way to interest the masses in musical training.[63] In Petrograd, by

---

60. Igor' Il'inskii, *Sam o sebe* (Moscow, 1961), pp. 96–97.
61. Wolkonsky, *My Reminiscences*, vol. 2, pp. 221–22; and Khodasevich, *Literaturnye stat'i*, pp. 326–29.
62. *Griadushchee*, no. 4 (1919), p. 13.
63. G. Liubimov, "Narodnye orkestry i ikh znachenie v muzy

contrast, the music division was in the hands of a young composer, Ianis Ozolin, who thought the organization should create revolutionary songs. He and his supporters took a dim view of Moscow's programs, which they found too conservative.[64] In Kologriv, where the music studio was headed by a Petrograd conservatory graduate, Mariia Shipova, the approach was entirely conventional. She taught her students piano, violin, and songs by the classical Russian composers.[65]

This broad range of offerings was not unique to music. The Petrograd Proletkult was greatly influenced by Mgebrov's training in the symbolist theater of Vera Komissarzhevskaia. The main figures in Mgebrov's performances were allegorical ones such as those in the play *Legend of the Communard*, in which the heroes bore names like "Wisdom" and "Truth."[66] By contrast, the Moscow Proletkult theater was first led by Valentin Smyshliaev, who came from the Moscow Art Theater. His productions bore the unmistakable stamp of Stanislavsky's method acting.[67] In Saratov art courses were led by an avant-garde painter who advocated abstract art.[68] Moscow workshops were split acrimoniously between instructors who taught portrait painting and still lives and the aggressive

---

kal'nom prosveshchenii mass," *Gorn*, no. 2/3 (1919), pp. 99–105; A. D. Kastal'skii, "K voprosu ob organizatsii muzykal'nykh zaniatii v tsentral'noi studii Moskovskogo Proletkul'ta," in *Muzykal'naia zhizn' Moskvy v pervye gody posle Oktiabria*, ed. S. R. Stepanova (Moscow, 1972), pp. 283–84.

64. See for example Vladimir Kirillov's critique of Moscow's approach in *Protokoly pervoi konferentsii*, pp. 127–28.

65. Report on Kologriv music studios, TsGALI f. 1230, op. 1, d. 1278, ll. 13, 22 ob.

66. On Mgebrov's background see V. E. Rafilovich, ed., *Istoriia sovetskogo teatra* (Leningrad, 1933), vol. 1, p. 238. For a description of this play see James R. von Geldern, *Festivals of the Revolution, 1917–1920: Art and Theater in the Formation of Soviet Culture* (forthcoming), chapter 4.

67. See V. Smyshliaev, "O rabote teatral'nogo otdela Moskovskogo Proletkul'ta," *Gorn*, no. 1 (1918), p. 54; and idem, "Opyt instsenirovki stikhotvoreniia Verkharna 'Vostanie,' " *Gorn*, no. 2 (1919), pp. 82–90.

68. *Vzmakhi*, no. 2 (1920), p. 81.

advocates of production art, who believed that conventional forms should be abandoned for techniques more closely tied to industrial production.[69]

The integral involvement of intellectuals in Proletkult work offered the movement many advantages, including an experienced staff and a broad range of artistic influences. As the scattered memoirs of Proletkult participants suggest, members sincerely appreciated the training they received.[70] But these valued skills themselves could prove confining when the old intelligentsia's conception of proletarian culture—whether realist, avant-gardist, or symbolist—determined the content of local work.

Workers' Control?

During the Civil War years many revolutionary hopes for the establishment of proletarian leadership in politics, economics, and social life were disappointed. The government needed the services of intellectuals and experts in order to survive and was willing to compensate them well for their aid. By the end of the war many workers complained about the domination of specialists and bureaucrats in factories, unions, government bureaucracies, and the Communist Party. They protested that the ubiquitous influence of nonworkers marked a betrayal of the proletarian revolution.

The failure of workers' control has been examined most carefully at the factory level.[71] Workers began to take over

69. See the lively discussion of artistic programs at the central Proletkult meeting, July 5, 1919, TsGALI f. 1230, op. 1, d. 3, ll. 52–53 ob. On production art in the Proletkult see Chapter 5.

70. See Shtraukh, "Dva Sergeia Mikhailovicha," pp. 69–72; "Vospominaniia P. N. Zubovoi," TsGALI f. 1230, op. 2, d. 14; and L. Granat and N. Varzin, *Aktery-agitatory, boitsy* (Moscow, 1970), pp. 112–76.

71. See Paul H. Avrich, "The Bolshevik Revolution and Workers' Control in Russian Industry," *Slavic Review*, vol. 22, no. 1 (1963); William Husband, *Workers' Control and Centralization in the Russian Revolution: The Textile Industry of the Central Industrial Region*,

factories as a defensive measure to secure jobs when the Russian economy began its long spiral downward on the eve of the February Revolution. From the outset there were many competing definitions of workers' management. Some factories wanted to liquidate all nonproletarian supervisors; in others workers simply hoped to found mechanisms to supervise the administration. As the revolution and Civil War progressed, increasing demands for labor discipline and productivity, coming from the army, the Communist Party, state economic agencies, and unions, narrowed the sphere of proletarian power. This narrowing eventually resulted in the imposition of one-man management and an industrial structure that allowed little room for local governance.

However, the collapse of this movement was not simply the result of state centralization at the expense of proletarian autonomy. Experiments in worker management failed badly in many factories, particularly in those where unskilled labor predominated. Control committees discovered that they lacked the expertise to carry out supervisory tasks.[72] Calls for skilled experts, for increased labor discipline, and for better central management of the economy came from workers themselves as well as from state and party organizations.[73] The condition of the working class, weakened through revolu-

1917–1920, The Carl Beck Papers in Russian and East European Studies, no. 403 (Pittsburgh, 1985); David Mandel, *The Petrograd Workers and the Fall of the Old Regime* (New York, 1983); idem, *The Petrograd Workers and the Soviet Seizure of Power* (New York, 1984); Thomas Remington, *Building Socialism in Bolshevik Russia: Ideology and Industrial Organization, 1917–1921* (Pittsburgh, 1984), pp. 23–47; William G. Rosenberg, "Workers and Workers' Control in the Russian Revolution," *History Workshop*, no. 5 (1978); idem, "Russian Labor and Bolshevik Power after October," *Slavic Review*, vol. 44, no. 2 (1985), pp. 213–38; Carmen Sirianni, *Workers' Control and Socialist Democracy: The Soviet Experience* (London, 1982); and S. A. Smith, *Red Petrograd* (Cambridge, Eng., 1983).

72. This point is particularly emphasized in Husband, *Workers' Control*, pp. 34–43.

73. See Smith, *Red Petrograd*, pp. 246–52.

tion and war, combined with the disastrous state of the economy to contribute to the failure of workers' control.

The Proletkult's own attempt to promote proletarian leadership was on a much more modest scale. Its primary goal was to foster workers' independence within its own circles and studios. Yet even this limited experiment met with questionable results, as was clearly illustrated by the presence of intellectuals at all levels of the organization. As in the case of factory councils, this pattern can in part be traced to the severe economic and political disruptions of the early Soviet years. The Civil War weakened the proletariat's cultural vanguard, the very constituency for whom the organization was intended. But external factors alone were not to blame. Proletkult participants voluntarily chose a skilled and experienced leadership, often at the expense of class purity.

The visible role of intellectuals in the Proletkult was a source of conflict in many local organizations. According to one report in *Proletarian Culture* trade unionists in the provinces frequently complained that intellectuals held too much power. Disputes emerged over whether the new culture would be made "from above" by intellectuals or "from below" by the workers themselves.[74] As one speaker at a Moscow conference protested, it seemed that the organization was led by representatives of the bourgeoisie, people without any understanding of the proletarian milieu or proletarian creativity. In the provinces they called the Proletkult "Intelligentkult."[75]

These tensions could lead to bitter power struggles. The Communist Party division in Orsha, Mogilev province, shut down the local Proletkult because it reportedly had no work-

74. "Khronika Proletkul'ta," *Proletarskaia kul'tura*, no. 6 (1919), p. 30.

75. V. A. Razumov, "Rol' rabochego klassa v stroitel'stve sotsial-isticheskoi kul'tury v nachale revoliutsii i v gody grazhdanskoi voiny, 1917–1920," in *Rol' rabochego klassa v razvitii sotsialisticheskoi kul'tury*, ed. M. P. Kim and V. P. Naumov (Moscow, 1967), pp. 18–19. The speaker is identified as a student named Efremenkov.

ers in it. In the town of Brasovo, Orel province, participants threatened to expel all intellectuals because they wanted too much power. The vice president of the Kologriv Proletkult was ousted when a rival candidate exposed him as an intellectual careerist who had worked his way into proletarian organizations under false pretenses.[76]

Intellectuals also resisted the Proletkult's attempts to make use of their talents. Numerous local organizations complained that they had trouble attracting and keeping a trained staff. When the Izhevsk organization was restructured under worker leadership, the new presidium still wanted the help of the local intelligentsia, but its help was difficult to procure. The Proletkultists there complained that the technical staff had undermined comradely relations by asking for higher wages.[77] An organization in the village of Tomna reported that it had extreme difficulties finding teachers. It had invited the local intelligentsia to take part, but no one responded.[78]

However, some of the battles that appeared to center on workers' control were in fact conflicts between different groups of intellectuals who claimed to represent workers' interests. In the Petrograd Proletkult, for example, a struggle developed between two factions advocating different theatrical programs. The young director Dmitrii Shcheglov, a proponent of realism, was called to task for diverging from the symbolist direction of other Petrograd studios. According to Shcheglov's memoirs, Samobytnik-Mashirov, the proletarian leader of the Petrograd organization, criticized him for the independent direction of his classes and then berated himself for giving an intellectual so much control. Shcheglov recalled

76. "Khronika Proletkul'ta," *Proletarskaia kul'tura*, no. 6 (1919), p. 30; "Rost Proletkul'ta," *Proletarskaia kul'tura*, no. 9/10 (1919), p. 31; and the correspondence from the Kologriv organization to the center, November 5, 1919, TsGALI f. 1230, op. 1, d. 1278, ll. 43–44.

77. Report on the Izhevsk Proletkult for 1919–1920, TsGALI f. 1230, op. 1, d. 1221, ll. 1–1 ob., 11 ob.–12; and *Proletarskaia kul'tura*, no. 17/19 (1920), p. 89.

78. Questionnaire from the Tomna Proletkult, 1920, TsGALI f. 1230, op. 1, d. 117, l. 34.

that he did not say anything at all in response. "Why? Because I really never had worked in a factory and did not have the merits that my Proletkult comrades had."[79]

He was bitter, however, when Lebedev-Polianskii visited the Petrograd organization and chided participants there for giving intellectuals undue influence. The national president singled out Shcheglov for criticism and told him that he should emulate the proletarian methods of the head theater director, Mgebrov. Shcheglov noted with sarcasm that both of these representatives of the workers' interests, Lebedev-Polianskii and Mgebrov, were in fact intellectuals.[80] This struggle was over aesthetics but was couched in the language of workers' control.

This incident once again reveals the malleability of the Proletkult's class-based language. When Shcheglov opposed the aesthetic direction of the Petrograd organization, he was singled out as a suspect intellectual. But the social origins of intellectual friends went unnoticed. Just as participants altered the definition of "worker" to fit the organization's heterogeneous membership, they stretched the meanings of "intellectual" and "specialist" to suit their needs. They even devised new categories for those who had earned their trust and sympathy.

One can see this quite clearly in the answers to a 1921 central questionnaire that asked local leaders to determine whether "specialists" or "Proletkultists" were in charge of artistic studios. This questionnaire would have been an easy way to distinguish between intellectual and worker leaders, but that is not how the participants applied the categories. Instead, they were perfectly willing to give intellectuals the title of Proletkultist. The organization in Belev, for example, reported that its art studio was led by a Proletkultist when the intellectual Timofei Katurkin was in charge.[81] This flexible

79. D. Shcheglov, "U istokov," in *U istokov: Sbornik*, ed. I. P. Skachkov (Moscow, 1960), p. 70.
80. Ibid., p. 75.
81. Local questionnaire, TsGALI f. 1230, op. 1, d. 118, l. 7 ob.; and

use of social labels was a creative solution to a difficult problem: a simple way for participants to acknowledge the intellectuals' contributions without relinquishing proletarian control was to rename the nonworkers as part of the movement.

The Proletkult was not an organization in which intellectuals led and workers followed. Instead it was an elaborate system of mixed management. Its advocates pointed to the movement's real successes, to the national leaders who came from the proletariat, and to the strong worker presence on its local governing boards. The central Proletkult forcefully argued that it kept much tighter control over experts than did any other Soviet institution.[82] But critics found ample evidence to the contrary. The obvious discrepancy between the Proletkult's claims to proletarian hegemony and its much more modest accomplishments made it highly vulnerable to charges of hypocrisy. It also graphically illustrated how difficult it was to promote cultural creation without granting considerable power to the bearers of cultural expertise.

Defining equitable relations between workers and intellectuals was one of the oldest and most persistent problems of the Russian socialist movement, a problem that began with the inception of socialism and continued well into the Soviet period. Proletkultists were keenly aware of these tensions and devised a number of rules and regulations to minimize them. However, their solutions were clearly inadequate. The obstacles, which previous generations had also faced, remained the same. The lower classes had to be educated to assume positions of power, but who would restrict the influence of the educators?

Certainly the Proletkult never gave up its commitment to

---

a local report on studio work, d. 1581, ll. 28–28 ob., cited in V. V. Gorbunov, "Oktiabr' i nachalo kul'turnoi revoliutsii na mestakh," in *Velikii Oktiabr'*, ed. Iu. A. Poliakov (Moscow, 1978), pp. 71–72.

82. "Neobkhodimoe ob"iasnenie," TsGALI f. 1230, op. 1, d. 51, l. 6.

workers' control. Class exclusivity defined the organization and justified its existence in the Soviet state. At the same time, however, these principles were artfully suspended to integrate intellectuals sympathetic to the organization's goals. There were definite advantages to this arrangement; participants gained skills they never could have achieved without the aid of skilled cultural workers.

Still, the integration of the old intelligentsia raised serious and debilitating problems for the movement. It undermined the Proletkult's demand for institutional autonomy because the justification for independence was to protect its class identity. It also raised fundamental questions about what proletarian culture should or could be—something given to workers from above or something made by workers from below. At the very least, the large-scale involvement of artists and intellectuals ensured that the culture of the future would bear the marks of those who had been trained in the prerevolutionary past.

1. Aleksandr Bogdanov, whose writings on proletarian culture inspired the Proletkult movement. Source: *Pod znamenem marksizma*, no. 4 (1928).

2. Valerian Pletnev, playwright and Proletkult president from December 1920 until August 1932. Source: *Pechat' i revoliutsiia*, no. 7 (1927).

3. The presidium of the national Proletkult organization elected at the first national conference, September 1918. Sitting from left to right: Fedor Kalinin, Vladimir Faidysh, Pavel Lebedev-Polianskii, Aleksei Samobytnik-Mashirov, I. I. Nikitin, Vasilii Ignatov. Standing from left to right: Stefan Krivtsov, Karl Ozol-Prednek, Anna Dodonova, N. M. Vasilevskii, Vladimir Kirillov.

Source: *Protokoly pervoi Vserossiiskoi konferentsii proletarskikh kul'turno-prosvetitel'nykh organizatsii, 15–20 sentiabria, 1918 g.*, ed. P. I. Lebedev-Polianskii (Moscow, 1918).

4. Delegates to the first national Proletkult conference sitting under a banner that reads "Long Live the International Proletkult."
Source: *Protokoly pervoi Vserossiiskoi konferentsii proletarskikh kul'turno-prosvetitel'nykh organizatsii, 15–20 sentiabria, 1918 g.*, ed. P. I. Lebedev-Polianskii (Moscow, 1918).

5. Members of the Petrograd Proletkult drama studio performing a collective reading of Walt Whitman's poem "Europe."
Source: *Plamia*, no. 21 (1918).

6. A choral class in the Petrograd Proletkult.
Source: *Plamia*, no. 9 (1918).

7. A scene from Valerian Pletnev's play *Lena*, which is about the strike that led to the Lena Massacre. The play is being staged by the First Workers' Theater in Moscow.
Source: Huntly Carter, *The New Theatre and Cinema of Soviet Russia* (London, 1924).

8.   A scene from Ostrovsky's play *Enough Simplicity for Every Wise Man*. The play was radically revised by Sergei Eisenstein and Sergei Tretiakov for the First Workers' Theater. The poster reads: "Religion is the Opiate of the People."
Source: Huntly Carter, *The New Theatre and Cinema of Soviet Russia* (London, 1924).

9. A draft of a panel by the artist Ia. M. Guminer to decorate the Smolnyi Institute in Petrograd for the first anniversary of the revolution. The caption reads: "Proletkult—Proletarian Creation Guarantees the World Commune."

Source: I. M. Bibikova and N. I. Levchenko, *Agitatsionno-massovoe iskusstvo: Oformlenie prazdnestv* (Moscow, 1984), vol. 2.

10. A sketch of a banner for the Moscow Province Textile Workers' Union designed by members of the Moscow Proletkult art studios. An example of production art, the banner was to be made from materials characteristic of the textile trade and to have moving parts that evoked the workings of spinning machines.

Source: *Gorn*, no. 7 (1922).

11. A cover for the Moscow Proletkult journal *Create!* (*Tvori!*) by the proletarian artist Aleksandr Zugrin. The top caption reads "Proletarians of all lands, unite!"
Source: *Tvori!*, no. 2 (1921).

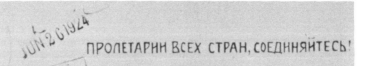

ПРОЛЕТАРИИ ВСЕХ СТРАН, СОЕДИНЯЙТЕСЬ!

ГОРН

КНИГА 1-(6)

ВСЕРОССИЙСКИЙ
ПРОЛЕТКУЛЬТ
1922

12. A cover for the Moscow Proletkult journal *Furnace*
(*Gorn*) by the proletarian artist Aleksandr Zugrin. The drawing, "At the Furnace," shows a blacksmith at his anvil, a very
common image in Proletkult art.
Source: *Gorn*, no. 6 (1922).

ПРОЛЕТАРИИ ВСЕХ СТРАН, СОЕДИНЯЙТЕСЬ!

ГОРН

КНИГА 2-(7)

ВСЕРОССИЙСКИЙ

ПРОЛЕТКУЛЬТ

1922

13. An illustration from the cover of the Moscow Proletkult journal *Furnace* (*Gorn*) commemorating the fifth anniversary of the Proletkult.
Source: *Gorn*, no. 7 (1922).

5

Iron Flowers
Proletkult Creation in the Arts

I am not in gentle nature
Among the blooming bowers.
Under the smokey sky in the factory
I forged iron flowers.
Mikhail Gerasimov,
"Zheleznye tsvety"

This poem by Mikhail Gerasimov exemplifies the best-known genre of Proletkult artistic practice during the early revolutionary years. Its proletarian imagery was meant to set it apart from the art of the bourgeoisie, which was dedicated to gentle nature. Instead Gerasimov exalted iron flowers as a uniquely working-class image of beauty. The laborer in the midst of the factory milieu was both the subject and the creator of this new form.

Not all Proletkult productions evoked the life and labor of the working class in such a simple and direct way. Proletarian art, like proletarian class identity, was given many different meanings. Three very broad understandings competed with one another during the Civil War years. The revolutionary romanticism of proletarian artists such as Gerasimov certainly constituted the most distinctive direction. Creations ideally would be by, for, and about workers and would employ images drawn from factory life. Although best developed in literature, this approach also flourished in music, in the form of "revolutionary hymns," in posters and paintings, and in plays that depicted the heroic struggles of the working class.

The Proletkult also attracted a small but influential group of avant-garde artists who were determined to break with the stylistic conventions of bourgeois art and culture. This trend was most noticeable in the visual arts, where important groups rejected "easel art" and "museum art" altogether and devised programs to unify cultural creation with factory production. Experimental theater, which turned against realistic methods, and experimental music, where artists devised new tonal systems, also gained small followings. Here the definition of proletarian culture was largely oppositional; these creations, in theory at least, marked a radical departure from prerevolutionary artistic schools.

By far the most common activity in Proletkult cultural sectors, however, was to offer training and education in Russia's prerevolutionary cultural heritage. In this task the organization continued the work of educational societies, people's houses, and cooperatives formed long before 1917. According to this definition of proletarian culture the Proletkult would bring culture, especially the elite *kul'tura* of the nineteenth century intelligentsia, to the laboring masses.

None of these approaches represented a clearly defined artistic school. Those writers and painters who praised the factory milieu in their work accused one another of pursuing revolutionary content at the expense of revolutionary form. Avant-gardists faced the charge that their experiments forced culture out of the average worker's reach. And even those who saw the organization as an educational society did not agree on the proper content of the cultural heritage they hoped to transmit.

The movement's eclecticism disturbed many participants, yet it was precisely this diversity that contributed to its remarkable popularity. The Proletkult was simultaneously van-

guardist and populist, agitational and educational, a continuation of prerevolutionary trends and an attempt to make
something entirely new. Its programs gave stenographers poetry recitations, house painters piano lessons, and machinists
the chance to become professional actors. At its most utopian
the organization promised to break down the barriers between the cultured elite and the uncultured masses. It offered
the optimistic message that even the humblest member of
society could become a cultural creator and help to articulate
what the new culture of revolutionary Russia was to be.

In the Studio and at the Front:
The Locus of Proletkult Creation

Proletkult cultural practice was expansive and indeed extended beyond the fine arts to club work, science, and efforts
to transform the fabric of family life.[1] Nonetheless, training in
the arts formed the core of Proletkult local activities. The
Proletkult united a vast array of programs, including lecture
series, seminars, studios, exhibitions, theaters, orchestras,
and even workshops in circus technique. Each local organization was supposed to have at least four artistic sectors in
theater, music, literature, and art, popularly known by the
abbreviations *teo, muzo, lito,* and *izo.*

Offerings varied widely from place to place, determined by
local funding, the tastes of members, and the skills of their
instructors. Some organizations, particularly those in the two
capitals, had an impressive array of famous artists to assist
them. In others participants were on their own. Better endowed groups sponsored a broad range of classes and lectures, but poorer circles could only afford very limited programs. The Tula Proletkult music section had a symphony
orchestra, a brass band, an orchestra for folk instruments, and
special classes in solo and operatic singing. By contrast, the

---

1. I discuss these projects in the next chapter.

small and embattled Archangel Proletkult could only support a choir.[2]

Theater led all other artistic forms in popularity, a phenomenon hardly limited to the Proletkult. Many bemused and critical intellectuals, such as the writer Viktor Shklovskii, marveled at the general craze for theater among the Russian lower classes. "No one knows what to do with drama circles. They are propagating like protozoa. Not the lack of fuel, nor the lack of food, nor the Entente—no, nothing can stop their growth."[3] The stage's attraction was partly because of familiarity; the extensive network of people's theaters in the late nineteenth and early twentieth centuries had already paved the way. Drama was also a collective form that proved particularly well-suited to the agitational tasks of the revolution and Civil War. Often performed without costumes or sets, popular theater required little more than a bare room and the imaginations of the actors and the audience.

The Proletkult's musical sectors also inspired large followings. Here too familiarity was part of the appeal; choral singing was a standard part of Russian elementary education.[4] Some Proletkultists consciously based their work on Russian folk music as a means to attract participants. Others built their repertoire around popular proletarian tunes that had played an important part in workers' social and organizational lives before the revolution.[5] Choirs, the most common

2. "Iz otcheta Tul'skogo gubernskogo Proletkul'ta," *Proletarskoe stroitel'stvo*, no. 2 (1919), p. 27; and the report of the Archangel music division in 1921, *Tsentral'nyi Gosudarstvennyi Arkhiv Literatury i Iskusstva* [henceforth cited as TsGALI] f. 1230, op. 1, d. 145, ll. 3–3 ob.

3. Viktor Shklovskii, *Khod konia: Sbornik statei* (Berlin, 1923), p. 59. For additional commentary on the importance of theater see Serge Wolkonsky, *My Reminiscences*, trans. A. E. Chamot (London, 1924), vol. 2, p. 219; and Marc Slonim, *Russian Theater from the Empire to the Soviets* (Cleveland, 1961), p. 241.

4. Jeffrey Brooks, *When Russia Learned to Read* (Princeton, 1985), p. 50.

5. On prerevolutionary workers' songs see A. I. Nutrikhin, ed.,

musical grouping, required very few resources, especially if the repertoire was based on well-known songs.

The literature and fine arts sectors were generally smaller and less stable. Unlike theater and music, these forms were not inherently performing arts that encouraged group participation. Instead painting, drawing, and writing depended on individual talent and initiative in a more central way. They also relied on precious paper, an extremely rare commodity during the Civil War. One instructor complained that his art classes were having a difficult time because there were not enough pencils, erasers, or paint, and there was no paper at all.[6] Writing circles in the provinces often could not publish their work because paper was in short supply, and they also complained about the dearth of trained teachers. The Rybinsk Proletkult, which had a very lively theater, did not even open a literature section during the Civil War. "A [literature] studio is essential but has been delayed because we lack a good instructor," the local president lamented.[7]

The heart of Proletkult artistic activity was the studio, or workshop, where members gathered to develop their creative skills. Although the central leadership was very concerned about the form and content of studio work, local circles had no standard structure. Some operated like open classrooms, where interested participants could come and go as they pleased, but others required entrance auditions and recommendations from current members. One aspiring proletarian actor in a Moscow Proletkult drama studio was initially almost rejected because his examiners did not believe his reci-

---

Pesni russkikh rabochikh (vosemnadtsatyi-nachalo dvadtsatogo veka) (Moscow and Leningrad, 1962), pp. 5–38. For a description of songs in the context of factory life see Semen Kanatchikov, *A Radical Worker in Tsarist Russia*, trans. and ed. Reginald E. Zelnik (Stanford, 1986), pp. 19, 37–38, 48–49.

6. Report from the Kologriv Proletkult, TsGALI f. 1230, op. 1, d. 1278, l. 11 ob.

7. From a 1919 questionnaire, TsGALI f. 1230, op. 1, d. 117, l. 6.

tation of a Nekrasov poem showed sufficient artistic taste.[8] In Petrograd theater workshops quickly developed a hierarchical structure. At the lowest level were district and factory groups, followed by citywide studios, which were open only by audition. At the top was the central Proletkult theater, which paid its actors the minimum wage for factory workers in return for their full-time participation.[9]

Ideally, workshops were run collectively by the students, who set the curriculum and determined their creative direction. Scattered reports describing the internal workings of studios reveal that group presentations and critiques were a common pedagogical tool. One intellectual observer, after watching members of Moscow literary studios read and discuss their work, concluded: "In Proletkult studios a new, comradely, unified artistic environment is taking shape and precisely such an environment . . . usually is the soil that nurtures the sprouts of a new, young art."[10] The Kostroma Proletkult leadership demanded that theater studios be run entirely by the participants. "The artistic professionalism of the old theater must be exchanged for the work of proletarian drama collectives."[11]

These descriptions of collective work notwithstanding, many Proletkult studios were organized as conventional art classes, where trained instructors taught their charges the basics of drawing, singing, and acting. Valentin Smyshliaev, a Proletkult theater expert who came from the Moscow Art Theater, schooled his students in the principles of Stanislavsky's method acting. A piano teacher in Kologriv took role

8. V. Grigorev, "Nikolai Sedel'nikov v studii," *Tvori!*, no. 3/4 (1921), pp. 52–53.

9. A. A. Mgebrov, *Zhizn' v teatre* (Moscow and Leningrad, 1933), vol. 2, pp. 408–10.

10. M. T., "V Moskovskom Proletkul'te," *Narodnoe prosveshchenie*, no. 32 (1919), p. 20.

11. "Organizatsiia Kostromskogo Proletkul'ta," *Sbornik Kostromskogo Proletkul'ta*, no. 1 (1919), p. 109.

in her classes and kept a close record of her students' progress. In Tambov the musician Vasilev-Buglai shaped the Proletkult's first choir from the remnants of a church chorus. He not only planned what the choir would sing, he also arranged to give his students classes in political economy.[12]

At the end of the Civil War the Proletkult was harshly criticized for its "isolated laboratory methods," which supposedly cut off its work from the population at large. However, Proletkult studios were never really laboratories in any meaningful sense of the word. To begin with, artistic collectives were not stable enough to form a cohesive creative environment. Both the staff and the student body changed constantly because of wartime recruitments, housing and heating crises, and uncertain funding. A Moscow district art studio first opened in 1918 with almost one hundred students, but as the winter descended most abandoned the unheated quarters. A few months later only a dedicated core of twenty-five was left that was willing to brave the cold.[13] Leaders of the small Parfenev Proletkult in Kostroma province complained that their most talented instructors and members had departed for the front in the summer of 1919.[14]

The word "laboratory" implies that studio work was carefully monitored and perfected before it was brought to light, but this was not the case. Instead participants presented their creations to the public at every opportunity. Art studios, for example, made posters, banners, and emblems for unions and helped to decorate agitational trains and boats. In the summer of 1919 the Tula art workshop published a proud production report announcing that its students had made five

12. V. Smyshliaev, "Opyt instsenirovka stikhotvoreniia Ver-kharna 'Vosstanie,' " *Gorn*, no. 2 (1919), pp. 82–90; a report by the Kologriv instructor Rozova, 1919, TsGALI f. 1230, op. 1, d. 1278, ll. 79–82; and Dmitrii Vasil'ev-Buglai, "Na fronte v 1918 godu," *Sovetskaia muzyka*, no. 2 (1940), pp. 12–15.

13. E. Lozovaia, "O raionnom Moskovskom Proletkul'te," *Vestnik zhizni*, no. 6/7 (1919), p. 141.

14. Report to the central organization, July 29, 1919, TsGALI f. 1230, op. 1, d. 1279, l. 33.

hundred posters for the Communist Party, fifty-two for the teachers' union, and three for local cooperatives. In addition, they had produced one hundred portraits of revolutionary leaders. The Tambov Proletkult, which offered very extensive and well-staffed art classes, directed all of its energies to poster design during the Civil War.[15]

Agitational tasks dictated much of the organization's artistic production. Local studios not only made posters and banners but also took part in revolutionary festivals. Proletkult workshops were integrally involved in staging the first celebrations in 1918. On May Day in Petrograd Proletkultists took charge of the Smolnyi Institute and the surrounding square, focal points of the day's festivities. They also planned the opening of their main center, the Palace of Proletarian Culture, to coincide with the holiday. The Moscow Proletkult was just as visible at the first anniversary of the revolution. It decorated central parts of the city and provided entertainment for the high point of the celebration, Lenin's unveiling of a monument to the martyrs of the revolution.[16]

Not restricting themselves to the home front, Proletkult studios took to the road to perform for Red Army troops. The larger organizations in Petrograd, Moscow, Tambov, and Tula organized special "front studios," well equipped with rousing

15. "Iz otcheta Tul'skogo gubernskogo Proletkul'ta o studiinykh i obshe-organizatsionnykh rabotakh," *Proletarskoe stroitel'stvo*, no. 2 (1919), pp. 27–28; and V. Mikhailov, *Khudozhniki Tambovskogo kraia: Istoricheskii ocherk razvitiia izobrazitel'nogo iskusstva na Tambovshchine* (Leningrad, 1976), pp. 45–46.

16. On festivals in general see Christel Lane, *The Rites of Rulers: Ritual in Industrial Society* (New York, 1981), pp. 161–66; and James R. von Geldern, *Festivals of the Revolution, 1917–1920* (forthcoming), especially chapters 1 and 2. On Proletkult involvement see A. Raikhenstein, "1 maia i 7 noiabria 1918 goda v Moskve," in *Agitatsionno-massovoe iskusstvo pervykh let Oktiabria*, ed. E. A. Speranskaia (Moscow, 1971), pp. 129–30; I. Rostovtseva, "Uchastie khudozhnikov v organizatsii i provedenii prazdnikov 1 maia i 7 noiabria v Petrograde v 1918 godu," in ibid., pp. 40, 63–64; and Vasilii Ignatov, "Otkrytie Dvortsa Proletarskoi Kul'tury," *Griadushchee*, no. 3 (1918), pp. 4–5.

theatrical and musical repertoires that toured the front lines during the Civil War.[17] An aspiring young actress, P. N. Zubova, went south with the Moscow Proletkult's Second Front Troupe in the fall of 1920. She recalled her adventures with a sense of excitement, even though she slept on floors in train stations and never got enough to eat.[18] These trips were not without danger. Kotia Mgebrov-Chekhan, the nine-year-old son of the directors of the Petrograd Proletkult theater, was killed as the Petrograd troupe was touring the Western Front.[19]

This ebullient cultural activity did not result in a coherent cultural program. Even the most sympathetic observers remarked on the incipient, preparatory nature of most Proletkult production during the Civil War. As one reviewer of an art exhibit concluded, the paintings did not yet display a new form of cultural creation. Instead, they were "the rich black soil from which a new art will grow."[20]

The Proletkult as Culture Bearer

Of all the criticisms leveled against the Proletkult, the charge of cultural nihilism was the most persistent. Alarmed observers listened to the Proletkult's most radical proponents and concluded that the organization really meant to toss out Russia's cultural heritage and start anew. When Lenin included this accusation in his list of Proletkult sins, it became enshrined in most Soviet scholarship.[21]

17. "Petrogradskii Proletkul't," *Griadushchee*, no. 7/8 (1919), p. 30; *Griadushchaia kul'tura*, no. 6/7 (1919), pp. 1–2, 28; and "Proletkul't i front," *Tvori!*, no. 1, (1920), p. 19.

18. "Vospominaniia P. N. Zubovoi," TsGALI f. 1230, op. 2, d. 14, ll. 4–5.

19. A. Gutorovich, "A korolevu otpravim v kabak!" *Teatral'naia zhizn'*, no. 14 (1966), p. 21.

20. I. Iasinskii, "Vystavka avtodidaktov," *Griadushchee*, no. 4 (1918), inside front cover.

21. V. V. Gorbunov, the foremost Soviet scholar on the Proletkult, calls nihilism one of its major failings, *V. I. Lenin i Proletkul't*

To be sure, there were extremists in the Proletkult who claimed to reject the accumulated knowledge of prerevolutionary society. "In the name of our tomorrow we will burn the Raphaels, destroy the museums, and trample on the flowers of art," wrote Vladimir Kirillov in "We," the most famous poem associated with the Proletkult.[22] However, this mood of exuberant destruction does not capture the movement as a whole. Bogdanov, much vilified in Soviet sources as a dangerous nihilist, urged workers to study their cultural heritage in order to discover what was important to them and what was not.[23] The programs he helped to structure in Capri, Bologna, and later in the Proletkult had substantial historical components designed to introduce students to cultural tradition and criticism.

The extremely quotable flamboyant statements uttered by some Proletkult participants were often tempered by a more modest recognition that they could not really expect to build their new culture from scratch. "There are no 'older brothers,'" proclaimed the writer Pavel Bessalko. "The worker-poet should create, not study." But he also acknowledged that a real proletarian artist needed to know the history of culture,

---

(Moscow, 1974), p. 5. See also G. K. Fedotova, "Prakticheskaia deiatel'nost' Proletkul'ta v oblasti khudozhestvennoi samodeiatel'nosti," *Sbornik trudov Moskovskogo gosudarstvennogo instituta kul'tury*, vol. 23 (1973), p. 136; R. V. Kandaura, "Bor'ba V. I. Lenina i partii protiv vliianiia A. A. Bogdanova na Proletkul't," in *Iskusstvo soiuznykh respublik k piatidesiati-letiiu obrazovaniia SSSR* (Leningrad, 1972), pp. 35–39; and S. I. Martynova, "Problema kollektivizma v literaturnykh sporakh 20-kh godov," in *Problema lichnosti i obshchestva v sovremennoi literature i iskusstve*, ed. S. M. Petrov, V. I. Borshchukov, and A. V. Karaganov (Moscow, 1967), pp. 70–75. For a Western study that emphasizes the Proletkult's rejection of Russia's cultural heritage see John E. Bowlt, "Russian Art in the Nineteen Twenties," *Soviet Studies*, vol. 22, no. 4 (1971), pp. 578–79.

22. Vladimir Kirillov, "My," in *Stikhotvoreniia i poemy*, by Vladimir Kirillov (Moscow, 1970), p. 35.

23. See A. A. Bogdanov, "Proletariat i iskusstvo," *Protokoly pervoi Vserossiiskoi konferentsii proletarskikh kul'turno-prosvetitel'nykh organizatsii, 15–20 sentiabria, 1918 g.*, ed. P. I. Lebedev-Polianskii (Moscow, 1918), p. 76; and idem, *O proletarskoi kul'ture, 1904–1924* (Moscow, 1924), pp. 142–57.

religion, and art.[24] The editors of the Smolensk journal *Labor and Creation* (*Trud i tvorchestvo*) proudly insisted that they would destroy the useless culture of the past in order to build a new one. However, in the very same issue the head of the literary studio announced a contest for the best sonnet, that venerable old literary form, to be judged by a local professor.[25]

The label "culture bearer" surely would have offended Proletkult leaders because they associated it with the philanthropic efforts of the liberal intelligentsia. Nonetheless, much of the organization's work bore a distinct similarity to the activities of prerevolutionary cultural centers. Evenings of recitations, plays, and songs often included historical lectures. When the Petrograd theater studio gave a reading of Walt Whitman's poems, the director Mgebrov introduced it with a speech on Whitman's significance in world literature.[26] Musical performances were conceived as a way to train the tastes of the audience and were accompanied by lectures on the life and times of the featured composer. Proletkult publications sought to acquaint their audiences with the classics of world culture, as had self-education journals before the revolution. Tver's *Proletkult* contained articles on the works of Victor Hugo and Tiuchev. The Kologriv publication *Life of the Arts* (*Zhizn' iskusstv*) commemorated the work of Chekhov. Even the radical Petrograd journal *The Future* published short pieces on Walt Whitman, Dobroliubov, and Nekrasov.[27]

The tried-and-true classics common in workers' and people's theaters before the revolution dominated local stages. The most popular plays were by Ostrovsky, Gogol, Chekhov, and, sometimes, Gorky. For example, the Polekova factory

24. P. Bessal'ko, "O forme i soderzhanii," *Griadushchee*, no. 4 (1918), p. 4.

25. "Ot redaktsii," and "Kuznitsa poetov," *Trud i tvorchestvo*, no. 1 (1919), pp. 22, 17–18.

26. *Severnaia Kommuna*, August 2, 1918, p. 4.

27. *Proletkul't* (Tver), no. 3/4 (1919), pp. 22–25, 28–29; *Zhizn' iskusstv*, no. 3 (1918), pp. 29–31; and *Griadushchee*, no. 5 (1918), p. 12; no. 9 (1918), pp. 17–18; no. 7/8 (1919), pp. 25–27.

Proletkult's repertoire consisted of works by these authors and also included one by Cervantes. In 1918 a small village organization in Tambov province reported proudly that it had just put on its first production of Ostrovsky plays.[28]

For those who were interested in founding a new proletarian theater this reliance on an older repertoire was disappointing. However, even the most iconoclastic experts acknowledged that Proletkultists needed to know and appreciate some of the classics. Platon Kerzhentsev, whose influential book *Creative Theater* (*Tvorcheskii teatr*) went through five editions from 1918 to 1923, insisted that proletarian theaters should eschew prerevolutionary work as much as possible.[29] But because new plays were in short supply, he also drew up lists of acceptable classic works.[30] One list, compiled for the Moscow soviet theater commission, included plays by Aristophanes, Aeschylus, Shakespeare, Lope de Vega, and Schiller.[31]

Proletkult music studios tried to give their members a broad education. Some of Russia's finest musicians taught in the Proletkult, including Reinhold Glière in Petrograd, Grigorii Liubimov and Arsenii Avraamov in Moscow, and Dmitrii Vasilev-Buglai in Tambov.[32] Even the small town of Belev had two instructors who had formerly taught violin and voice at the Petrograd conservatory.[33] Local groups gave classes in musical theory, solo singing, and composition, along with

28. On Polekova see a 1920 questionnaire, TsGALI f. 1230, op. 1, d. 117, l. 51; and on Tambov see "Khronika Proletkul'ta," *Proletarskaia kul'tura*, no. 9/10 (1919), p. 59; no. 15/16 (1920), pp. 81–82.

29. P. M. Kerzhentsev, *Tvorcheskii teatr*, (Moscow, 1918), pp. 77–82, 95–110; and idem, *Revoliutsiia i teatr* (Moscow, 1918), pp. 34–36.

30. Kerzhentsev, *Revoliutsiia i teatr*, p. 48; and *Protokoly pervoi konferentsii*, pp. 45–46, l22.

31. "Spisok p'es, rekomendovannykh Moskovskoi repertuarnoi komissiei," *Tsentral'nyi Gosudarstvennyi Arkhiv RSFSR* [henceforth cited as TsGA RSFSR] f. 2306, op. 2, d. 357, ll. 38–38 ob. For provincial lists see *Zori*, no. 1 (1918), pp. 17–18 and TsGALI f. 1230, op. 1, d. 1279, ll. 24–24 ob.

32. For biographies of these Proletkult instructors see *Muzykal'naia entsiklopediia* (Moscow, 1973–1981).

33. V. V. Gorbunov, "Oktiabr' i nachalo kul'turnoi revoliutsii na

instruction in a range of instruments from the violin to the balalaika. In Tambov, which had a rich musical program, piano lessons were the most popular offering of all; over four hundred students signed up for them in the first months of 1919.[34] Although many choirs chose revolutionary songs, the classics were also represented. Choral evenings included works by Bach and Schumann, and orchestral performances often featured classical Russian composers like Mussorgsky.[35]

In Moscow folk music formed the core of musical education. The main director, Aleksandr Kastalskii, believed that folk songs were the best way to draw the masses to musical training.[36] Once attracted, participants would then be introduced to folk instruments, classical instruments, and a wide range of music classes. Moscow Proletkult students could choose from many different activities, including orchestras for folk instruments, an impressive program of classes in musical theory, and classical concerts.[37]

Fine arts studios also integrated a strong historical component. Instructors took students to museums to examine drawing, painting, and sculpture. In the workshop participants were taught to sketch live models, still lives, and landscapes. As in other media, the Proletkult gained the services of many impressive art instructors, such as the famous sculptor Sergei Konenkov and the well-known art professor Timofei Katurkin.[38] The range of art courses could be quite impressive, from

mestakh," in *Velikii Oktiabr'*, ed. Iu. A. Poliakov (Moscow, 1978), p. 72; and *Rubezhi*, no. 1 (1922), p. 82.

34. *Griadushchaia kul'tura*, no. 4/5 (1919), pp. 25–26.

35. A. M. S., "O muzykal'nykh programmakh," *Proletarskaia kul'tura* (Tiflis), no. 1 (1919), p. 23; and "Tverskii Proletkul't," TsGALI f. 1230, op. l, d. 1525, l. 11.

36. A. D. Kastal'skii, "K voprosu ob organizatsii muzykal'nykh zaniatii v tsentral'noi studii Moskovskogo Proletkul'ta," in *Muzykal'naia zhizn' Moskvy*, ed. S. R. Stepanova (Moscow, 1972), pp. 283–84; and B. Krasin, "Zadachi muzykal'nogo otdela," *Gorn*, no. 1 (1918), p. 59.

37. See Roslavets's report on the Moscow Proletkult's music division in July 1920 in Stepanova, *Muzykal'naia zhizn' Moskvy*, p. 291.

38. On Konenkov see *Gorn*, no. 2/3 (1919), p. 127; on Katurkin

simple drawing classes to lessons in architecture and stage design.[39]

To enrich the work of beginning writers, literary divisions sponsored lecture series and seminars. Tambov studios gave classes in the theory of poetic creation, along with the history of drama and prose. In Moscow interested students could choose courses on the history of culture, the literature of the nineteenth century, and the history of the theater, among many other offerings.[40] Vladislav Khodasevich, a very disgruntled lecturer in the Moscow Proletkult, gave seminars on Pushkin's work.[41]

Many aspiring Proletkult authors took the nineteenth century classics as their models rather than the stirring themes of the revolution. In the pages of provincial publications one can find works that seem far removed from the social conflagration of the Civil War. A poem called "Here and There," published in Kologriv's *Life of the Arts*, sounded like the conscience-stricken call of the prerevolutionary intelligentsia. It contrasted the life of the decadent rich to that of the poor.

> Here—a night without hope, a night without end.
> There—a bacchanalian feast and wonderful dreams.
> Oh, great, magnanimous, and eternal God,
> When will we all become equals?[42]

Other authors avoided politics altogether. They composed lyric incantations of nature, filled with winter skies and passing thunderstorms. Leonid Tsinovskii, the self-educated son of Petrograd factory workers, was a Red Army propagandist,

---

see the delegate list to the 1921 national congress, TsGALI f. 1230, op. 1, d. 144, l. 127.

39. *Griadushchaia kul'tura*, no. 3 (1919), p. 25; and *Proletkul't* (Tver), no. 1/2 (1919), p. 45.

40. On Tambov see *Griadushchaia kul'tura*, no. 4/5 (1919), inside back cover; on Moscow see N. Pavlovich, "Rabota literaturno-izdatel'skogo otdela," *Gorn*, no. 1 (1918), pp. 44–45.

41. V. Khodasevich, *Literaturnye stat'i i vospominaniia* (New York, 1954), pp. 325–31.

42. Chaika, "Zdes' i tam," *Zhizn' iskusstv*, no. 3 (1918), p. 7.

Communist Party member, and Proletkult leader. In the midst of the revolutionary upheaval, he published these lines:

> In pearl strands under a bridal veil,
> In robes of woven silver,
> The white grove of birch trees
> Stands immovably frozen
> As if bewitched by a dream.[43]

The prevalence of prerevolutionary forms in Proletkult workshops, publications, and public performances discouraged many of those who hoped to find the foundations for original, autonomous creative work. Lebedev-Polianskii, the Proletkult president, was very disappointed by the writing in provincial journals. Not only was it stylistically weak, but he also felt that it depicted the revolution in "purely democratic," nonproletarian terms.[44] The futurists, who believed themselves to be the real creators of revolutionary culture, faulted the Proletkult at every opportunity for its cultural conservatism.[45]

Without a doubt, Proletkult studios helped to inculcate respect for prerevolutionary high culture, thereby contributing to the elevation of that culture within Soviet society. Nikolai Roslavets, who taught in the Moscow organization, wrote a positive assessment of the movement's accomplishments in 1924, long after it had been discredited and had sunk into relative insignificance. In his view the Proletkult had attracted the best intellectuals and offered the masses serious artistic training. "Now we can say with conviction that precisely the Proletkult should be given the honor of saving Russian artistic culture."[46]

43. L. Tsinovskii, "Sad," *Tsvety truda* (Archangel, 1922), p. 10. On Tsinovskii's background see "Lichnaia anketa," TsGALI f. 1230, op. 1, d. 118, ll. 60–61.

44. P. I. Lebedev-Polianskii [V. Polianskii, pseud.], "Poeziia sovetskoi provintsii," *Proletarskaia kul'tura*, no. 7/8 (1919), pp. 43–49, 56–57.

45. See, for example, O. M. Brik, "Nalet na futurizm," *Iskusstvo kommuny*, no. 10 (1919), p. 3.

46. Nikolai Roslavets, "Sem' let Oktiabria v muzyke," *Muzykal'naia kul'tura*, no. 3 (1924), pp. 184–86, quotation p. 184.

Nonetheless, it would be wrong to conclude that Prolet-kultists were merely engaged in a process of assimilation. Through their efforts students transformed the artistic material to which they were exposed. Participants made their "conservative" repertoire revolutionary by placing it in new contexts. Ostrovsky plays performed on an open stage for Red Army soldiers conveyed a different meaning than the same works put on by a professional troupe. Exposure to the arts in itself had an emancipatory power. As one woman worker from a Proletkult club in Kostroma explained:

In this fine building we pass the best days of our lives. We rest from daily labor and cares, studying all that is good and worthy, studying things we never knew or saw before. Comrade workers! Remember that we used to live as oppressed slaves. We did not understand what music was, what literature was, and many other fine things. Now in our club we workers study subjects that were once unknown to us. Now we understand that we are people like everyone else and that we have even more right to live than others because everything is made by our hands.[47]

Worker-Centered Art

Clearly not all Proletkultists were content to study the culture of the past; many hoped to find a distinctive working-class art that would embody the spirit of socialism. The aesthetics of this genre were never very clearly defined, even by the organization's most enthusiastic advocates. For Bogdanov proletarian creation would evolve from the labor process and express the workers' collective ethos; it would serve as a means to organize and articulate the proletariat's unique vision of the world. But these principles offered few guidelines for either form or content.[48] Lebedev-Polianskii was only slightly more

47. V. Pashkina, in "Vpechatleniia rabochikh ot klubnoi zhizni," *Sbornik Kostromskogo Proletkul'ta*, no. 1 (1919), p. 38.
48. See A. A. Bogdanov, "Chto takoe proletarskaia poeziia," *Proletarskaia kul'tura*, no. 1 (1918), pp. 12–22; idem, "Proletariat i iskusstvo," *Protokoly pervoi konferentsii*, pp. 72–79; and idem, *O proletarskoi kul'ture*, pp. 104–99.

specific. He believed that the new art had to focus on the city and the workplace as the loci of the proletariat's creative powers.[49]

The worker-centered art composed by Proletkult writers, painters, musicians, and playwrights came in many different forms. Most was stylistically conservative and followed standard artistic conventions. But in contrast to the classics, Proletkult artists crafted poems, songs, plays, and paintings that lauded the powers and virtues of the victorious proletariat and depicted the future of the revolution in grandiose, utopian terms. Critics of the 1920s and 1930s, who sought either more realism or more innovation, named this genre "revolutionary romanticism."[50]

This celebratory style was best developed in literature, where many worker-writers had begun their publishing careers long before the revolution. The best-known Proletkult authors, Pavel Bessalko, Mikhail Gerasimov, Vladimir Kirillov, Aleksei Samobytnik-Mashirov, and Ilia Sadofev, helped to set the tone for workers' literature during the Civil War. Their work was not all of a piece, nor was it sui generis. Numerous literary critics have traced the influence of Lermontov, Nekrasov, Verkhaeren, Whitman, Briusov, Blok, and Maiakovskii in Proletkult creations.[51]

Nonetheless, these authors did address common themes

49. P. I. Lebedev-Polianskii [V. Polianskii, pseud.], "Motivy rabochei poezii," *Proletarskaia kul'tura*, no. 3 (1918), pp. 1–12.

50. See, for example, A. Voronskii, "O gruppe pisatelei 'Kuznitsa,' " *Krasnaia nov'*, no. 13 (1923), pp. 297–312; A. Lezhnev, "Proletkul't i proletarskoe iskusstvo," *Krasnaia nov'*, no. 19 (1924), pp. 272–87, no. 20 (1924), pp. 268–82; and V. Sytyrin, "O blagorodnykh predkakh, neblagorodnykh potomkakh," *Na literaturnom postu*, no. 3 (1930), pp. 15–30.

51. I. S. Eventov, ed., *Poeziia v bol'shevistskikh izdaniiakh, 1901–1917* (Leningrad, 1967), pp. 39–40; K. V. Driagin, *Pateticheskaia lirika proletarskikh poetov ephokhi voennogo kommunizma* (Viatka, 1933), pp. 93–119; and Martynova, "Problema kollektivizma," pp. 59–68.

that made their work distinctive. The revolution was central to their writing. It was presented as a festival made by and for the proletariat. They looked to the glorious future that socialism would initiate. Most important, they used their work to praise workers and workers' collectives, often in inventive and hyperbolic language. Workers were giants, titans, and masters capable of anything. As Vladimir Kirillov wrote in his poem "To the Proletariat":

> O, many-faced (*mnogolikii*) ruler of the world
> Your faith—reason; your strength—labor.
>   . . .
> Beneath your dark shirt, in your stern heart
> You carry the sun of a new life.[52]

In Proletkult writing symbols of progress and beauty were drawn from the lives of industrial laborers, something apparent in the titles of many poems: "Iron Flowers" (Gerasimov), "The Iron Messiah" (Kirillov), "Machine Paradise" (Samobytnik-Mashirov), "We Grow from Iron" (Gastev). Industrial imagery was so predominant that one contemporary critic called proletarian writers' work "machinism."[53]

The literature of this older generation of Proletkult authors dominated the most important journals in the two capitals and was given a central place in provincial publications as well. Aspiring new writers looked to the creations of their established colleagues, who took their didactic functions very seriously. The editorial board of Petrograd's *The Future*, led by Bessalko, Kalinin, Kirillov, and Samobytnik-Mashirov, published rejection notices that betray their sense of purpose and also their sense of superiority. "Save your time and ours, comrades," one such notice read. "There is no point wasting time reading or writing poems like the ones you have sent. They are hopelessly weak." Prospective authors were often

52. Vladimir Kirillov, "Proletariatu," in *Stikhotvoreniia i poemy*, by Vladimir Kirillov, p. 33.

53. L. N. Kleinbort, *Ocherki narodnoi literatury, 1880–1923 gg.: Belletristiki* (Leningrad, 1924), p. 267.

taken to task for using old and dated imagery, but the most critical responses were saved for those who addressed "non-proletarian" themes. One who bemoaned his fate was admonished, "That's a hopeless task, comrade. To struggle with fate is like fighting with windmills. The proletariat believes in the power of collective reason, not in fate." They taunted another who sent in a poem titled "To My Weary Soul." In the editors' opinion such intellectual rubbish did not belong on the pages of a proletarian journal.[54]

The industrial imagery so important to the first generation of Proletkult authors was emulated in the provinces. In journals with names such as *Glow of the Factories* (*Zarevo zavodov*), *The Hammer* (*Molot*), and *Our Furnace* (*Nash Gorn*) provincial writers praised the factory, workers' collectives, and the glorious future of socialism, which was to be built by proletarian hands. As one Proletkultist in Saratov wrote:

> Here they are, these calloused hands!
> These huge rakes
> That pierce the depths of the earth
> With fingers of red steel!
>
> Here they are, these calloused hands!
> They will build a home
> For freedom, art, and science
> With no room for pain or suffering.[55]

Proletarian poetry was used as a model for other artistic forms. One of the first Proletkult plays, Vasilii Ignatov's *Dawn of the Proletkult* (*Zori Proletkul'ta*), was actually a compendium of popular poems tied together by symbolic figures, among them a young girl in red representing the Communist Party.[56] Well-known poems were also put to music to create what was

54. *Griadushchee*, no. 1 (1919), p. 24; no. 2/3 (1919), p. 32.

55. Sergei Stradnyi, "Ruki," from *Pod Oktiabrem*, a Saratov Proletkult publication, reprinted in Z. S. Papernyi and R. A. Shatseva, eds., *Proletarskie poety pervykh let sovetskoi epokhi* (Leningrad, 1959), pp. 452–53.

56. L. Tamashin, *Sovetskaia dramaturgiia v gody grazhdanskoi voiny* (Moscow, 1961), pp. 44, 52.

known as "revolutionary hymns," a favorite method in the Petrograd Proletkult. At the opening of the main Proletkult building in Petrograd on May 1, 1918, the choir, under the direction of the composer Ianis Ozolin, performed "Workers' Palace" ("Rabochii dvorets") to the words of Aleksandr Pomorskii's poem and "May Day" ("Pervyi mai") to the words of Kirillov's poem.[57] The central Proletkult leader Fedor Kalinin was so impressed by this approach that he wanted revolutionary hymns to form the basis of the Proletkult's musical curriculum.[58]

Proletkult writers also tried their hands at plays, creating agitational and inspirational works that depicted workers' struggles in the revolution and Civil War. One of the most successful was *The Bricklayer* (*Kamenshchik*) by Pavel Bessalko, who had studied with Lunacharskii in Paris.[59] This play is an allegorical tale about an architect who designs tall buildings and the worker who executes his plans. The architect is afraid of heights and dies trying to overcome his fears. When the revolution begins, the bricklayer, who has now studied architectural theory, assumes his former employer's job. He starts to construct a huge "tower of the commune," a revolutionary tower of Babel that will end national divisions between workers and inspire a single international language. The play discusses themes dear to the hearts of Proletkult theorists, including the need for workers to take over the tasks of intellectuals. As one laborer tells the protagonist, "It is good that you studied the art of building. Workers will trust you to construct the tower. You are ours; we are proud that you are one of our own."[60] The play ends as the bricklayer scales the

57. V. Ignatov, "Otkrytie Dvortsa Proletarskoi Kul'tury," *Griadushchee*, no. 3 (1918), pp. 4–5.

58. Proletkult central committee meeting, July 5, 1919, TsGALI f. 1230, op. 1, d. 3, ll. 71 ob.–72.

59. Bessalko, who died of typhus in early 1920, is commemorated in A. V. Lunacharsky, *Revolutionary Silhouettes*, trans. and ed. Michael Glenny (New York, 1968), pp. 149–53.

60. P. Bessal'ko, *Kamenshchik, Plamia*, no. 33 (1918), pp. 2–7, quotation p. 6.

tower to place a red flag at the top. A popular favorite in Proletkult organizations, *The Bricklayer* was also used as a model for theatrical improvisations in the Red Army.[61]

Valerian Pletnev, an important Moscow leader and head of the national Proletkult after 1920, became one of the organization's best-known playwrights. His theme was the history of the workers' struggle and the evolution of the revolutionary movement in Russia. By 1921 Pletnev's plays were standard fare in many provincial organizations and workers' clubs.[62] Among his most popular works were the following: *The Avenger* (*Msititel'*), a heroic tale of self-sacrifice during the last days of the Paris Commune that was inspired by the work of the French author Léon Cladel; *Strikes* (*Stachki*), based on a story by Aleksei Gastev about youths who engage in a labor protest in prerevolutionary Russia; *Improbable, but Possible* (*Neveroiatno, no vozmozhno*), a farce about the Provisional Government; and *Lena*, about workers' lives during the strike that led up to the Lena massacre.[63]

The Civil War itself became the subject matter of Proletkult drama. Pavel Arskii, from the Petrograd organization, wrote a short agitational piece, *For the Red Soviets* (*Za krasnye sovety*), depicting an assault by White forces on a peasant village and their brutalization of women and children. It was used by the Petrograd troupe and by the Red Army to discourage desertion.[64] When the Moscow Proletkult went to the Polish front in

61. A. Z. Iufit, ed., *Russkii sovetskii teatr, 1917–1921: Dokumenty i materialy* (Leningrad, 1968), pp. 318–19.

62. See local Proletkult questionnaires sent to the center in 1921, TsGALI f. 1230, op. 1, d. 118, ll. 27, 46, 9; and A. K. Kolesova, "Prakticheskaia deiatel'nost' rabochego kluba v 1917–1920 godakh," *Uchenye zapiski Moskovskogo gosudarstvennogo instituta kul'tury*, vol. 17 (1968), p. 244.

63. V. F. Pletnev, *Lena* (Rostov on Don, 1921); idem, *Mstitel'* (Moscow, 1922); idem, *Neveroiatno, no vozmozhno* (Moscow, 1921); and idem, *Stachki* (Moscow, 1921).

64. Pavel Arskii, *Za krasnye sovety*, in *Pervye sovetskie p'esy*, ed. V. F. Pimenov (Moscow, 1958), pp. 489–99; and L. A. Pinegina, *Sovetskii rabochii klass i khudozhestvennaia kul'tura, 1917–1932* (Moscow, 1984), p. 203.

1920, the traveling studio devised a special play, *Pan Bunia*, to expose the corruption of the Polish landlords.[65]

Like theater groups, music collectives were quick to discover an appropriate revolutionary repertoire. Choirs performed popular prerevolutionary workers' songs of struggle, such as "The Red Banner" ("Krasnoe znamia") and "Boldly Keep Step, Comrades" ("Smelo, tovarishchi, v nogu"),[66] along with "The Internationale" and "The Marseillaise." They also devised new lyrics for well-known tunes. For example, Pavel Arskii supplied verses that could be sung to "The Internationale":

> Rise up, all of toiling Russia.
> Rise up, our giant, our titan.
> Yours—all the working masses.
> Yours—the workers of all lands.[67]

Vasilev-Buglai composed a rousing political message for the popular gypsy ballad "White Acacias."[68]

In the visual arts many Proletkult participants tried to discover a simple, realistic style based on working-class themes. "The body of the working man, here is the ideal of future sculpture," read one explanation of a proletarian aesthetic.[69] An intellectual instructor in a Saratov art studio defined workers' art as the expression of monumental content through clear and simple forms. In his view such an approach grew organically from workers' life experiences. "Each worker's broad hand decisively and energetically draws the charcoal across the paper; it powerfully and boldly kneads and shreds the clay. The reason for [the workers'] special traits is not hard to explain. Since childhood these joiners, turners,

65. S. Margolin, *Pervyi Rabochii teatr Proletkul'ta* (Moscow, 1930), p. 24.

66. These songs were first published in the late nineteenth century, Nutrikhin, *Pesni russkikh rabochikh*, pp. 191–94, 227.

67. Pavel Arskii, "Gimn," *Plamia*, no. 2 (1918), p. 7.

68. Vasil'ev-Buglai, "Na fronte," p. 14.

69. "Khronika Proletkul'ta," *Proletarskaia kul'tura*, no. 6 (1918), p. 31.

and carpenters have made things out of wood or iron and have shaped them into the necessary forms."[70]

Although many believed that realism was the proper form for proletarian creation, sympathetic critics tried to distinguish between proletarian realism and the dominant modes of nineteenth century art. In the words of the art professor A. A. Sidorov, "The realism of the Proletkult is of course not the old detailed kind, bound to nature. In the faces of these portraits and in the colors of these landscapes one discerns an effort to become masters of nature, to subjugate nature to [the workers'] plans."[71] Others gave a more honest account of Proletkultists' intellectual debts. The Proletkult instructor Lev Pumpianskii, in a review of a Petrograd exhibit of proletarian art, noted the primitive nature of many of the paintings, but he also found much to praise. In the works by soldiers, sailors, proofreaders, and house painters Pumpianskii saw elements of naturalism, impressionism, and the *lubok* tradition of Russian art. He was particularly moved by one artist, a hall porter named Andreev, whose paintings evoked the naive folk style of Henri Rousseau and Nataliia Goncharova.[72]

In their search for unique proletarian forms many participants brusquely rejected artistic paths that they associated with alien classes. Platon Kerzhentsev, the theater expert, was a sharp critic of the "bourgeois" opera and ballet, sentiments echoed in some Proletkult publications.[73] Boris Krasin of Moscow worried that workers would be corrupted by the "petty-bourgeois" musical tastes of the lower classes, particularly popular gypsy songs.[74] Playwrights denounced the

70. Instruktor, "V studiiakh izobrazitel'nykh iskusstv," *Zarevo zavodov*, no. 2 (1919), p. 55.

71. A. A. S. [A. A. Sidorov], "Vystavka Moskovskogo Proletkul'ta," *Tvorchestvo*, no. 7/10 (1920), p. 45.

72. Lev Pumpianskii, "Iskusstvo i sovremennost'. Ocherk tretii: Proletarskie khudozhniki," *Plamia*, no. 39 (1919), pp. 10–14, especially p. 12.

73. Kerzhentsev, *Revoliutsiia i teatr*, pp. 30–31; Pinegina, *Sovetskii rabochii klass*, p. 109.

74. *Protokoly pervoi konferentsii*, p. 46.

"frivolous" repertoires chosen by many local theaters, including farces and humorous entertainments. These opinions lent a censorious, moralistic tone to many Proletkult pronouncements on aesthetics, but they did not dictate the content of local work.[75]

Proletkult art critics saved their most vicious attacks for "futurism," a blanket term indiscriminately (and inaccurately) applied to impressionism, cubism, nonfigurative artistic forms, and various types of literary and theatrical experiments. These styles were rejected not because they were new but because they were old; they had begun before the revolution and were promoted by "bourgeois artists," which made them unsuitable forms for the proletariat.[76] A recurrent theme in Proletkult criticism was that futuristic forms were too difficult for workers to comprehend. "First and foremost, as the positive sum of collective sensibilities, feelings, and experiences," wrote the intellectual Ilia Trainin, "proletarian

75. The Petrograd Proletkult, for example, sponsored an opera workshop taught by professional singers, *Griadushchee*, no. 7/8 (1920), p. 22.
76. See F. I. Kalinin, "O futurizme," *Proletarskaia kul'tura*, no. 7/8 (1919), pp. 41–43; P. Bessal'ko, "Futurizm i proletarskaia kul'tura," *Griadushchee*, no. 10 (1918), pp. 10–12; S. Kluben, "Proletkul't i komfut," *Griadushchaia kul'tura*, no. 4/5 (1919), pp. 14–17; I. Trainin, "Proletarskoe iskusstvo i futurizm," *Zarevo zavodov*, no. 2 (1919), pp. 29–37; S. Spasskii, "Itogi futurizma," ibid., pp. 42–45; K. Mikhailov, "Izobrazitel'noe iskusstvo i futurizm," ibid., pp. 52–54; Karl Ozol'–Prednek, "Proletarskoe iskusstvo—revoliutsionnoe iskusstvo," *Proletkul't* (Tver), no. 1 (1919), pp. 26–29; L. T[oom], "Eshche slovo o futurizme," *Vzmakhi*, no. 1 (1919), p. 115; O. Olenev, "Nakonets-to," *Gudki*, no. 1 (1919), pp. 17–19; Vak, "Teatr Moskovskogo soveta," *Gudki*, no. 2 (1919), pp. 19–20; and Vladimir Chumarev, "O prirode futurizma," *Zori griadushchego*, no. 5 (1922), pp. 117–24. The articles by Sergei Spasskii and Lidiia Toom were guarded defenses of futurism. For further discussions of this debate see Bengt Jangfeldt, *Majakovskij and Futurism, 1917–1921* (Stockholm, 1976), pp. 74–84 and Gerd Wilbert, " 'Linke' Kunst und Proletkul't in Sovetrussland, 1918–1919," in *Von der Revolution zum Scriftstellerkongress: Entwicklungsstrukturen und Funktionsbestimmungen der russischen Literatur und Kultur zwischen 1917 und 1934*, ed. G. Erler et al. (Berlin, 1979), pp. 230–47.

art is clear and understandable to everyone."[77] Art could not claim to be collective if the collective could not grasp it.

Efforts to create a worker-centered art were not universally well received by the artistic community. Critics found much of the Proletkult's work amateurish, eclectic, and highly derivative.[78] The most complete demolition was at the hands of the much-maligned futurists, who could find nothing new or valuable in Proletkult work. The self-proclaimed worker vanguard was just reusing the tired clichés of heroism and realism, insisted David Sterenberg. To create a truly proletarian art, one needed more than tales of the lives of labor. The essential ingredient was a new, inventive, and revolutionary artistic form.[79] Despite the bad blood between futurists and the Proletkult, it was a message that at least some participants took to heart.

Revolutionary Experiments

The intricate relationship between artistic form and content was not a central theme for Proletkult artists and critics during the early Soviet years. Indeed, many participants seemed to believe that art with a revolutionary content—new words to old ballads, new images in the ode or sonnet, or even old plays in new contexts—was a sufficient expression of the proletarian spirit. Bogdanov, a foe of stylistic innovation, insisted that true socialist art would be "simple in form but enormous in content." He protested against some works by proletarian artists that were stylistically so complex that even intellectu-

77. I. Trainin, "Proletarskoe iskusstvo i futurizm," *Zarevo zavodov*, no. 2 (1919), p. 36.

78. See, for example, L. Kleinbort's comments on Proletkult art exhibits in I. Matsa, L. Reingardt, and L. Rempel', eds., *Sovetskoe iskusstvo za 15 let: Materialy i dokumentatsii* (Moscow, 1933), pp. 51–53.

79. D. P. Sterenberg, "Kritikam iz Proletkul'ta," *Iskusstvo kommuny*, no. 10 (1919), p. 30. See also O. M. Brik, "Dovol'no soglashatel'stva!" ibid., no. 6 (1919), p. 1.

als had a hard time grasping them.[80] Ilia Trainin, another opponent of experimentation, believed that proletarian art first and foremost meant a revolution in content. From this a new form would eventually emerge.[81]

However, a vocal minority in the movement was convinced that revolutionary messages needed innovative modes of expression. They sought new formal methods that would distinguish their creative products from those of other classes. In the field of music, for example, the Moscow Proletkult opened a small scientific and technical sector where experimental musicians like Arsenii Avraamov and Nikolai Roslavets worked to create a seventeen-note scale. They also studied the use of industrial objects as instruments, anticipating the concerts of factory whistles sponsored in part by the Proletkult during the 1923 celebration of the revolution.[82] The local music studio in Penza put on a "collective concert" without a conductor in 1920, a forerunner of the leaderless orchestras that gained popularity later in the decade.[83]

Literature circles tried their hands at collective writing projects, one venture that had the hearty endorsement of the central organization. A Moscow studio produced a collective poem, "In Memory of the Fallen," to honor those killed in an attack on the Moscow party center in the fall of 1919.[84] Mikhail Gerasimov worked together with Sergei Esenin and Sergei Klychkov to compose a poem commemorating Sergei Ko-

80. "Zasedaniia pervogo Vserossiiskogo soveshchaniia proletarskikh pisatelei," May 10, 1920, TsGALI f. 1638 [Vsesoiuznoe obshchestvo proletarskikh pisatelei "Kuznitsa"], op. 3, d. 1, ll. 1–2. See also "Pervyi Vserossiiskii s"ezd proletarskikh pisatelei," *Kuznitsa*, no. 7 (1920), p. 35.

81. I. Trainin, "Proletarskoe iskusstvo i futurizm," *Zarevo zavodov*, no. 2 (1919), p. 36.

82. "Iz otcheta uchenogo sekretariia Nauchno-technicheskogo podotdela," in Stepanova, *Muzykal'naia zhizn' Moskvy*, pp. 292–94; and Arsenii Avraamov, "Simfoniia gudkov," *Gorn*, no. 9 (1923), pp. 109–16.

83. *Proletarskaia kul'tura*, no. 17/19 (1920), p. 89.

84. "Pamiati pogibshikh," in Papernyi and Shatseva, *Proletarskie poety*, p. 423.

nenkov's monument to the martyrs of the revolution. The poem was then put to music and performed by the Moscow Proletkult choir when the sculpture was unveiled in November 1918.[85]

Theater workshops also experimented with collective works. In Rybinsk members wrote, directed, and performed an agitational play called *Don't Go* (*Ne khodi*), which depicted the confrontation of a Red Army soldier with his wife who did not want him to fight in the Civil War. Central leaders continually cited this play as the best example of collective creation, and it became a standard part of the Proletkult's theatrical repertoire.[86] In Saratov a club theater put on improvisational evenings. People in the audience would shout out themes, such as "taking over an apartment" or "why I became a Communist," and studio members would act them out on stage.[87] Improvisation became the basis of all theatrical work in Proletkult clubs during the New Economic Policy; members were encouraged to create their own skits and mock trials about the problems of everyday life.[88]

Collective readings were another innovation employed by drama studios, a solution to the problem of repertoire and to the poor preparation of Proletkult students for public performances. The head of the Petrograd theater, Mgebrov, was an enthusiastic supporter of this technique. He adapted nondramatic material for the stage, fashioning poetry into elaborate scripts with very detailed choreography. Individuals read small parts of the poems, but the majority of the work was declaimed by the chorus. Mgebrov hailed this as an original, collective artistic form.[89]

85. M. Gerasimov, S. Esenin, and S. Klychkov, "Kantata," *Zarevo zavodov*, no. 1 (1919), pp. 24–25; and Raikhenstein, "1 maia i 7 noiabria 1918 goda v Moskve," p. 102.

86. "Khronika Proletkul'ta," *Proletarskaia kul'tura*, no. 20/21 (1921), p. 53; and V. Smyshliaev, "Rabota teatral'nogo sektsii," *Biulleten' vtorogo s"ezda Proletkul'tov*, no. 2 (1921), p. 32.

87. *Proletarskaia kul'tura*, no. 15/16 (1920), p. 79.

88. See Chapter 8.

89. Mgebrov, *Zhizn' v teatre*, vol. 2, pp. 321–31, esp. p. 323. See

Moscow theatrical studios launched their own experiments, opening a special division for "tonal-plastic movement" in 1920. Based on rigorous physical training and group readings, tonal plastics aimed to educate actors to work together as a mass, a rejection of the individualistic methods of Stanislavsky's theater. In late 1920 Sergei Eisenstein, who was later to become a film director, introduced the avant-garde director Vsevolod Meyerhold's system of biomechanics. It made integrated movement and conscious body control, rather than subconscious feeling, the basis of acting. Neither technique originated in the Proletkult. Meyerhold developed the basic principles of biomechanics years before the revolution, and tonal plastics drew on the ideas of the Swiss composer and choreographer Jaques-Dalcroze.[90] However, Proletkultists saw both techniques as methods to create a new collective theater.

Despite widespread denunciations of futurism, select local circles produced "futurist" work. The art section in the short-lived Proletkult in Barnaul was led by Nikolai Tarabukin, who was influenced by the work of Malevich and Altman. When Tarabukin went to Moscow to work for Narkompros's experimental Institute for Artistic Culture, he also became an instructor in the Moscow Proletkult.[91] The Saratov art division was led by the avant-garde artist V. Iustinskii, who believed that the proletariat had to find new artistic forms. He designed the completely abstract cover for the Saratov Proletkult publication, *Waves* (*Vzmakhi*).[92] This journal, and espe-

---

von Geldern, *Festivals*, chapter 1, for a description of Mgebrov's first collective reading.

90. See Marjorie L. Hoover, *Meyerhold: The Art of the Conscious Theater* (Amherst, 1974), pp. 75–91; and D. Zolotnitskii, *Zori teatral'nogo Oktiabria* (Leningrad, 1976), pp. 344–59.

91. V. L. Soskin, *Ocherki istorii kul'tury Sibiri v gody revoliutsii i grazhdanskoi voiny* (Novosibirsk, 1965), pp. 254–55. Tarabukin became an important contributor to the Proletkult journal published during the New Economic Policy, *Rabochii klub*.

92. On V. Iustinskii see E. Speranskaia, "Materialy k istorii oformleniia pervykh revoliutsionnykh prazdnestv v Saratove i Nizh-

cially its cover, got a very unfavorable review in *Proletarian Culture* for its "futuristic tendencies." Despite this critique, the Saratov organization did not change its direction. In a 1920 report one participant complained, "I do not know why they have stuck a futurist label on our art studios. They should be glad that our students do not demand teachers from the old school."[93]

Some Proletkult students found their way to modern styles on their own. A young peasant woman who worked with Timofei Katurkin in Belev was amazed by the paintings of Picasso and Matisse she discovered when invited to a conference in Moscow. This exposure convinced her that she had to go to study in France, where she eventually became a professional painter and married Fernand Léger.[94] A Moscow member, Aleksandr Zugrin, became one of the Proletkult's most visible artists. Although his teachers were realists, Zugrin's work sometimes showed the influence of cubism. His engravings and linoleum cuts adorned the covers and pages of journals such as *Furnace* (*Gorn*), *Create!* (*Tvori!*), and *Creation* (*Tvorchestvo*), as well as the book jackets of many collections of proletarian poems.[95]

Artistic experiments got their widest acceptance when the Moscow Proletkult gave its support to production art, a direction first suggested by the avant-gardist Olga Rozanova in 1918.[96] Rather than making rarefied objects for museums or

---

nem Novgorode," in *Agitatsionno-massovoe iskusstvo pervykh let Oktiabria*, ed. E. A. Speranskaia (Moscow, 1971), pp. 144, 152–53, 156.

93. "Doklad otdela izobrazitel'nykh iskusstv," *Vzmakhi*, no. 2 (1920), p. 81.

94. Maksim Vladimirov, "Chudesa chelovecheskie," *Nedelia*, no. 32 (1974), pp. 6–7.

95. V. Khmeleva, "Khudozhnik-rabochii A. I. Zugrin," *Rabochii zhurnal*, no. 3/4 (1924), pp. 139–43, esp. p. 141; and N. Tarabukin, "Proletarskii khudozhnik," ibid., pp. 135–38.

96. On Rozanova's involvement in the Proletkult see Camilla Gray, *The Russian Experiment in Art, 1868–1922* (London, 1976), p. 245; and Christina Lodder, *Russian Constructivism* (New Haven, 1983), p. 259.

the beautification of private spaces, the advocates of this approach believed that proletarian artists should turn their attention to the public sphere. They should bring an aesthetic sense to the mass production of objects for general use, for example, textiles and furniture.[97]

In the first issue of *Furnace*, published in mid-1918, the Moscow art studio organizers explained that the main goal of production art was the fusion of artistic creation and industry. Unions should send the Proletkult talented workers who would then be trained in artistic skills closely connected to their trades. Builders would be taught architecture and weavers textile design.[98] Such a course would lead to the end of "bourgeois" forms like museum art and easel art, argued Boris Arvatov, one of the foremost theorists of this pragmatic aesthetic. He became involved in the Moscow Proletkult in 1919 and under his influence art studios increasingly turned toward practical and industrial design.[99]

Production art appealed to Proletkultists because it was firmly grounded in the factory, which gave it good proletarian credentials. This approach aimed to bring art into daily life, fulfilling the Proletkult's promise to change the function of art in society. Proponents of this highly utilitarian direction rejected the strict delineation between art and life and also that between artists and other producers. By focusing on objects with obvious social uses, including posters and banners, production art helped to justify the Proletkult's existing emphasis on agitational forms.

Initially, only some Moscow art studios embraced production art, but it steadily gained influence. In 1919 Anna Dodonova urged the national organization to pursue this direc-

97. See Lodder, *Russian Constructivism*, pp. 75–76, 103.

98. "Plan organizatsii izobrazitel'nogo otdela Moskovskogo proletariata," *Gorn*, no. 1 (1918), pp. 66–67.

99. On Arvatov see Hans Günther and Karla Hielscher, "Zur proletarischen Produktionskunst Boris I. Arvatovs," in *Kunst und Produktion*, by Boris Arvatov, ed. and trans. H. Günther and K. Hielscher (Munich, 1972), pp. 116–33.

tion in all its artistic programs. She contended that many workshops were in danger of perpetuating a "handicraft" (*kustarnyi*) approach to art. Rather than continuing in the old way, it was imperative to tie art to industry.[100] Eventually, production art was accepted as the Proletkult's official aesthetic platform, a move that was resisted by many local circles that found it too utilitarian and cold.[101] Although this approach never completely dominated local practice, the central Proletkult's endorsement revealed the organization's affinity to the avant-garde, a link that would only become stronger in the 1920s.

Artistic Mastery and Professionalization

During the early Soviet years the Proletkult was a remarkably vital cultural institution, and it was also remarkably eclectic. It had no unified aesthetic direction; in its far-flung network of studios and clubs it produced both some of the most conservative and some of the most radical cultural creations. But there was another source of confusion. The participants also could not decide what the precise purpose of the organization was. For many local circles the Proletkult served as a comprehensive cultural training program for the lower classes. This inclusive vision was opposed by other members who hoped the Proletkult would provide the most talented students with enough skills and resources to discover the culture of the future.

Some of the harshest criticisms of Proletkult work came from within its own ranks. Participants worried about the low quality of production and the weaknesses of local training

100. Protocol from the July 5, 1919, central committee meeting, TsGALI f. 1230, op. 1, d. 3, ll. 52–53 ob.

101. See the resolutions on art at the 1920 and 1921 national gatherings, "Rezoliutsii sektsii izobrazitel'nykh iskusstv," *Proletarskaia kul'tura*, no. 17/19 (1920), pp. 81–82; "Proletkul't i ego zadachi v izobrazitel'nom iskusstve," *Biulleten' vtorogo s"ezda*, no. 2, pp. 40–51, esp. pp. 45–46; and the discussions at the June 1922 national plenum, TsGA RSFSR f. 2313, op. 1, d. 19, ll. 29–30.

programs. They also feared that the constant demands for agitational performances lowered artistic standards. As the Moscow leader Arvatov mournfully reflected in late 1920, "It's funny to say this, but it remains a fact: up until now the proletariat has not given even one performance the way it wanted to give it."[102]

One obvious solution to these problems was to direct the organization's limited resources to fewer students, who would receive more intensive schooling than typical programs could provide. A dispute in Moscow in early 1919 over the creation of special workshops for scholarship students initiated a wide-ranging national debate over the issue of "professionalization."[103] Should the Proletkult allow all members to pursue their cultural interests alongside their usual occupations? Or should it instead help the most talented workers by freeing them from their jobs and giving them the skills to become professional artists? The foes of professionalization argued that worker-artists received their inspiration from the factory. They should not abandon this source of strength, nor should they distance themselves from the broad mass of laborers. Those on the other side of the argument countered that one condemned aspiring proletarian artists to mediocrity if they had to stay at their benches. Without full-time attention to their own cultural development, they would never get the preparation necessary to create an art that could rival that of other classes.

Distrust of hierarchical privilege was widespread in the

---

102. B. Arvatov, "Na povorote," *Tvori!*, no. 1 (1920), p. 12.

103. V. Pletnev, "O professionalizme," *Proletarskaia kul'tura*, no. 7/8 (1919), pp. 31–37; P. M. Kerzhentsev, "Metody raboty Proletkul'ta," *Proletarskaia kul'tura*, no. 6 (1919), p. 20; idem, "O professionalizme," *Gorn*, no. 2/3 (1920), pp. 69–70; Ivan Eroshin, "O professionalizme v iskusstve," *Gudki*, no. 5 (1919), pp. 15–17; and F. Kalinin, "O professionalizme rabochikh v iskusstve," *Proletarskaia kul'tura*, no. 7/8 (1919), pp. 29–31. For an expanded discussion see Lynn Mally, "Egalitarian and Elitist Visions of Cultural Transformation: The Debate in the Proletkul't Movement," in *Culture et révolution*, ed. Marc Ferro and Sheila Fitzpatrick (Paris, 1989), pp. 137–46.

Proletkult, and professionalization sparked a number of passionate objections. One writer in the Samara journal *Glow of the Factories* denounced the notion of artistic genius itself as a degenerate remnant of capitalism. The purpose of the revolution was to bring out the creative potential in everyone. Organizers of the very radical Kostroma Proletkult insisted that proletarian culture would be made by the working class as a whole, not by gifted "loners" (*edinochki*) who stood outside their class.[104] A theater enthusiast in Tambov claimed that the old method of elevating the artist above the public was passé. "Together with the old theater, the old actor, [that is,] the actor-parrot (*akter-popugai*), is disappearing. In his place will come the actor-creator, the actor-amateur." The author used the term *liubitel'*, an amateur or a dilettante, as a positive description.[105]

Nonetheless, selective programs such as scholarships provided easy answers for local groups facing financial problems and constant student turnover. Such methods also appealed to the most ambitious studio members, who worried that the organization might overlook their needs. One worker-participant in a Moscow literary studio, Ivan Eroshin, complained that after a day in the factory he hardly had the energy for nightly lessons in the Proletkult. In his view physical and mental labor did not mix. "Let us live with our art so that our brain and blood, our whole selves, are imbued with it; then we can strike the most powerful weapon from our enemy's hands."[106]

Even before the issue of professionalization was officially resolved, a group of working-class authors left the movement to start a rival organization, charging that the Proletkult did

104. V. Libert, "Proletarskoe iskusstvo," *Zarevo zavodov*, no. 2 (1919), pp. 27–29; and "Organizatsiia Kostromskogo Proletkul'ta," *Sbornik Kostromskogo Proletkul'ta*, no. 1 (1919), p. 107.

105. R., "O revoliutsii teatra," *Griadushchaia kul'tura*, no. 4/5 (1919), p. 22.

106. Ivan Eroshin, "O professionalizme v iskusstve," *Gudki*, no. 5 (1919), pp. 15–17, quotation p. 17.

not pay enough attention to their professional needs. In February 1920 Mikhail Gerasimov opened a circle for proletarian literature under the aegis of Narkompros and took five other Moscow poets along with him. According to these poets the Proletkult inhibited their creative growth because it slighted formal training and ignored the special demands of the most talented. From his base in Narkompros Gerasimov opened a new journal, *The Foundry* (*Kuznitsa*), and gathered a group of writers around it. This group was known as the "Smithy" or the "Kuznitsy."[107] They used the Narkompros division as a base to expand plans for a proletarian writers' union that would devote itself to the interests of professional working-class authors.

Initially, this rupture did not greatly threaten the Proletkult. Many talented authors, including Kirillov and Samobytnik-Mashirov, joined the Smithy but did not break their ties to the Proletkult. By the time the groundwork for the new union was laid the two groups had reached an uneasy compromise. The union would not attempt to rival or eclipse the Proletkult; instead it would devote itself primarily to discrete professional issues, such as payment scales. In return the Proletkult central committee offered moral and limited financial support.[108] Despite the compromise, this altercation graphically illustrated how loosely the Proletkult's following was bound

107. On the Kuznitsy see Edward J. Brown, *The Proletarian Episode in Russian Literature, 1928–1932* (New York, 1953), pp. 8–13; L. M. Farber, *Sovetskaia literatura pervykh let revoliutsii, 1917–1920 gg.* (Moscow, 1966), pp. 94–105; Barbara Kerneck, "Die Lyriker der 'Kuznica,' 1920–1922: Entstehung und Auflösung einer Gruppe," in *Von der Revolution zum Schriftstellerkongress*, ed. G. Erler et al. (Berlin, 1979), pp. 269–89; Robert A. Maguire, *Red Virgin Soil: Soviet Literature in the 1920's* (Princeton, 1968), pp. 156–59; N. V. Zakharchenko, " 'Kuznitsa' i Proletkul't," in *Pisatel' i literaturnyi protsess*, ed. I. M. Toibin (Dushanbe, 1974), vol. 2, pp. 27–46; idem, "Kogda i kak obrazovalas' 'Kuznitsa,' " *Filologicheskie nauki*, no. 4 (1973), pp. 15–27; and Viacheslav Zavalishin, *Early Soviet Writers* (New York, 1958), part 3.

108. "Pervyi s"ezd proletarskikh pisatelei," *Kuznitsa*, no. 7 (1920), pp. 32–34.

together. A dispute over artistic training was enough to split the organization apart.

Professionalization was finally placed on the national agenda at the 1920 Proletkult congress, an event that also marked a turning point in the debate over artistic programs. Lunacharskii gave the keynote address on this controversial topic, arguing that proletarian ideology had already penetrated Soviet life to such an extent that it made no sense to restrict aspiring worker-artists to the factory. However, he warned that professionalism for workers could not take the same forms that it had under capitalism. It did not mean that the organization would abandon its commitment to the broad masses.[109]

This was not an isolated resolution. The conference delegates also gave official approval to local groups wishing to sponsor elite artistic studios and scholarship programs. In addition, the delegates supported the formation of a selective national Proletkult studio in Moscow that would begin work in the theater. Here, too, the resolutions had a somewhat cautious tone. One organizer, Stefan Krivtsov, demanded that scholarship students be required to take part in union and party work so that they would retain their class ties.[110]

Demands for higher artistic quality and expertise accompanied these endorsements of professionalization. "Turn away from dilettantism and amateurism to mastery and professionalism," read the 1920 congress resolutions on literature. Similar sentiments were echoed for music, theater, and the visual arts as well.[111] In a comprehensive statement on the

109. P. I. Lebedev-Polianskii [V. Kunavin, pseud.], "Vserossiiskii s"ezd Proletkul'ta," *Proletarskaia kul'tura*, no. 17/19 (1920), p. 75; and A. Lunacharskii, "O professionalizme rabochikh v iskusstve," ibid, p. 80.

110. "Tezisy tov. V. V. Ignatova po organizatsii Tsentral'noi Areny Proletarskogo Tvorchestva," TsGALI f. 963 [Gosudarstvennyi teatr imeni V. Meierkhol'da], op. 2, d. 58, l. 3; and S. Krivtsov, "Rezoliutsiia organizatsionnoi sektsii," *Proletarskaia kul'tura*, no. 17/19 (1920), p. 83.

111. *Proletarskaia kul'tura*, no. 17/19 (1920), pp. 80–82, quotation p. 80.

arts issued at the end of 1920 central leaders proclaimed: "All students should learn that without grasping the mechanics of art, without mastery, their creative expression will be weak; they often will only discover an already-discovered America."[112]

Along with calls for mastery came much more explicit instructions on the kind of art that Proletkultists should pursue. The movement would offer rigorous studio training, but its primary function was to produce original creative art. Visual art studios would make banners, decorations, and implement the principles of production art. Literature studios would write song lyrics, new plays, and agitational slogans for festivals. Music workshops would put composition before performances. Finally, theater circles would conceive a new, proletarian repertoire.[113] Although these proposals fell far short of a systematic aesthetic, they did show that the central leadership was eager to rid the Proletkult of some of its cultural eclecticism. It also was a clear step away from one of the most important functions of the Proletkult during the Civil War— to offer large and varied audiences a chance to learn about and perform the Russian classics.

Professionalization was the logical result of the Proletkult's commitment to a new proletarian intelligentsia. In the words of one central resolution, "If we are not afraid to take the proletariat from the bench to run the government, then there is no reason to worry that workers' specialization in artistic creation will lead to a rift with their class."[114] By embracing this direction the Proletkult also followed patterns set by other revolutionary institutions. The advocates of egalitarianism and decentralization in the army, state bureaucracies, and the Communist Party all faced defeat by the end of the Civil War.[115] What is interesting in this case is the ambivalent

112. "Blizhaishchie zadachi Proletkul'ta," *Proletarskaia kul'tura*, no. 20/21 (1921), pp. 27–35, quotation p. 30.

113. Ibid.

114. "Tretii s"ezd Vserossiiskogo soveta Proletkul'ta," *Proletarskaia kul'tura*, no. 13/14 (1920), p. 86.

115. See Mark von Hagen, *The Red Army and the Revolution* (forth-

nature of the Proletkult's endorsement. Members made clear that they wanted a new kind of professional artist, one who would not lose contact with the laboring population. But nonetheless, by emphasizing the importance of professional standards the leadership undermined the contributions of those who wrote, acted, composed, and painted after working hours—those "dilettantes" who had built the movement during the Civil War years.

———

Proletkultists tried to discover new forms of artistic expression without clear blueprints to tell them how to proceed. The fact that no distinctive genre of proletarian art emerged from their efforts is hardly surprising. Proletkultists experimented with a variety of artistic approaches, and in so doing they were aided by an impressive professional staff. However, the organization was not a catalyst for the creation of a unique proletarian culture; rather it was a mirror reflecting the heterogeneous cultural world of the early Soviet years.

The cultural diversity of the movement was deeply troubling to many members and particularly to the national leaders, who began to restrict its range by the end of the Civil War. They gave their support to special programs, such as production art, that contradicted the tastes of some local followers. At the same time, they endorsed scholarship programs and elite studios to provide serious training to a select few. These were all methods to improve the organization's cultural output; still, they narrowed both its aesthetic and its social scope. Even before the Proletkult began its rapid decline during the New Economic Policy, a decline precipitated by political attacks and funding shortages, the movement had em-

coming), chapters 2 and 3; and Robert Service, *The Bolshevik Party in Revolution, 1917–1923: A Study in Organizational Change* (London, 1979), pp. 134–58.

braced programs guaranteed to limit its popular appeal.[116] It ceded the creation of proletarian culture to the most talented, to the artists and intellectuals who claimed a proletarian title but who had left the smokey sky in the factory behind.

116. See Gabriele Gorzka, A. *Bogdanov und der russische Prolet-kult* (Frankfurt am Main, 1980), pp. 46–59.

6

Proletarian Utopias
Science, Family, and Daily Life

The Proletkult proposed an expansive, utopian agenda to transform Russia in the wake of the revolution. "A new science, art, literature, and morality, in short, a new proletarian culture, conceived in the ranks of the industrial proletariat, is preparing a new human being with a new system of emotions and beliefs," proclaimed Pavel Lebedev-Polianskii in 1918.[1] Proletarian culture, the soul of socialism, would emerge everywhere, and thus the Proletkult would have a foothold everywhere as well.

There was a utopian element to all revolutionary visions of the new society. Peasant dreamers prophesied a world without cities, and labor radicals foresaw factories without foremen. Leftist artists wanted to destroy museums and bring art to the streets and the homes of the common man.[2] Even Lenin, the most pragmatic of politicians, was briefly infected with

1. P. I. Lebedev-Polianskii [V. Polianskii, pseud.], "Pod znamia Proletkul'ta," *Proletarskaia kul'tura*, no. 1 (1918), p. 3.
2. See Richard Stites, *Revolutionary Dreams* (New York, 1989); Katerina Clark, "The City versus the Countryside in Soviet Peasant Literature of the Twenties: A Duel of Utopias," in *Bolshevik Culture*, ed. Abbott Gleason, Peter Kenez, and Richard Stites (Bloomington, 1985), pp. 175–89; and René Fueloep-Miller, *The Mind and Face of Bolshevism*, trans. F. S. Flint and D. T. Tait (New York, 1965).

this spirit; in his famous work *State and Revolution* he depicted a governmental structure so simple and transparent that any cook could run the state. Proletkultists, as the self-proclaimed creators of the culture of the future, were inherently utopian. They were convinced that they could usher in the perfect society and the perfect culture, both of which would be based on shared human values rather than class prejudices. "I believe we nurse the future with our hard toil," declared the proletarian poet Vasilii Aleksandrovskii. "Exert your mind and muscles, harden yourself with labor's fire, so that Russia's resurrection will spread to the whole world."[3]

To realize these lofty goals, Proletkult enthusiasts aspired to change far more than artistic creation. The positive, collectivist values that shaped a new art were to permeate all of life—the work place, the school, and the home. They hoped to alter the structure of knowledge and the very fabric of daily existence. These projects were truly utopian; they aimed at perfection but eluded all practical methods of implementation. Still, their articulation shows the breadth of the Proletkult's vision: love, learning, friendship, and community would all come to express the spirit of the socialist age.

Proletarian Science

Given the Proletkultists' fascination with machines and the work environment, it is hardly surprising that some participants became enamored of the idea of a proletarian science. This idea proved to be one of the movement's most controversial proposals, exciting horrified responses from those who believed that the very notion of a class-specific science called the immutable dictates of nature into question.[4] Repeated

3. V. D. Aleksandrovskii, "Veriu ia—my griadushchee vynianchim," in *Proletarskie poety pervykh let sovetskoi epokhi*, ed. Z. S. Papernyi and R. A. Shatseva (Leningrad, 1959), pp. 102–3.
4. See, for example, the comments of a Tver medic, *Pervaia Tverskaia gubernskaia konferentsiia kul'turno-prosvetitel'nykh organizatsii* (Tver, 1919), p. 24.

assurances that the Proletkult did not intend to challenge Newton's laws often fell on deaf ears.[5]

The theory that evoked such passion was the brainchild of Aleksandr Bogdanov. Although Bogdanov was a medical doctor and was convinced of technology's guiding role in social evolution, he did not address himself to the natural sciences alone. The Russian word for science, *nauka*, like the German word *Wissenschaft*, applies to all scholarly disciplines, from studies of literature to physics. Bogdanov aimed to bring all knowledge into a single organized system that he called "tectology," or the science of organization.[6]

For Bogdanov all forms of science, even the most rarefied and abstract branches, reflected and sustained the social system that generated them. The way that scientific knowledge was structured, transmitted, and ultimately applied under capitalism helped to solidify the capitalist order. Bogdanov believed that the basic purpose of science was to organize labor power. Although capitalists applied scientific knowledge to bolster their own exploitative labor practices, the socialist system with the proletariat at the helm would restructure scientific knowledge to suit its radically altered social and economic goals. "The working class needs a *proletarian* science," insisted Bogdanov in his most famous essay on the subject. "This means a science that is acceptable, understandable, and accountable to [the proletariat's] life mission, a science that is organized from the proletariat's point of

5. See M. N. Smit, "Proletarizatsiia nauki," *Proletarskaia kul'tura*, no. 11/12 (1919), pp. 27–33, esp. p. 31.

6. For explanations of Bogdanov's organizational science see Zenovia A. Sochor, *Revolution and Culture* (Ithaca, 1988), pp. 45–56; Ilmari Susiluoto, *The Origins and Development of Systems Thinking in the Soviet Union* (Helsinki, 1982), pp. 46–69; Alexander S. Vucinich, *Science in Russian Culture, 1861–1917* (Stanford, 1970), pp. 446–54; and idem, *Social Thought in Tsarist Russia: The Quest for a General Science of Society, 1861–1917* (Chicago, 1976), pp. 206–30. For a highly critical view see Dominique Lecourt, *Proletarian Science? The Case of Lysenko*, trans. Ben Brewster (London, 1977), pp. 137–62.

view, one that is capable of leading [the proletariat's] forces to struggle for, attain, and implement its social ideals."[7]

The advocates of a new science did not reject the achievements of past generations, but they felt that the proletariat would have to apply this knowledge in a different way. When a critic charged that both the bourgeoisie and the working class would use the same methods to cure disease, Aleksei Samobytnik-Mashirov countered that this was not necessarily true. Capitalists used prescriptions and medicine, but the proletariat would examine the social causes of illness and combat them through better health care and medical insurance.[8]

However, Bogdanov and his supporters had more than a socially conscious application of acquired knowledge in mind. They insisted that the working class would fundamentally restructure scientific information. Science under capitalism was overly specialized, fragmented, and arcane. The proletariat would synthesize knowledge into one unified, monistic system and tie it to life and labor.[9] To achieve this goal, scientific learning could not simply be popularized or democratized because such an approach only meant transmitting accepted truths in an easily accessible form. Nor was it sufficient to proletarianize the institutions of higher learning. Instead science had to be *socialized*; it would be altered and reexamined to meet the needs of a well-organized social system.[10] In the words of a character from Bogdanov's utopian novel, *Engineer Menni*, "The proletariat must master [science] by changing it. In the hands of workers it must become much

7. A. A. Bogdanov, "Nauka i rabochii klass," 1918, reprinted in *O proletarskoi kul'ture, 1904–1924*, by A. A. Bogdanov (Moscow, 1924), pp. 200–221, quotation p. 208.

8. *Protokoly pervoi Vserossiiskoi konferentsii proletarskikh kul'-turno-prosvetitel'nykh organizatsii, 15–20 sentiabria, 1918 g.*, ed. P. I. Lebedev-Polianskii (Moscow, 1918), p. 39.

9. Bogdanov, "Nauka i rabochii klass," pp. 213–15.

10. Ibid., pp. 216–18; and M. N. Smit, "Blizhaishchie etapy proletarizatsii nauki," *Proletarskaia kul'tura*, no. 17/19 (1920), p. 79.

simpler, more harmonious and vital. Its fragmentation must be overcome, it must be brought closer to the labor that is its primary source."[11]

To realize this ambitious agenda, Bogdanov proposed to start proletarian universities that would be based on his own experiences in workers' educational circles and in the Capri and the Bologna schools.[12] He chose the title "university" because it evoked the kind of universalist knowledge he hoped to achieve. The explicit class label was meant to distinguish the new institutions from both elitist schools and "people's universities," which were open to the population at large. As Bogdanov's colleague Mariia Smit explained, proletarian universities would not fit workers into old educational systems, nor would they simply try to train revolutionary agitators. Their purpose was to prepare proletarian leaders, to create "the brain of the working class."[13]

The national Proletkult and numerous local groups enthusiastically embraced these proposals.[14] However, they were not alone in their passion for scientific education. During the first years of Soviet power institutions of higher learning proliferated at a dazzling rate.[15] Not only state organs but also unions, factories, cooperatives, and many other groups at the

11. A. A. Bogdanov, *Engineer Menni*, in *Red Star*, by A. A. Bogdanov, ed. Loren R. Graham and Richard Stites, trans. Charles Rougle (Bloomington, 1984), p. 187.

12. A. A. Bogdanov, *Kul'turnye zadachi nashego vremeni* (Moscow, 1911), pp. 69–74; and idem, "Proletarskii universitet," *Proletarskaia kul'tura*, no. 5 (1918), pp. 9–21.

13. M. N. Smit, "Proletarizatsiia nauki," *Izvestiia TsIK*, June 8, 1919.

14. See the Moscow Proletkult's endorsement of proletarian universities, *Pervaia Moskovskaia obshchegorodskaia konferentsiia proletarskikh kul'turno-prosvetitel'nykh organizatsii, 23–28 fevralia, 1918 goda* (Moscow, 1918), pp. 6–8; and the national organization's endorsement, *Protokoly pervoi konferentsii*, p. 42.

15. On early Soviet education see Oskar Anweiler, *Geschichte der Schule und Pädagogik vom Ende des Zarenreichs bis zum Beginn der Stalin Ära* (Berlin, 1964), esp. pp. 78–153; Sheila Fitzpatrick, *The Commissariat of Enlightenment* (Cambridge, Eng., 1970); N. Hans and S. Hessen, *Educational Policy in Soviet Russia* (London, 1930);

grass roots contributed to this remarkable expansion. The Proletkult could not even claim a monopoly on the title of "proletarian university," which was used by many other sponsors.[16]

The Proletkult's first short-lived experiment in higher education began in the spring of 1918 with the opening of the Moscow Proletarian University. Its curriculum had a very Bogdanovian flavor. The school journal, which only survived one issue, announced that the institution aimed to reassess the culture of the past in light of the proletariat's collective spirit. Significantly, it also contained Bogdanov's best-known treatise on proletarian science.[17] But the Proletkult shared leadership of the school with the city soviet and the local Narkompros division. A three-way fight to control the staff and the course offerings brought about its early demise. Bogdanov blamed its failure on internal factors. He felt that the faculty members had not worked together and that the student body, composed mainly of white-collar employees, had not expressed a proletarian point of view.[18]

After this false start the Proletkult opened another school

R. H. Hayashida, "Lenin and the Third Front," *Slavic Review*, vol. 28, no. 2 (1969), pp. 314–24; David Lane, "The Impact of the Revolution on the Selection of Students for Higher Education," *Sociology*, no. 7 (1973), pp. 241–52; F. Lilge, "Lenin and the Politics of Education," *Slavic Review*, vol. 27, no. 2 (1968), pp. 230–57; James C. McClelland, "Bolshevik Approaches to Higher Education, 1917–1921," *Slavic Review*, vol. 30, no. 4 (1971), pp. 818–31; and idem, "The Utopian and the Heroic: Divergent Paths to the Communist Educational Ideal," in *Bolshevik Culture*, ed. Abbott Gleason, Peter Kenez, and Richard Stites (Bloomington, 1985) pp. 114–30.

16. See V. Smushkov, "Narodnye universitety," *Vneshkol'noe obrazovanie* (Moscow), no. 2/3 (1919), columns 34–43.

17. *Izvestiia Moskovskogo proletarskogo universiteta*, no. 1 (1918), pp. 1–10.

18. On the university's closure see the July 13, July 24, and August 6, 1918, minutes for the collegium of proletarian culture in Narkompros, *Tsentral'nyi Gosudarstvennyi Arkhiv RSFSR* [henceforth cited as TsGA RSFSR] f. 2306, op. 17, d. 1, ll. 2–3, 6–6 ob.; A. A. Bogdanov, "Proletarskii universitet," *Proletarskaia kul'tura*, no. 5 (1918), pp. 15–16.

that followed Bogdanov's educational ideals more closely. He was intimately involved in the curriculum planning for this new institution, and his detailed course outlines provide a glimpse of how he hoped to realize a proletarian science. The school had three levels, each lasting one year. During the first year, designed as an orientation course, students would be introduced to methods of scientific inquiry and taught how to express themselves in a written and oral fashion. They would survey the natural scientific disciplines, including mathematics, physics, chemistry, and physiology, in order to assess the contributions each had made to the labor process. Wherever possible, Bogdanov wanted to use experiments and hands-on techniques as pedagogical tools, not just lectures or textbooks. After this basic grounding in the natural sciences students would turn to the study of society. The curriculum included classes in economics, Russian history, socialism, and the structure of the state and the economy. Here, too, Bogdanov stressed a personalized, participatory approach. Students would use original documents and case studies to gain a sense of historical development and struggle.[19]

After the first year of introductory courses, Bogdanov's aversion to specialized programs became even more pronounced. Rather than presenting each subject separately, he proposed a thematic study plan. The second year opened with an overview of the methodological techniques of scientific investigation, the principles of evolution, the basic theories of energy, and the ways that biology could be applied to the labor process. Students then turned to the social sciences, beginning with a course that examined the history of technology in society. The cycle ended with a class on dialectical materialism as the foundation for a general scientific approach to the world. Bogdanov's integrated, monistic approach to science and society was most apparent in his proposals for the final year. Students were expected to mesh their

19. A. A. Bogdanov, "Proletarskii universitet," *Proletarskaia kul'tura*, no. 5 (1918), pp. 17–19.

knowledge into an encyclopedic system, culminating their work with a course called "The General Organization of Science."[20]

To avoid the problems of the first university, the Proletkult set out to find a working-class clientele. Both Proletkult and Narkompros journals publicized application requirements for the new school. Students were supposed to be recommended by working-class organizations, very broadly defined to include unions, soviets, and the Red Army. Workers and poor peasants were eligible, but white-collar workers were encouraged to go elsewhere. One article by Stefan Krivtsov, a central Proletkult leader, gave a clear explanation of the university's unique pedagogical approach. The university would not teach narrow specialties, nor would it try to create "mandarins of science." Instead, the school would encourage "builder-engineers engaged in all aspects of human endeavor."[21]

In March 1919 the Proletkult's experimental school opened with much pomp and circumstance in Moscow. It was named the Karl Liebknecht University, after the recently assassinated German Spartacist leader. Lunacharskii, Bukharin, and an Austrian representative from the Third International spoke at the opening celebration.[22] Bogdanov claimed that student selection had indeed followed the guidelines set by the central organization and that the four hundred participants came mainly from the working class and peasantry, with only a handful from the laboring intelligentsia. The scant published biographical information about a few of the students tends to confirm his assessment.[23]

The Karl Liebknecht University only flourished for a few

20. Ibid., pp. 19–22.
21. S. Krivtsov, "Proletarskii universitet," *Vneshkol'noe obrazovanie* (Moscow), no. 1 (1919), pp. 18–30, quotation p. 20.
22. "Torzhestvennoe otkrytie proletarskogo universiteta," *Izvestiia TsIK*, March 25, 1919.
23. Bogdanov, cited in *Izvestiia TsIK*, May 17, 1919; and M. F., "82 pokazaniia: Ankety sredi studentov Moskovskogo proletarskogo universiteta," *Proletarskaia kul'tura*, no. 11/12 (1919), pp. 48–57.

months before it was summarily shut down in late July 1919. Its president, N. V. Rogzinskii, who came from the Adult Education Division in Narkompros, felt that its curriculum and staff did not really express the needs of the proletariat. Instead, he proposed that the university be merged with the Sverdlov courses, which offered short-term classes for soviet and party agitators, in order to create a new institution called the Sverdlov Communist University. Although technically a merger, this proposal really meant the total loss of Proletkult control because the Communist Party Central Committee and Narkompros were to take charge of the new school.[24] Party officials explained the step as a temporary measure caused by the demands of the Civil War.[25] However, Bogdanov's innovative educational approach must have also prompted the action. Once the Sverdlov University opened in early 1920, its first president, V. I. Nevskii, went out of his way to denounce the idea of a proletarian university in general and Bogdanov's theory of organizational science in particular.[26]

Bogdanov's unusual curriculum was hardly tested during the university's brief existence, and student questionnaires published after its demise gave mixed reviews. Some students made modest statements about their experience. "I learned what I had to read and how to understand what I read," asserted one participant. But others offered a more positive assessment. "I am entirely convinced that it is necessary to develop a new scientific method," concluded an enthusiastic student. "Only in this way will it be possible to take the valuable and necessary elements from bourgeois culture in order

24. *Izvestiia TsIK*, May 17, 1919; and "K zakrytiiu proletarskogo universiteta," *Proletarskaia kul'tura*, no. 9/10 (1919), pp. 56–59, esp. p. 57. See also Fitzpatrick, *Commissariat*, pp. 101–3.

25. See Elena Stasova's announcement to the Proletkult central committee, August 2, 1919, *Tsentral'nyi Gosudarstvennyi Arkhiv Literatury i Iskusstva* [henceforth cited as TsGALI] f. 1230, op. 1, d. 3, l. 101.

26. V. I. Nevskii, *Otchet raboche-krest'ianskogo Kommunisticheskogo universiteta imeni Ia. M. Sverdlova* (Moscow, 1920), p. 7.

to create and strengthen genuine proletarian culture and ideology."[27]

Many of the former students certainly cared enough about the school to protest its sudden closure. In a poignant letter to the Proletkult central committee, they questioned whether the new school would really meet their needs. The Karl Liebknecht University had aimed to educate proletarian intellectuals in a rigorous three-year program, but the Sverdlov University planned to train agitators in only four months.[28] But one critic writing in *Izvestiia* argued that this was precisely the point. The state needed agitators, not self-styled proletarian leaders. Paraphrasing Marx, S. Novikov claimed that the former proletarian university had hoped to teach students to have a revolutionary worldview, but the new Communist university would teach them how to change the capitalist world into a socialist one.[29]

The failure of the Karl Liebknecht University certainly did not put an end to Proletkult experiments in proletarian science. Various provincial organizations opened their own schools that were intended to educate the working class in a new spirit. "All over Russia a wave to build workers' universities is spreading," exclaimed one central organizer in 1919. In Orel workers donated wages from an extra day's work to finance such a venture. New proletarian institutes of higher learning opened in Smolensk, Tula, Penza, Sormovo, Tsaritsyn, and Balashov.[30]

However, many of these schools were not directly controlled by the Proletkult, nor did they follow Bogdanov's

27. M. F., "82 pokazaniia," *Proletarskaia kul'tura*, no. 11/12 (1919), pp. 48–58, quotations pp. 50, 51.

28. Ibid., pp. 52–58; and "Vypiska iz protokola obshchego sobraniia studentov byv. Moskovskogo proletarskogo universiteta," TsGALI f. 1230, op. 1, d. 3, ll. 103–103 ob.

29. S. Novikov, "Kommunisticheskii universitet," *Izvestiia TsIK*, June 17, 1919.

30. "Khronika Proletkul'ta," *Proletarskaia kul'tura*, no. 6 (1919), pp. 31–33, quotation p. 31.

elaborate educational plans. Tver's "Karl Marx University of Proletarian Culture," founded at a provincial Proletkult conference in 1919, is a good example. From the very beginning the local Narkompros division jointly sponsored the project and the school opened its doors to white-collar employees as well as to industrial workers and peasants. The curriculum, which was hardly innovative, included classes in foreign languages, economics, and accounting.[31]

These provincial experiments distressed Bogdanov because he felt they corrupted his image of proletarian science. Most of the new institutions really did not deserve the name they gave themselves, he complained. They were just "people's universities" offering basic educational courses to a variety of social classes. Although there was certainly nothing wrong with such an endeavor, it hardly contributed to the development of a new science. His own curriculum was not intended as a rigid system, but in order to earn the title of proletarian university an institution had to attempt to unify and reassess scientific knowledge.[32]

With their efforts to create unique proletarian institutions of higher learning largely frustrated, central Proletkult leaders began to pursue a different course. They proposed that local groups open "science studios," similar to the artistic workshops that most already offered. Mariia Smit, an enthusiastic advocate of proletarian science, gave a detailed description of these circles at the Proletkult national congress in 1920. They were to attract some forty to fifty participants, all from the industrial proletariat. Ideally, these workers were to have long years of factory experience behind them that had earned them leading roles in the labor movement. Because of the nature of the subject matter, Smit conceded that the in-

31. *Pervaia Tverskaia gubernskaia konferentsiia*, p. 55; *Proletkul't* (Tver), no. 1/2 (1919), pp. 43, 47. See similar accounts of other provincial efforts in *Proletarskaia kul'tura*, no. 13/14 (1920), p. 89; no. 15/16 (1920), p. 87.
32. A. A. Bogdanov, "O provintsial'nykh proletarskikh universitetakh," *Proletarskaia kul'tura*, no. 9/10 (1919), pp. 53–56.

structors would most likely have to be intellectuals, but she insisted that they be Marxists with close ties to factory labor. She also sketched out the curriculum: a very modified version of the program for proletarian universities. Students would be introduced to mathematics, physics, technology, biology, political economy, and the theories of proletarian culture.[33]

Science studios were never very popular with local organizations, perhaps in part because the center only proposed them just as the Proletkult began its rapid decline at the end of 1920. They obviously also posed burdensome staffing problems for groups that already lacked skilled personnel. In addition, the intended clientele was the most advanced and politically sophisticated workers, a commodity always in short supply.

Spontaneous attempts to start science divisions in the provinces came up with many of the same results as provincial proletarian universities. They were long on introduction and short on synthesis. The science section in the Smolensk Proletkult, for example, claimed that it would "eradicate the division between science and labor and investigate new scientific methods."[34] But its practice did not bear out these promises. A group of local teachers and doctors gave lectures on biology, bacteriology, and sanitary problems, along with discussions about current problems, such as "Why We Don't Have Bread."[35]

Bogdanov's reaction to local programs of this sort was predictably negative. He personally censured the work of the "Socialist Education Division" in the Petrograd Proletkult, which offered classes in foreign languages, mechanics, and construction.[36] At a Proletkult central committee meeting in

33. M. N. Smit, "Blizhaishchie etapy proletarskoi kul'tury," *Proletarskaia kul'tura*, no. 17/19 (1920), pp. 32–40; on Bogdanov and science studios see *Proletarskaia kul'tura*, no. 20/21 (1921), p. 36.

34. "Provintsial'nye proletkul'ty," *Narodnoe obrazovanie*, no. 31 (1919), p. 21.

35. "Zerkalo studii," *Trud i tvorchestvo*, no. 1 (1919), p. 14.

36. "Otchet o deiatel'nosti otdela obshchesotsialisticheskogo

August 1919 Bogdanov argued that there was nothing at all socialist about the division's curriculum. He was particularly offended by the group's plan to take a trip to America to study technology. Following Bogdanov's recommendations, the central committee directed that the division be closed without delay.[37]

The development of proletarian science was resisted on many levels; it was stymied by the hostility of state organs, by staffing problems, and also by the commonplace tastes of local members and teachers. Although the issue remained on the Proletkult's agenda, the methods for its realization were constantly scaled down. A handful of local science studios took shape during the first years of the New Economic Policy, but they were short-lived and offered a very small range of courses.[38] At the national level a central science circle opened in 1921. Although sponsored by the central committee, it had none of the ambitions of Bogdanov's proletarian university. Most of the courses were in the arts and political education; only a handful touched on the natural sciences. The overarching interdisciplinary courses, which were the trademark of Bogdanov's inventive curriculum, were missing altogether.[39]

Proletkult organizers finally turned to workers' clubs as the primary vehicle to impart scientific education. These popular institutions could reach a larger audience than either the Proletkult studios or the universities and thus seemed to be able to bring the promise of a new science to the masses. Yet by the time the Proletkultists set out on this course during the New Economic Policy their educational agenda had shrunk yet

obrazovaniia za pervoe polugodie 1919 goda," *Griadushchee*, no. 5/6 (1919), pp. 30–31.

37. August 12, 1919, Proletkult central committee meeting, TsGALI f. 1230, op. 1, d. 3, l. 69.

38. For a discussion of local studios see the Proletkult plenum, June 28, 1922, TsGA RSFSR f. 2313, op. 1, d. 19, ll. 22–22 ob.; for the curriculum of the Rzhev science studio see *Gorn*, no. 6 (1922), pp. 155–56.

39. For the course plan see "Otchet po rabotam Nauchnoi Kollegii," *Gorn*, no. 8 (1923), p. 238.

again. The courses they proposed dealt with the rudiments of socialist theory, economic planning, and rational labor practices.[40] This was hardly an education for utopia that would shatter conventional perceptions of the world.

The Proletarian Family

In their writings on social values and social mores Proletkult theorists emerged as thoughtful critics of the proletarian family, which they felt inculcated the class-alien values of careerism, competition, and individualism. Proletkult analyses revealed a clear understanding of the influence of the family on social behavior. However, they also exposed a deep hostility to the privacy of the home and hearth. The family was viewed primarily as a negative force that posed a powerful threat to proletarian collectivism. Thus Proletkultists proposed to circumvent the family by drawing all family members into the public, collective world of the labor movement.

Before 1917 the Russian socialist movement, like its European counterparts, gave scant attention to family issues. It was widely held that the emancipation of women would inevitably follow in the wake of a socialist revolution, just as expanding labor opportunities for women would restructure family patterns. In the meantime most Russian socialists did not believe that these problems were of burning importance. Only with great difficulty and perseverance did some women organizers convince the Social Democratic Party to develop programs geared specifically to women workers.[41]

40. See, for example, "Obshchestvenno-nauchnyi kruzhok," *Rabochii klub*, no. 1 (1924), pp. 5–9; and V. F. Pletnev, *Rabochii klub: Printsipy i metody ego raboty*, 2d ed. (Moscow, 1925), pp. 22–38. For more on club education during the New Economic Policy see Chapter 8.

41. On the organizing efforts of the Social Democratic Party among working women see Richard Stites, *The Women's Liberation Movement in Russia: Feminism, Nihilism and Bolshevism, 1860–1930* (Princeton, 1978), esp. pp. 233–78; Rose L. Glickman, "The Russian Factory Woman, 1880–1914," in *Women in Russia*, ed. Dorothy At-

Radicals in the Proletkult had a better record on these issues than many of their Bolshevik counterparts. Although the student participants at the Capri and Bologna schools were all men, Aleksandra Kollontai came to Bologna to lecture on agitation among women workers.[42] In his Vperedist writings Aleksandr Bogdanov attacked the narrowness of proletarian family life. His utopian novel *Red Star*, written to popularize his political and social theories, was in part about the redefinition of sexual roles he felt the revolution would bring. Children were raised communally on socialist Mars. Women, freed from the tyranny of the home, held the same jobs as men and even looked similar to them. The Martian Netti, the book's heroine, was a gifted doctor and intergalactic explorer. Bogdanov's utopia held no place for the nuclear family.[43]

When the Bolsheviks came to power, they made the family a key part of their broad social agenda by purging family law of its most oppressive qualities. Divorce was simplified, abortion legalized, and economic provisions dictated equal pay for equal work. Women activists founded a special division of the Communist Party, the Zhenotdel, to ensure that women were informed of their new rights and encouraged to take leadership roles.[44] These measures met resistance from men, who

---

kinson, Alexander Dallin, and Gail Lapidus (Stanford, 1977), pp. 79–83; idem, *Russian Factory Women: Workplace and Society, 1880–1914* (Berkeley, 1984), pp. 242–80; and Anne Bobroff, "The Bolsheviks and Working Women, 1905–1920," *Soviet Studies*, vol. 26, no. 4 (1974), pp. 540–67.

42. S. Livshits, "Partiinaia shkola v Bolon'e, 1910–1911 gg.," *Proletarskaia revoliutsiia*, no. 3 (1926), p. 133.

43. Bogdanov's 1911 article, "Sotsializm v nastoiashchem," addressed family matters. See Bogdanov, *O proletarskoi kul'ture*, pp. 94–99. See also Bogdanov, *Red Star*, pp. 23–140, esp. pp. 68–74.

44. On the Zhenotdel see Stites, *The Women's Liberation Movement in Russia*, pp. 317–46; Carol Eubanks Hayden, "The Zhenotdel and the Bolshevik Party," *Russian History*, vol. 3, no. 2 (1976), pp. 150–73; and idem, "Feminism and Bolshevism: The Zhenotdel and the Politics of Women's Emancipation in Russia, 1917–1930" (Ph.D. diss., University of California, Berkeley, 1979).

were reluctant to give up their privileged position inside and outside the home, and also from women, who saw state measures as a frightening threat to the security that marriage had provided.[45] But for some, like the Bolshevik feminist Aleksandra Kollontai, the revolutionary programs did not go far enough. Like Bogdanov, she envisioned a society where the nuclear family would no longer be a social necessity.[46]

In the early Soviet debate on the family's future many Proletkult members sided with the radicals. They wanted to see the family's social functions, and particularly its child-rearing responsibilities, replaced by public organs, a course that would lead to the end of the old family. However, there was a curious gap between ends and means. Neither national nor local organizations developed realistic programs to implement their ideas. Bogdanov's own views were symptomatic. Although he offered a cogent criticism of the family's debilitating power,[47] he did not suggest how to move from the individualist tyranny of the old system to the communalist society depicted in his novels.

The failure of Proletkult organizations to place the proletarian family at the center of their practice was in part owing to these organizations' roots in the prerevolutionary socialist movement. Many local groups grew from a base in union and

45. On the social consequences of Bolshevik family laws see Barbara Evans Clements, "The Birth of the New Soviet Woman," in *Bolshevik Culture*, ed. Abbott Gleason, Peter Kenez, and Richard Stites (Bloomington, 1985), pp. 220–37; Beatrice Farnsworth, "Village Women Experience the Revolution," in Gleason, Kenez, and Stites, *Bolshevik Culture*, pp. 238–60; and Wendy Goldman, "Freedom and its Consequences: The Debate on the Soviet Family Code of 1926," *Russian History*, vol. 11, no. 4 (1984), pp. 362–88.

46. Barbara Evans Clements, *Bolshevik Feminist: The Life of Aleksandra Kollontai* (Bloomington, 1979), pp. 149–77, 225–41; and Alexandra Kollontai, *Selected Writings*, ed. and trans. Alix Holt (New York, 1977), pp. 113–50, 201–92. For a broad range of contemporary views on the family see William G. Rosenberg, ed., *Bolshevik Visions* (Ann Arbor, 1984), pp. 73–141.

47. See A. A. Bogdanov, *Elementy proletarskoi kul'tury v razvitii rabochego klassa* (Moscow, 1920), pp. 48–49.

factory clubs, which served mainly a male clientele. Efforts to solicit female participation before 1917 had been at best half-hearted.[48] Numerous Proletkultists retained these views after the revolution. When Pavel Lebedev-Polianskii examined the role of Proletkult clubs at the first national conference in 1918, he assumed that they would serve as a refuge from the family. He argued that each club needed a library because workers' apartments were too small and dark and the eager learner was too often interrupted by the noise of children. "It is imperative to create an atmosphere in the club where a person can learn to work in public life, freed from the clutches of petty family life."[49] Just what would happen to those left behind in the dismal, noisy apartment—presumably women and children—did not seem to concern him.

Proletkult artistic products reinforced this image of the working class and its institutions as an adult male sphere. The most common representation of the worker evoked in verse, placards, and song was the mighty male blacksmith with muscled arms and calloused hands, a recurrent theme in Western European socialist art as well.[50] The only family that really mattered was the surrogate family of the working class, with the conviviality of the shop floor and the warmth of workers' organizations. This surrogate family was almost exclusively a male preserve. Women and children were minor, almost missing, themes in the factory-centered thematic of Proletkult creation. "I am the son of labor," proclaimed one proletarian author.[51] Mikhail Gerasimov reserved his most tender lyrics for the workplace. In one poem he evoked his beloved factory under its kerchief of smoke with its melodious steel voice.[52] It was the factory, not a woman, that was the

48. See I. N. Kubikov, "Uchastie zhenshchin-rabotnits v klubakh," *Vestnik kul'tury i svobody*, no. 2 (1918), pp. 34–37.

49. *Protokoly pervoi konferentsii*, p. 96.

50. On Western European imagery see Eric Hobsbawm, "Man and Woman in Socialist Iconography," *History Workshop Journal*, no. 6 (1978), pp. 121–38.

51. Martyn, "Ia syn truda," *Krasnoe utro*, no. 1 (1919), p. 18.

52. Mikhail Gerasimov, "Vozvrashchenie," in *Stikhotvoreniia*, by Mikhail Gerasimov (Moscow, 1959), pp. 95–96.

object of his desire. In other works women only served to restrain male action in the world, as in the popular Civil War play *Don't Go* (*Ne khodi*), in which the heroine begged her husband not to join the Red Army.[53]

Because Proletkult leaders presented the organization as the cultural vanguard of the working class, they had no pressing reason to find an innovative way to restructure the family. The movement could only include the family if it extended itself to women workers, but women were traditionally much less skilled members of the proletariat. Russian working women also had very poor literacy levels because they had had far fewer educational opportunities open to them before the revolution. The prejudices of parents, fellow workers, and even women themselves often led to the attitude that female education was an unnecessary luxury.[54] For many male workers and political activists women remained a symbol of the unformed, superstitious attitudes that the working class had to leave behind.[55]

The solutions Proletkult participants devised to transform the proletarian family revealed the privileged position they tendered the male-dominated world of socialist institutions and also their deep-seated suspicions of female authority inside the home. They aimed to minimize the family's power by drawing women and children into the Proletkult and, wherever possible, by replacing private tasks with public ones. This policy would serve a dual function; it would reeducate women to accept their new role under socialism while limiting the family's ability to distort the values of future generations.

Discussions about the family were often really discussions about women and the power that they had to destroy the goals

53. See "Khronika Proletkul'ta," *Proletarskaia kul'tura*, no. 20/21, p. 53. For a similar view of women see Il'ia Sadof'ev, "Nashel," *Griadushchee*, no. 12/13 (1920), pp. 4–8.

54. Glickman, *Russian Factory Women*, pp. 132–45.

55. See S. A. Smith, *Red Petrograd* (Cambridge, Eng., 1983), pp. 192–97; and Clements, "The Birth of the New Soviet Woman," pp. 220–25.

of the revolution. Numerous Proletkult commentators insisted that women had to be taught to value what the revolution had to offer them.[56] Most important, female participants had to learn to change their limited perspective on society, the family, and the home because women were the main inculcators of class-alien values. As one orator at the national congress in 1918 insisted, the best way to eradicate petty-bourgeois attitudes in daily life was to reeducate women in Proletkult programs.[57]

Yet even the most modest step in this program, encouraging women workers and working-class wives to join Proletkult activities, was not seriously addressed by many local organizations. A handful of intellectual women headed important local groups and earned a place on the national governing board, but local records show that female participants were always in the minority.[58] When P. N. Zubova joined a theatrical troupe touring the front lines in 1920, only two other women accompanied her.[59] Some groups had no female members at all.[60]

Those organizations with a more successful record of female participation made a special effort to gain women's interest. The Proletkult in Kostroma, a textile town with a high percentage of women workers, had fairly high female participation rates in its main club. The club organizer, M. A. Rostopchina, made sure that the agitators who tried to get women to join were women themselves, and she also planned

56. See, for example, Ivan Knizhnik, "Na grany novoi kul'tury," *Griadushchee*, no. 11 (1920), p. 2; I. Fuks, "Rabotnitsa v svete novoi kul'ture," *Griadushchaia kul'tura*, no. 3 (1919), pp. 14–15; and P. Rabochii, "Zhenskoe tvorchestvo," *Zori griadushchego*, no. 1 (1922), pp. 121–22.

57. *Protokoly pervoi konferentsii*, pp. 98–99.

58. See, for example, "Svedeniia o studiitsakh Izhevskogo Proletkul'ta," TsGALI f. 1230, op. 1, d. 1221, l. 73; and "Spisok studiitsev," Tver, 1921, d. 1525, ll. 66–69.

59. "Vospominaniia P. N. Zubovoi," TsGALI f. 1230, op. 2, d. 14, l. 3.

60. *Proletkul't* (Tver), no. 3/4 (1919), p. 54.

special reading circles aimed specifically at women workers. According to published participation figures these efforts bore fruit. In the beginning most club users were male, but soon the number of women rose until they constituted 35 percent of the members and on any given day might make up 40 percent of those using club facilities.[61]

The Tula Proletkult initially also reached out to include female members. Vasilii Ignatov and his collaborator, the local party leader Grigorii Kaminskii, appealed directly to women in the organization's first announcement:

Comrade women workers! If in the past you were beaten down and exhausted, now even for you a new day has begun. Now you, together with your fathers, husbands, and brothers, can take part in the building of a new Communist life with equal rights. Don't turn away from them. Don't shut yourself off as you once did in your rooms, corners, and basements. Come bravely to your Proletkult. Give it your leisure time and take a creative part in building class cultural values. Come, and don't be ashamed of your age, your semiliteracy, or even your complete illiteracy.[62]

The elaborate membership rules drawn up in early 1919 censured male behavior that might offend women, such as rude language, teasing, and the use of insulting nicknames.[63]

But experiences in Tula illustrated that it took more than progressive rules or posters to raise female participation figures. Although the Tula organization quickly developed diverse cultural studios, among them even a workshop for circus techniques, there was no general educational division and no literacy programs for those semiliterate women to whom

61. M. Rostopchina, "Kul'tura nasha," *Sbornik Kostromskogo Proletkul'ta*, no. 1 (1919), pp. 8–10, 15, 19–20, 28–29.
62. "Ot Proletkul'ta k Tul'skomu proletariatu," 1919, TsGALI f. 1230, op. 1, d. 1536, l. 74. On the drafting of this appeal see N. A. Milonov, "O deiatel'nosti Tul'skogo Proletkul'ta," in *Aktual'nye voprosy istorii literatury*, ed. Z. I. Levinson, N. A. Milonov, and A. F. Sergeicheva (Tula, 1969), p. 147.
63. "Ustav," 1919, TsGALI f. 1230, op. 1, d. 1536, l. 1.

the poster was addressed. In 1921 only eight out of fifty-four studio participants were women.[64]

Faced with evidence of low female participation, some of the movement's members fell back on the common panaceas prevalent in early Soviet writings on the family: as socialism took hold and technology evolved, family problems would automatically be resolved. "Even now the woman worker remains in very bad conditions," lamented one writer in Tambov, "and it is our responsibility to try to free her from them." But the only solution the author proposed was the vague hope that machines would someday take over women's more unpleasant household tasks, like mending and laundry.[65]

Although the status of women remained a marginal issue for many members, the fate of proletarian children sparked more interest. Women embodied all the problems of the past, but children were the hope of the future. When addressing the problems of the young, Proletkultists revealed yet another mark against the old family: it inhibited the radical potential of children. In the opinion of one Petrograd activist, Elena Bagdateva, the Proletkult had to become involved in child care to shield young people from the harmful effects of "the petty-bourgeois mother, the money-grubbing father, and the bigoted grandmother."[66] The school and the workplace should become as important to children as the family. The Moscow Proletkult even passed a "Declaration of Children's Rights," which guaranteed that children could pick their own form of education, their own religion, and could even leave their parents if they chose.[67] Some took these ideas to their logical conclusion. They wanted the Proletkult to assume responsibility for all proletarian children by taking them from their

64. Statistics on Tula studio participants, December 15, 1921, TsGALI f. 1230, op. 1, d. 1538, ll. 28–29.

65. I. Fuks, "Zhenshchina v svete novoi kul'tury," *Griadushchaia kul'tura*, no. 3 (1919), pp. 14–15, quotation p. 14.

66. E. Bagdat'eva, "Detskii Proletkul't," *Griadushchee*, no. 6 (1918), p. 14.

67. *Moskovskaia konferentsiia*, p. 39.

homes at an early age. This was necessary, according to one male participant, in order to combat the conservative influence of their parents, especially their mothers.[68]

Such grandiose schemes far surpassed Proletkult resources and would hardly have been sanctioned by either Narkompros or working-class families themselves. A more modest course taken by some local circles was to open special "Children's Proletkults" (*Detskie Proletkul'ty*), which catered to young people ages eight to sixteen. The most successful of these opened in Tula in 1919.[69] It even published its own newspaper, staffed and edited by the young participants themselves.

The contents of the Tula paper, titled *Children's Proletkult* (*Detskii Proletkul't*), reveal young people's hostility to the confines of conventional family life. Enthusiastic revolutionary youths expressed their hopes for a special proletarian culture for children that would be based on a highly developed sense of children's self-worth and autonomy. In these articles children and youth appeared as the real revolutionaries who needed to inspire recalcitrant, backward adults to revolutionary acts. "We have to do more than awaken and organize other children," wrote one fourteen-year-old girl. "We have to awaken and organize our fathers, mothers, older brothers, and sisters to come to the defense of the revolution."[70] According to the organization's young leader, Dmitrii Pozhidaev, the Children's Proletkult would liberate young people from the despotism of the petty-bourgeois family and give them useful social tasks.[71]

Although no other provincial organization developed a net-

68. *Protokoly pervoi konferentsii*, pp. 62–71, 53.

69. Report from V. V. Ignatov, July 8, 1919, TsGALI f. 1230, op. 1, d. 1538, ll. 9 ob.–10.

70. Aleksandra Vagina, "Tovarishchi-deti," *Detskii Proletkul't*, no. 4 (1920), p. 2; see also A. Sokolova, "K rabochim," ibid., no. 1 (1919), p. 3.

71. D. Pozhidaev, "Detskii gubernskii Proletkul't," *Proletarskoe stroitel'stvo*, no. 2 (1919), pp. 28–29.

work as large as Tula's, many sponsored special activities for children. The Rybinsk and Syzran Proletkults had separate children's sectors, and the Tver, Rzhev, Vladikavkaz, and Pushkinskii raion groups opened children's studios.[72] Some factory circles supported child-care facilities. According to one organizer in Cheliabinsk, the most enthusiastic response to his attempt to found a Proletkult came from the female secretary of the local soviet, who told him that mothers wanted to start groups for their children.[73]

None of this, however, amounted to a consistent or coherent policy. Proletkult programs were simply not equal to the colossal task of social transformation. Like many other early Soviet radicals, Proletkult organizers assumed that the family would wither away on its own as its basic child-rearing tasks were assumed by state and workers' institutions. "It seemed to us that the bourgeois world had crashed down and that its remains—former family and property relations, the dependence of women, and even the 'domestic economy'—were already buried forever," reminisced a woman who had attended the first Zhenotdel congress in 1918. "Reading the reports and resolutions of this congress now, one is simply astonished [to see] the ease with which they projected the complete transformation of the old world, state sponsored child-rearing, changes in marital relations, the destruction of the domestic economy, and so on."[74]

By the start of the New Economic Policy it was obvious that

72. Local questionnaires from Rybinsk, TsGALI f. 1230, op. 1, d. 117, ll. 96–97; from Syran, d. 114, l. 125; and from Tver, d. 1527, l. 55. For Rzhev see *Griadushchee*, no. 9/12 (1921), p. 100; and for Vladikavkaz see *Proletkul't* (Vladikavkaz), no. 1 (1919), p. 13.

73. There were child-care facilities at the Tula Armaments Works and the Tomna factory in Kineshma; see the local questionnaires in TsGALI f. 1230, op. 1, d. 1540, ll. 4–4 ob. and d. 117, l. 34. On efforts to start child-care in Cheliabinsk see the May 25, 1920, report by a local organizer, d. 1238, l. 5 ob.

74. V. Golubeva, "Vserossiiskii s"ezd rabotnits i krest'ianok," *Kommunistka*, no. 11 (1923), p. 18. See also Hayden, "Feminism and Bolshevism," p. 139.

old social mores could not be so easily uprooted. The state was not going to take over all of the home's functions, and the family would not melt away on its own. Only then did Proletkultists begin to take the need for pragmatic measures more seriously, rather than loudly predicting the family's demise. Focusing their efforts primarily on workers' clubs, Proletkult organizers tried to devise methods to increase female participation, such as offering day-care centers and special discussion groups that addressed women's needs. Once in the club women would be taught about socialism and the accomplishments of the revolution and would also receive special courses in child-rearing.[75]

Most of these suggestions hardly challenged socially accepted gender roles; women were exhorted to become better socialists by becoming better socialist mothers. Rather than proposing that men assume part of the onerous burden of housework, Proletkult literature suggested that women form collective kitchens and rationalize their labor in the home. These proposals were light years away from the world of Bogdanov's Martian heroine, but they did acknowledge that the working class was made up of both men and women, something earlier proletarian circles had been loath to do.

Clubs—The Public Hearth

During the early Soviet years Proletkultists looked more and more to clubs as their major tool to transform social habits and values. There is a certain irony in this approach because, unlike proletarian universities, clubs were not utopian constructs. Instead they were old and venerable working-class institutions. They had served as an important focal point in workers' political and cultural lives long before the October

75. See, for example, V. F. Pletnev, "Zadachi i metody raboty kruzhka po bytu," *Rabochii klub*, no. 1 (1924), pp. 29–31; and M. R. [M. A. Rostopchina], "Rabota kluba po bytovom fronte," *Rabochii klub*, no. 2 (1924), pp. 37–38.

Revolution because they provided a place to gather, hear lectures, read books, and, if need be, to disguise political activity under the cover of cultural work. In the first years of Soviet power clubs were very popular and were sponsored by an impressive array of local groups.[76] Many Proletkults, including the first organization in Petrograd, owed their existence in large part to the efforts of club members.

Clubs appealed to Proletkult activists because they could link cultural creation to issues that directly affected workers' daily lives. During the hard years of the Civil War clubs served as a home away from home for many laborers facing rapidly deteriorating living conditions.[77] They offered food, warmth, and conviviality in a period of great social dislocation. The hostility that Proletkult theorists already felt for the privacy of the home and the individualism of family values was transformed into a positive endorsement of clubs as a "public hearth" (*obshchestvennyi ochag*).[78] For some, clubs served as a model for the future socialist society.[79]

Because of their ties to local communities, clubs were attractive to many national institutions seeking a closer rela-

76. On clubs in the revolutionary period see G. E. Bylin, "Rabochie kluby i kul'turno-prosvetitel'nye komissii profsoiuzov i fabzavkomov Petrograda v mirnyi period razvitiia revoliutsii," *Uchenye zapiski VPSh VTsSPS*, vol. 2 (1970), pp. 108–18; Gabriele Gorzka, "Proletarian Culture in Practice: Workers' Clubs in the Period 1917–1921," in *Essays in Soviet History*, ed. J. W. Strong (forthcoming); A. K. Kolesova, "Deiatel'nost' rabochikh klubov po Kommunisticheskomu vospitaniiu trudiashchikhsia v 1917–1923 gg." (Candidate dissertation, Moscow State University, 1969); idem, "Prakticheskaia deiatel'nost' rabochego kluba v 1917–1920 godakh," *Uchenye zapiski Moskovskogo gosudarstvennogo instituta kul'tury*, vol. 17 (1968), pp. 231–49; and I. N. Kubikov, "Rabochie kluby v Petrograde," *Vestnik kul'tury i svobody*, no. 1 (1918), pp. 34–37.
77. Gorzka, "Proletarian Culture in Practice." See also idem, "Alltag der städtischen Arbeiterschaft in Sowjetrussland, 1918–1921," *Archiv für Sozialgeschichte*, no. 25 (1985), pp. 137–57.
78. The term is Mikhail Zverev's, "Klub ili obshchestvennyi ochag," *Griadushchee*, no. 5/6 (1919), p. 23.
79. Stefan Krivtsov, *Protokoly pervoi konferentsii*, p. 90; and A., "Rabochie kluby," *Proletkul't* (Vladikavkaz), no. 1 (1919), p. 15.

tionship to the laboring population and to the industrial proletariat in particular. During the Civil War and the first years
of the New Economic Policy Narkompros, the Communist
Party, the national union organization, and the Proletkult all
competed for influence in club networks in order to forge links
to "the broad mass of workers." Because most clubs offered
some form of lectures and classes, they were an attractive
vehicle for those who wished to imbue the masses with the
new socialist spirit.

Initially, Proletkultists advocated a loose affiliation with
existing clubs in the hope that the clubs could serve as a
training ground for their activities. Delegates to the Moscow
Proletkult conference in February 1918 argued that city clubs
could prepare members for more rigorous creative activity.
They should have tea rooms, cafeterias, and reading rooms for
general use. The Proletkult's job would be to oversee cultural
work in these independent bodies, which would be tied to, but
not part of, its own apparatus.[80]

However, this path proved too modest for the central leaders, who quickly outlined an ambitious plan for a special kind
of Proletkult club. Fedor Kalinin proposed an ideal intellectual environment, almost like a small university, where workers could find information on union affairs, government programs, and legal problems. Clubs would offer myriad cultural
stimuli and studios as well as lectures and study circles. The
range of activities was to be so broad that Kalinin called the
club "a universal studio for the practical realization of the
proletarian cultural program, a living laboratory that em-
braces all aspects of workers' lives."[81] In other words, he
hoped to turn the club into an intensive study center, leaving
little time for leisure. This distinctive approach gained an
official stamp of approval at the first national conference in
1918. Local organizations were advised to form a special club

80. *Moskovskaia konferentsiia*, pp. 8–14.
81. F. Kalinin, "Rabochii klub," *Proletarskaia kul'tura*, no. 2
(1918), pp. 13–15, quotation p. 13.

division (*klubnyi otdel* or *klubo*) and start their own clubs, which would serve as "the heartbeat and brain of the working class."[82]

According to central guidelines Proletkult clubs had to provide extensive educational services, including classes in the social sciences, art history, law, and socialist theory. In addition, they were supposed to offer a broad array of creative artistic workshops.[83] Yet another crucial function of the club was the transformation of daily life (*byt*) to reflect the values of socialism. In this area, however, the center issued no specific instructions; presumably, new patterns of social interaction and collectivity would emerge in the laboratory of the club itself.

The national organization devoted considerable resources to club expansion, even financing groups that were not formally part of the Proletkult network.[84] Its ambitious demands for highly structured programs encouraged some local organizations to try to centralize all proletarian clubs under Proletkult control, including those sponsored by other organizations. Such actions, however, met concerted opposition, particularly from the Adult Education Division in Narkompros. The Petrograd Proletkult, for example, founded a club division that helped to supply some 120 city clubs in 1919.[85] But Narkompros quickly challenged the Proletkult's role and installed itself as the main coordinator of city clubs by the following year.[86]

82. *Protokoly pervoi konferentsii*, pp. 49, 90–100, quotation p. 90.

83. See "Primernyi ustav rabochego kluba," *Proletarskaia kul'-tura*, no. 7/8 (1919), pp. 62–67.

84. See, for example, the discussion on funding for the Moscow club "Third International," TsGALI f. 1230, op. 1, d. 3, ll. 35, 37.

85. "Rezoliutsiia klubnoi sektsii po dokladu t. Kudelli," *Gria-dushchee*, no. 5/6 (1919), pp. 28–29; and *Vneshkol'noe obrazovanie* (Petrograd), no. 4/5 (1919), pp. 70–71.

86. *Petrogradskaia obshchegorodskaia konferentsiia rabochikh klubov: Stenograficheskii otchet* (Petrograd, 1920), pp. 3, 12. For a similar conflict in Moscow see Vladimir Faidysh's March 10, 1919, report in the Moscow Proletkult, TsGALI f. 1230, op. 1, d. 35, l. 2;

Efforts at centralization also backfired because they undermined the clubs' community base. The Moscow Proletkult conducted a study of factory clubs in 1920 and concluded that they were not at all well organized: instead of operating disparate, poorly funded groups factories should consolidate their resources and open regional city clubs that could serve several factories at once.[87] But the cure proved worse than the disease. When club activists formed larger regional circles, they discovered that the new circles were too far away from the workplace and thus were inaccessible to many workers because of the poor state of public transportation. The Moscow division was forced to admit that its rationalization attempts had been a failure.[88]

One of the best documented and most successful Proletkult circles was the First Workers' Socialist Club in Kostroma. It helped members find apartments, furniture, food, and also served as a general information center.[89] In addition to these practical functions, it offered lectures on a variety of topics, from physics to agriculture, and also sponsored literacy courses and artistic studios. The published responses of Kostroma club members were filled with enthusiastic praise. "Our comrades fill up the room," wrote one. "The piano starts playing. The telephone rings. The lecturer begins his talk. I listen and absorb everything into my head and try not to lose anything new and bright."[90]

Although most other circles could not match the variety of Kostroma's programs, they nonetheless were popular gathering spots for the laboring population. Workers and employees supported clubs through dues, payroll deductions, and special

---

Izvestiia TsIK, January 11, 1919, p. 4; and *Gorn*, no. 2/3 (1919), pp. 126–27.

87. *Gorn*, no. 2/3 (1919), pp. 126–27; no. 5 (1920), pp. 71–80, 86–87.

88. *Gudki*, no. 1 (1919), p. 4; no. 2 (1919), p. 27; and *Gorn*, no. 5 (1920), pp. 86–87.

89. M. Rostopchina, "Kul'tura nasha," *Sbornik Kostromskogo Proletkul'ta*, no. 1 (1919), pp. 6, 10.

90. "Vpechatleniia rabochikh ot klubnoi zhizni," ibid., p. 36.

fees for public events. Club cafeterias were an important source of food in hungry cities and towns, and when supplies were scarce, attendance suffered. Libraries distributed newspapers, journals, and books, and program committees offered lectures, classes, and discussion groups. At the Kamenka factory "Proletklub" workers and employees took part in artistic circles, literacy courses, and listened to lectures on scientific themes like "What is Electricity?" Popular public readings familiarized members with the works of Tolstoi, Gogol, Lermontov, and even *Uncle Tom's Cabin*.[91]

Despite this evidence of a lively network, central organizers were often dissatisfied with local accomplishments. One problem was that many Proletkults had no clubs at all. This was the case in Kolpino and Polekova, even though both had fairly successful artistic studios. The same was true for the larger groups in Archangel and Ekaterinburg.[92] Organizers directed familiar complaints to Moscow. They did not have the staff, the funds, or the space to open clubs. One Tver activist reported that work there had gotten off to a very slow start because neither of the city's major factories could provide rooms for club activities.[93]

But existing clubs did not please the critics either. These circles were faulted either because of their "strictly educational" approach or because of the low level of their cultural work. The ideal mix of education, creation, and conviviality was difficult to find.[94] At the Proletkult club in the Pudemskii factory, Viatka province, there were no lectures or special classes. The only educational component consisted of public readings from *Proletarian Culture*. Instead, activities revolved around a lively theater that performed classic and contempo-

91. April 1, 1919, protocol of a local club meeting, TsGALI f. 1230, op. 1, d. 1265, l. 25.

92. Local questionnaires from Kolpino, TsGALI f. 1230, op. 1, d. 430, l. 93; from Polekova, d. 117, l. 51; from Archangel, d. 117, ll. 77–77 ob.; and from Ekaterinburg, d. 117, ll. 80–80 ob.

93. "Klubnoe delo v Tveri," *Proletkul't* (Tver), no. 3/4 (1919), pp. 35–36.

94. See, for example, P. Knyshov, "O soderzhanii klubnoi raboty," *Gorn*, no. 4 (1919), pp. 55–57.

rary plays.[95] In the Ivanovo-Voznesensk Proletkult clubs offered basic educational courses and little else. The organizers complained that they could not sustain creative workshops because there were not enough instructors and the participants were poorly prepared.[96]

The most serious criticism of all, however, was that local club work was frivolous, thereby perpetuating petty-bourgeois attitudes. In the opinion of central organizers Russian workers' clubs had always been distinguished by their serious nature, as opposed to Western European clubs, which were little more than bars.[97] This sober view made club workers even more intolerant of groups that served primarily as friendly spots to eat, drink, talk, and, worst of all, dance. Stefan Krivtsov, who wrote frequently on club life in *Proletarian Culture*, continually railed against circles that served as teahouses, dance halls, "or worse." "In place of a club in Iaroslavl they ended up with a cookhouse," lamented Krivtsov. "The same goes for the club in Petrovsk. They named it after comrade Lenin and it should have the clearest and loftiest goals, such as the unification of workers and the awakening of their interest in and love for art. Instead, they have some sort of free love unions."[98]

These censorious attitudes only grew more pronounced as the Proletkult faced increasing competition from its cultural rivals. In late 1920 Narkompros transformed its Adult Education Division into the Chief Committee for Political Education, or Glavpolitprosvet, which tried to take control of all forms of club activity.[99] As the Proletkult's influence began to

95. Local questionnaire, TsGALI f. 1230, op. 1, d. 117, l. 58.

96. "Material k istorii Proletkul'ta," TsGALI f. 1230, op. 1, d. 1245, ll. 6–7; local questionnaire, d. 117, l. 50 ob.

97. O. Zol', "Kluby—iacheiki proletarskoi klassovoi samodeiatel'nosti," *Griadushchee*, no. 5 (1918), p. 9; and *Protokoly pervoi konferentsii*, p. 91.

98. "Khronika Proletkul'ta," *Proletarskaia kul'tura*, no. 7/8 (1919), p. 68. See also *Proletarskaia kul'tura*, no. 5 (1918), p. 41; no. 6 (1919), p. 34; no. 11/12 (1919), pp. 61–62.

99. On the formation of Glavpolitprosvet see Fitzpatrick, *Commissariat*, pp. 186–96. On Glavpolitprosvet and Proletkult club work

wane, its leaders made ever more strident efforts to distinguish their clubs from those of other institutions in order to provide a justification for the Proletkult's continued independence. Proletkult clubs were superior to union and Narkompros circles, argued the central leadership, because they placed creative work at the center of their programs. They alone were committed to changing the patterns of everyday life.[100] The national leadership explicitly stated that Proletkult clubs were intended to facilitate artistic and scientific discovery, not to meet the rudimentary demands of poorly educated participants.[101]

The transformation of daily life and daily habits became an ever more common theme for Proletkult club activists, particularly during the first years of the New Economic Policy. Proletkult leaders worried that the reinvigoration of capitalist trading would encourage petty-bourgeois behavior. Clubs, however, could be a bulwark against this danger. They would serve as the "basic creative cell for the proletarianization of daily life."[102] But in a marked shift from the Civil War years, the values that were to emerge were predefined. In a more forceful fashion than ever before Proletkult organizers prescribed the proper forms of proletarian behavior that the clubs were meant to imbue: mores would change as workers became more punctual, more sober, and more knowledgeable about politics and the economy.

At the heart of Proletkult club work lay curious contradictions. On the one hand, the clubs were the movement's last bastion of experimentation, the places where science, the family, and daily life were to be immutably altered. On the other hand, Proletkult leaders seemed determined to under-

see A. K. Kolesova, "Preodolenie v deiatel'nosti rabochikh klubov vliianiia oshibochnykh teorii Proletkul'ta," *Uchenye zapiski Moskovskogo gosudarstvennogo instituta kul'tury*, vol. 15 (1968), p. 317.

100. See *Proletarskaia kul'tura*, no. 17/19 (1920), p. 82.

101. See "Deklaratsiia, priniataia plenumom Vserossiiskogo Ts. K. Proletkul'ta 19 dekabria 1920," *Griadushchee*, no. 4/6 (1921), p. 58.

102. Ibid.

mine the very elements that made these circles popular. Although praising clubs for their ties to the broad masses, Proletkultists called for demanding programs that depended on highly literate and well-prepared participants. Although they valued the clubs' roots in local communities, they tried to centralize and standardize their work. They singled out clubs as the best expression of workers' creativity and independence but nonetheless began to dictate the very values such autonomy was meant to achieve.

———————

Proletkultists were inspired by a vision of the future that lent a utopian fervor to all they undertook. When described by the organization's enthusiasts, even ordinary cultural events like piano lessons and science lectures had the potential to transform the world. Although this transcendent image of the new society was never abandoned, the Proletkult's utopianism was significantly muted during the first years of Soviet power. Proponents of proletarian science moved away from grand schemes; instead they turned to modest courses meant to encourage political awareness and labor discipline. The critics of the family quickly stopped waiting for its demise; they devised limited plans to rationalize household chores. Those who offered a hazy promise of socialist habits and mores recast in the fire of revolution ended up with agitational campaigns to promote sobriety and punctuality.

This loss of revolutionary fervor was not unique to the Proletkult. Communist Party activists who believed they had seen the end of private ownership and private trade had to accept the sobering initiation of the New Economic Policy. The critics of political bureaucracies witnessed a speedy centralization process that set their dream of a stateless society off into the unknown future. The advocates of educational experiments who hoped to erase the distinction between mental and physical labor were challenged by the pragmatic needs of the Soviet economy. Everywhere political activists raised their voices against utopian luxuries—the luxury of worker-run factories, of egalitarian schooling, and even the "luxury of discussion and argument," Lenin's way to discourage oppositional tendencies within the party.[103] The Civil War, with its peculiar mix of hardship and heroism, had nurtured radical schemes. But when the hard task of reconstruction began, such schemes seemed oddly unsuited to the task.

The Proletkult's shift in tactics was in part a conscious strategy as its participants came to realize that the revolution would not undermine old social institutions as thoroughly as they had hoped. Rather than vainly predicting the end of the family or blaming women for their backwardness, they chose the slower road of inclusion and education. Instead of starting elaborate and expensive new institutions, they shifted the locus of educational work to their own clubs.

Nonetheless, this new course was not entirely voluntary. Club activists proposed ever more specialized programs as a way to distinguish their work from other groups and thus protect the independence of their circles. Bogdanov's plans for an innovative proletarian university were not even given a chance to be tested. The organization's pragmatism reflected the rapidly shrinking sphere allotted to it by its cultural competitors. By the end of the Civil War both Narkompros and the Communist Party had grown impatient with the Proletkult's ambitious cultural agenda and were eager to expedite its retreat from utopia.

103. *Desiatyi s"ezd Rossiiskoi Kommunisticheskoi partii: Stenograficheskii otchet* (Moscow, 1921), p. 2.

7

The Proletkult in Crisis

In October 1920, just as the worst of the Civil War was past, Proletkult delegates gathered in Moscow to discuss what seemed to be the bright future of their cause. The organization's mass base promised to grow as the new era of peace saw the return of workers to the factories. The national leaders were convinced that Proletkult work would improve in quality now that the agitational tasks of the war were over. They even foresaw international expansion and support. But these optimistic projections were quickly undermined. By the conclusion of the conference the Communist Party Central Committee forced the Proletkult to give up its independence and become part of the state's cultural bureaucracy, thereby initiating a period of precipitous decline for the organization.

The Communist Party's assault on the Proletkult is often presented as the logical result of Lenin's longstanding animus against Bogdanov.[1] Although certainly a factor, this animus alone cannot explain the timing or the vehemence of the party's actions. Bogdanov, after all, had taken part in the Proletkult from the very beginning, and he retained a leading

---

1. See, for example, Robert C. Williams, *The Other Bolsheviks* (Bloomington, 1985), pp. 185–87.

position a full year after its subordination. Proletkult autonomy, not Bogdanov, was the prime target of the central committee's attacks in the fall of 1920, when the imminent end to
the war marked yet another crisis for the new regime. Despite
the hardships, the Civil War had worked as a cohesive force
for the Soviet state. Many potential critics feared the Whites
more than the Bolsheviks and thus put aside their doubts
until the outcome was certain. But as the war drew to a close,
debates about the future of the country began anew. Emergency solutions to military problems lost their primary
justification. Union activists began to clamor for a more central role in economic planning. Critical factions within the
Communist Party called for reorganization and decentralization. In response the party leadership moved quickly to undercut potentially troublesome groups, among them the Proletkult.

A central issue in the heated political discussions that
began in 1920 was the future role of proletarian institutions.
The state had mobilized (and eventually militarized) Russian
labor during the war while restricting labor unions mainly to
disciplinary tasks. Although labor leaders accepted these
conditions in the context of the military crisis, once a Red
victory seemed certain some began to chafe against them.
Trade unionists were particularly opposed to plans to continue labor militarization into the postwar period to meet the
new emergency of economic reconstruction. These proposals
aimed to fuse the unions with the state bureaucracy.[2]

This course was most vehemently rejected by the leftist
trade union activists known as the Workers' Opposition. With
a following in the Metalworkers' Union, in Moscow, Samara,
the Urals, and the Ukraine, the Workers' Opposition de-

2. On the trade union debates see Edward Hallett Carr, *The
Bolshevik Revolution, 1917–1923* (New York, 1952), vol. 2, pp. 198–
227; Robert V. Daniels, *Conscience of the Revolution* (New York,
1960), pp. 119–36; Jay B. Sorenson, *The Life and Death of Soviet Trade
Unionism, 1917–1928* (New York, 1969), pp. 106–28; and Thomas
Remington, *Building Socialism in Bolshevik Russia* (Pittsburgh,
1984), pp. 92–101.

manded that the trade unions be granted real independence and the power to control the economy. Their insistence on autonomy sounded very similar to Proletkult demands. Indeed, the major theoretical statement of the Workers' Opposition, written by Aleksandra Kollontai, coincided with the Proletkult's vision of the Soviet order on many levels. The Workers' Opposition attacked the prevalence of nonworkers, particularly specialists, within the Soviet system; its solution to the growing bureaucratization in the party and the state was to allow more room for workers' independent action (*samodeiatel'nost'*), a key word in the Proletkult vocabulary.[3] The members of the Workers' Opposition also criticized internal party organization, insisting that the Bolshevik leadership pay more attention to the rank and file and introduce wider discussion and debate.[4] Another critical faction, the Democratic Centralists, shared some of these complaints, arguing that the party was overcentralized.[5] Although the Democratic Centralists and the Workers' Opposition did not unite around their common grievances, the appearance of such vocal critics worried the party leadership and eventually led to the ban on factions at the Tenth Party Congress in 1921.

   In addition to this dissent among their allies, the Bolsheviks also had to ponder the daunting problem of the Russian peasantry. During the Civil War peasant sympathy for the regime's land programs had been worn thin by grain requisitions at gunpoint. In the summer of 1920 the peasantry in Tambov province erupted in a partisan war against Soviet power that helped to convince the government that forced requisitions could not long continue. It was painfully clear

   3. A. Kollontai, *Rabochaia oppozitsiia* (Moscow, 1921), pp. 37–45.
   4. Indeed, Kollontai insisted on more *glasnost'*, a demand with a very contemporary sound, ibid., p. 44.
   5. On the Democratic Centralists see Robert Service, *The Bolshevik Party in Revolution, 1917–1923* (London, 1979), pp. 51–53, 144–46; and Ekkehard Klug, "Die Gruppe des Demokratischen Zentralismus und der 10. Parteitag der KPR(b) im März 1921," *Jahrbücher für die Geschichte Osteuropas*, vol. 35 (1987), pp. 36–58.

that the state had to shift to noncoercive economic measures if it were to forge a modicum of support for the regime.

As they pondered new economic approaches, government leaders also began to give even greater consideration to propaganda and education as a way to imbue the population with a unified, pro-Soviet spirit. In August 1920 the Communist Party created a special division of agitation and propaganda, usually known as Agitprop, to oversee all Soviet institutions involved in political education.[6] At the same time, Narkompros created its own section for political enlightenment, Glavpolitprosvet, out of its former Adult Education Division.[7] Because the exact duties of these two new groups were not clearly defined, they were potentially in conflict. Nonetheless, their almost simultaneous creation illustrated the appearance of a new emphasis on political education as a way to cement the social order.

Although the Proletkult had mainly worked as a loyal propagandist for the Red cause during the Civil War, it nonetheless embodied potentially threatening principles. Its insistence on autonomy had an ominous ring at a time when other groups were making their own case for independence and authority. Its claims to a large following among rank-and-file workers made it a possible candidate for opposition. Finally, it oversaw a broad network of cultural and political education programs theoretically free from party and state control. Thus, with or without Bogdanov's provocative presence, Lenin had ample motivation to turn against the movement as the country made its rocky transition from war to peace.

The End of Proletkult Autonomy

From its inception the Proletkult had faced local challenges to its independence from labor unions, local party committees,

6. Peter Kenez, *The Birth of the Propaganda State* (Cambridge, Eng., 1985), pp. 124–25.
7. Sheila Fitzpatrick, *The Commissariat of Enlightenment* (Cambridge, Eng., 1970), pp. 166–76.

and state organs. Narkompros workers were its most persistent critics. Nadezhda Krupskaia, head of the Adult Education Division and, later, Glavpolitprosvet, never saw any justification for Proletkult autonomy because she did not think the organization served any special cultural function. Instead, it was a "completely ordinary educational organization, its practice and class composition hardly distinguishable from Narkompros organizations."[8] Since 1918 Krupskaia had tried to absorb the Proletkult into the Adult Education Division, raising the issue at every opportunity. In May 1919, at the first national conference of adult education workers, she determined that because the Proletkult was in essence an adult education organization, it belonged under the aegis of Narkompros. With her encouragement the delegates voted overwhelmingly to tie the Proletkult to her division.[9]

This decision provoked protests from local Proletkult organizations. One disgruntled Proletkultist in Tambov querulously inquired why the state kept reopening an issue that had long been settled.[10] The presidium of the Ivanovo-Voznesensk organization expressed anger and bewilderment. How could anyone object to an independent working-class organization? "Proletkults have firmly established their organizations in factories and plants and have taken hold among the working class. If we eliminate them, we will uproot the basis of cultural-educational activity among the workers."[11]

To clear up the confusion, representatives from Narkompros and the Proletkult met in June 1919 to define the terms of their relations yet again. Lunacharskii, Krupskaia, and Lebedev-Polianskii agreed to a compromise that seemed to offer

8. N. K. Krupskaia, "Neskol'ko slov o Proletkul'te," in *Pedagogicheskie sochineniia v desiati tomakh*, by N. K. Krupskaia (Moscow, 1961), vol. 7, p. 60.

9. "O Proletkul'te," *Vneshkol'noe obrazovanie* (Moscow), no. 4/6 (1919), columns 171–72; and *Izvestiia TsIK*, May 13, 1919.

10. S. Kluben', "Proletkul't i Narobraz," *Griadushchaia kul'tura*, no. 6/7 (1919), pp. 19–21.

11. "Svedeniia, kasaiushchiesia deiatel'nosti Proletkul'ta," *Tsentral'nyi Gosudarstvennyi Arkhiv RSFSR* [henceforth cited as TsGA RSFSR] f. 2306, op. 17, d. 9, ll. 1–4, quotation l. 3.

something for everyone. Local Proletkults were to become subsections of local Adult Education Divisions, which partially confirmed the decision of Krupskaia's section. However, they could continue to conduct their work independently with their own separate budgets.[12] This ambiguous ruling did little to resolve the issue. In some towns, such as Tver, Proletkult workers came to an amiable agreement with the Adult Education Division.[13] But conflicts persisted in many other localities. State representatives were hardly satisfied, and when the Adult Education Division began its reorganization in the summer of 1920 many of its officials perceived this as an opportunity to take full charge of Proletkult operations.[14]

Until 1920 the Communist Party did not officially take sides in these skirmishes over the Proletkult's status. Because there were no firm guidelines, Proletkult-party relations varied from one locality to the next. Whereas in Tula the provincial party committee helped to found the Proletkult and confirmed its leadership, in Tambov Proletkultists confronted hostility from party members, who believed that the organization was a frivolous distraction from serious social responsibilities.[15]

But as it became clear that the Civil War was coming to a close, the Communist Party Central Committee abruptly ended its official silence and began to express concern about the Proletkult's status. Lenin was chiefly responsible for this change. Initially, he had seemed to approve of the new organization, which he viewed as a way to educate workers to assume positions of authority in the state.[16] However, once he

12. June 10, 1919, circular from the Proletkult division in Narkompros, *Tsentral'nyi Gosudarstvennyi Arkhiv Literatury i Iskusstva* [henceforth cited as TsGALI] f. 1230, op. 1, d. 240, l. 3. The decision was publicized in many Proletkult journals. See, for example, *Proletkul't* (Tver), no. 3/4 (1919), pp. 19–20.

13. *Proletarskaia kul'tura*, no. 15/16 (1920), pp. 75, 83.

14. Fitzpatrick, *Commissariat*, p. 176.

15. For Tula see the August 1918 minutes of a provincial party meeting, TsGALI f. 1230, op. 1, d. 1536, l. 8; on Tambov see B. V., "O rabote Proletkul'ta," *Griadushchaia kul'tura*, no. 4/5 (1919), p. 18.

16. See Lenin's greeting to the first Proletkult congress, "Pis'mo

took notice of the scope of Proletkult activities, he became much more critical and began to formulate his own ideas about cultural transformation. Although he would not finalize his thoughts on culture until the last years of his life, already in 1919 Lenin began to attack what he felt were the mistaken priorities in Proletkult work.[17]

Lenin was a cultural conservative whose own tastes tended toward the Russian classics. He took a dim view of the many avant-gardist experiments engendered by the revolution. Rather than squandering resources on such projects, Lenin believed that the state had to address Russia's cultural backwardness, especially its low literacy levels and poor work habits. To overcome these obstacles, the new regime had to make use of the cultural foundation inherited from capitalism and employ the experts that capitalism had trained. "We have to build socialism from that culture," he insisted. "We have no other materials."[18] Speaking out at the 1919 conference of adult education workers, Lenin proclaimed his opposition to "all kinds of intellectual inventions (*vydumki*), all kinds of 'proletarian culture.' "[19] The real evidence of proletarian cul-

---

prezidiumu konferentsii proletarskikh kul'turno-prosvetitel'nykh organizatsii," *Protokoly pervoi Vserossiiskoi konferentsii proletarskikh kul'turno-prosvetitel'nykh organizatsii, 15–20 sentiabria, 1918 g.,* ed. P. I. Lebedev-Polianskii (Moscow, 1918), p. 3.

17. For Lenin's ideas on culture in the last years of his life see Moshe Lewin, *Lenin's Last Struggle* (London, 1975), pp. 113–14. There is a large literature comparing Lenin's understanding of culture with Proletkult views. For the most useful see Peter Gorsen and Eberhard Knödler-Bunte, *Proletkult: System einer proletarischen Kultur* (Stuttgart, 1974), vol. 1, esp. pp. 76–102; I. S. Smirnov, "Leninskaia kontseptsiia kul'turnoi revoliutsii i kritika Proletkul'ta," in *Istoricheskaia nauka i nekotorye problemy sovremennosti,* ed. M. I. Gefter (Moscow, 1969), pp. 63–85; V. V. Gorbunov, "Kritika V. I. Leninym teorii Proletkul'ta ob otnoshenii k kul'turnomu naslediiu," *Voprosy istorii KPSS,* no. 5 (1968), pp. 83–93; idem, *Lenin i sotsialisticheskaia kul'tura* (Moscow, 1972), esp. pp. 169–213; and Zenovia A. Sochor, *Revolution and Culture* (Ithaca, 1988), chapters 5 and 6.

18. V. I. Lenin, "Uspekhi i trudnosti sovetskoi vlasti," 1919, in *Polnoe sobranie sochinenii,* by V. I. Lenin, 5th ed. (Moscow, 1969), vol. 38, p. 54.

19. V. I. Lenin, "Ob obmane naroda lozungami svobody i raven-

ture would be effective organization to supply the devastated country with coal and bread.

Narkompros's critique of the Proletkult centered on Proletkult practice. Krupskaia, in particular, pointed to the rudimentary and unexceptional nature of much Proletkult work and used this contention as the justification to call for its subordination. Lenin, by contrast, was offended by Proletkult theory, even though it often had little to do with Proletkult practice. He opposed his own pragmatic thoughts on culture to the "harebrained" conceptions of Proletkultists. As soon as Lenin entered the fray, the organization was threatened both for what it was and for what it wanted to be.

Bogdanov's continued commitment to proletarian culture worried Lenin as well. In the early years of Soviet power Bogdanov published widely, and his writings clearly influenced some prominent party leaders, including Bukharin.[20] When Lenin discovered that Bogdanov had issued a new edition of his book *Empiriomonism*, which had been so important in their prerevolutionary altercations, he promptly planned a new edition of his own critique. Published in the fall of 1920, Lenin's *Materialism and Empiriocriticism* had a new preface by V. I. Nevskii, who had already attacked Bogdanov in the controversy over the Proletkult's proletarian university in Moscow. Although Nevskii did not mention the Proletkult explicitly, he sharply criticized Bogdanov's recent writings, including articles that had appeared in *Proletarian Culture*.[21]

However, it was not until Lenin discovered disturbing evidence about the Proletkult movement's size and grandiose ambitions that he moved to force its subordination. During the Second Comintern Congress in August 1920 Proletkultists founded an international branch of their organization with Lunacharskii at its head. Its stated aspiration was to spread

---

stva," in *V. I. Lenin o literature i iskusstve*, 7th ed., ed. N. Krutikov (Moscow, 1986), p. 289.

20. This point is made convincingly by John Biggart, "Bukharin and the Origins of the Proletarian Culture Debate," *Soviet Studies*, vol. 34, no. 2 (1987), pp. 229–46, esp. pp. 231–32.

21. V. I. Nevskii, "Dialekticheskii materializm i filosofiia mertvoi

proletarian culture around the world.[22] Apparently alarmed by the Proletkult's pretensions, Lenin wrote Mikhail Pokrovskii, second in command of Narkompros, with some urgent questions.[23] What was the legal status of the Proletkult? Who were its leaders? Where did it get its funding? What had it accomplished? Pokrovskii replied that the Proletkult was an independent organization under Narkompros control. Lenin also received reports about its leaders, finances, and cultural programs from the central Proletkultists Vladimir Faidysh and Vasilii Ignatov. They did not, however, pass on widespread doubts about the cohesiveness of the organization or the mixed social composition of its membership. Instead they wrote that the Proletkult united some four hundred thousand proletarians.[24]

Faced with news of an autonomous organization that claimed such a significant working-class following, Lenin quickly took steps to end its independence. The Proletkult national congress, scheduled to meet in Moscow from October 5 to October 12, 1920, provided him with an opportunity. He charged Lunacharskii to inform delegates that their organization would now be absorbed by Narkompros. But Lunacharskii, who had long defended Proletkult interests, went back on the agreement; his speech to the Proletkult congress contained no mention of a pending change in the organization's status.[25] Lenin reacted immediately, calling a series of Polit-

---

reaktsii," in *Sochineniia*, by V. I. Lenin, 3d ed. (Moscow, 1931), vol. 13, pp. 317–24.

22. "Mezhdunarodnyi biuro Proletkul'ta," *Izvestiia TsIK*, August 14, 1920. On the bureau in general see *Proletarskaia kul'tura*, no. 15/16 (1920), pp. 3–6 and no. 17/19 (1920), pp. 2–5.

23. Although there is no direct evidence to prove that Lenin read the article and was moved to take action because of it, the case for this causal chain is made convincingly by Smirnov, "Leninskaia kontseptsiia kul'turnoi revoliutsii," pp. 71–73. Once Lenin had subordinated the Proletkult to Narkompros, he disbanded the International Bureau, ibid., p. 81.

24. Notes by V. P. Faidysh and V. V. Ignatov in *Lenin o literature*, p. 542.

25. For a summary of Lunacharskii's speech see *Proletarskaia*

buro meetings to discuss the Proletkult and to draw up proposals for its subordination.[26] From this point on Lenin circumvented Lunacharskii and dealt directly with the central Proletkult's faction of party members, headed by Valerian Pletnev.

The national Proletkult had strong ties to the Communist Party. A full two-thirds of the conference delegates were Communists, as were all national leaders, except Bogdanov.[27] Nonetheless, they were not immediately convinced that the party's action was justified. Representatives from the Proletkult met with Lenin while the Politburo was working out its proposals. According to Lenin's notes of the meeting, they did not understand how Proletkult autonomy posed a threat to anyone.[28] The party faction had trouble convincing the assembled delegates to accept the central committee's proposal, which only passed after long debate and appeals to party discipline.[29]

Eventually, however, the Proletkult congress approved a five-point statement drafted by the Communist Party Central Committee.[30] The resolution made the Proletkult into a divi-

---

kul'tura, no. 17/19 (1920), p. 78. Lunacharskii later claimed that his remarks were misinterpreted, but there is no evidence to support this contention. See Fitzpatrick, *Commissariat*, pp. 177–78.

26. On the machinations behind the scenes at the Politburo meetings see V. V. Gorbunov, "Bor'ba V. I. Lenina s separatistskimi ustremleniiami Proletkul'ta," *Voprosy istorii KPSS*, no. 1 (1958), pp. 33–35. For the text of Lenin's original proposal, softened by Bukharin, see *Lenin o literature*, pp. 301–2. On Bukharin's intervention see Biggart, "Bukharin," pp. 233–34.

27. *Griadushchee*, no. 12/13 (1920), p. 22; and "Neobkhodimoe ob"iasnenie," TsGALI f. 1230, op. 1, d. 51, l. 6.

28. Gorbunov, "Bor'ba V. I. Lenina s separatistskimi ustremleniiami Proletkul'ta," pp. 34–35. In a widely quoted memoir of the meeting, first published in 1967, Anna Dodonova claimed that party members were quickly swayed by Lenin, but Lenin's notes indicate otherwise. Dodonova also exaggerated the number of party members at the congress; see A. Dodonova, "Iz vospominanii o Proletkul'ta," in *Lenin o literature*, pp. 500–503.

29. *Proletarskaia kul'tura*, no. 17/19 (1920), p. 78; and *Griadushchee*, no. 12/13 (1920), p.22.

30. "Rezoliutsii po organizatsionnomu voprosu, vnesena Kom-

sion of the Narkompros bureaucracy that was accountable to the party for the content of its work. Perhaps to sweeten the pill, the party instructed Narkompros to ensure that the proletariat had the opportunity for free creative work within its establishments, which seemed to imply that Proletkult artistic activity might continue more or less unchanged.

This was only the opening gambit, however, in a long process of reorganization. A special plenum of the Communist Party Central Committee met many times in the late fall of 1920 to determine more precise guidelines for Proletkult work and to draft an explanation of the new situation for local party and Proletkult activists. The end result was the central committee decree "On the Proletkults," published in *Pravda* on December 1, 1920. The decree was less an explanation than a denunciation; it excoriated Proletkult leaders, its organizational practice, and the movement's understanding of its cultural mission.[31]

The *Pravda* letter was scathingly critical of the Proletkult's demand for autonomy, which it portrayed as a petty-bourgeois attempt to establish an institutional base outside of Soviet power. Proletkult independence had attracted many socially alien elements, among them futurists, decadents, and proponents of "idealist and anti-Marxist philosophies." Although Bogdanov was not directly mentioned, he was also a target. The central committee linked the Proletkult to "anti-Marxist, God-building" groups of intellectuals who were now trying to manipulate the working class with their "semibourgeois philosophical 'systems' and schemes." The party would have done something sooner had it not been hindered by the military emergency. Now that the Civil War was ending, it could finally turn its attention to the important problems of culture and education.[32]

The central committee then appealed to the working-class

munisticheskoi fraktsiei po predlozheniiu TsK RKP," *Proletarskaia kul'tura*, no. 17/19 (1920), pp. 83–84.

31. "O Proletkul'takh: Pis'mo TsK RKP," *Pravda*, December 1, 1920, reprinted in *Lenin o literature*, pp. 408–10.

32. Ibid.

masses, who had been fed "Machism and futurism" under the guise of proletarian culture. The party in no way wanted to stop efforts by worker-intellectuals to improve themselves in the arts. Rather, it hoped that these efforts would be placed in the hands of the laboring classes so that the workers' government could help the workers' intelligentsia.[33] When read between the lines, this statement deftly turned Proletkult leaders into the very bourgeois intellectuals they claimed to oppose. The party, not the Proletkult, emerged as the defender of "real, authentic" proletarian culture.[34]

This attack proved to have much more serious consequences for the movement than the formal loss of autonomy that had been approved at the national congress. The precise terms of the Proletkult's new bureaucratic status evolved slowly through lengthy and complicated agreements with state, union, and party organs. In the meantime, the party's critique appeared in the foremost newspaper in the country. Unlike previous criticisms, the *Pravda* letter discredited the organization on political grounds. In the hard winter of 1920–1921, when hunger riots and strikes erupted throughout the country, the Proletkult was branded as a potentially dangerous, anti-Soviet institution.

Responding with shock and outrage, the Proletkult central leadership drew up a response, "An Unavoidable Explanation," which it tried to publish in *Pravda* without success.[35] This document revealed the enormous gap between Proletkultists' self-perceptions and the central committee's views. It began somewhat disingenuously, expressing gratitude to the party for finally showing an interest in Proletkult work. But the rest of the text refuted the substance and purpose of the party's letter point by point. The Proletkult was loyal to the party and the Soviet regime, something clearly shown

33. Ibid.
34. Ibid., p. 410.
35. "Neobkhodimoe ob"iasnenie," TsGALI f. 1230, op. 1, d. 51, l. 6. On publication efforts see *Lenin o literature*, p. 545.

by the large number of Communists in the organization. It did not shelter "anti-Marxist" groups; in fact it kept better control over its specialists than did other Soviet institutions. The presidium also insisted that the Proletkult did not promote "Machists and God-builders" because both Bogdanov and Lunacharskii had long since abandoned these ideas. Bogdanov's works were now published by government and party presses, and he was an instructor at the party-controlled Sverdlov University. Lunacharskii had inspired enough confidence to be appointed Commissar of Enlightenment. As for the charge of endorsing futurism, they had openly denounced such trends.[36]

Proletkultists were dismayed that the party had decided to print an attack that was filled with such unexpected accusations. They had heard rumors that the letter was a reaction to agitation within the Proletkult protesting the loss of institutional autonomy, but "we do not know of any publicly printed statement of this kind." In conclusion, they held out hope for better, more fruitful relations between the Proletkult and the party in the future.[37] But this plea had no effect, nor did a special delegation that urged Lenin to change his mind.[38] Its avenues for protest now exhausted, the Proletkult had no choice but to begin a painful process of reassessment.

Reorganization and Decline

The Proletkult's subordination to Narkompros irrevocably altered the movement's place in Soviet cultural life. Its claim to be the "third path" to proletarian power, bombastic in the best of times, now had lost all credence. Although few participants wanted the organization to assume a modest role as a

36. "Neobkhodimoe ob"iasnenie."
37. Ibid.
38. On the delegation see *Proletarskaia kul'tura*, no. 20/21 (1921), p. 33; and F. Volgin's memoirs, published first in *Krasnyi Krym*, January 21, 1921, and reprinted in *Lenin o literature*, pp. 503–4.

Narkompros subsection, it was difficult for them to articulate a new mission within the narrow limits set by the party and the state. To make matters worse, the party's intervention sparked discord within the organization and between the Proletkult and its numerous cultural competitors.

The first efforts to define a new identity began at a national plenum in mid-December 1920. Called to discuss the practical consequences of the party's letter, the plenum resulted in a new central leadership. Lebedev-Polianskii, the national president, found himself in a minority at the meeting. He opposed handing over discussions about organizational status to the Proletkult's party faction, perhaps because this would have excluded Bogdanov, who was not a party member. Moreover, he did not even want to consider any fundamental changes in the Proletkult's cultural direction. When his proposals were soundly defeated, Lebedev-Polianskii tendered his resignation, a move that was quickly accepted.[39]

Writing under the pseudonym of V. Kunavin shortly after his resignation, Lebedev-Polianskii took the opportunity to express his views on the Proletkult's subordination in the Narkompros journal *Creation* (*Tvorchestvo*). He did not attack the party for its intervention, but he did wonder why it had chosen to move against the Proletkult when trade unions remained independent. As always, Lebedev-Polianskii was most critical of the state bureaucracy. The Proletkult was not strong enough to imbue Narkompros with the proletarian energy it so desperately needed; instead, it might easily acquire all of Narkompros's problems. Already Proletkult work was too similar to state programs, and unification would only increase the danger that the Proletkult would lose its distinctive character. The Proletkult should turn to factories and solicit a pure proletarian following. It should eschew education and propaganda and pursue scientific research and

39. See the minutes of the December plenum in *Proletarskaia kul'tura*, no. 20/21 (1921), pp. 32–34; and Dodonova, "Iz vospominanii," in *Lenin o literature*, pp. 502–3.

creative programs. Only such a path would save it from disappearing forever inside the state bureaucracy.[40]

With Lebedev-Polianskii's departure the Proletkult lost its most stalwart defender of autonomy. His place was filled by Valerian Pletnev, the same energetic playwright from Moscow who had led the party faction to accept the Proletkult's subordination. A former worker, Pletnev had never been part of the Vpered circle, and his presence seemed designed to reassure Proletkult critics. His first step was to begin a rigorous reevaluation of Proletkult practice that addressed many of the Communist Party's complaints.[41] Under Pletnev's guidance the national organization decided to use the Proletkult's forces to help rebuild Soviet society in the wake of the Civil War. The Proletkult would devote part of its energies to "production propaganda," an idea proposed by Glavpolitprosvet to popularize labor discipline. It would also work to implement the party's cultural and political programs.[42]

But in crucial areas the restructured leadership refused to acquiesce to the party's critique. Significantly, Pletnev made no effort to remove Bogdanov from national prominence. Bogdanov participated in at least part of the December plenum and was a delegate to the 1921 national convention. The next issue of *Proletarian Culture* prominently displayed one of his articles on "organizational science."[43] And despite the Com-

40. P. I. Lebedev-Polianskii [V. Kunavin, pseud.], "V novykh usloviiakh: O Proletkul'takh," *Tvorchestvo*, no. 11/12 (1920), pp. 37–39.

41. For the organization's new program, initiated under Pletnev's leadership, see "Blizhaishchie zadachi Proletkul'ta," *Proletarskaia kul'tura*, no. 20/21 (1921), pp. 27–32; and a slightly longer version, "Deklaratsiia priniataia plenumom Vserossiiskogo Ts. K. Proletkul'ta 19 dek., 1920 g.," *Griadushchee*, no. 4/6 (1921), pp. 53–59. For a thoughtful analysis of this shift that concentrates on internal Proletkult dynamics see Gabriele Gorzka, *A. Bogdanov und der russische Proletkult* (Frankfurt am Main, 1980), pp. 46–55.

42. "Deklaratsiia," *Griadushchee*, no. 4/6 (1920), pp. 54, 55, 57–58. See Krupskaia's proposal for production propaganda in Glavpolitprosvet, *Pedagogicheskie sochineniia*, vol. 7, pp. 73–82.

43. See *Proletarskaia kul'tura*, no. 20/21 (1921), p. 36, and the delegate list for the 1921 congress, TsGALI f. 1230, op. 1, d. 144, l. 116. See

munist Party's hostile polemics against the Proletkult's approach, the plenum maintained its commitment to proletarian culture. Indeed, national leaders proclaimed that Proletkult ideas had to be publicized even more broadly in order to intensify the struggle against bourgeois culture and bourgeois life-styles. Nor would Proletkultists limit themselves to work in artistic studios alone, a frequent demand by Narkompros activists. Instead, Proletkultists reaffirmed the importance of clubs; they also insisted that the organization needed to expand its very small network of science studios, a proposal championed by Bogdanov himself.[44] Thus the decisions of the December plenum made clear that even without institutional autonomy the Proletkult intended to remain the proletariat's cultural advocate.

In taking these strong positions the national leaders of the Proletkult seemed unaware that the cultural and political landscape was changing rapidly around them. The Proletkult was not the only organization to face severe party scrutiny. Narkompros itself was in the throes of reorganization by the winter of 1920. Because of party intervention, Glavpolitprosvet became a much more ambitious enterprise, theoretically taking charge of all political education for Narkompros, the soviets, the trade unions, the army, and the Proletkult. This expansion made Glavpolitprosvet a much more formidable adversary than the Adult Education Division had ever been.[45]

Trade unions also felt the sting of reorganization. In March 1921 the momentous Tenth Party Congress ended their pretensions to a powerful economic role. Against the backdrop of the Kronstadt rebellion and other threats to Bolshevik power, the Workers' Opposition, labeled as a dangerous syndicalist

---

also A. A. Bogdanov, "Ocherki organizatsionnoi nauki," *Proletarskaia kul'tura*, no. 20/21 (1921), pp. 3–19.

44. "Deklaratsiia," *Griadushchee*, no. 4/6 (1921), pp. 54, 58. The national leadership confirmed Bogdanov's plans for a national science studio in May 1921, *Proletarskaia kul'tura*, no. 20/21 (1921), p. 36.

45. Fitzpatrick, *Commissariat*, pp. 186–209.

deviation, was easily defeated. Although unions retained their formal independence, their duties were henceforth restricted mainly to didactic tasks. They were to be the schools of communism, transmission belts between the Communist Party and the proletarian masses. And the more their economic duties declined, the more the unions began to emerge as serious competitors to the Proletkult in the fields of culture and education.

The introduction of the New Economic Policy made it even harder for the Proletkult to maintain its former position. Inaugurated at the Tenth Party Congress, the New Economic Policy marked the beginning of a fiscal crisis for all state institutions. The government abandoned forced requisitions from the peasantry, which dramatically lowered state revenues. As a result, there was less funding for all state services, social services in particular. Narkompros's share of the budget declined from 9.4 percent in 1920 to 2.2 percent in 1921.[46]

Despite these ominous signs, Pletnev began negotiations to preserve what he could of the Proletkult's independence. A savvy bargainer, he obtained permission from Narkompros to maintain Proletkult clubs as long as they registered with Glavpolitprosvet. In addition, he gained grudging approval for the idea of science studios. Most important, Pletnev won the theoretical assurance that local organizations could retain control over their own budgets.[47] He also bargained with the trade unions. At the national trade union convention in May 1921, where labor leaders confirmed their new role as the schools of communism, Pletnev was on hand to defend Proletkult interests. "Socialist culture can only grow from a foundation built by workers themselves," he exclaimed to an ap-

46. Fitzpatrick, *Commissariat*, p. 291. On the budgetary implications of the New Economic Policy see R. W. Davies, *The Development of the Soviet Budgetary System* (Cambridge, Eng., 1958), pp. 50–58.

47. See Pletnev's comments on his negotiations with Glavpolitprosvet and Narkompros at the second Proletkult congress, *Biulleten' vtorogo s"ezda Proletkul'tov*, no. 1, pp. 57–60, 65; no. 2, pp. 90, 94.

plauding audience.[48] At a special gathering of union cultural workers a few months later he convinced them to send particularly talented workers to Proletkult studios. In return he promised to let Proletkult factory organizations be counted as part of the unions' cultural apparatus.[49]

These bureaucratic wranglings were designed to protect the Proletkult's cultural territory, but they did very little to safeguard its extensive provincial networks. Indeed, there were signs that the central Proletkult saw the initial stages of the crisis as an opportunity to cleanse the organization of its troublesome elements, its nonproletarian members, and its stubbornly independent local factions. When Pletnev appeared at a meeting for trade union cultural workers in September 1921, at least half of the three hundred Proletkult divisions that had existed just a year before had already disappeared. Nonetheless, he referred to this decline as "normal." "When the slogan of proletarian culture was spread to the masses, Proletkults started growing like mushrooms even in places where there were no preconditions for creative cultural work, which we want to spread primarily among the industrial proletariat."[50]

While the center tried to save the Proletkult's institutional integrity, the complex network established during the Civil War was rapidly disintegrating. At the local level the Proletkult's loss of independence made it an easy target for rival circles that wanted to expand their cultural resources. Many Politprosvet divisions interpreted their new power as an excuse to disband Proletkult operations. The Kologriv circle, for example, was summarily closed by the local Politprosvet office.[51] Narkompros workers also resorted to harassment,

48. *Chetvertyi Vserossiiskii s"ezd professional'nykh soiuzov, 17–25 maia 1921 goda: Stenograficheskii otchet* (Moscow, 1921), vol. 2, pp. 89–90, quotation p. 90.

49. *Biulleten' pervoi Vserossiiskoi konferentsii po kul'turno-prosvetitel'noi rabote profsoiuzov* (Moscow, 1921), no. 2, pp. 3–6; no. 3, pp. 4–5.

50. Ibid., no. 2, p. 3.

51. Telegram from the Kologriv Proletkult to the central organization, January 3, 1921, TsGALI f. 1230, op. 1, d. 1278, l. 83.

refusing to hand over Proletkult funds. In addition, they sometimes absorbed parts of local organizations' infrastructure, particularly their clubs.[52]

The exceedingly critical tone of the Communist Party's attack turned many local Communists against local Proletkult organizations. In Iaroslavl the party committee closed down Proletkult operations. Local leaders in Saratov reported that Proletkult-party relations had soured so much after December 1920 that the party had decided to close down several regional circles. Proletkultists in Samara and Tver complained that responsible workers who were party members had been assigned other duties. These reassignments seriously depleted these organizations' staffs.[53]

Unions also began to look at the Proletkult as a source of supplies and staff. In Tver, for example, labor leaders tried to take over all Proletkult clubs. The Samara union bureaucracy attempted to subordinate the entire organization as part of its cultural apparatus. In Orenburg the Proletkult faced such hostility from the local party committee that it voluntarily surrendered to union control for its own protection.[54]

But it was the fiscal consequences of the New Economic Policy that had the most detrimental effects of all. Because most local organizations had never established financial independence, they were exceedingly vulnerable when government resources dried up. Many had enjoyed some help from local allies, but now these allies faced their own constraints. During the Civil War the Shuia factory Proletkult had re-

52. On general conflicts over clubs see *Biulleten' vtorogo s"ezda*, no. 2, pp. 12–13. On finances see the reports from local organizations at the February 1922 Proletkult plenum, TsGALI f. 1230, op. 1, d. 146, ll. 8 ob., 11 ob.

53. Iaroslavl, *Biulleten' vtorogo s"ezda*, no. 1, p. 4; Saratov, Tver, and Samara, reports at the February 1922 Proletkult plenum, TsGALI f. 1230, op. 1, d. 146, ll. 8, 12, 10 ob.

54. Tver, report by Vladislava Lie at the February 1922 plenum, TsGALI f. 1230, op. 1, d. 146, l. 12; Samara, report by A. S. Shein at the February plenum, d. 146, l. 10 ob.; Orenburg, "Plan ob"edineniia Orenproletkul'ta s kul'totdelom G.S.P.S." and a letter to the Proletkult central committee, d. 1235, ll. 25, 36 ob.

ceived free rent, heat, and lighting from the factory management. But with the new financial policies of 1921, which
required balanced factory budgets, the plant demanded payment for these services.[55]

The financial crisis at the center meant decreased funds all
along the organizational chain. Because the central Proletkult
secured its own needs first, it had significantly less to send to
provincial and city groups. They in turn had less to pass on to
those circles that were dependent on them. The lowest level
organizations, factory Proletkults and clubs, suffered the
most. Under these circumstances small town circles with
weak or nonexistent ties to the national bureaucracy simply
disappeared. Local Proletkults carried on their own internal
purges, closing down affiliates they could no longer support or
those that appeared to be conducting "strictly educational
work."[56] The Tver provincial Proletkult encompassed four circles in 1920; by the end of 1921 only one remained.[57]

The situation of the Ivanovo-Voznesensk Proletkult in the
first year of the New Economic Policy illustrates how financial hardships and cultural rivalries worked together to undermine the organization. Problems began in early 1921. With
the status of the Proletkult now in question the Ivanovo-
Voznesensk branch began to have difficulties with the local
party bureau and with unions. Local leaders complained that
party criticism had driven some workers away. Because of
financial problems, the Proletkult had to reduce its stipends
for studio members to such a low level that it could no longer
support those with families. The Textile Workers' Union, once
an ally, now challenged Proletkult control of factory clubs.

55. Local questionnaire, 1921, TsGALI f. 1230, op. 1, d. 117, l. 69
ob.

56. See the report of the Tula provincial Proletkult, July 15, 1921,
TsGALI f. 1230, op. 1, d. 1538, l. 25 ob.

57. Report by the local president at the second Tver provincial
conference, 1921, TsGALI f. 1230, op. 1, d. 1525, l. 20; "O sostoianii
rabot Tverskogo Proletkul'ta k I/X 22 [October 1, 1922]," d. 1527, l.
35.

Even the intervention of the city's Politprosvet division on the Proletkult's behalf could not mitigate union hostility. The local president, Olga Vladimirova, painted a very depressing picture. Club work was dying out and studio participants had stopped receiving rations. "Students are literally starving," she concluded.[58]

In Smolensk cultural activities were also severely restricted during 1921. The organization had no particular problems with other local groups, but it also received no help; funds from the center were simply not enough to cover costs. The Proletkult had to reduce its membership from two hundred to eighty-five and to shut down both the literature and music studios. Its one remaining regional affiliate in Iartsevo was about to close because the local Politprosvet refused to hand over funds. The Iartsevo president blamed both the central and the provincial Proletkults for his plight. They should have sent money or at least instructions on how to help his organization survive.[59]

These examples show how little central negotiations had done to stave off local crises. Indeed, some participants began to wonder if national leaders were interested in the Proletkult's continued survival as a mass organization. Despite the alarming news coming in from the provinces, Pletnev could still describe the Proletkult's decline in 1921 as "normal," a choice of words that implied that the expansion during the Civil War had been somehow abnormal. According to this interpretation the crisis was in fact an opportunity to cleanse the organization of its alien elements. However, Pletnev would soon be shocked to discover that the Proletkult's collapse had only just begun.

58. "Material k istorii Proletkul'ta," TsGALI f. 1230, op. 1, d. 1245, ll. 6, 16; Vladimirova's report on the Ivanovo-Voznesensk Proletkult, February 2, 1922, d. 146, l. 7 ob.

59. Questionnaire for the 1921 conference, TsGALI f. 1230, op. 1, d. 118, ll. 33, 11; report by the Proletkult head A. I. Smirnov, February 1922, d. 146, l. 11 ob.; "Anketa o roli, zadachakh i tseliakh Proletkul'ta," March 1922, d. 118, l. 62.

The Cultural Vanguard

In the fall of 1921 Proletkult delegates gathered for yet another national congress, but this time a very different mood prevailed than just a year before. The sharp decline in resources and the resulting drop in membership had severely strained the relations between the central organization and its provincial affiliates. As if these problems were not enough, the organization faced renewed questions about its political reliability.

The first crisis broke even before the conference opened. An anonymous pamphlet titled *We are Collectivists* (*My—kollektivisty*) came to the attention of the Proletkult central leadership and the Communist Party Central Committee. The authors, whose identity has never been established, declared themselves a Communist Party faction with links to the Proletkult and the Workers' Opposition. They denounced the New Economic Policy, accused the Communist Party of abandoning the principles of socialism and the dictatorship of the proletariat, and claimed Bogdanov and the Vperedist tradition to be the real inspiration for communism and for the Proletkult movement.[60]

The Communist Party's reaction was swift. Bukharin published an attack in *Pravda* that called the platform an example of "Bogdanovian Menshevism" and denounced Bogdanov for his passive and false approach to revolutionary change. A small number of people, he warned, wanted to make the Proletkult the basis of a Menshevik revival.[61] Although the Politburo reaffirmed its earlier rulings on political orthodoxy

---

60. Excerpts from the document are cited in V. V. Gorbunov, *V. I. Lenin i Proletkul't* (Moscow, 1974), pp. 172–74; N. Bukharin, "K s"ezdu Proletkul'ta," *Pravda*, November 22, 1921; and L. N. Suvorov, "Iz istorii bor'by V. I. Lenina i partii bol'shevikov protiv bogdanovskoi 'organizatsionnoi nauki,' " *Filosofskie nauki*, no. 3 (1966), pp. 87–89.

61. N. Bukharin, "K s"ezdu Proletkul'ta," *Pravda*, November 22, 1921; Biggart, "Bukharin," pp. 236–37.

within the Proletkult, the Proletkult's party faction published its own statement, rejecting all attempts to use the organization for "narrow group interests."[62]

The anonymous pamphlet altered the official Proletkult stance toward its most important theorist. Although Bogdanov was present as a delegate at the November gathering, he was not reelected to the Proletkult governing board. It was at this time, not in 1920, that Bogdanov was relieved of his national position.[63] Unlike Bukharin and other party critics, Pletnev never denounced Bogdanov by name, except to acknowledge that the collectivists looked to his work for inspiration. Still, he was quick to distance the Proletkult from charges of "collectivist" sympathies.

The collectivist platform was quickly pushed to the sidelines of the Proletkult conference. It is not even clear how much support it ever received. Nonetheless, the collectivists' denunciation of party policies under the New Economic Policy forced Proletkult leaders to address this dramatic shift in the country's course. By initiating an era of class compromise the New Economic Policy challenged the very reason for the Proletkult's existence. How would an organization devoted to the pursuit of proletarian dictatorship justify itself in this new social environment?

Pletnev attempted to turn this obvious weakness into a strength. He insisted that the Proletkult was more important than ever precisely because of the New Economic Policy. The economic shift encouraged the petty bourgeoisie to consolidate its alien ideology. Therefore, workers' organizations had to unite in an army against such influences, with the Proletkult taking the lead. If the New Economic Policy marked a retreat in economics and politics, the Proletkult would not

62. The November 18, 1921, ruling is in TsGALI f. 1230, op. 1, d. 14, l. 104. It was published in *Pravda* on November 23, 1921, under the title "Resoliutsiia fraktsii s"ezda Proletkul'ta."

63. See the delegate list for the 1921 national congress, TsGALI f. 1230, op. 1, d. 144, l. 116, and *Biulleten' vtorogo s"ezda*, no. 2, p. 93.

allow a retreat on the ideological front.[64] In essence, he argued that the New Economic Policy provided the Proletkult with a new and powerful justification for its continued existence.

This remarkable self-confidence in the face of hostile criticism also marked Pletnev's dealings with local Proletkult affiliates. He was determined to establish central control over local work, thereby annihilating the long-standing animosities between Moscow and the provinces. His preferred tactic was to ignore local problems altogether, brushing aside complaints that the central and Moscow organizations were appropriating most of the scarce resources for themselves.[65]

Pletnev continued to assert that institutional decline thus far had been positive and had cleansed the Proletkult of the alien elements that had crept in during the Civil War. Although it was true, he granted, that organizations like the one in the small town of Iarensk, Vologda province, were dying out, this was a positive development because there were no workers in those organizations anyway. "Maybe there is one shoemaker who is somehow organized, but that does not give us the right to have a Proletkult; we are an organization for the industrial proletariat."[66] Making the message even clearer, Pletnev proclaimed: "At the present time, under these conditions, the Proletkult cannot be a mass organization. It is and will be an organization for cultural and creative forces of the vanguard of the proletarian masses."[67]

This vanguardist vision dominated the discussions on creative work as well. None of the suggestions advanced by national leaders was suitable for a mass organization. In her presentation on club work Raisa Ginzburg stressed the need for advanced, well-educated proletarian participants. Similarly, in a long and complex lecture on the theater, Valentin

64. *Chetvertyi s"ezd professional'nykh soiuzov*, p. 83; and *Biulleten' vtorogo s"ezda*, no. 2, pp. 73–74.
65. *Biulleten vtorogo s"ezda*, no. 1, pp. 18–21.
66. Ibid., p. 13.
67. Ibid., no. 2, p. 77. See also ibid., no. 1, p. 39.

Smyshliaev derisively condemned most provincial theatrical practices and insisted that the Proletkult had to back experimental projects. And Ilia Trainin, outlining existing practices in the visual arts, suggested that the Proletkult open a central training school with a rigorous four-year program.[68]

The vanguardism of Kirillov's speech on literature was particularly extreme. He wanted to disband all provincial studios and use the money to support a handful of excellent students in Moscow. Because the financial situation of even the best students was desperate, why waste money on the provinces? "The severe, cruel facts of life have shown us that those things that we hoped and dreamed about in our work are very, very far away." Rather than squandering money on untalented workers, the Proletkult should support those who had already proven themselves.[69] This radical elitism was too much even for Pletnev, who argued that the Proletkult had to remain open to those workers who dreamed of one day becoming artists.[70]

As with earlier efforts, congress resolutions outlining new relations with unions and Narkompros did little to resolve local hostilities.[71] The Communist Party was also ambivalent. In late November the Politburo sent a circular to local party committees with a mixed message about future cooperation. It urged local bureaus to support the Proletkult as "one of the party's mechanisms (*apparaty*) for satisfying the proletariat's cultural demands," hardly an enthusiastic backing. At the same time, it directed Communists within the Proletkult to cleanse the organization of petty-bourgeois elements, collectivists, and the remnants of Bogdanov's philosophy.[72]

68. On clubs see ibid., no. 1, pp. 12–16; on theater see ibid., pp. 17–40, esp. pp. 23, 33; on music see ibid., pp. 51–69; on art see ibid., pp. 40–51, esp. p. 49.

69. Ibid., no. 2, pp. 2–6, quotation p. 2.

70. Ibid., pp. 7–8.

71. See reports from local Proletkults at the June 1922 Proletkult plenum discussions, TsGA RSFSR f. 2313, op. 1, d. 19, ll. 2–4; 9–9 ob.; 44–46.

72. This November 22, 1921, statement is in TsGALI f. 1230, op. 1, d. 51, l. 7, and reprinted in *Lenin o literature*, p. 410.

Finances remained the most serious problem of all, and the Proletkult's contradictory relationship to the state was only exacerbated by the fiscal crisis. Throughout its history the Proletkult had demanded independence while simultaneously insisting that the government foot the bill. But now Narkompros's resources were dwindling, and the Proletkult's continued demands for more money and more freedom of action hardly encouraged generosity. By the beginning of 1922 even national leaders had to acknowledge that the organization was in desperate straits. Appealing to Glavpolitprosvet for more funds, they claimed that they could now support no more than fifty or sixty local organizations. Any further reduction would endanger the cause of proletarian culture and the Proletkult's struggle against petty-bourgeois ideology.[73]

Finally acknowledging the gravity of the situation, in February 1922 the Proletkult leadership organized a central committee plenum. By now, all traces of optimism had faded. The delegates, from fifteen provincial cities as well as Moscow and Petrograd, were faced with the prospect of carrying out an organizational purge. The main item on the agenda was to compose a list of organizations the central Proletkult could still support. Only thirty-eight existing organizations made it on the list, with twelve new ones slated for opening (or reopening) in particularly important industrial areas.[74]

The process of elimination appears to have been fairly simple. Organizations that had not maintained close ties to the center, like those in Klin and Kursk, were struck from the list, as were those in areas without large proletarian populations. The plenum also eliminated groups that had not developed "successful" cultural programs as well as those with such

73. "Zaiavlenie," January 10, 1922, TsGA RSFSR f. 2313, op. 1, d. 19, l. 1.
74. "Dlia svedeniia vsekh uchrezhdenii i organizatsii RSFSR," February 5, 1922, TsGALI f. 1230, op. 1, d. 49, ll. 12–12 ob.; "Spisok Proletkul'tov utverzhdennykh plenumom Tsentral'nogo komiteta Vserossiiskogo Proletkul'ta, 2–5 fevralia, 1922 g.," d. 121, l. 2.

serious financial problems that they required significant central support to remain in operation. The Omsk Proletkult (not represented at the conference) was summarily closed because it was in difficult financial straits and was said to have weak ties to local workers.[75] Leonid Tsinovskii, the representative from Archangel, chronicled a long history of external opposition and internal disputes in his city. With no local resources for the Proletkult to draw on the future of the Archangel organization lay in the hands of the plenum. Another local leader, Nikolai Beliaev, recounted how the Tambov Proletkult, one of the first groups, had declined at the end of the Civil War and now faced extinction unless the center promised more aid. Both the Archangel and Tambov circles were victims of the reorganization.[76]

Through this radical retrenchment the center hoped to redirect Proletkult resources to the best local organizations and to find funds for new groups in important industrial areas. The plenum also intensified the process of centralization. New allocations of staff and support openly favored Moscow and the central Proletkult administration. Narkompros had authorized rations for one thousand staff members and fifteen hundred student scholarships in 1922. The plenum gave 435 staff rations (43.5 percent) and 690 scholarships (46 percent) to Moscow and the central studios. Talented workers from the provinces would have to make their way to the capital, concluded the national Proletkult leader Vladimir Faidysh.[77]

Despite their scale even these reductions proved unrealistic. By mid-1922 Glavpolitprosvet had lowered ration sub-

75. V. L. Soskin and V. P. Butorin, "Proletkul't v Sibiri," in *Problemy istorii sovetskoi Sibiri*, ed. A. S. Moskovskii (Novosibirsk, 1973), pp. 137–38.

76. Protocols of the February 1922 plenum, TsGALI f. 1230, op. 1, d. 146, ll. 9 ob.–10 ob.; 7–7 ob.; 19 ob.–20.

77. On staffing and scholarships see Pletnev's report at the February 1922 plenum, TsGALI f. 1230, op. 1, d. 146, ll. 2–2 ob.; on the distribution of rations, ll. 21 ob.–22. For Faidysh's comments see l. 21 ob.

sidies by yet another third,[78] and local organizations complained that they were not receiving even these small
amounts. None of the new organizations planned at the February plenum was ever opened and local closures continued.
Of the twenty-six factory organizations on the official list,
only ten were still in operation by the end of 1922.[79]

Continual financial difficulties forced the central organization to reassess its position once again. The plans at the February plenum had a certain logic to them—support the stron-
gest organizations at the expense of the weak and reach out to
areas with large factory populations. But there was no way to
portray the continued collapse in a positive light. Reports
from the provinces were grim. Local organizations were dissolving because there was no money and no one left to lead
them. For example, despite the fact that it had the support of
local workers, the Rostov on Don Proletkult had closed because it had no funds and repeated requests for staff had gone
unanswered. The remaining students had left for Narkompros
studios or the local workers' faculty. The Kuznetsov Proletkult shut down for similar reasons, even though the center
had singled out Kuznetsov as a particularly important area
for Proletkult work.[80]

At this point Pletnev and his colleagues agreed that it was
senseless to apply to either Narkompros or the Communist
Party for more aid. The only possible source of funds remaining was the union cultural bureaucracy. In order to gain more
energetic labor support Pletnev proposed yet another national
congress in the fall of 1922, this one to coincide with the fifth
national trade union convention.[81] There was no more cutting

78. See the letter by Vladimir Faidysh to Glavpolitprosvet, August 22, 1922, TsGA RSFSR f. 2313, op. 1, d. 19, l. 67.
79. Compare the February 1922 list in TsGALI f. 1230, op. 1, d.
121, l. 2 ob. to figures for late 1922 in *Gorn*, no. 7 (1922), p. 160.
80. Reports from the June 26–29, 1922, central plenum, TsGA
RSFSR f. 2313, op. 1, d. 19, ll. 2–26.
81. On a new agreement with unions see TsGA RSFSR f. 2313, op.
1, d. 19, ll. 2–5, 19 ob.–20 ob.; on a new conference, ll. 37, 21–30.

to be done, and there were no more reorganizational schemes to be tried. Nonetheless, the Proletkult president still harbored the hope that if he could make his case eloquently enough, the organization would find the resources to help it survive.

On the Ideological Front:
The Proletarian Culture Debates

By the fall of 1922 the Proletkult was a small and embattled organization, only a shadow of the movement that had claimed almost half a million members two years before. Its membership had fallen to just over twenty-five hundred students organized in twenty local circles.[82] Its once impressive publication network had collapsed. Excluded from the state budget, *Proletarian Culture* put out its last issue in 1921.[83] The Moscow-based *Furnace*, now representing the national organization, was the Proletkult's only remaining major journal.

Yet despite its drastically reduced size, the Proletkult became the subject of a major debate in the Soviet press. To be sure, by now the Proletkult hardly posed enough of a threat to initiate such controversy. But these discussions were only partly about the fate of the organization. They were also a test of the very notion of proletarian culture and provided an excellent vehicle to discuss some of the "burning questions" that the New Economic Policy had raised for the Communist Party and the state. What was the correct way to bring about the cultural transformation of Soviet Russia? Who posed a greater danger—experts and intellectuals trained under capitalism or a backward and disaffected working class?

This broad discussion of proletarian culture, approved by the Politburo itself, gave Pletnev a remarkable chance to take

82. "O Proletkul'te," *Gorn*, no. 7 (1922), pp. 160–61.
83. Minutes of June 29, 1922, Proletkult plenum, TsGA RSFSR f. 2313, d. 19, ll. 33–33 ob.

the Proletkult's case to the nation.[84] Although the organization was a suspect ally, its outspoken critique of bourgeois ideology won it some sympathy among those who shared the Proletkultists' concern that the New Economic Policy might inaugurate a period of bourgeois reaction. Such fears were raised repeatedly at the Eleventh Party Congress, and Bukharin, writing in the prestigious party journal *Under the Banner of Marxism* (*Pod znamenem marksizma*), warned that history had offered many examples of a vanquished people imposing their culture on the conquerors.[85] If the Proletkult did not have the right answers, for people like Bukharin, at least it raised the right questions.

Understandably, Pletnev was particularly concerned about the Proletkult's future, which he saw as synonymous with the future of proletarian culture. His opening article, "On the Ideological Front," was an extensive statement of Proletkult beliefs and philosophy. If Marxists were hostile to the Proletkult, that was simply because they did not understand it. Proletarian culture was the necessary antithesis to bourgeois culture, the necessary step before a real classless culture for all humanity could be achieved. Although proletarian culture would necessarily incorporate elements from all that had come before, it would relentlessly struggle against bourgeois individualism. The Proletkult was historically necessary to fight against bourgeois ideology.[86] The New Economic Policy was not mentioned explicitly in the article, but there were

84. On the decision to start the series see *Lenin o literature*, p. 546. Pletnev's contribution consisted of three articles, "Na ideologicheskom fronte," *Pravda*, September 22, 1922; "O desnitse i shuitse Proletkul'ta," *Pravda*, October 17, 1922; and "V Proletkul'te," *Pravda*, October 20, 1922.

85. See Biggart, "Bukharin," pp. 237–41; and N. Bukharin, "Burzhuaznaia revoliutsiia i revoliutsiia proletarskaia," *Pod znamenem marksizma*, no. 7/8 (1922), pp. 61–82, esp. p. 79. Biggart argues that this article was the real beginning of the debate.

86. V. F. Pletnev, "Na ideologicheskom fronte," *Pravda*, September 22, 1922, reprinted with Lenin's criticisms in *Lenin o literature*, pp. 304–11.

transparent polemics against it everywhere. Pletnev spoke out against class compromise, the use of experts, and the participation of the peasantry, the bourgeoisie, and the intelligentsia in his organization. Proletarian culture, the necessary antidote to the current ills of the country, could only be made by the workers' hands.

"On the Ideological Front" was also a plea for more faith in the proletariat's creative powers. The working class had the force to conceive a new science and art, "even in this wild, uncultured, semiliterate, and impoverished country." Using strikingly Bogdanovist language, Pletnev defended the notion of proletarian science by insisting that the proletariat had to find new systems of knowledge, new ties between the disciplines, and a monistic understanding of the world. Moving from science to art, he proclaimed that the new culture must be made by worker artists, people who aimed to change the world, not just to beautify it. Perhaps the Proletkult had not made much progress in the four years of its existence, but one had to remember that the bourgeoisie had taken five centuries to develop its culture. "Should we consider the first experimental steps in this direction as utopian, as an unnecessary luxury?" he asked rhetorically.[87]

Pletnev answered his own question one month later. In an article entitled "In the Proletkult," he reiterated and expanded his description of Proletkult practice, praising its literary achievements, its theatrical output (especially his own plays), and its new trend toward production art. He also incorporated a novel explanation for the Proletkult's decline. The organization had grown much too large by late 1920 and the center could not provide enough resources to support such an extensive network. Therefore, from the 1920 congress onward it had deliberately reduced the number of local affiliates until there were only thirty-eight by November 1921.[88] By citing these deflated figures, which contradicted those he had

87. Ibid., quotations pp. 308, 309.
88. V. F. Pletnev, "V Proletkul'te," *Pravda*, October 20, 1922.

put forward a year before, the Proletkult president apparently hoped to show that his demands for continued state support were reasonable and modest, and that the collapse of the national network had taken place at least in part by design. He ended with a plea for continued subsidies: the effects of the New Economic Policy in 1922 had reduced the Proletkult well below its 1921 level. Now there were only twenty organizations and requests were coming from industrial areas to open new ones. He had heard rumors that the government might remove state support altogether. "If there is a wish to kill the Proletkult, then taking away government support will surely accomplish this."[89]

But this emotional defense served only to mobilize the Proletkult's opponents. Nadezhda Krupskaia was the first to respond. Although she did not dispute that the revolution would inspire a new class ideology, she separated the issue of proletarian culture from the Proletkult organization, which was too limited, too cut off from the masses, and too uncritical of bourgeois art to create a new culture. The proletariat did not come to power to lord it over other classes; instead it had to convince them of the rightness of its views. The Proletkult had much to be proud of, according to Krupskaia, for its studios had introduced many workers to artistic education. But she denied that it had created a uniquely proletarian art, and she rejected the idea that such an art, when it did emerge, would be made by workers alone. Proletarian culture would come from life itself; it could not be "hatched."[90]

Krupskaia's criticisms were mild compared to Lenin's. Outraged by Pletnev's first article, Lenin immediately sent off a protest to Bukharin for publishing it in *Pravda*. He then began to plan with Iakov Iakovlev, second in command at Agitprop, for a full-scale onslaught against Pletnev.[91] Iakov-

89. Ibid.
90. Nadezhda Krupskaia, "Proletarskaia ideologiia i Proletkul't," *Pravda*, October 8, 1922, reprinted in her *Pedagogicheskie sochineniia*, vol. 7, pp. 139–44.
91. *Lenin o literature*, pp. 311, 411.

lev's long response, written with Lenin's aid, found nothing of value in Pletnev's defense of Proletkult work. Pletnev's ideas on science were silly and mystical. The Proletkult had no business insisting on a rigid, class-exclusive approach. Now was the time to make peace with the peasantry and the specialists. Iakovlev also lashed out at the Proletkult's artistic practice, particularly its plays.[92]

The most interesting part of this sustained critique was the picture it painted of the Russian proletariat. Iakovlev doubted that the present-day working class had the knowledge or the experience to fulfill the tasks that Pletnev described. His opponent showed absolutely no appreciation of the cultural conditions of present-day Russia, chided Iakovlev. There were aspects of bourgeois culture that were definitely needed to fight against Russia's cultural backwardness (*nekul'turnost'*). The years of war and revolution had robbed the proletariat of its best elements, leaving semiliterates, peasants, and speculators (*meshochniki*) in their place. Instead of these "real" workers, who still prayed to the holy mother on the shop floor, Pletnev offered a fantastic vision of the working class. "Some elements of 'fantasy' were unavoidable, especially in the first period of the revolution when the working class of Russia shook the entire edifice of the bourgeois world with its mighty blows." But now the time for fantasy was over, Iakovlev concluded.[93]

Such a somber assessment of the proletariat and its skills echoed Lenin's own disparaging comments at the Eleventh Party Congress, where he insisted that Russian factories were now filled with all kinds of "accidental elements."[94] This analysis led Lenin to reject the whole idea of proletarian culture, a new step in the controversy. Before the country could

92. Iakovlev's two-part article, first printed in *Pravda* on October 24 and 25, 1922, is reprinted in *Lenin o literature*, pp. 411–23.
93. Ibid., p. 415.
94. See Sheila Fitzpatrick, "The Bolsheviks' Dilemma: Class, Culture and Politics in the Early Soviet Years," *Slavic Review*, vol. 47, no. 4 (1988), pp. 599–613.

even consider tossing out what was false in the heritage of capitalism, it had to attain those accomplishments necessary for socialism, such as literacy and a disciplined work ethic.[95] As Lenin wrote in one of his last articles, "Better Fewer, But Better," flippant talk of proletarian culture had blinded too many people to the country's cultural inadequacies. "For a start we should be satisfied with real bourgeois culture; for a start we should avoid the cruder types of prebourgeois culture, that is, bureaucratic culture and serf culture, etc. In matters of culture, haste and sweeping measures are most harmful."[96]

This acrimonious discussion accomplished exactly the opposite of what Pletnev had hoped. Although the organization was not disbanded, its upcoming conference was canceled and the Politburo voted to make it financially self-supporting. It would only provide enough funds to insure that the Proletkult did not collapse entirely.[97] Addressing this move at a Politprosvet conference a month later, Lunacharskii assumed a bittersweet tone. He conceded that the Proletkult turned out to be more expensive than expected and had brought few concrete results. But if the organization did not survive, they would have to find another way to allow the most talented workers to find their own approach to culture, science, and education.[98]

The result of the new cutbacks, predictably enough, was that the Proletkult shrank still further. By November 1922 the central organization had concluded that it did not have enough funds to cover heating costs for local organizations.

95. See Lewin, *Lenin's Last Struggle*, pp. 110, 113–14.

96. V. I. Lenin, "Luchshe men'she, da luchshe," in *Polnoe sobranie sochinenii*, by V. I. Lenin, 5th ed. (Moscow, 1970), vol. 45, p. 389.

97. Gorbunov, *Lenin i Proletkul't*, p. 195.

98. *Biulleten' tretego s"ezda Politprosvetov RSFSR* (Moscow, 1922), no. 1, pp. 4–5. See also Lunacharskii's contribution to the proletarian culture debate, "Eshche o voprose proletarskoi kul'ture," *Izvestiia TsIK*, November 3, 1922, reprinted in *Sobranie sochinenii v vos'mi tomakh*, by A. V. Lunacharskii, ed. I. I. Anisimov (Moscow, 1967), vol. 7, pp. 288–93.

By December it was running a deficit. In January 1924 there were only eleven Proletkult organizations left in the entire Soviet Union.[99] The ideological aftershocks of these debates were just as severe. They put all advocates of working-class creativity on the defensive in the early years of the New Economic Policy. But for the Proletkult their effects were even more disruptive. Proletarian creation and artistic expression were now separated from the Proletkult as a social and cultural movement.

The short, simple answer to the question of why the Proletkult declined is obvious: financial hardships were the primary cause. From late 1920 onward the organization experienced one cutback after another, and each one had serious effects on the range and quality of Proletkult activities. But this abbreviated answer only conceals another question. Why did state, party, and local institutions end their financial support? To answer this question, we must unravel a complex tangle of practical and ideological explanations.

At a very basic level the Proletkult's demise seems almost predetermined. Members of the Communist Party's central leadership, and Lenin in particular, distrusted any institution that demanded independence, from trade unions and party factions to opposing political parties. They could hardly be expected to tolerate an organization that not only aspired to autonomy but also claimed a large proletarian following. In addition, Lenin had a special grievance against the organization he associated with Bogdanov. Once he took note of the size and scope of Proletkult activities in the fall of 1920, the organization was fated for radical change.

The end of the Civil War and the introduction of the New Economic Policy only hastened the Proletkult's collapse. The

99. November and December 1922 meetings of the Proletkult presidium, TsGALI f. 1230, op. 1, d. 9, ll. 3–4; "Sostav Proletkul'tov i rukovodiashchikh organov," TsGALI f. 1230, op. 1, d. 121, l. 51.

New Economic Policy marked the beginning of fiscal austerity measures for all state organs as the country struggled to recover from the long years of war. In the process most educational and cultural institutions suffered severe cutbacks. But it is also fair to say that the Proletkult was singled out as a special victim. Given the changing needs of the Soviet state and its shrinking assets, the government was hardly willing to finance an organization with dubious cultural accomplishments and a suspect political reputation.

The New Economic Policy also marked a change in the ideological climate of the Soviet Union. It initiated an era in which the radical language of class war was increasingly out of place. The party encouraged alliances between workers and peasants and between workers and the experts needed to rebuild an ailing economy. Of course the Proletkult had included experts and peasants in its activities from the outset; it was never an exclusively proletarian organization. Still, central leaders had always loudly condemned the participation of other social groups. Their class-exclusive pronouncements were part of a general chorus during the Civil War, but now they appeared querulous and even dangerous.

Proletkult leaders continued to portray themselves as stalwart defenders of proletarian culture, but they no longer had a large movement behind them to help them realize their goals. A few thousand participants, no matter what their quality, could hardly evoke the same messianic, enthusiastic appeal as the rambling, chaotic organization of the Civil War years. It did not seem utopian to think that such small numbers could change the ethical and cultural basis of an entire society. Instead it seemed quixotic. The institution that had placed proletarian culture on the revolutionary agenda in 1917 was pushed to the sidelines and was no longer able to claim a formative role in Soviet cultural life.

8

The Proletkult as Postscript, 1923–1932

The Proletkult never recovered from the attacks leveled against it in the early 1920s. Despite considerable effort, participants could not overcome its poor reputation as a politically suspect and socially restrictive organization. The membership shrank still further during the New Economic Policy as the Proletkult struggled to define a place for itself in the new cultural and political environment. To be sure, during the First Five-Year Plan, when the state's direct appeals to the working class rekindled proletarian movements, the Proletkult began to expand again. But even then it was overshadowed by newer cultural organizations that had much closer ties to the regime.

In contrast to the Civil War years, the period of the New Economic Policy did not favor proletarian cultural projects. In its search for talent and resources to help rebuild the wartorn country the government extended itself to social groups that had been alienated during the bitter years of the Civil War. Both the peasantry and parts of the intelligentsia benefited from this change of policy, but many workers experienced worsening conditions.[1] Groups like the Proletkult,

1. On state policies toward workers during the New Economic Policy see William J. Chase, *Workers, Society, and the Soviet State: Labor and Life in Moscow, 1918–1929* (Urbana, 1987).

with their message of working-class hegemony and proletarian dictatorship, raised dissonant themes out of step with the dominant ideology of the 1920s.

Nonetheless, new cultural unions seeking proletarian forms of expression took shape in all artistic media. The Proletarian Writers' Union, known by its acronym VAPP, was an aggressive advocate of working-class literature. A special group for proletarian music, RAPM, was founded, and artists opened the Association of Revolutionary Russian Artists, AKhRR. The theater also had its circles, including the Blue Shirt (Siniaia Bluza) and the Theater of Working Class Youth (TRAM).[2]

Although they were reluctant to acknowledge it, these groups owed a debt to the Proletkult. Their participants believed that art was a powerful ideological weapon through which to organize society. In their search for uniquely proletarian artistic forms they believed they could help consolidate working-class power. And like the Proletkult, these new organizations had tenuous ties to the class that they claimed to represent. Less than a quarter of VAPP's members were industrial workers in 1928.[3]

Despite these similarities, there were marked differences between the Proletkult and its successors. The new circles were concerned with specific artistic media, but the Proletkult viewed culture broadly as a combination of art, ideology, and daily life. None of the organizations established during

2. On these groups see Edward J. Brown, *The Proletarian Episode in Russian Literature, 1928–1932* (New York, 1953); Hubertus Gassner and Eckhardt Gillen, eds., *Zwischen Revolutionskunst und sozialistischen Realismus: Kunstdebatten in der Sowjetunion von 1917 bis 1934* (Cologne, 1979); I. M. Gronskii and V. N. Perel'man, eds., *AKhRR—Assotsiatsiia Khudozhnikov Revoliutsionnoi Rossii: Sbornik vospominanii, statei, dokumentov* (Moscow, 1973); L. A. Pinegina, *Sovetskii rabochii klass i khudozhestvennaia kul'tura, 1917–1932* (Moscow, 1984); and Boris Schwarz, *Music and Musical Life in Soviet Russia*, Rev. ed. (Bloomington, 1983), chapters 3–5.

3. "Na Vserossiiskom s"ezde proletarskikh pisatelei," *Na literaturnom postu*, no. 19 (1928), p. 71.

the New Economic Policy could boast the same large follow-ing as the early Proletkult, and none manifested the same political independence. Each had close ties to state and party institutions: AKhRR worked with the Red Army; some circles of VAPP made party membership a requirement to join; RAPM was sponsored in part by the state publishing house; and TRAM was allied with the Komsomol.[4]

Proletarian culture remained a controversial issue in the 1920s; debates about its significance and place in Soviet cul-tural life continued unabated. The foes of working-class art found an eloquent advocate in Leon Trotsky, who insisted that the whole concept had no place in Marxist historical develop-ment. Although the bourgeoisie had developed its culture over centuries, the transition period between capitalism and so-cialism would be too short for the proletariat to find its own unique modes of artistic expression.[5] Trotsky's views were elaborated in well-funded state journals like *Red Virgin Soil* (*Krasnaia nov'*), edited by the brilliant critic Aleksandr Voron-skii. Voronskii's publication served as a forum for talented nonproletarian authors, known as "fellow travelers," and also for those who had a skeptical view of working-class creation.[6]

However, the new artistic groups did not suffer in silence. Instead, led by the Proletarian Writers' Union, they clamored loudly for more party support and for a dominant position in Soviet cultural life. VAPP's major journals—*On Guard* (*Na*

4. On AKhRR see Elizabeth Valkenier, *Russian Realist Art* (Ann Arbor, 1977), pp. 150–52; on VAPP see Brown, *The Proletarian Epi-sode*, pp. 12–20; on RAPM see Schwarz, *Music and Musical Life*, p. 54; on TRAM see V. Mironova, *TRAM: Agitatsionnyi molodezhnyi teatr, 1920–1930kh godov* (Leningrad, 1977).

5. Leon Trotsky, "Proletarian Art and Proletarian Culture," in *Literature and Revolution*, by Leon Trotsky (Ann Arbor, 1975), pp. 184–214.

6. The classic study of this important journal is Robert A. Ma-guire, *Red Virgin Soil* (Princeton, 1968). For examples of the journal's stance on proletarian literature see A. Voronskii, "O gruppe 'Kuz-nitsa,' " *Krasnaia nov'*, no. 13 (1923), pp. 297–312; on the visual arts see Fedorov-Davydov, "Tendentsii sovremennoi russkoi zhivopisi v svete sotsial'nogo analiza," *Krasnaia nov'*, no. 23 (1924), pp. 329–48.

postu), succeeded by *On Literary Guard* (*Na literaturnom postu*)—tirelessly attacked Voronskii and Trotsky in the 1920s. But the many artistic unions never presented a united front. Divided by serious aesthetic differences and internal power struggles, they lashed out against one another almost as much as they did against the fellow travelers.

In the ongoing cultural debates the Proletkult served as a negative reference point. Its theoretical foundation and cultural practices had been explicitly denounced by Lenin, and his statements were periodically reprinted during the New Economic Policy. Because Lenin had linked the very idea of proletarian culture to the Proletkult and Bogdanov, other groups, especially the vocal and combative VAPP, spent considerable energy trying to show how their conception of proletarian art and ideology differed from Bogdanovism and the Proletkult's "false laboratory methods."[7] Inevitably, such tactics weakened the Proletkult's position, even among potential allies. It became a convenient scapegoat for those new organizations that wished to deflect hostility from their own efforts to define a proletarian culture.

The Proletkult's Social Program

During the 1920s the two cardinal principles of Proletkult organization, autonomy and independent action (*samostoiatel'nost'* and *samodeiatel'nost'*), were finally separated as the organization abandoned any pretense of institutional autonomy. Despite this momentous shift in its founding principles, national leaders still believed that the organization was the main defender of workers' creative independence. Within the Proletkult's small studios and theaters members conducted innovative artistic experiments. At the same time they also tried to reach out to the laboring population at large by offer-

7. See, for example, G. Lelevich, "O marksizme, bogdanovshchine, proletarskoi literature i t. Rumii," *Na postu*, no. 6 (1925), columns 171–88.

ing their services as researchers and instructors to working-class clubs.

Eager to end its suspect political status, the Proletkult struggled to establish its trustworthiness as a loyal, proparty organization. When a small circle of workers, inspired in part by Bogdanov's thought, formed an underground circle called "Workers' Truth" (*Rabochaia pravda*) in 1922–1923, prominent party members pointed to this as yet more evidence of the Proletkult's fundamentally flawed theories.[8] Proletkult leaders publicly took the party's side, announcing that Workers' Truth was alienated from real life, had no understanding of Marxist theory, and could not grasp the dialectical development of proletarian culture. The Communist Party was neither hierarchical nor authoritarian, as the Workers' Truth group charged. Instead the party ensured workers' collective interaction and self-government.[9]

But these attempts at political conformity did nothing to halt the organization's rapid decline. There were only eleven Proletkult circles left in the Soviet Union in 1924, and early in the following year the Proletkult in Tver, one of the oldest, shut its doors, liquidated by the local party division.[10] This dramatic reduction did not leave a distilled proletarian essence. Only 20 percent of the 412 workshop participants in 1924 came directly from the factory, although 33 percent more came from a proletarian background.[11] These figures

8. See I. Vardin's comments at a party press section meeting in May 1924 in *Voprosy kul'tury pri diktature proletariata: Sbornik* (Moscow and Leningrad, 1925), pp. 127–28. On Workers' Truth see Frits Kool and Erwin Oberländer, eds., *Arbeiterdemokratie oder Parteidiktatur* (Freiburg, 1967), pp. 264–73; Robert V. Daniels, *Conscience of the Revolution* (New York, 1960), p. 204; and N. I. Demidov, *Iz istorii bor'by Kommunisticheskoi partii za chistotu sotsialisticheskoi ideologii v period NEPa* (Moscow, 1960), pp. 9–10.

9. "Proletarskaia kul'tura: Tezisy pod redaktsiei Nauchnoi Komissii Proletkul'ta," *Al'manakh Proletkul'ta*, p. 21.

10. Minutes of the January 20, 1925, meeting of the central Proletkult presidium, *Tsentral'nyi Gosudarstvennyi Arkhiv Literatury i Iskusstva* [henceforth cited as TsGALI] f. 1230, op. 1, d. 19, l. 7.

11. *Al'manakh Proletkul'ta*, p. 187.

changed little in the later years of the New Economic Policy; in 1928 only 49 percent of the students in creative workshops could claim any ties at all to the industrial working class.[12]

With their own networks so badly depleted, Proletkultists had to devise other ways to reach out to the proletarian population. As during the Civil War, they turned to clubs as their main link to the masses. By now the organization had lost control of most of its own clubs, but it provided instructors, information, and detailed guidelines for cultural work to union, factory, and Narkompros circles. Proletkult art studios crafted posters, banners, and slogans for club events. The central organization sponsored a director's workshop to train aspiring actors and directors for club theaters; it also sponsored a special program designed to educate club leaders.[13]

To popularize club work, the Proletkult replaced *Furnace*, its only national publication, with a new journal called *Workers' Club* (*Rabochii klub*) in 1924. Unlike previous ventures, this journal was not addressed to Proletkult members and sympathizers alone. Instead, it was aimed at a broad audience of club workers and was filled with advice on organizational techniques, political education, and cultural events. Through this publication Proletkultists hoped to reach a large readership with the message that Soviet workers needed a rigorous and well-planned club agenda. The most frequent contributors were seasoned Proletkult club activists, including Raisa Ginzburg, M. A. Rostopchina, and Valerian Pletnev.

The ideal club of Proletkult design contained many small circles (*kruzhki*). Each circle was quite specialized, but together they addressed a broad array of topical issues, including science, the family, sports, atheism, and military training. Political education received special emphasis. In the pages of *Workers' Club*, Proletkult activists instructed readers about

12. "Sotsial'nyi i partiinyi sostav tvorcheskikh kollektivov, 1927–1928," TsGALI f. 1230, op. 1, d. 298, l. 21.
13. *Rabochii klub*, no. 3/4 (1924), p. 77; and "Organizatsionnye-instruktorskie kursy pri TsK Vserossiiskogo Proletkul'ta," *Rabochii klub*, no. 7 (1924), p. 37.

revolutionary history and current politics. Begun in the year of Lenin's death, the journal devoted special attention to the fallen hero, advocating "Lenin corners" within each club.[14] Contributors proposed special evenings of political games in which club members could test their knowledge of party history and Marxist theory. In a marked about-face peasant issues now received much positive attention. Clubs were advised to open "peasant circles" and "peasant corners" to prepare workers for agitation in the countryside.[15]

Through clubs Proletkultists hoped to continue their efforts to transform the patterns of daily life and to change the "worker-philistine" (*rabochii-obyvatel'*) into a conscious class member.[16] Much of the writing on proletarian habits had a familiar ring; as during the Civil War, Proletkult activists admonished club members to give up their frivolous leisure-time pursuits, such as drinking and dancing. However, they proposed different methods to achieve the old ends. To raise female attendance, for example, the editors of *Workers' Club* suggested an impressive array of programs, from day-care centers and lavish celebrations of International Women's Day to sewing circles.[17] Women had been a missing theme in Civil War creative works, but now the Proletkult proposed theatrical scenarios addressing the problems of divorce, child-rearing, and family law. One such sketch depicted a trial in which a man refused to accept responsibility for impregnating his companion. In order to cast doubts on his paternity, he con-

14. See, for example, "Leninskie ugolki v klubakh," *Rabochii klub*, no. 5 (1924), pp. 47–48. On Lenin corners in general see Nina Tumarkin, *Lenin Lives! The Lenin Cult in Soviet Russia* (Cambridge, Mass., 1983), pp. 126–27, 222–24.

15. V. Pletnev, "Vnimanie derevne," *Rabochii klub*, no. 10/11 (1924), pp. 5–8; and R. Ginzburg, "Rabochii klub—litsom v derevne!" *Rabochii klub*, no. 14 (1925), pp. 3–6.

16. Iu. L., "Obshchestvenno-nauchnyi kruzhok," *Rabochii klub*, no. 1 (1924), pp. 5–9.

17. A. Zhilin, "Raskrepostim rabotnitsu," *Rabochii klub*, no. 10/11 (1924), pp. 67–69; "Den' Rabotnits," *Rabochii klub*, no. 15 (1925), pp. 60–63; and V. Pletnev, "Rabota sredi zhenshchin v klube," *Rabochii klub*, no. 25 (1926), pp. 4–7.

vinced his male friends to testify that they had also slept with her. In a Solomon-like decision the judge made all the men responsible for the child's financial welfare.[18]

New campaigns to change proletarian sensibilities were also added to the roster. Proletkultists urged workers to turn away from religion and join in the struggle for atheism by participating in antireligious festivities, such as "Komsomol Easter" and "Komsomol Christmas."[19] To achieve more labor discipline and higher industrial productivity, Proletkultists supported the work of the Scientific Organization of Labor (Nauchnaia Organizatsiia Truda, or NOT). Clubs should teach workers the value of time, admonished the avant-garde artist Nikolai Tarabukin. Leisure, like everything else, had to be learned.[20] To insure a strong and healthy working class, the Proletkult also became an enthusiastic advocate of physical education.

This ambitious social and political agenda was to be conveyed in large part through the medium of creative work. In the ideal club of Proletkult design, theater, music, literature, and art all became active forces in daily life. Proletkultists were strong supporters of participatory artistic forms, such as "living journals," "living newspapers," and "agitational courts" (*agit sudy*). Club members were instructed to design their own scenarios for these multimedia presentations using newspaper articles and current disputes in their workplace, neighborhood, and home. *Workers' Club* is filled with model scenarios based on timely issues, including the rise of fascism, worker-peasant relations, and antireligious campaigns. Some combined these themes in a humorous way, as in one sketch in which physical education advocates go to a village to chal-

18. Arkhip, "Priataly kontsy—popali v ottsy," *Rabochii klub*, no. 5 (1924), pp. 34–37.

19. M. Maiorskii, "Antireligioznyi kruzhok," *Rabochii klub*, no. 3/4 (1924), pp. 6–12; and A. Ivanov, "Komsomol'skoe rozhdestvo," *Rabochii klub*, no. 10/11 (1924), pp. 12–16.

20. Nikolai Tarabukin, "Vremia v klube," *Rabochii klub*, no. 1 (1924), pp. 32–33.

lenge the local priest and interest his daughter in their cause.[21]

Despite their efforts to provide practical services for labor organizations, Proletkultists encountered criticism of their day-to-day activities from the trade union cultural bureaucracy. Union organizers believed that the Proletkult placed too much emphasis on creative work at the expense of very basic educational programs, like literacy. They also feared that the kinds of clubs the Proletkult proposed could not possibly interest most workers, because they remained isolated and exclusive "laboratories." Proletkultists, however, complained that union cultural work was poorly planned, unsystematic, and devoted largely to frivolous entertainments.[22]

The Proletkult was soon forced to take trade unionists' criticisms to heart because in July 1925 the organization was shifted from Narkompros to union control.[23] As a result of this new arrangement, *Workers' Club* opened its pages to more reports from local union circles and began to recommend that clubs simplify their cultural offerings and devote more time to basic educational tasks. In an attempt to reach out to more workers, particularly adults, Proletkult club experts expressed an unusual concern for simple comforts, such as a pleasant club environment, better food in the buffet, and free tea.[24] Economic themes also gained more prominence. Mem-

21. Ia. Semenov, "Fizkul'tura v derevne," *Rabochii klub*, no. 15 (1925), pp. 43–53.

22. See S. Levman, "Proletkul't i profsoiuzy," *Vestnik truda*, no. 1 (1924), pp. 93–102, and Raisa Ginzburg's outraged response, "Nashi raznoglasiia v klubnoi rabote," *Rabochii klub*, no. 8 (1924), pp. 3–7. For an analysis of these disputes see John Hatch, "The Politics of Mass Culture: Workers, Communists, and Proletkul't in the Development of Workers' Clubs, 1921–1925," *Russian History*, vól. 13, no. 2/3 (1986), pp. 119–48.

23. "O Proletkul'te," *Pravda*, June 18, 1925; and V. Pletnev and F. Seniushkin, "Polozhenie o formakh sviazi Proletkul'ta s profsoiuzami," in *Leningradskii Proletkul't na tret'em fronte* (Leningrad, 1928), pp. 34–35.

24. S. Krepusko, "Pochemu vzrozlyi rabochii ne idet v klub," *Ra-*

bers were exhorted to pay more attention to the tasks of economic reconstruction and to consider ways to raise industrial productivity.[25]

In order to improve the quality of club work the Proletkult conducted numerous surveys and studies of local activities, compiling pamphlets and organizational guides. When asked, the organization also provided art instructors for union clubs. One Proletkult theater specialist completely reshaped the artistic program at the "Metallist" club in Leningrad. He convinced participants to give up their largely classical repertoire and to compose their own productions on themes such as "The Red Wedding" instead.[26] In Moscow a special research group called the "Club Cabinet" planned curricula for union cultural training programs.

For the Proletkult, clubs were centers to nurture and strengthen workers' creative autonomy. In their voluminous publications Proletkult activists continually underscored the importance of independent action. Artistic workshops were not supposed to rely on professional teachers or to follow the lead of professional artistic schools. Ideally, they would incorporate the real problems of daily life in works created by and for the participants themselves. Discussion groups and classes were intended to address issues directly concerning the members, rather than following rigid course outlines. In short, proletarian clubs were not supposed to resemble conventional educational programs, where activities were planned without student participation.

Nonetheless, there was a strong didactic, even patronizing,

---

bochii klub, no. 25 (1926), pp. 25–35; and I. Mazin, "Odin chainyi opyt," ibid., pp. 36–39.

25. See, for example, M. Rostopchina, "Ocherednye zadachi kluba," *Rabochii klub*, no. 32 (1926), pp. 3–6. For similar trends in Komsomol clubs see Peter Gooderham, "The Komsomol and Worker Youth: The Inculcation of 'Communist Values' in Leningrad during NEP," *Soviet Studies*, vol. 34, no. 4 (1982), pp. 506–28.

26. "Teatral'naia rabota kluba 'Metallist' v Leningrade," *Rabochii klub*, no. 30/31 (1926), pp. 97–98.

streak in Proletkult instructions. The organization printed and distributed scenarios for agitational courts and living newspapers, effectively undercutting the idea that members should write their own. In the proposals for political classes and discussion circles they included suggested questions and even suggested answers, along with bibliographies of required readings.[27] The transformation of "worker-philistines" into "conscious" workers was not left to chance or to the vagaries of individual interpretation. Through the medium of creative work Proletkult club programs aimed to educate a healthy, sober, loyal, and industrious working class.

Artistic Practice

The Proletkult's politically conventional club programs contrasted sharply with the innovative work it conducted in its own theaters and creative workshops. In comparison with the Civil War years its artistic agenda became much more homogeneous. The national organization finally had enough power to impose a fairly unified aesthetic direction that was enforced by constant inspections of provincial groups.[28] National guidelines endorsing production art and experimental forms finally prevailed, moving the organization toward the artistic left. In a clear indication of this shift artists and writers from the futurist camp, including Nikolai Chuzhak and Sergei Tretiakov, gained influence in Proletkult central studios. The futurist journal *LEF* noted this with some pride in one of its early issues.[29] Although leaders like Pletnev contin-

27. See, for example, V. Zlatov, "Kul'trazvlecheniia v klube," *Rabochii klub*, no. 2 (1924), p. 28; M. R., "Voprosy dlia polit-igr," *Rabochii klub*, no. 12 (1924), pp. 22–24.

28. In the fall of 1924, for example, Dodonova and Pletnev visited the Ivanovo-Voznesensk, Leningrad, and Kharkov organizations to inspect their work; see the minutes of the September 2, 1924, meeting of the central Proletkult presidium, TsGALI f. 1230, op. 1, d. 16, l. 20.

29. "Proletkul't," *LEF*, no. 2 (1923), p. 173.

ued to object to the label "futurist," the Proletkult nonetheless became an ally of the avant-garde.[30]

Theater, always the most popular art form, became the arena for the Proletkult's greatest experimental successes. By 1927 the organization supported workers' theaters in six Soviet cities outside of the capital.[31] The First Workers' Theater in Moscow, opened in 1921, shaped an interesting repertoire. The offerings were still eclectic, ranging from *Dawn of the Proletkult*, a compendium of proletarian poetry first composed in 1918, to Pletnev's realistic *Lena*. However, standard prerevolutionary classics disappeared entirely. In their place came the inventive work of Sergei Eisenstein, who became active in the Proletkult theater in 1921.

A student of Vsevolod Meyerhold, one of the most innovative directors of the early Soviet years, Eisenstein introduced many new techniques to the Proletkult. The most fruitful was Meyerhold's system of biomechanics. Advocates of this system argued that it would work like Taylorism in industry and make acting into a controlled, scientific process.[32] From his mentor, Eisenstein also took a love of the circus, pantomime, parody, and the grotesque—"minor forms" that Meyerhold believed were rooted in popular theater and culture.

Working together with the futurist writer Sergei Tretiakov, Eisenstein directed three striking experimental plays in 1923–1924. The first was an adaptation of Ostrovsky's *Enough Simplicity for Every Wise Man*, completely rewritten by Tretiakov.[33] This production moved the setting to contemporary émigré Paris and employed circus techniques, buffoonery, and even film (Eisenstein's first) to surprise and engage the

30. On this shift see John Willett, *Art and Politics in the Weimar Period, 1917–1933: The New Sobriety* (New York, 1978), p. 42.

31. V. Pletnev, "Za rabochii teatr," *Rabochii klub*, no. 41 (1927), pp. 3–8.

32. See Marjorie L. Hoover, *Meyerhold: The Art of the Conscious Theater* (Amherst, 1974), pp. 100–110, 311–15.

33. On Eisenstein in the Proletkult see Karla Hielscher, "S. M. Eisensteins Theaterarbeit beim Moskauer Proletkult, 1921–1924," *Aesthetik und Kommunikation*, no. 13 (1973), pp. 64–75.

audience. The next production, also a collaboration between Eisenstein and Tretiakov, was *Are you Listening, Moscow?* (*Slyshish', Moskva?*), a chilling agitational play about the rise of fascism in Germany. Using methods to promote suspense and terror, Eisenstein and Tretiakov induced the audience to identify with the events depicted on the stage. In the final scene viewers enthusiastically joined in the storming of a fascist tribunal.[34] Eisenstein's last major work in the Prolet-kult was *Gas Masks* (*Protivogazy*), a performance staged in the Moscow gas works without any decorations or set designs.[35]

After *Gas Masks* Eisenstein left the Proletkult for film production, although his first major film, *Strike* (*Stachka*), was completed with help from Valerian Pletnev and the First Workers' Theater collective.[36] The major directors who followed him in both the Moscow and Leningrad Proletkult theaters—Aleksei Gripich, Lazar Kritsberg, and Naum Loiter—had also studied with Meyerhold.[37] Throughout the 1920s the First Workers' Theater in Moscow employed techniques inherited from Meyerhold, especially the biomechanical method and the extensive use of the grotesque, pantomime, and satire, an approach that set the standard for all provincial branches.[38]

In the visual arts the Proletkult also shed some of its diversity and embraced the principles of the artistic left. The production art approach finally prevailed during the New Economic Policy. As a symbol of this shift, in the spring of 1922 the central art studio in Moscow closed its painting workshop.[39] Boris Arvatov became the most eloquent spokesman

34. S., "Slyshish', Moskva?" *LEF*, no. 4 (1924), p. 217.
35. *Al'manakh Proletkul'ta*, p. 186.
36. Jay Leyda, *Kino: A History of the Russian and Soviet Film*, 3d ed. (Princeton, 1983), p. 181.
37. See D. Zolotnitskii, *Budni i prazdniki teatral'nogo Oktiabria* (Leningrad, 1978), pp. 12, 43; and S. Margolin, *Pervyi Rabochii teatr Proletkul'ta* (Moscow, 1930), p. 56.
38. See "O rabote Proletkul'tov RSFSR, 1925–1926," TsGALI f. 1230, op. 1, d. 45, ll. 37–40 for provincial theatrical repertoires.
39. "Zhivopisnye masterskie," *Gorn*, no. 8 (1923), p. 242.

for the arts, praising the virtues of artistic creation tied to practical needs. He declared that easel art, museums, and purely decorative forms were dead.[40] Instead, art studios turned to utilitarian tactics, designing posters, book jackets, union emblems, and decorations for revolutionary festivals.[41]

In comparison with the visual arts and theater the Proletkult's work in literature was modest. It could not compete with the expanding number of proletarian writers' organizations or with the growing workers' correspondent movement encouraged by the party press. Local groups urged club activists to teach practical skills, such as journalistic technique, speech writing, and how to prepare scripts for agitational courts that were based on experiences from workers' daily lives. However, the task of publishing and promoting imaginative literature passed into other hands.

The Proletkult's presence in the musical world also declined. Some local groups, like one in Georgia, developed popular choirs and orchestras, but the national Proletkult did not sponsor a central music studio. The work that remained also tended to the left. In 1923 the Moscow Proletkult, led by the experimental musician Arsenii Avraamov, staged a concert of factory whistles to celebrate the anniversary of the revolution. The Leningrad Proletkult organized a jazz band, which promoted the "sports trot" to dislodge popular enthusiasm for the fox-trot.[42]

Participants in Proletkult workshops and studios were supported by scholarships in the 1920s, and most pursued their artistic work full time. The First Workers' Theater in Moscow was particularly successful in promoting its young artists to

40. Boris Arvatov, "Iskusstvo v systeme proletarskoi kul'tury," in *Na putiakh iskusstva: Sbornik statei*, ed. V. M. Bliumenfel'd, V. F. Pletnev, and N. F. Chuzhak (Moscow, 1926), pp. 9–33.

41. See the designs for May Day tribunals in 1925, *Rabochii klub*, no. 16/17 (1925), pp. 53–54.

42. Arsenii Avraamov, "Simfoniia gudkov," *Gorn*, no. 9 (1923), pp. 109–16; *Leningradskii Proletkul't na tret'em fronte*, p. 26; and Pavel Marinchik, *Rozhdenie Komsomol'skogo teatra* (Leningrad and Moscow, 1963), p. 175.

professional careers. The future National Artists of the Soviet Union, Maksim Shtraukh and Iuliia Glizer, as well as the famous film star Grigorii Aleksandrov all got their start in this organization.[43]

Nonetheless, the Proletkult continued to display ambivalence toward professionalization. Its artistic programs were idiosyncratic; they were designed to take their inspiration from nonprofessional circles.[44] More important, they were not integrated into the general Soviet educational system. When someone graduated from a workers' faculty or party school, it was clear what that meant, complained one participant from Ivanovo-Voznesensk. However, the social significance of Proletkult training was not immediately apparent to him. "I have to leave the Proletkult to join up with some Meyerhold or one of his many assistants or go to some VKhUTEMAS [Higher State Artistic and Technical Workshops] just to find out if I am or will become a real actor or artist with a credential in my pocket."[45]

When the Proletkult switched to trade union contrnl in 1925, its creative work came under closer scrutiny. In general, union leaders were critical of the Proletkult's agitational and experimental style. They urged it to follow the paths of established professional groups more closely, particularly in the theater.[46] This evoked some positive responses from journalists in *Workers' Club*, who argued that proletarian audiences were growing tired of "naked agitation" and longed for well-developed characters and a clear plot line. However, central Proletkult leaders resolutely resisted conventional repertoires. Club theaters should stage agitational trials or com-

43. Margolin, *Pervyi Rabochii teatr*, pp. 58–59.
44. V. Bliumenfel'd, "Teorabota Lenproletkul'ta," *Rabochii klub*, no. 28 (1926), pp. 34–37.
45. Khoral, "Na bol'nye temy," TsGALI f. 1230, op. 1, d. 1245, ll. 57–59, quotation l. 59. Some of his colleagues accused him of cowardly, petty-bourgeois behavior for this statement. See ibid., ll. 50–56.
46. "Vsesoiuznoe kul'tsoveshchanie pri VTsSPS," *Rabochii klub*, no. 29 (1926), pp. 51–53.

pose literary montages from public documents and newspapers, urged V. M. Bliumenfeld of the Leningrad Proletkult. Valerian Pletnev believed that scripts of any kind would soon be a thing of the past.[47]

Within its own workshops and theaters the Proletkult showed no signs of adopting more conservative methods under trade union management. Although the Workers' Theater retreated somewhat from its experiments under Eisenstein, it had a completely contemporary repertoire and considered itself part of the artistic left. Production art still held sway. Workshops employed the popular method of photomontage, and Moscow studios, under the direction of Aleksandr Rodchenko, designed ingenious multipurpose furniture for clubs.[48] Festivals were a focal point for much local activity. In 1927 the Leningrad Proletkult helped to map out an elaborate three-day agenda for the tenth anniversary of the revolution. The program incorporated displays of military hardware, historical scenes from the revolution, and mass performances of physical exercises and games.[49]

Despite this evidence of vitality, the Proletkult remained on the margins of cultural life in the 1920s. During the festivities marking the first decade of the revolution, numerous reviewers gave an appreciative account of the Proletkult's contributions to Soviet culture. But the articles had the tone of a postmortem, looking back at an institution that had outlived its usefulness. In his assessment of a decade of Soviet litera-

47. V. Bliumenfel'd, "Litmontazh," *Rabochii klub*, no. 32 (1926), pp. 19–26; and A. V. Lunacharskii, R. A. Pel'she, and V. F. Pletnev, eds., *Puti sovremennogo teatra* (Moscow, 1926), pp. 51–53.

48. L. P., "Izo Rabota Leningradskogo Proletkul'ta za 10 let," in *Sovetskoe iskusstvo za 15 let: Materialy i dokumentatsii*, ed. I. Matsa, L. Reingardt, and L. Rempel' (Moscow, 1933), pp. 279–82; Ia. Tugendkhol'd, "Sovremennyi plakat," *Pechat' i revoliutsiia*, no. 8 (1926), pp. 61–62; A. R., "Zapisnaia knizhka LEFa," *Novyi LEF*, no. 6 (1927), p. 5; and I. Chkannkov and N. Serov, "Klubnaia mebel'," *Rabochii klub*, no. 50 (1928), pp. 30–38.

49. I. M. Bibikova and N. I. Levchenko, *Agitatsionno-massovoe iskusstvo: Oformlenie prazdnestv* (Moscow, 1984), vol. 1, pp. 162–66.

ture the influential critic Viacheslav Polonskii concluded that
the Proletkult had helped to awaken the creative power of the
working class. "No errors by Proletkult leaders and ideologues
can lessen the enormous significance of the movement, which
attracted many gifted representatives from proletarian youth,
if only for a short time."[50] It was clear from his tone that he
felt its short time had long since passed.

The First Five-Year Plan: Expansion and Demise

The end of the New Economic Policy and the advent of rapid industrialization and collectivization in the late 1920s
marked a profound change in Soviet social life. Groups favored during the New Economic Policy, especially the peasantry and parts of the educated elite, found their status
abruptly and radically altered. The regime now shunned its
former allies and turned to the working class, in rhetoric if not
always in policy, as the main buttress for the industrialization
drive. The language of class conflict, severely limited during
the 1920s, revived in the lexicons of political activists.

The First Five-Year Plan had profound cultural ramifica-
tions. During the 1920s the Soviet government had endorsed
a policy of relative cultural pluralism, thereby gaining the
support of many artists and intellectuals who were at best
lukewarm supporters of the new regime. Their knowledge and
expertise were considered essential to realizing Lenin's vision
of a cultural revolution, that is, the gradual dissemination of
literacy and education to the broadest possible public. However, this incremental approach was abruptly altered in the
late 1920s. The state's change in direction put cultural experts
on the defensive and disrupted established educational programs. Cultural revolution, in its new aggressive transmogri-
fication, became a medium for class conflict, a way for the

50. V. Polonskii, "Literaturnoe dvizhenie Oktiabr'skogo desiati-
letiia," *Pechat' i revoliutsiia*, no. 7 (1927), pp. 15–80, quotation p. 38;
see also P. Markov, "Teatr," in ibid., pp. 149–50.

regime to motivate and justify its assaults on the intelligentsia and the peasantry.[51]

The many cultural circles advocating proletarian artistic forms not only welcomed these new policies but also helped to give them teeth. The Proletarian Writers' Union, especially its radical Russian division, the Russian Association of Proletarian Writers (RAPP), stepped up attacks against bourgeois culture, this time with some effectiveness. Voronskii, Lunacharskii, and others who defended "fellow travelers" and independent intellectuals quickly fell from grace. In language similar to that of the Civil War RAPP and its allies now demanded proletarian hegemony in the cultural sphere.

Proletkultists also embraced the new direction. In a substantial article on the meaning of cultural revolution, Valerian Pletnev argued that without a radical shift in cultural values, industrialization would not succeed. He insisted that it was essential for the country to rationalize industry, revise its educational system, and rid itself of the corrupt influence of bureaucrats, kulaks, and capitalists. The masses had to be excited and drawn into industrialization through cultural creation; they needed a new literature, film, and theater as well as new forms of propaganda to involve them in the great push for economic change.[52]

During the First Five-Year Plan all proletarian cultural circles were on the upsurge. RAPP increased its membership by 80 percent from 1930 to 1931; the number of TRAM affiliates expanded fivefold from 1929 to 1932.[53] The Proletkult also experienced some positive change: the membership in

51. See Sheila Fitzpatrick, ed., *Cultural Revolution in Russia, 1928–1931* (Bloomington, 1978), esp. Sheila Fitzpatrick, "Cultural Revolution as Class War," pp. 8–40.

52. V. Pletnev, "O kul'turnoi revoliutsii," *Rabochii klub*, no. 53/54 (1928), pp. 3–13.

53. Katerina Clark, "Little Heroes and Big Deeds: Literature Responds to the First Five Year Plan," in *Cultural Revolution in Russia, 1928–1931*, ed. Sheila Fitzpatrick (Bloomington, 1978), p. 196; and Mironova, *TRAM*, p. 6.

existing organizations increased, the percentage of workers rose, and the national network grew to include new circles in areas like Stalingrad and parts of Siberia.[54]

Topical themes dominated the Proletkult's creative work. New circles in Siberia sent out agitational troupes to perform at construction sites and collective farms.[55] Proletkult theaters performed contemporary plays, for example, Aleksandr Bezymenskii's *The Shot* (*Vystrel*), which had been made famous by the Meyerhold Theater. In the play young workers expose party corruption and unmask a group of Trotsky's supporters. Another play, *Without Regard to Individuals* (*Nevziraia na litsa*), featured a Komsomol member who valiantly resists the management of a large department store and reveals its unethical practices.[56]

Although the Proletkult showed signs of rejuvenation during the years of the "Stalin revolution," it could not reclaim its old position. It had neither the funding nor the staff to inspire the same broad following that it had had in the Civil War years. Moreover, its artistic direction was at odds with the aesthetic approaches favored by the regime. The Proletkult embraced a theater inspired by Meyerhold, a visual arts based on constructivism, and literary methods that tended toward documentation and a literature of fact. All these techniques came under attack as "formalistic" methods during the First Five-Year Plan. The Communist Party Central Committee even singled out the Siberian Proletkult for censure because it took a critical stand toward the work of Maxim Gorky.[57]

54. Minutes of the July 3, 1931, meeting of the central Proletkult presidium, TsGALI f. 1230, op. 1, d. 23, ll. 1, 8; and T. A. Khavina, "Bor'ba Kommunisticheskoi partii za Proletkul't i rukovodstvo ego deiatel'nost'iu, 1917–1932 gg." (Candidate diss., Leningrad State University, 1978), p. 152.

55. Pinegina, *Sovetskii rabochii klass*, p. 95; and *Kunst in die Produktion: Sowjetische Kunst während der Phase der Kollektivierung und Industrialisierung, 1927–1933* (Berlin, 1977), p. 22.

56. *Pechat' i revoliutsiia*, no. 5/6 (1930), p. 95; ibid., no. 3 (1930), p. 87.

57. "O vystupleniiakh sibirskikh literatorov i literaturnykh or-

But the Proletkult's most significant handicap remained its poor political reputation. RAPP, the most powerful cultural organization, attacked Proletkult theory and practice in a manner that harkened back to Lenin's original accusations. In their journal *On Literary Guard*, RAPP members denounced the Proletkult as a carcass of the revolution and accused it of being inspired by the false "Menshevik" ideas of Aleksandr Bogdanov. It had never produced much good work because its members totally rejected Russia's cultural heritage and held a romantic view of the revolution. The contemporary Proletkult was beneath their notice; its adherents were nothing more than the executors of a deceased movement who were circling around the sarcophagus.[58]

The ascendancy of proletarian cultural groups ended almost as quickly as it began. Their domination of cultural life depended on a state-sponsored shift in the social climate that openly favored the working class. By 1931 the government began a hasty retreat from the anti-intellectual positions it had sanctioned at the beginning of the plan. It instituted a series of laws designed to bolster the position of "bourgeois" experts and the technical intelligentsia, who had been severely ostracized both by state organs and by workers' cultural groups. Wage differentials favoring the better educated were introduced and the massive affirmative action programs, a central feature of the First Five-Year Plan's educational policy, were drastically curtailed.[59]

These dramatic reversals quickly affected the organiza-

ganizatsii protiv Maksima Gor'kogo," in *KPSS o kul'ture, prosveshchenii i nauke: Sbornik dokumentov*, ed. V. S. Viktorov (Moscow, 1963), pp. 201–2.

58. See V. Sytyrin, "O blagorodnykh predkakh, neblagodarnykh potomkakh, o legomyslennom povedenii poslednikh," *Na literaturnom postu*, no. 2 (1930), pp. 26–30; and idem, "Blagodarnost'," ibid., no. 8 (1930), pp. 20–23. See also Iu. Libedinskii, "O proletarskom teatre," *Rabochii i teatr*, no. 2 (1932), pp. 4–5.

59. Fitzpatrick, "Cultural Revolution as Class War"; idem, *Education and Social Mobility in the Soviet Union, 1921–1934* (Cambridge, Eng., 1979), pp. 209–33; and Kendall E. Bailes, *Technology and Society under Lenin and Stalin* (Princeton, 1978), pp. 159–87.

tions advocating proletarian culture. As at the start of the New Economic Policy, these groups' messages of proletarian hegemony were no longer welcome. RAPP, which had demanded a privileged position, became a special target of party criticism. It was charged with hounding sympathetic noncommunist writers, producing vulgar and inconsistent criticism, and promoting poor artistic products.[60] Although RAPP and its allies had been exposed to such attacks before, this time it was the prelude to their dissolution.

In April 1932 the Communist Party issued a directive that disbanded all literary and cultural circles. The document had a neutral title, "On the Restructuring of Literary and Artistic Organizations," but it was aimed specifically at the proletarian circles that had dominated cultural life during the First Five-Year Plan.[61] The party acknowledged the service of these groups, which had helped to foster a new generation of artists from the fields and factories. However, the directive charged that their activities had now become too narrow and sectarian, thus hindering the further development of socialist art. They would be replaced by professional unions open to artists of all classes.

This resolution marked the end of the many cultural circles that had evolved from 1917 to 1932, among them the Proletkult. These circles liquidated their operations, dividing up their staff and resources. Most affiliates of TRAM, the active youth theater, were absorbed into the Komsomol. Members of the Russian Association for Proletarian Musicians, RAPM, offered their services to the new musicians' union.[62] The Proletkult, the oldest and at one time the most inclusive of all these

60. Brown, *The Proletarian Episode*, pp. 188–89; Herman Ermolaev, *Soviet Literary Theories, 1917–1934* (Berkeley, 1963), pp. 106–18; and S. Sheshukov, *Neistovye revniteli: Iz istorii literaturnoi bor'by 20-kh godov* (Moscow, 1970), pp. 302–13.

61. "O perestroike literaturno-khudozhestvennykh organizatsii: Postanovlenie TsK VKP(b) ot 23 aprelia 1932 g.," in Gronskii and Perel'man, *AKhRR—Assotsiatsiia Khudozhnikov Revoliutsionnoi Rossii*, pp. 329–30.

62. Mironova, *TRAM*, pp. 92–104; and Schwarz, *Music and Musical Life*, p. 112.

groups, quietly handed over its assets to the trade union cultural bureaucracy; in August 1932 it ceased to exist.[63]

After dissolving the many contentious groups that had dominated Soviet cultural life, the regime began to formulate an official Soviet aesthetic, "socialist realism." This elusive genre bore some similarities to Proletkult cultural theories. Like Bogdanov, the shapers of socialist realism believed that art served an active social role. They also insisted that cultural creation be simple, clear, and easily accessible to the masses, characteristics that echoed at least part of the Proletkult's artistic platform during the Civil War. But at this point similarities ended. Proletkultists believed that culture in the broadest sense was a means to awaken creative independence and to express proletarian class consciousness. By contrast, the advocates of socialist realism saw art as a didactic medium through which to educate the toiling masses in the spirit of socialism.[64] Either implicitly or explicitly, they rejected the premise of a unique class culture that spoke to and for the proletariat.

Instead, socialist realism was intended to convey the values of all groups in Soviet society. Its purpose was to give "poetic shape to the spiritual experience of the socialist man who is now coming into being," to quote Bukharin's effusive phrase.[65] Proletkultists had always maintained that their ultimate goal was to create the foundation for a human culture transcending class boundaries; proletarian class culture was necessary as the penultimate step before that final end. Now socialist realism claimed to have achieved this classless ideal.

63. Khavina, "Bor'ba Kommunisticheskoi partii za Proletkul't," pp. 156–57; and Pinegina, *Sovetskii rabochii klass*, p. 118.

64. See the resolutions passed at the 1934 Writers' Congress, *Soviet Writers' Congress, 1934: The Debate on Socialist Realism and Modernism in the Soviet Union* (London, 1977), p. 275. For an innovative study of socialist realism that stresses its didactic nature see Katerina Clark, *The Soviet Novel: History as Ritual* (Chicago, 1985).

65. *Soviet Writers' Congress*, p. 255.

The new aesthetic was presented as the expression of a new and more advanced stage of historical development, a move toward a classless society.[66] The state's adoption of this new direction turned proletarian culture, supposedly the harbinger of the future, into the culture of the past.

66. On the links between socialist realism and a new classless interpretation of Soviet society see Ermolaev, *Soviet Literary Theories*, pp. 140–43; and Hans Günther, *Die Verstaatlichung der Literatur: Entstehung und Funktionsweise des sozialistischen-realistischen Kanons der sowjetischen Literatur der 30er Jahren* (Stuttgart, 1984), p. 12.

Conclusion

"Culture is not a luxury," wrote one Moscow Proletkult participant in 1920.[1] No words could better serve as the motto for the movement as a whole. Bogdanov first used them in his writings on art and culture before the revolution.[2] Lunacharskii repeated them when he moved to start the first Proletkult circle in 1917. No matter what the political condition of the country, he insisted, culture was too vital an arena to be ignored.[3] When defending the organization against political attacks, Valerian Pletnev employed the same phrase, pleading that the Proletkult not be viewed as a luxury that could be cast aside.[4]

Of course, on a fundamental level the Proletkult's opponents did not believe that culture was a luxury either. Instead, they questioned how best to turn what Pletnev called "this wild, uncultured, semiliterate, and impoverished country"[5] into a cultured society. The state chose a pragmatic approach, using its elaborate bureaucratic networks to transmit basic

1. O. Radanskii, "Zadachi proletarskoi kul'tury," *Gorn*, no. 2/3 (1920), p. 39.

2. See, for example, A. A. Bogdanov, "Vozmozhno li proletarskoe iskusstvo?" 1914, in *O proletarskoi kul'ture, 1904–1924*, by A. A. Bogdanov (Moscow, 1924), pp. 104–16.

3. P. N. Amosov et al., eds., *Oktiabr'skaia revoliutsiia i fabzavkomy* (Moscow, 1927), vol. 1, pp. 235–37.

4. V. Pletnev, "Na ideologicheskom fronte," *Pravda*, September 27, 1922.

5. Ibid.

education, labor discipline, and respect for the Russian classical tradition. In its varied programs the Proletkult contributed to this process as well by opening literacy classes and introductory courses in the sciences and humanities. In its workshops, theaters, and choirs it helped to familiarize the population with the prerevolutionary classics.

And yet, at least in the opinion of its most passionate advocates, the Proletkult was never meant to serve as a mere "culture bearer." Instead, its task was to found a new cultural order, an order dominated by a proletarian class spirit. Although no one could articulate just what shape this new culture would take, Proletkultists set incredibly ambitious goals. They wanted an art that would inspire society to productive labor and break down the boundaries between refined culture and daily life. They sought a new science that would integrate all knowledge into a harmonious whole and yet still be accessible to the population at large. They hoped to create a new proletarian intelligentsia that could completely subsume the old intelligentsia but not lose its ties to the working class. It was this utopian agenda that so offended pragmatists like Lenin, who saw such proposals as "harebrained" extravagances that the state could ill afford.

During its long tenure the Proletkult's expansive cultural goals narrowed markedly. Already during the Civil War, local circles abandoned many of their basic educational functions in order to conserve resources and attract a more advanced and gifted membership. The rich and eclectic artistic offerings, from folk music choirs to tonal-plastic studios, were gradually limited as the organization embraced a more unified cultural direction. Grandiose plans to transform science, the family, and daily life were scaled down to projects with much more modest ambitions. Instead of changing proletarian mores Proletkultists tried to restructure club workshops. Instead of addressing inequities inside the proletarian home they reached out to female participants with the promise of sewing circles.

This contraction of the movement's cultural mission was

partly the result of internal politics. Most central leaders had never wanted to provide hygiene lectures or literacy classes and were more than happy to leave these tasks to state institutions. Nor did they aspire to serve all of the laboring masses. In their view the Proletkult's real constituency was the proletariat's cultural vanguard, not the diverse social mix of the Civil War years. As the national organization gained more influence, it intervened in local operations to enforce its own vision of the Proletkult's goals. At the same time, many participants began to lose faith in their ability to transform long-standing habits and institutions, at least in the sweeping manner that they had first predicted. As Kirillov lamented in 1921, "The severe, cruel facts of life have shown us that those things we hoped and dreamed about in our work are very, very far away."[6]

External opposition also forced the organization to narrow its sights. The Proletkult never was a laboratory, isolated from the rest of Soviet society. It flourished with the aid and support of many allies, including unions, soviets, and parts of the Narkompros bureaucracy. When the Communist Party turned against it, the Proletkult's coalition of support dissolved. With the advent of the New Economic Policy there were fewer funds available for all cultural projects, but money was particularly scarce for an organization with controversial cultural and political goals. The Proletkult's dwindling programs reflected its dwindling resources. It had neither the funds nor the staff to support the wide network that had prospered during the early years.

As the Proletkult's cultural offerings declined, so too did its political ambitions. Once the organization was subordinated to the state, its controversial claim to be the equal of trade unions and the Communist Party was hardly tenable. Indeed, Proletkult autonomy was always a fragile construct, one that proved very easy to undermine. Although it gained the movement many followers, it also earned the Proletkult the party's

6. *Biulleten' vtorogo s"ezda Proletkul'tov*, no. 2 (1921), p. 3.

animosity. During the New Economic Policy members were much more cautious. The Proletkult named itself the main protector of workers' creative independence, but it no longer posed even a rhetorical threat to state or party authority.

The Proletkult spanned three distinct stages of early Soviet history: the revolution and Civil War, the New Economic Policy, and the radical changes inaugurated by the First Five-Year Plan. Only in the first period was it a major actor in the country's cultural life. Its tenure as a mass organization lasted almost as long as the war itself. The movement began its rapid expansion in the fall of 1918, in one of the first difficult phases of the war. By the late fall of 1920, as the war was ending, Narkompros took control and the Proletkult movement began its swift decline. Undoubtedly the conflict had facilitated Proletkult growth, because the heroic, combative atmosphere of the Civil War years encouraged many to believe that a new social order might be quickly and easily achieved. The organization's utopian cultural agenda fit the spirit of the times.

Because the political structure of the new state was not yet firmly in place, the Proletkult's controversial political ideas did not initially excite broad opposition. Members believed that it was possible, even desirable, to create new institutions that fully supported the regime but still remained outside state control. In 1918 such notions were already problematic, but they could still find some support within Narkompros and the Communist Party. Moreover, despite its claims to independence, the Proletkult provided valuable services for the government. It sponsored pro-Soviet educational programs and joined forces with other groups to enhance the cultural offerings available to the population at large. More important, the movement devoted considerable energy to agitation for a Red victory, both on the home front and on the battlefields.

The social upheavals of the early revolutionary years also encouraged the movement's growth. The Civil War called traditional social categories into question and disrupted established notions of social hierarchy. Despite the militant class-exclusive language so common in Proletkult pronouncements, participants defined the proletariat in the broadest possible way. In this period of social flux, when the very parameters of the working class were shifting, local organizations ignored class strictures and recruited a very broad social coalition. The Proletkult grew as quickly as it did because its appeal extended far beyond the industrial working class. In essence, it was a plebeian, not a proletarian, movement.

After the Civil War the Proletkult confronted a much less hospitable social and political climate. It faced aggressive new competitors in the arts and found few allies. The organization's following shrank rapidly, at least in part because it had less to offer prospective members. Certainly, by the 1920s those who had joined to take French lessons or to study mechanical drawing had better funded and less controversial options at their disposal. With its limited resources the Proletkult's claims to safeguard workers' ideology against the pernicious influences of the New Economic Policy could hardly inspire much confidence. Indeed, the continuing discussions about proletarian culture were only marginally addressed to the Proletkult. It was a negative reference point, a symbol of the past.

Although the atmosphere changed during the First Five-Year Plan, briefly giving proletarian cultural circles a new lease on life, the Proletkult never reclaimed its former role. The state-sponsored utopianism of the late 1920s and early 1930s was of a different sort than the expansive spirit of the Civil War, a change that Proletkult programs graphically showed. During the revolution the organization proposed to reshape the cultural foundations of society. During the First Five-Year Plan it looked for new ways to put culture to work to facilitate the industrialization drive.

The Proletkult began with extravagant promises, and measured against these goals its accomplishments were disappointing. Its ambitious social programs were never realized. The idea of a unique proletarian science inspired little support. Within its own circles representatives from the old intelligentsia held powerful posts, and "new intellectuals" like Kalinin and Gerasimov did not display much solidarity with their less advanced worker-comrades. Even in the arts, efforts to find distinctive working-class forms were stymied because participants could not agree on a representative proletarian genre. Proletkult creative production left few marks on future Soviet culture. Already in the 1920s, many regarded its brand of revolutionary romanticism as a curiosity, the expression of a phase of the revolution that had come and gone. By the 1930s critics denounced its innovative work in the visual arts and theater as utilitarian and formalistic.

But if we judge the Proletkult by such demanding standards alone, we undervalue what it did achieve. The very variety of Proletkult programs, so maddening to central leaders, was evidence of local ingenuity and creativity. Proletkult organizers, even those who did nothing more than open a cultural center, provided important services to their communities. They offered workers, peasants, and white-collar employees a chance to take art classes, listen to science lectures, and put their creative energies to work for the Soviet cause. In the better endowed organizations students came into contact with some of the finest artists in the country. Finally, the very existence of the movement encouraged debates about the political structure of the new state and the role of the working class within it.

The Proletkult did not found a culture of the future. However, it embodied the euphoric optimism of the early years of the revolution, an optimism that fostered the belief that any cook could run the state, any union could manage the economy, and any worker could write a sonnet. This utopian vision did not survive the 1920s, but it was a crucial part of a revolution that sought to transform culture as well as political and economic life.

Bibliography

Archival Sources

Tsentral'nyi Gosudarstvennyi Arkhiv Literatury i Iskusstva (TsGALI)
Fond 963. Gosudarstvennyi teatr imeni V. Meierkhol'da.
Fond 1230. Proletarskie kul'turno-prosvetitel'nye organizatsii (Proletkul't).
Fond 1372. Vladimir Timofeevich Kirillov.
Fond 1638. Vsesoiuznoe obshchestvo proletarskikh pisatelei "Kuznitsa."
Tsentral'nyi Gosudarstvennyi Arkhiv RSFSR (TsGA RSFSR)
Fond 2306. Narkompros.
Fond 2313. Glavpolitprosvet.

Proletkult Journals and Collections

Al'manakh Proletkul'ta. Moscow, 1925.
Biulleten' pervoi Kavkazsko-Donskoi konferentsii proletarskikh kul'turno-prosvetitel'nykh organizatsii, 25–28 sentiabria, 1920 goda (Armavir), 1920, nos. 1–6.
Biulleten' vtorogo s"ezda Proletkul'tov, 1921, nos. 1–2.
Bliumenfel'd, V. M., V. F. Pletnev, and N. F. Chuzhak, eds. *Na putiakh iskusstva: Sbornik statei*. Moscow, 1926.
Detskii Proletkul't (Tula), 1919–1921, nos. 1–9.
Gorn (Moscow), 1918–1923, nos. 1–9.
Griadushchaia kul'tura (Tambov), 1918–1919, nos. 1–7.

Griadushchee (Petrograd), 1918, nos. 1–10; 1919, nos. 1–7/8; 1920, nos. 1/2–12/13; 1921, nos. 1/3–9/12.

Gudki (Moscow), 1919, nos. 1–6.

Krasnoe utro (Orel), 1919, no. 1.

Leningradskii Proletkul't na tret'em fronte. Leningrad, 1928.

Literaturnyi al'manakh. Petrograd, 1918.

Metody raboty Proletkul'ta. Rostov on Don, 1920.

Mir i chelovek (Kolpino), 1919, no. 1.

Molot (Orenburg), 1920, no. 1.

Nash gorn (Bezhitsa), 1919, no. 1.

Pereval: Populiarnyi literaturno-khudozhestvennyi i nauchnyi zhurnal (Petrograd), 1922, no. 1.

Pervaia Moskovskaia obshchegorodskaia konferentsiia proletarskikh kul'turno-prosvetitel'nykh organizatsii, 23–28 fevralia, 1918 goda: Tezisy, rezoliutsii. Moscow, 1918.

Pervaia Tverskaia gubernskaia konferentsiia kul'turno-prosvetitel'nykh organizatsii: Protokoly zasedanii. Tver, 1919.

Petrogradskaia obshegorodskaia konferentsiia proletarskikh kul'turno-prosvetitel'nykh organizatsii. Moscow, 1918.

Proletarskaia kul'tura (Moscow), 1918–1921, nos. 1–21.

Proletarskaia kul'tura (Tiflis), 1919, no. 1.

Proletarskii den' kul'tury: V den' prazdnika kul'tury, 6. avgusta, 1919. Kiev, 1919.

Proletkul't (Vladikavkaz), 1919, no. 1.

Proletkul't: Tverskoi vestnik proletarskoi kul'tury (Tver), 1919, nos. 1–4.

Proletkul'tvorets (Moscow), 1920, no. 1.

Protokoly pervoi Vserossiiskoi konferentsii proletarskikh kul'-turno-prosvetitel'nykh organizatsii, 15–20 sentiabria, 1918 g. Edited by P. I. Lebedev-Polianskii. Moscow, 1918.

Rabochii klub (Moscow), 1924–1928, nos. 1–59/60.

Rubezhi (Belev), 1922, no. 1.

Sbornik Kostromskogo Proletkul'ta (Kostroma), 1919, nos. 1–2.

Sbornik pamiati F. I. Kalinina. Rostov on Don, 1920.

Troika. Smolensk, 1921.

Trud i tvorchestvo (Smolensk), 1919, no. 1.

Tsvety truda. Archangel, 1922.

Tvori! (Moscow), 1920–1921, nos. 1–4.

Vzmakhi: Zhurnal sbornik Proletkul'ta (Saratov) 1919, no. 1; 1920, no. 2.

Zarevo zavodov (Samara), 1919, nos. 1–2.

Zhenshchina i byt. Moscow, 1926.

Zhizn' iskusstv (Kologriv), 1918, nos. 1–4.

Zori (Klin), 1918, no. 1.

Zori griadushchego (Kharkov), 1922, nos. 1–5.

Contemporary Newspapers and Journals

Iskusstvo kommuny, 1918–1919, nos. 1–19.

Izvestiia Moskovskogo proletarskogo universiteta, 1918, no. 1.

Izvestiia TsIK, 1917–1928.

Krasnaia nov', 1922–1931.

Kuznitsa, 1920–1921, nos. 1–7.

LEF, 1923–1924.

Na literaturnom postu, 1926–1932.

Na postu, 1923–1925.

Novaia zhizn', 1917.

Novyi LEF, 1927–1928.

Pechat' i revoliutsiia, 1922–1930.

Plamia, 1918–1920.

Pravda, 1917–1932.

Proletarskoe iskusstvo (Velikii Ustiug), 1919, nos. 1–11.

Proletarskoe stroitel'stvo (Tula), 1919–1920, nos. 1–10.

Rabochaia gazeta, 1917.

Rabochii mir, 1918–1919.

Rabochii put', 1917.

Severnaia kommuna: Izvestiia Petrogradskogo soveta rabochikh i krasnoarmeiskikh deputatov, 1918.

Vneshkol'noe obrazovanie (Moscow), 1919, nos. 1–6.

Vneshkol'noe obrazovanie (Petrograd), 1919–1920, nos. 1–5.

Vpered, 1910–1911, nos. 1–3.

Vpered (Geneva), 1915–1917, nos. 1–6.

Published Proceedings and Document Collections

Amosov, P. N., et al., eds. *Oktiabr'skaia revoliutsiia i fabzav-komy: Materialy po istorii fabrichno-zavodskikh komitetov.* 2 vols. Moscow, 1927.

Belaia, A. O., ed. *Iz istorii sovetskoi esteticheskoi mysli, 1917–1932: Sbornik dokumentov.* Moscow, 1980.

Biulleten' pervoi Vserossiiskoi konferentsii po kul'turno-prosve-titel'noi raboty profsoiuzov. Moscow, 1921.

Biulleten' piatogo Vserossiiskogo s"ezda profsoiuzov. Moscow, 1922.

Biulleten' tretego s"ezda Politprosvetov RSFSR. Moscow, 1922.

Biulleten' Vserossiiskogo soveshchaniia Politprosvetov, 1–8 noiabria, 1920 g. Moscow, 1920.

Brodskii, N. L., ed. *Literaturnye manifesty ot simvolizma k Okti-abriu.* Moscow, 1929. Reprint, edited by Karl Eimerma-cher. Munich, 1969.

Chetvertyi Vserossiiskii s"ezd professional'nykh soiuzov, 17–25 maia, 1921 goda: Stenograficheskii otchet. Moscow, 1921.

Chugaev, D. A., ed. *Rabochii klass sovetskoi Rossii v pervye gody diktatury proletariata: Sbornik dokumentov i materia-lov.* Moscow, 1964.

Dekrety sovetskoi vlasti. Vol. 1. Moscow, 1957.

Desiatyi s"ezd Rossiiskoi Kommunisticheskoi partii: Stenogra-ficheskii otchet. Moscow, 1921.

Deviatyi s"ezd Rossiiskoi Kommunisticheskoi partii: Stenogra-ficheskii otchet, 29 marta–4 aprelia 1920 g. Moscow, 1920.

Eimermacher, Karl, ed. *Dokumente zur sowjetischen Literatur-politik, 1917–1932.* Stuttgart, 1972.

Ermakov, A. F., comp. "Lunacharskii i Proletkul't." *Druzhba narodov,* no. 1 (1968), pp. 242–47.

Gausman, A., ed. *Rezoliutsii i postanovleniia 4-ogo s"ezda prof-soiuzov.* Tiflis, 1921.

Gronskii, I. M., and V. N. Perel'man, eds. *AKhRR—Assotsia-tsiia Khudozhnikov Revoliutsionnoi Rossii: Sbornik vospo-minanii, statei, dokumentov.* Moscow, 1973.

Iufit, A. Z., ed. *Russkii sovetskii teatr, 1917–1921: Dokumenty i materialy.* Leningrad, 1968.

Kool, Frits, and Erwin Oberländer, eds. *Arbeiterdemokratie oder Parteidiktatur*. Freiburg, 1967.

Lorenz, Richard, ed. *Proletarische Kulturrevolution in Sowjetrussland, 1917–1921: Dokumente des "Proletkult."* Translated by Uwe Brügmann and Gert Meyer. Munich, 1969.

Matsa, I., L. Reingardt, and L. Rempel', eds. *Sovetskoe iskusstvo za 15 let: Materialy i dokumentatsii*. Moscow, 1933.

Mints, I. I., B. D. Galperina, G. L. Sobolev, and V. I. Startsev, eds. *Fabrichno-zavodskie komitety Petrograda v 1917 godu: Protokoly*. Moscow, 1982.

Odinnadtsatyi s"ezd RKP(b), mart-aprel' 1922 goda: Stenograficheskii otchet. Moscow, 1961.

Pervyi Vserossiiskii s"ezd sovetov rabochikh i soldatskikh deputatov. 2 vols. Moscow, 1930.

Petrogradskaia obshchegorodskaia konferentsiia rabochikh klubov: Stenograficheskii otchet. Petrograd, 1920.

Rosenberg, William G., ed. *Bolshevik Visions: First Phase of the Cultural Revolution in Soviet Russia*. Ann Arbor, 1984.

Sed'moi s"ezd Rossiiskoi Kommunisticheskoi partii: Stenograficheskii otchet. Moscow and Petrograd, 1923.

Shestoi s"ezd RSDRP (bol'shevikov): Protokoly, avgust 1917 goda. Moscow, 1958.

Smirnov, I. S., comp. "K istorii Proletkul'ta." *Voprosy literatury*, no. 1 (1968), pp. 113–24.

———. "Tsennoe priznanie: Pis'ma proletkul'tovtsa V. V. Ignatova K. S. Stanislavskomu, S. M. Eizenshteinu, V. E. Meierkhol'du." *Teatr*, no. 12 (1976), pp. 45–51.

Soviet Writers' Congress, 1934: The Debate on Socialist Realism and Modernism in the Soviet Union. London, 1977.

Stepanova, S. R., ed. *Muzykal'naia zhizn' Moskvy v pervye gody posle Oktiabria, Oktiabr' 1917–1920: Khronika, dokumenty, materialy*. Moscow, 1972.

Tret'ia Vserossiiskaia konferentsiia professional'nykh soiuzov, 3–11 iulia (20–28 iunia staryi stil') 1917 goda: Stenograficheskii otchet. Moscow, 1927. Reprint, edited by Diane Koenker. Millwood, N.Y., 1982.

Tretii s"ezd sovetov rabochikh, krestian'skikh i krasnoarmei-skikh deputatov Tul'skoi gubernii. Tula, 1919.

Viktorov, V. S., ed. *KPSS o kul'ture, prosveshchenii i nauke: Sbornik dokumentov.* Moscow, 1963.

Volkova, V., comp. "Materialy Proletkul'ta v TsGALI." *Voprosy literatury,* no. 1 (1958), pp. 168–83.

Vosmoi s"ezd RKP(b), 18–23 marta, 1919 g. Moscow, 1933.

Books, Articles, and Dissertations

Abramov, Ia. V. *Nashi voskresnye shkoly: Ikh proshloe i nastoiashchee.* St. Petersburg, 1900.

Alekseev, A. D., ed. *Istoriia russkoi sovetskoi muzyki.* Moscow, 1956.

Andronov, S. A., ed. *KPSS vo glave kul'turnoi revoliutsii v SSSR.* Moscow, 1972.

Anweiler, Oskar. *Geschichte der Schule und Pädagogik in Russland vom Ende des Zarenreichs bis zum Beginn der Stalin Ära.* Berlin, 1964.

——— . *The Soviets: The Russian Workers', Peasants' and Soldiers' Councils, 1905–1921.* New York, 1974.

Arskii, Pavel. *Za krasnye sovety.* In *Pervye sovetskie p'esy,* edited by V. F. Pimenov. Moscow, 1958.

Arvatov, Boris. "Iskusstvo v sisteme proletarskoi kul'tury." In *Na putiakh iskusstva: Sbornik statei,* edited by V. M. Bliumenfel'd, V. F. Pletnev, and N. F. Chuzhak. Moscow, 1926.

——— . *Kunst und Produktion.* Translated and edited by H. Günther and K. Hielscher. Munich, 1972.

Avrich, Paul H. "Bolshevik Opposition to Lenin: G. T. Miasnikov and the Workers' Group." *Russian Review,* vol. 43, no. 1 (1984), pp. 1–29.

——— . "The Bolshevik Revolution and Workers' Control in Russian Industry." *Slavic Review,* vol. 22, no. 1 (1963), pp. 47–63.

——— . *Kronstadt, 1921.* New York, 1974.

——— . "Russian Factory Committees in 1917." *Jahrbücher für Geschichte Osteuropas,* vol. 11 (1963), pp. 161–82.

Baevskii, D. A. *Rabochii klass v pervye gody sovetskoi vlasti, 1917–1921 gg.* Moscow, 1974.

Bailes, Kendall E. "Alexei Gastev and the Controversy over Taylorism, 1918–1924." *Soviet Studies*, vol. 29, no. 3 (1977), pp. 373–94.

——— . *Technology and Society under Lenin and Stalin: Origins of the Soviet Technical Intelligentsia.* Princeton, 1978.

Baklanova, I. A. *Rabochie Petrograda v period mirnogo razvitiia revoliutsii.* Leningrad, 1978.

Balibanovich, E. "M. Gor'kii i 'Pervyi sbornik proletarskikh pisatelei.' " *Oktiabr'*, no. 10 (1934), pp. 206–11.

Ballestrem, Karl G. "Lenin and Bogdanov." *Studies in Soviet Thought*, vol. 9 (1969), pp. 283–310.

Barren, Stephanie, and Maurice Tuchman, eds. *The Avant-Garde in Russia, 1910–1930: New Perspectives.* Los Angeles, 1980.

Bessal'ko, P. *Kamenshchik. Plamia*, no. 33 (1918), pp. 2–7.

Bessal'ko, P., and F. Kalinin. *Problemy proletarskoi kul'tury.* Petrograd, 1919.

Bibikova, I. M., and N. I. Levchenko. *Agitatsionno-massovoe iskusstvo: Oformlenie prazdnestv.* 2 vols. Moscow, 1984.

"Bibliografiia literaturnykh rabot P. I. Lebedeva-Polianskogo." *Literaturnoe nasledstvo*, vol. 55 (1947), pp. 611–26.

Biggart, John. " 'Anti-Leninist Bolshevism': The *Forward* Group of the RSDRP." *Canadian Slavonic Papers*, vol. 23, no. 2 (1981), pp. 134–53.

——— . "Bukharin and the Origins of the Proletarian Culture Debate." *Soviet Studies*, vol. 34, no. 2 (1987), pp. 229–46.

——— . "Marxism and Social Anthropology: A Proletkul't Bibliography on the 'History of Culture' (1923)." *Studies in Soviet Thought*, vol. 24 (1982), pp. 1–9.

Bikhter, A. M. "U istokov russkoi proletarskoi poezii." In *U istokov russkoi proletarskoi poezii*, edited by R. A. Shatseva and O. E. Afonina. Moscow, 1965.

Bobroff, Anne. "The Bolsheviks and Working Women, 1905–1920." *Soviet Studies*, vol. 26, no. 4 (1974), pp. 540–67.

Bogdanov, A. A. *Elementy proletarskoi kul'tury v razvitii rabochego klassa: Lektsii, prochitannye v Moskovskom Proletkul'te vesnoi 1919 g.* Moscow, 1920.

————. *Iskusstvo i rabochii klass.* Moscow, 1918.

————. *Kul'turnye zadachi nashego vremeni.* Moscow, 1911.

————. *Novyi mir.* 3d ed. Moscow, 1920.

————. *O proletarskoi kul'ture, 1904–1924.* Moscow, 1924.

————. *Red Star: The First Bolshevik Utopia.* Edited by Loren R. Graham and Richard Stites. Translated by Charles Rougle. Bloomington, 1984.

————. "Religion, Art and Marxism." *The Labour Monthly,* vol. 6, no. 9 (1924), pp. 489–97.

————. *A Short Course of Economic Science.* London, 1923.

———— [Maksimov, pseud.]. "Sotsializm v nastoiashchem." *Vpered,* no. 2 (1911), cols. 59–71.

————. *Vvedenie v politicheskuiu ekonomiiu.* 2d ed. New York, n.d.

————. "The Workers' Artistic Inheritance." *The Labour Monthly,* vol. 6, no. 9 (1924), pp. 549–56.

Bol'shaia sovetskaia entsiklopediia. Moscow, 1926–1947.

Bonnell, Victoria E. *Roots of Rebellion: Workers' Politics and Organizations in St. Petersburg and Moscow, 1900–1914.* Berkeley, 1983.

————. "Urban Working Class Life in Early Twentieth Century Russia: Some Problems and Patterns." *Russian History,* vol. 8, no. 3 (1981), pp. 360–78.

Bowlt, John E. "Russian Art in the Nineteen Twenties," *Soviet Studies,* vol. 22, no. 4 (1971), pp. 575–94.

————. "The Society of Easel Artists (OST)." *Russian History,* vol. 9, no. 2/3 (1982), pp. 203–26.

Breitenburg, S., ed. *Dooktiabr'skaia Pravda ob iskusstve i literature.* Moscow, 1937.

Briusova, N. "Massovaia muzykal'no-prosvetitel'naia rabota v pervye gody posle Oktiabria." *Sovetskaia muzyka,* no. 6 (1947), pp. 46–55.

Brooks, Jeffrey. "Popular Philistinism and the Course of Russian Modernism." In *Literature and History: Theoretical*

Problems and Russian Case Studies, edited by Gary Saul Morson. Stanford, 1986.

———. "Readers and Reading at the End of the Tsarist Era." In *Literature and Society in Tsarist Russia*, edited by William Mills Todd III. Stanford, 1978.

———. *When Russia Learned to Read: Literacy and Popular Literature, 1861–1917*. Princeton, 1985.

Brown, Edward J. *The Proletarian Episode in Russian Literature, 1928–1932*. New York, 1953.

Brügmann, Uwe. *Die russischen Gewerkschaften in Revolution und Bürgerkrieg, 1917–1919*. Frankfurt am Main, 1972.

Bugaenko, P. A. *A. V. Lunacharskii i literaturnoe dvizhenie 20-kh godov*. Saratov, 1967.

———. "A. V. Lunacharskii i Proletkul't." In *Problemy razvitiia sovetskoi literatury 20-kh godov*, edited by P. A. Bugaenko. Saratov, 1963.

Bukharin, N. "Burzhuaznaia revoliutsiia i revoliutsiia proletarskaia." *Pod znamenem marksizma*, no. 7/8 (1922), pp. 61–82.

Burbank, Jane. *Intelligentsia and Revolution: Russian Views of Bolshevism, 1917–1922*. New York, 1986.

Bylin, G. E. "Iz istorii kul'turno-prosvetitel'noi deiatel'nosti profsoiuzov i fabzavkomov Petrograda v period podgotovki Oktiabr'skogo vooruzhennogo vosstaniia." *Uchenye zapiski VPSh VTsSPS*, vol. 1 (1969), pp. 114–23.

———. "Kul'turno-prosvetitel'naia deiatel'nost' profsoiuzov i fabzavkomov Petrograda v period ot fevralia k Oktiabriu 1917 goda." Candidate dissertation, Moscow State University, 1971.

———. "Rabochie kluby i kul'turno-prosvetitel'nye komissii profsoiuzov i fabzavkomov Petrograda v mirnyi period razvitiia revoliutsii." *Uchenye zapiski VPSh VTsSPS*, vol. 2 (1970), pp. 108–18.

Carr, Edward Hallett. *The Bolshevik Revolution, 1917–1923*. 3 vols. New York, 1951–1953.

Carter, Huntly. *The New Spirit in the Russian Theatre, 1917–1928*. London, 1929.

————. *The New Theatre and Cinema of Soviet Russia*. London, 1924.

Chamberlin, William Henry. *The Russian Revolution*. 2 vols. New York, 1965.

Chase, William J. *Workers, Society, and the Soviet State: Labor and Life in Moscow, 1918–1929*. Urbana, 1987.

Chemodanova, E. M., ed. *Prechistenskie rabochie kursy: Pervyi rabochii universitet v Moskve: Sbornik statei i vospominanii*. Moscow, 1948.

Clark, Katerina. "The City versus the Countryside in Soviet Peasant Literature of the Twenties: A Duel of Utopias." In *Bolshevik Culture: Experiment and Order in the Russian Revolution*, edited by Abbott Gleason, Peter Kenez, and Richard Stites. Bloomington, 1985.

————. "Little Heroes and Big Deeds: Literature Responds to the First Five Year Plan." In *Cultural Revolution in Russia, 1928–1931*, edited by Sheila Fitzpatrick. Bloomington, 1978.

————. *The Soviet Novel: History as Ritual*. Chicago, 1985.

Clements, Barbara Evans. "The Birth of the New Soviet Woman." In *Bolshevik Culture: Experiment and Order in the Russian Revolution*, edited by Abbott Gleason, Peter Kenez, and Richard Stites. Bloomington, 1985.

————. *Bolshevik Feminist: The Life of Aleksandra Kollontai*. Bloomington, 1979.

————. "Working-Class and Peasant Women in the Russian Revolution, 1917–1923." *Signs*, vol. 8, no. 2 (1982), pp. 215–35.

Cohen, Stephen F. *Bukharin and the Bolshevik Revolution: A Political Biography, 1888–1938*. New York, 1975.

Crouch, Eugene Garland, Jr. "The Theory and Practice of A. A. Bogdanov's Proletcult." Ph.D. dissertation, University of North Carolina, Chapel Hill, 1973.

Daniels, Robert V. *The Conscience of the Revolution: Communist Opposition in Soviet Russia*. New York, 1960.

————. *Red October: The Bolshevik Revolution of 1917*. New York, 1967.

Davies, R. W. *The Development of the Soviet Budgetary System*. Cambridge, Eng., 1958.

Davydov, Iu. N. "Leninskaia kritika otnosheniia Bogdanova k filosofskoi traditsii." *Voprosy filosofii*, no. 6 (1959), pp. 111–22.

Dement'ev, A. G., ed. *Ocherki istorii russkoi sovetskoi zhurnalistiki, 1917–1932 gg.* Moscow, 1966.

Dement'eva, N. V. "O nekotorykh osobennostiakh estetiki i gnoseologii Proletkul'ta: Bogdanovskaia konseptsiia 'kollektivnogo opyta.'" *Pisatel' i zhizn'*, vol. 3 (1971), pp. 124–37.

Demidov, N. I. *Iz istorii bor'by Kommunisticheskoi partii za chistotu sotsialisticheskoi ideologii v period NEPa*. Moscow, 1960.

Denisova, L. F. "V. I. Lenin i Proletkul't." *Voprosy filosofii*, no. 4 (1964), pp. 49–59.

Diament, Kh. Ia. *Profsoiuzy na kul'turnom fronte: Ocherki Moskovskoi raboty*. Moscow, 1923.

Dregenberg, H. J. *Die sowjetische Politik auf dem Gebiet der bildenden Kunst von 1917–1934*. Berlin, 1972.

Dreiden, S. *Muzyka revoliutsii*. 2d ed. Moscow, 1970.

Driagin, K. V. *Pateticheskaia lirika proletarskikh poetov epokhi voennogo kommunizma*. Viatka, 1933.

Drobizhev, V. Z. "Sotsialisticheskoe obobshchestvlenie promyshlennosti v SSSR." *Voprosy istorii*, no. 6 (1964), pp. 43–64.

Dzeniskevich, A. R., ed. *Istoriia rabochikh Leningrada*. Vol. 2. Leningrad, 1972.

Ehrenburg, Ilya. *First Years of Revolution, 1918–1921*. Translated by Anna Bostock. London, 1962.

Elwood, Ralph Carter. "Lenin and the Social Democratic Schools for Underground Party Workers, 1909–11." *Political Science Quarterly*, vol. 81, no. 3 (1966), pp. 370–91.

Engelstein, Laura. *Moscow, 1905: Working Class Organization and Political Conflict*. Stanford, 1982.

Erler, Gernot. "Revolution und Kultur." *Aesthetik und Kommunikation*, no. 19 (1975), pp. 92–106; no. 20 (1975), pp. 9–25.

Ermakov, A. F. "A. V. Lunacharskii i sozdanie Proletkul'ta." In *Aktual'nye voprosy istorii marksistskoi literaturnoi kritiki,* edited by P. A. Bugaenko. Kishenev, 1975.

Ermakov, V. T. "Ideinaia bor'ba na kul'turnom fronte v pervye gody sovetskoi vlasti." *Voprosy istorii,* no. 11 (1971), pp. 16–31.

——— . *Istoricheskii opyt kul'turnoi revoliutsii v SSSR.* Moscow, 1968.

——— . "Sovetskaia kul'tura kak predmet istoricheskogo issledovaniia," *Voprosy istorii,* no. 11 (1973), pp. 20–33.

Ermolaev, Herman. *Soviet Literary Theories, 1917–1934: The Genesis of Socialist Realism.* Berkeley, 1963.

Eventov, I. S., ed. *Poeziia v bol'shevistskikh izdaniiakh, 1901–1917.* Leningrad, 1967.

Farber, L. M. *Sovetskaia literatura pervykh let revoliutsii, 1917–1920 gg.* Moscow, 1966.

Farnsworth, Beatrice. "Village Women Experience the Revolution." In *Bolshevik Culture: Experiment and Order in the Russian Revolution,* edited by Abbott Gleason, Peter Kenez, and Richard Stites. Bloomington, 1985.

Fedin, Konstantin. *Sobranie sochinenii v deviati tomakh.* Vol. 9. Moscow, 1962.

Fediukin, S. A. *The Great October Revolution and the Intelligentsia.* Translated by Sinclair Lourit. Moscow, 1975.

——— . "Iz istorii bor'by s burzhuaznoi ideologiei v pervye gody NEPa." *Voprosy istorii KPSS,* no. 1 (1972), pp. 79–88.

——— . "Khudozhestvennaia intelligentsiia v pervye gody sovetskoi vlasti." *Istoriia SSSR,* no. 1 (1969), pp. 8–26.

——— . *Sovetskaia vlast' i burzhuaznye spetsialisty.* Moscow, 1965.

Fedotova, G. K. "Prakticheskaia deiatel'nost' Proletkul'ta v oblasti khudozhestvennoi samodeiatel'nosti." *Sbornik trudov Moskovskogo gosudarstvennogo instituta kul'tury,* vol. 23 (1973), pp. 127–62.

Fenner, Heinz. *Die Propaganda-Schulen der Bolschewisten: Ein Beitrag zur Vorgeschichte der Proletkultbewegung.* Berlin, 1920.

Ferro, Marc. *The Russian Revolution of February 1917*. Translated by J. L. Richards. Englewood Cliffs, N.J., 1972.

Fitzpatrick, Sheila. "The Bolsheviks' Dilemma: Class, Culture and Politics in the Early Soviet Years." *Slavic Review*, vol. 47, no. 4 (1988), pp. 599–613.

———. *The Commissariat of Enlightenment: Soviet Organization of Education and the Arts under Lunacharsky, 1917–1921*. Cambridge, Eng., 1970.

———. "Cultural Revolution as Class War." In *Cultural Revolution in Russia, 1928–1931*, edited by Sheila Fitzpatrick. Bloomington, 1978.

———. *Education and Social Mobility in the Soviet Union, 1921–1934*. Cambridge, Eng., 1979.

———. "The 'Soft' Line on Culture and its Enemies: Soviet Cultural Policy, 1922–1927." *Slavic Review*, vol. 33, no. 2 (1974), pp. 267–87.

———, ed. *Cultural Revolution in Russia, 1928–1931*. Bloomington, 1978.

Fomin, A. I. "Stanovlenie tsentral'nogo sovetskogo apparatagosudarstvennogo rukovodstva narodnym prosveshcheniem." *Voprosy istorii*, no. 12 (1976), pp. 17–29.

Fueloep-Miller, René. *The Mind and Face of Bolshevism: An Examination of Cultural Life in Russia*. Translated by F. S. Flint and D. F. Tait. New York, 1965.

Fueloep-Miller, René, and Joseph Gregor. *The Russian Theatre: Its Character and History with a Special Reference to the Revolutionary Period*. Translated by Paul England. New York, 1968.

Gaponenko, L. S. *Rabochii klass v 1917 godu*. Moscow, 1970.

Gassner, Hubertus, and Eckhardt Gillen, eds. *Zwischen Revolutionskunst und sozialistischen Realismus: Kunstdebatten in der Sowjetunion von 1917 bis 1934*. Cologne, 1979.

Gerasimov, Mikhail. *Stikhotvoreniia*. Moscow, 1959.

———. *Zavod vesennii*. Moscow, 1919.

Geyer, Dietrich. "Arbeiterbewegung und 'Kulturrevolution' in Russland." *Vierteljahreshefte für Zeitgeschichte*, vol. 10, no. 1 (1962), pp. 43–55.

Gill, Graeme J. *Peasant and Government in the Russian Revolution*. London, 1979.

Gimpel'son, E. G. *Sovetskii rabochii klass, 1918–1920 gg.: Sotsial'no-politicheskie izmeneniia*. Moscow, 1974.

————. *Sovety v gody inostrannoi interventsii i grazhdanskoi voiny*. Moscow, 1968.

————. *"Voennyi kommunizm": Politika, praktika, ideologiia*. Moscow, 1973.

Gleason, Abbott, Peter Kenez, and Richard Stites, eds. *Bolshevik Culture: Experiment and Order in the Russian Revolution*. Bloomington, 1985.

Glickman, Rose L. "The Russian Factory Woman, 1880–1914." In *Women in Russia*, edited by Dorothy Atkinson, Alexander Dallin, and Gail Lapidus. Stanford, 1977.

————. *Russian Factory Women: Workplace and Society, 1880–1914*. Berkeley, 1984.

Gol'denberg, M. "Sotsial'no-politicheskoe soderzhanie likvidatorstva," *Proletarskaia revoliutsiia*, no. 6/7 (1928), pp. 222–64.

Goldman, Wendy. "Freedom and its Consequences: The Debate on the Soviet Family Code of 1926." *Russian History*, vol. 11, no. 4 (1984), pp. 362–88.

Gooderham, Peter. "The Komsomol and Worker Youth: The Inculcation of 'Communist Values' in Leningrad during NEP." *Soviet Studies*, vol. 34, no. 4 (1982), pp. 504–28.

Gorbunov, V. V. "Bor'ba V. I. Lenina s separatistskimi ustremleniiami Proletkul'ta." *Voprosy istorii KPSS*, no. 1 (1958), pp. 29–40.

————. "Iz istorii bor'by Kommunisticheskoi partii s sektanstvom Proletkul'ta." In *Ocherki po istorii sovetskoi nauki i kul'tury*, edited by L. V. Koshman. Moscow, 1968.

————. "Iz istorii kul'turno-prosvetitel'noi deiatel'nosti Petrogradskikh bol'shevikov v period podgotovki Oktiabria." *Voprosy istorii KPSS*, no. 2 (1967), pp. 25–35.

————. "Kritika V. I. Leninym teorii Proletkul'ta ob otnoshenii k kul'turnomu naslediiu." *Voprosy istorii KPSS*, no. 5 (1968), pp. 83–93.

————. *Lenin i sotsialisticheskaia kul'tura: Leninskaia kontseptsiia formirovaniia sotsialisticheskoi kul'tury.* Moscow, 1972.

————. "Oktiabr' i nachalo kul'turnoi revoliutsii na mestakh." In *Velikii Oktiabr': Istoriia, istoriografiia, istochnovedenie,* edited by Iu. A. Poliakov. Moscow, 1978.

————. *V. I. Lenin i Proletkul't.* Moscow, 1974.

Gorelov, I. E. *Bol'sheviki i legal'nye organizatsii rabochego klassa.* Moscow, 1980.

Gor'kii, M. *Sobranie sochinenii v tridtsati tomakh.* Vol. 24. Moscow, 1953.

————. *Untimely Thoughts: Essays on Revolution, Culture and the Bolsheviks, 1917–1918.* Translated and edited by Herman Ermolaev. New York, 1968.

Gorodetskii, E. N. "Bor'ba narodnykh mass za sozdanie sovetskoi kul'tury, 1917–1920 gg." *Voprosy istorii,* no. 4 (1954), pp. 18–37.

Gorsen, Peter, and Eberhard Knödler-Bunte. *Proletkult: System einer proletarischen Kultur.* 2 vols. Stuttgart, 1974.

Gorzka, Gabriele. *A. Bogdanov und der russische Proletkult: Theorie und Praxis einer sozialistischen Kulturrevolution.* Frankfurt am Main, 1980.

————. "Alltag der städtischen Arbeiterschaft in Sowjetrussland, 1918–1921." *Archiv für Sozialgeschichte,* no. 25 (1985), pp. 137–57.

————. "Proletarian Culture in Practice: Workers' Clubs in the Period 1917–1921." In *Essays in Soviet History,* edited by J. W. Strong. Forthcoming.

Graham, Loren R. "Bogdanov's Inner Message." In *Red Star: The First Bolshevik Utopia,* by Alexander Bogdanov, edited by Loren R. Graham and Richard Stites. Bloomington, 1984.

————. *Science and Philosophy in the Soviet Union.* New York, 1971.

Granat, L., and N. Varzin. *Aktery-agitatory, boitsy.* Moscow, 1970.

Gray, Camilla. *The Russian Experiment in Art, 1868–1922.* London, 1976.

Grille, Dietrich. *Lenins Rivale: Bogdanov und seine Philosophie.* Cologne, 1966.

Grinval'd, Iakov. *Maksim Shtraukh.* Moscow, 1939.

Günther, Hans. "Proletarische und avantgardistische Kunst: Die Organizationsaesthetik Bogdanovs und die LEF Konzeption der 'lebenbauenden' Kunst." *Aesthetik und Kommunikation,* no. 12 (1973), pp. 62–75.

———. *Die Verstaatlichung der Literatur: Entstehung und Funktionsweise des sozialistischen-realistischen Kanons der sowjetischen Literatur der 30er Jahren.* Stuttgart, 1984.

Günther, Hans, and Karla Hielscher. "Zur proletarischen Produktionskunst Boris I. Arvatovs." In *Kunst und Produktion,* by Boris Arvatov, edited and translated by H. Günther and K. Hielscher. Munich, 1972.

Gurvich, A. R. "Artisticheskaia Moskva v 1917–1920 gg.: Iz vospominanii." *Novyi zhurnal,* no. 129 (1977), pp. 200–210.

Gutorovich, A. "A korolevu otpravim v kabak!" *Teatral'naia zhizn',* no. 14 (1966), pp. 20–21.

Haimson, Leopold. "The Problem of Social Identities in Early Twentieth Century Russia." *Slavic Review,* vol. 47, no. 1 (1988), pp. 1–28.

———. "The Problem of Social Stability in Urban Russia, 1905–1917." In *The Structure of Russian History,* edited by Michael Cherniavsky. New York, 1970.

———. *The Russian Marxists and the Origins of Bolshevism.* Boston, 1955.

Hans, N., and S. Hessen. *Educational Policy in Soviet Russia.* London, 1930.

Hasegawa, Tsuyoshi. *The February Revolution: Petrograd, 1917.* Seattle, 1981.

Hatch, John. "The Politics of Mass Culture: Workers, Communists, and Proletkul't in the Development of Workers' Clubs, 1921–1925." *Russian History,* vol. 13, no. 2/3 (1986), pp. 119–48.

Haupt, Georges, and Jean-Jacques Marie. *Makers of the Russian Revolution: Biographies of Bolshevik Leaders.* Translated by C. I. P. Ferdinand and D. M. Bellos. Ithaca, 1974.

Haupt, Georges, and Jutta Scherrer. "Gor'kij, Bogdanov, Lenin: Neue Quellen zur ideologischen Krise in der bolschewistischen Fraktion, 1908–1910." *Cahiers du monde russe et soviétique*, vol. 19 (1978), pp. 321–34.

Hayashida, R. H. "Lenin and the Third Front." *Slavic Review*, vol. 28, no. 2 (1969), pp. 314–24.

Hayden, Carol Eubanks. "Feminism and Bolshevism: The Zhenotdel and the Politics of Women's Emancipation in Russia, 1917–1930." Ph.D. dissertation, University of California, Berkeley, 1979.

———. "The Zhenotdel and the Bolshevik Party." *Russian History*, vol. 3, no. 2 (1976), pp. 150–73.

Hayward, Max, and Leopold Labedz, eds. *Literature and Revolution in Soviet Russia*. New York, 1963.

Hielscher, Karla. "S. M. Eisensteins Theaterarbeit beim Moskauer Proletkult, 1921–1924." *Aesthetik und Kommunikation*, no. 13 (1973), pp. 64–75.

Hobsbawm, Eric. "Man and Woman in Socialist Iconography." *History Workshop Journal*, no. 6 (1978), pp. 121–38.

Hoover, Marjorie L. *Meyerhold: The Art of the Conscious Theater*. Amherst, 1974.

Husband, William. *Workers' Control and Centralization in the Russian Revolution: The Textile Industry of the Central Industrial Region, 1917–1920*. The Carl Beck Papers in Russian and East European Studies, no. 403. Pittsburgh, 1985.

Iakovlev, B. *Kritik-boets: O P. I. Lebedeve-Polianskom*. Moscow, 1960.

Iakubovskii, Georgii. *Literaturnye portrety: Pisateli kuznitsy*. Moscow and Leningrad, 1926.

Ignatev, G. S. *Moskva v pervyi god proletarskoi diktatury*. Moscow, 1975.

Il'enkov, E. V. *Leninskaia dialektika i metafizika pozitivizma*. Moscow, 1980.

Il'ina, G. I. *Kul'turnoe stroitel'stvo v Petrograde*. Leningrad, 1982.

———. "Oktiabr' v Petrograde i khudozhestvennaia intelligentsiia." In *Oktiabr'skoe vooruzhennoe vosstanie v Petrograde: Sbornik statei*, edited by I. I. Mints. Moscow, 1980.

Il'inskii, Igor'. *Sam o sebe.* Moscow, 1961.

Iudin, P. *Marksizm-Leninizm o kul'ture i kul'turnoi revoliutsii.* Moscow, 1933.

Ivanov, L. M., ed. *Istoriia rabochego klassa Rossii, 1861–1900 gg.* Moscow, 1972.

Jangfeldt, Bengt. *Majakovskij and Futurism, 1917–1921.* Stockholm, 1976.

Jensen, Kenneth M. *Beyond Marx and Mach: Alexander Bogdanov's Philosophy of Living Experience.* Dordrecht, 1978.

Johansson, Kurt. *Aleksej Gastev: Proletarian Bard of the Machine Age.* Stockholm, 1983.

Johnson, Robert E. *Peasant and Proletarian: The Working Class of Moscow in the Late Nineteenth Century.* New Brunswick, N.J., 1979.

Joravsky, David. *Soviet Marxism and Natural Science.* New York, 1961.

Kabo, E. O. *Ocherki rabochego byta: Opyt monograficheskogo issledovaniia domashnego rabochego byta.* Moscow, 1928.

Kalinin, Fedor. *Ideologiia proizvodstva.* Moscow, 1922.

———. *Ob ideologii.* Moscow, 1922.

———. *Proletariat i tvorchestvo.* Moscow, 1922.

Kanatchikov, Semen. *A Radical Worker in Tsarist Russia: The Autobiography of Semen Ivanovich Kanatchikov.* Translated and edited by Reginald E. Zelnik. Stanford, 1986.

Kandaura, R. V. "Bor'ba V. I. Lenina i partii protiv vliiania A. A. Bogdanova na Proletkul't." In *Iskusstvo soiuznykh respublik k piatidesiati-letiiu obrazovaniia SSSR.* Leningrad, 1972.

Kanevets, T. M. "Kritika V. I. Leninym Proletkul'ta i otrazhenie 'proletkul'tovshchiny' v fizkul'turnom dvizhenii." *Uchenye zapiski Leningradskogo instituta fizkul'tury,* vol. 15 (1970), pp. 125–31.

Karpov, G. G. *Lenin o kul'turnoi revoliutsii.* Leningrad, 1970.

———. *O sovetskoi kul'ture i kul'turnoi revoliutsii SSSR.* Moscow, 1954.

Kastal'skii, A. D. "K voprosu ob organizatsii muzykal'nykh zaniatii v tsentral'noi studii Moskovskogo Proletkul'ta." In

Muzykal'naia zhizn' Moskvy v pervye gody posle Oktiabria, edited by S. R. Stepanova. Moscow, 1972.

Katuntseva, N. M. *Opyt SSSR po podgotovke intelligentsii iz rabochikh i krest'ian.* Moscow, 1977.

Kaun, Alexander. *Soviet Poets and Poetry.* Berkeley, 1943.

Keep, John L. H. *The Russian Revolution: A Study in Mass Mobilization.* New York, 1976.

Keldysh, Iu. V., ed. *Istoriia muzyki narodov SSSR.* Vol. 1, *1917–1932.* 2d. ed. Moscow, 1970.

Kemenov, V. S. "Leninskaia kritika makhizma i krizis sovremennogo burzhuaznogo iskusstva." *Voprosy filosofii,* no. 5 (1959), pp. 48–66.

Kenez, Peter. *The Birth of the Propaganda State: Soviet Methods of Mass Mobilization.* Cambridge, Eng., 1985.

———. *Civil War in South Russia, 1918: The First Year of the Volunteer Army.* Berkeley, 1971.

———. *Civil War in South Russia, 1919–1920: The Defeat of the Whites.* Berkeley, 1977.

Kerneck, Barbara. "Die Lyriker der 'Kuznica,' 1920–1922: Entstehung und Auslösung einer Gruppe." In *Von der Revolution zum Schriftstellerkongress: Entwicklungsstrukturen und Funktionsbestimmungen der russischen Literatur und Kultur zwischen 1917 und 1934,* edited by G. Erler, R. Grübel, K. Mänicke-Gyöngyösi, and P. Scherber. Berlin, 1979.

Kerzhentsev, P. M. *K novoi kul'ture.* Petrograd, 1921.

———. *Kul'tura i sovetskaia vlast'.* Moscow, 1919.

———. *Revoliutsiia i teatr.* Moscow, 1918.

———. *Tvorcheskii teatr: Puti sotsialisticheskogo teatra.* Moscow, 1918.

Khavina, T. A. "Bor'ba Kommunisticheskoi partii za Proletkul't i rukovodstvo ego deiatel'nost'iu, 1917–1932 gg." Candidate dissertation, Leningrad State University, 1978.

Khmeleva, V. "Khudozhnik-rabochii A. I. Zugrin." *Rabochii zhurnal,* no. 3/4 (1924), pp. 139–43.

Khodasevich, V. *Literaturnye stat'i i vospominaniia.* New York, 1954.

Kim, M. P. "Istoricheskii opyt kul'turnoi revoliutsii v SSSR." *Voprosy istorii,* no. 1 (1968), pp. 109–22.

————. *Kommunisticheskaia partiia: Organizator kul'turnoi revoliutstii v SSSR.* Moscow, 1955.

————. *Velikii Oktiabr' i kul'turnaia revoliutsiia v SSSR.* Moscow, 1967.

————, ed. *Kul'turnaia revoliutsiia v SSSR, 1917–1965 gg.* Moscow, 1967.

Kireeva, A. F. "Literaturnye gruppirovki 20-kh godov i Proletkul't." In *Iz istorii sovetskoi literatury 20-kh godov.* Ivanovo, 1963.

Kirillov, Vladimir. *Stikhotvoreniia i poemy.* Moscow, 1970.

Kiselev, A. L. "A. S. Serafimovich i Proletkul't." In *Sovetskaia literatura 20-kh godov.* Cheliabinsk, 1966.

Kleberg, Lars. " 'Peoples' Theater' and the Revolution: On the History of a Concept before and after 1917." In *Art, Society, Revolution: Russia, 1917–1921,* edited by N. A. Nilsson. Stockholm, 1979.

Kleinbort, L. N. *Ocherki narodnoi literatury, 1880–1923 gg.: Belletristiki.* Leningrad, 1924.

————. "Rukopisnye zhurnaly rabochikh." *Vestnik Evropy,* vol. 53, no. 3 (1917), pp. 275–98.

————. *Russkii chitatel'-rabochii: Po materialam sobrannym avtorom.* Leningrad, 1925.

Kline, George L. *Religious and Anti-Religious Thought in Russia.* Chicago, 1968.

Klug, Ekkehard. "Die Gruppe des Demokratischen Zentralismus und der 10. Parteitag der KPR(b) im März 1921." *Jahrbücher für die Geschichte Osteuropas,* vol. 35 (1987), pp. 36–58.

Knödler-Bunte, Eberhard. "Chronik zur politischen Entwicklung des Proletkult, 1917–1923." *Aesthetik und Kommunikation,* no. 5/6 (1972), pp. 153–90.

Knödler-Bunte, Eberhard, and G. Erler, eds. *Kultur und Kulturrevolution in der Sowjetunion.* Berlin, 1978.

Koenker, Diane. "The Evolution of Party Consciousness in 1917: The Case of the Moscow Workers," *Soviet Studies,* vol. 30, no. 1 (1978), pp. 38–62.

————. *Moscow Workers and the 1917 Revolution.* Princeton, 1981.

————. "Urban Families, Working Class Youth Groups and the 1917 Revolution in Moscow." In *The Family in Imperial Russia*, edited by David Ransel. Urbana, 1978.

————. "Urbanization and Deurbanization in the Russian Revolution and Civil War." *Journal of Modern History*, vol. 57, no. 3 (1985), pp. 424–50.

Kolesova, A. K. "Deiatel'nost' rabochikh klubov po Kommunisticheskomu vospitaniiu trudiashchikhsia v 1917–1923 gg." Candidate dissertation, Moscow State University, 1969.

————. "Prakticheskaia deiatel'nost' rabochego kluba v 1917–1920 godakh." *Uchenye zapiski Moskovskogo gosudarstvennogo instituta kul'tury*, vol. 17 (1968), pp. 231–49.

————. "Preodolenie v deiatel'nosti rabochikh klubov vliianiia oshibochnykh teorii Proletkul'ta," *Uchenye zapiski Moskovskogo gosudarstvennogo instituta kul'tury*, vol. 15 (1968), pp. 312–27.

Kollontai, A. *Rabochaia oppozitsiia*. Moscow, 1921.

————. *Selected Writings*. Edited and translated by Alix Holt. New York, 1977.

Kopanev, G. I., ed. *Geroi Oktiabria: Biografii aktivnykh uchastnikov podgotovki i provedeniia Oktiabr'skogo vooruzhennogo vosstaniia v Petrograde*. 2 vols. Leningrad, 1967.

Korolev, F. F. *Ocherki po istorii sovetskoi shkoly i pedagogiki, 1917–1920*. Moscow, 1958.

Kosarev, V. "Partiinaia shkola na ostrove Kapri." *Sibirskie ogni*, no. 2 (1922), pp. 63–75.

Krasnoshtanov, S. I. "Kritika Proletkul'ta o narodnom tvorchestve." In *Esteticheskie osobennosti fol'klora*, edited by L.E. Eliasov. Ulan-Ude, 1969.

Kratkaia literaturnaia entsiklopediia. Moscow, 1962–1978.

Kritsman, L. *Geroicheskii period Velikoi russkoi revoliutsii*. 2d ed. Moscow and Leningrad, 1926.

Krivtsov, S. "Pamiati A. A. Bogdanova." *Pod znamenem marksizma*, no. 4 (1928), pp. 179–86.

Krupskaia, N. K. *Pedagogicheskie sochineniia v desiati tomakh*. Moscow, 1957–1963.

————. *Vospominaniia o Lenine*. Moscow, 1957.

Kubikov, I. N. "Iskusstvo i otnoshenie k nemu rabochego klassa." *Nasha zaria*, no. 3 (1914), pp. 39–50.

―――. "Literaturno-muzykal'nye vechera v rabochikh klubakh." *Vestnik kul'tury i svobody*, no. 2 (1918), pp. 32–34.

―――. "Rabochie kluby v Petrograde." *Vestnik kul'tury i svobody*, no. 1 (1918), pp. 28–36.

―――. "Uchastie zhenshchin-rabotnits v klubakh." *Vestnik kul'tury i svobody*, no. 2 (1918), pp. 34–37.

Kulyshev, Iu. S., and V. I. Nosach. *Partiinaia organizatsiia i rabochie Petrograda v gody grazhdanskoi voiny, 1918–1920 gg.* Leningrad, 1971.

Kumanev, V. A. "Nekotorye problemy izucheniia kul'turnoi revoliutsii v SSSR." *Voprosy istorii*, no. 12 (1967), pp. 96–108.

Kunst in die Produktion: Sowjetische Kunst während der Phase der Kollektivierung und Industrialisierung, 1927–1933. Berlin, 1977.

Lane, Christel. *The Rites of Rulers: Ritual in Industrial Society.* New York, 1981.

Lane, David. "The Impact of the Revolution on the Selection of Students for Higher Education." *Sociology*, vol. 7 (1973), pp. 241–52.

Lapshin, V. P. *Khudozhestvennaia zhizn' Moskvy i Petrograda v 1917 godu.* Moscow, 1983.

Lebedev-Polianskii, P. I. "Kak nachinal rabotat' Narodnyi Komissariat Prosveshcheniia: Lichnye vospominaniia." *Proletarskaia revoliutsiia*, no. 2 (1926), pp. 49–61.

――― [V. Polianskii, pseud.]. "Russkie sotsial'shovanisty i zadacha revoliutsionnoi sotsial'demokratii." *Vpered*, no. 1 (1915), pp. 1–8.

――― [V. Kunavin, pseud.]. "V novykh usloviiakh: O Proletkul'takh." *Tvorchestvo*, no. 11/12 (1920), pp. 37–39.

Lecourt, Dominique. *Proletarian Science? The Case of Lysenko.* Translated by Ben Brewster. London, 1977.

Lenin, V. I. *Polnoe sobranie sochinenii.* 5th ed. Moscow, 1967–1970.

―――. *Sochineniia.* 3d ed. Moscow, 1928–1936.

————. *V. I. Lenin o literature i iskusstve.* 7th ed. Edited by N. Krutikov. Moscow, 1986.

Levin, I. D. *Rabochie kluby v dorevoliutsionnom Peterburge.* Moscow, 1926.

Levman, S. "Proletkul't i profsoiuzy." *Vestnik truda,* no. 1 (1924), pp. 93–102.

Lewin, Moshe. *Lenin's Last Struggle.* London, 1975.

Leyda, Jay. *Kino: A History of the Russian and Soviet Film.* 3d ed. Princeton, 1983.

Libedinskii, Iu. "O proletarskom teatre." *Rabochii i teatr,* no. 2 (1932), pp. 4–5.

Lidtke, Vernon. *The Alternative Culture: Socialist Labor in Imperial Germany.* New York, 1985.

Lieberstein, Samuel. "Technology, Work and Sociology in the USSR: The NOT Movement." *Technology and Culture,* vol. 16, no. 1 (1975), pp. 48–66.

Lilge, F. "Lenin and the Politics of Education." *Slavic Review,* vol. 27, no. 2 (1968), pp. 230–57.

Literaturnaia entsiklopediia. Moscow, 1929–1936.

Livshits, S. "Kapriiskaia partiinaia shkola, 1909 g." *Proletarskaia revoliutsiia,* no. 6 (1924), pp. 33–73.

————. "Partiinaia shkola v Bolon'e, 1910–1911 gg." *Proletarskaia revoliutsiia,* no. 3 (1926), pp. 109–44.

Lodder, Christina. *Russian Constructivism.* New Haven, 1983.

Lozovaia, E. "O raionnom Moskovskom Proletkul'te." *Vestnik zhizni,* no. 6/7 (1919), pp. 140–41.

Lunacharskii, A. V. "Ateisti." In *Ocherki po filosofii marksizma.* St. Petersburg, 1908.

————. *Kul'turnye zadachi rabochego klassa: Kul'tura obshchechelovecheskaia i klassovaia.* Petrograd, 1919.

————. *Ob intelligentsii: Sbornik statei.* Moscow, 1923.

————. *Revolutionary Silhouettes.* Translated and edited by Michael Glenny. New York, 1968.

————. *Sobranie sochinenii v vos'mi tomakh.* Edited by I. I. Anisimov. Vol. 7. Moscow, 1967.

————. *Velikii perevorot.* Petrograd, 1919.

————. *Vospominaniia i vpechatleniia.* Moscow, 1968.

Lunacharskii, A. V., and A. Khalatov. *Voprosy kul'turnogo stroitel'stva RSFSR*. Moscow, 1929.

Lunacharskii, A. V., A. Pel'she, and V. F. Pletnev. *Puti sovremennogo teatra*. Moscow, 1926.

L'vov-Rogachevskii, V. L. *Kniga dlia chteniia: Po istorii noveishei russkoi literatury*. Leningrad, 1924.

———. *Ocherki proletarskoi literatury*. Moscow, 1927.

———. *Raboche-krest'ianskie pisateli: Bibliograficheskii ukazatel'*. Moscow, 1926.

McClelland, James C. *Autocrats and Academics*. Chicago, 1978.

———. "Bolshevik Approaches to Higher Education, 1917–1921." *Slavic Review*, vol. 30, no. 4 (1971), pp. 818–31.

———. "Proletarianizing the Student Body: The Soviet Experience During the New Economic Policy." *Past and Present*, vol. 80 (1978), pp. 122–46.

———. "The Utopian and the Heroic: Divergent Paths to the Communist Educational Ideal." In *Bolshevik Culture: Experiment and Order in the Russian Revolution*, edited by Abbott Gleason, Peter Kenez, and Richard Stites. Bloomington, 1985.

———. "Utopianism versus Revolutionary Heroism in Bolshevik Policy: The Proletarian Culture Debate." *Slavic Review*, vol. 39, no. 3 (1980), pp. 403–25.

McVay, Gordon. *Esenin: A Life*. Ann Arbor, 1976.

Maguire, Robert A. *Red Virgin Soil: Soviet Literature in the 1920's*. Princeton, 1968.

Maier, C. S. "Between Taylorism and Technocracy." *Journal of Contemporary History*, vol. 5, no. 2 (1970), pp. 27–62.

Maksimov, A. A. *Sovetskaia zhurnalistika 20-kh godov: Kratkii ocherk zhurnal'noi periodiki*. Leningrad, 1964.

Malinin, A. S. *Lunacharskii o proletarskikh pisateliakh*. Minsk, 1965.

Maliuchenko, G. S. "Pervye teatral'nye sezony novoi epokhi." In *U istokov: Sbornik*, edited by I. P. Skachkov. Moscow, 1960.

Mally, Lynn. "Egalitarian and Elitist Visions of Cultural Transformation: The Debate in the Proletkul't Movement."

In *Culture et révolution,* edited by Marc Ferro and Sheila Fitzpatrick. Paris, 1989.

Mandel, David. "The Intelligentsia and the Working Class in 1917." *Critique,* no. 14 (1981), pp. 67–87.

————. *The Petrograd Workers and the Fall of the Old Regime: From the February Revolution to the July Days, 1917.* New York, 1983.

————. *The Petrograd Workers and the Soviet Seizure of Power: From the July Days, 1917, to July 1918.* New York, 1984.

Mänicke-Gyöngyösi, Krisztina. *"Proletarische Wissenschaft" und "Sozialistische Menschheitsreligion" als Modelle proletarischer Kultur.* Berlin, 1982.

Margolin, S. *Pervyi Rabochii teatr Proletkul'ta.* Moscow, 1930.

Marinchik, Pavel. *Rozhdenie Komsomol'skogo teatra.* Leningrad and Moscow, 1963.

Martynova, S. I. "Problema kollektivizma v literaturnykh sporakh 20-kh godov." In *Problema lichnosti i obshchestva v sovremennoi literature i iskusstve,* edited by S. M. Petrov, V. I. Borshchukov, and A. V. Karaganov. Moscow, 1967.

Matytsin, F. Ia. "Bor'ba V. I. Lenina protiv vul'garizatorskikh vozzrenii Proletkul'ta na iskusstvo." *Voprosy filosofii,* no. 1 (1953), pp. 111–25.

Mazaev, A. "Die 'Produktionskunst' des Proletkult." *Kunst und Literatur,* vol. 20 (1967), pp. 197–216.

Medynskii, E. N. *Vneshkol'noe obrazovanie: Ego znachenie, organizatsiia i tekhnika.* 3d ed. Moscow, 1918.

Mgebrov, A. A. *Zhizn' v teatre.* 2 vols. Moscow and Leningrad, 1933.

Mikhailov, V. *Khudozhniki Tambovskogo kraia: Istoricheskii ocherk razvitiia izobrazitel'nogo iskusstva na Tambovshchine.* Leningrad, 1976.

————. "V. I. Lenin i bor'ba s proletkul'tovskimi i futuristicheskimi izvrashcheniiami, 1919–1920 gg." *Iskusstvo,* no. 9 (1970), pp. 32–40.

Milonov, N. A. *Pisateli Tul'skogo kraia.* Tula, 1963.

————. "O deiatel'nosti Tul'skogo Proletkul'ta." In *Aktual'nye voprosy istorii literatury,* edited by Z. I. Levinson, N. A. Milonov, and A. F. Sergeicheva. Tula, 1969.

Mints, I. I. *God 1918*. Moscow, 1982.

―――. *Istoriia Velikogo Oktiabria*. 3 vols. Moscow, 1967–1973.

Mironova, V. *TRAM: Agitatsionnyi molodezhnyi teatr, 1920–1930kh godov*. Leningrad, 1977.

Mitel'man, M. *1917 god na Putilovskom zavode*. Leningrad, 1939.

Muratova, K. D. *Periodika po literature i iskusstvu za gody revoliutsii, 1917–1932*. Leningrad, 1933.

Muzykal'naia entsiklopediia. Moscow, 1973–1981.

Naimark, Norman M. *Terrorists and Social Democrats: The Russian Revolutionary Movement under Alexander III*. Cambridge, Mass., 1983.

Narodnyi Komissariat Vnutrennikh Del, RSFSR. *Goroda soiuzov SSSR*. Moscow, 1927.

Nevskii, V. A. *Kursy dlia podgotovki rabotnikov v rabochikh i krest'ianskikh klubakh*. Kostroma, 1919.

Nevskii, V. I. "Dialekticheskii materializm i filosofiia mertvoi reaktsii." In *Sochineniia*, by V. I. Lenin. 3d ed. Vol. 13. Moscow, 1931.

―――. *Otchet raboche-krest'ianskogo Kommunisticheskogo universiteta imeni Ia. M. Sverdlova*. Moscow, 1920.

Nosach, V. I., and O. I. Shkaratan. "Petrogradskie rabochie v bor'be za sotsialisticheskuiu kul'turu, Oktiabr' 1917–1918 gg." In *Ot Oktiabria k stroitel'stvu kommunizma: Sbornik statei*, edited by D. A. Baevskii. Moscow, 1967.

Nove, Alec. *An Economic History of the U.S.S.R.* Baltimore, 1969.

Novikov, V. "K istorii bor'by za sotsialisticheskuiu kul'turu: V. I. Lenin i diskussiia o proletarskoi kul'ture i Proletkul'te 1922 goda." *Voprosy literatury*, no. 3 (1967), pp. 27–48.

Nutrikhin, A. I., ed. *Pesni russkikh rabochikh (vosemnadtsatyi-nachalo dvadtsatogo veka)*. Moscow and Leningrad, 1962.

O'Connor, Timothy. *The Politics of Soviet Culture: Anatolii Lunacharskii*. Ann Arbor, 1983.

Orlovsky, Daniel T. "The Provisional Government and its Cultural Work." In *Bolshevik Culture: Experiment and Order in the Russian Revolution*, edited by Abbott Gleason, Peter Kenez, and Richard Stites. Bloomington, 1985.

Os'makov, N. V. *Russkaia proletarskaia poeziia, 1890–1917*. Moscow, 1968.

Ostroukhova, K. A. "Gruppa 'Vpered,' 1909–1917 gg." *Proletarskaia revoliutsiia*, no. 1 (1925), pp. 198–219.

———. "Otzovisty i ul'timatisty." *Proletarskaia revoliutsiia*, no. 6 (1924), pp. 14–32.

Otchet o rabote Politprosveta Narkomprosa. Moscow, 1920.

Ovtsin, Iu. I. *Bol'sheviki i kul'tura proshlogo*. Moscow, 1969.

Pankratova, A. M. *Fabrikräte in Russland: Der Kampf um die sozialistische Fabrik*. Translated by Karl Schlögel. Frankfurt am Main, 1975.

Papernyi, Z. S. *Samoe trudnoe*. Moscow, 1963.

Papernyi, Z. S., and R. A. Shatseva, eds. *Proletarskie poety pervykh let sovetskoi epokhi*. Leningrad, 1959.

Paquet, Alfons. *Im kommunistischen Russland: Briefe aus Moskau*. Jena, 1919.

Patrick, George Z. *Popular Poetry in Soviet Russia*. Berkeley, 1929.

Paul, Eden, and Cedar Paul. *Proletcult (Proletarian Culture)*. London, 1921.

Pedan, V. P. "O nekotorykh osobennostiakh esteticheskoi teorii Proletkul'ta (partiinost'—narodnost'—realizm)." In *Nekotorye voprosy Marksistko-Leninskoi filosofii*. Kharkov, 1964.

Pinegina, L. A. "Organizatsii proletarskoi kul'tury 1920-kh godov i kul'turnoe nasledie." *Voprosy istorii*, no. 7 (1981), pp. 84–94.

———. *Sovetskii rabochii klass i khudozhestvennaia kul'tura, 1917–1932*. Moscow, 1984.

Pinkevitch, Albert P. *The New Education in the Soviet Republic*. Translated by N. Perlmutter. London, 1930.

Pletnev, V. F. [V. Valerianov, pseud.]. "K voprosu o proletarskoi kul'ture." *Nasha zaria*, no. 10/11 (1913), pp. 35–41.

———. *Lena*. Rostov on Don, 1921.

———. *Mstitel'*. Moscow, 1922.

————. *Neveroiatno, no vozmozhno: Komediia v 3-kh de-istviiakh i 5-ti kartinakh*. Moscow, 1921.

———— [V. Valerianov, pseud.]. "Pervyi shag." *Bor'ba*, no. 7/8 (1914), pp. 44–46.

————. *Rabochii klub: Printsipy i metody raboty*. 2d ed. Moscow, 1925.

————. *Stachki: Intsenirovka po rasskazu Gasteva*. Moscow, 1921.

"Podpol'naia rabota v gody imperialisticheskoi voiny v Petrograde." *Krasnaia letopis'*, no. 2/3 (1922), pp. 116–43.

Potresov, A. "Kriticheskie nabroski: Eshche k voprosu o proletarskoi kul'ture." *Nasha zaria*, no. 2 (1914), pp. 88–99.

————. "Kriticheskie nabroski: O literature bez zhizni i o zhizni bez literatury." *Nasha zaria*, no. 4/5 (1913), pp. 63–69; no. 6 (1913), pp. 65–75.

————. "Otvet V. Valerianu." *Nasha zaria*, no. 10/11 (1914), pp. 41–48.

————. "Tragediia proletarskoi literatury." *Nasha zaria*, no. 6 (1913), pp. 65–75.

Priamkov, A. *Dooktiabr'skaia 'Pravda' o literature, 1912–1914 gg.* Moscow, 1955.

Prieberg, Fred K. *Musik in der Sowjetunion*. Cologne, 1965.

Puzyrev, V. G. " 'Proletkul't' na Dal'nem Vostoke." In *Iz istorii russkoi i zarubezhnoi literatury*, edited by V. N. Kasatkina, T. T. Napolona, and P. A. Shchekotov. Vol. 2. Saratov, 1968.

Rabinowitch, Alexander. *The Bolsheviks Come to Power: The Revolution of 1917 in Petrograd*. New York, 1976.

————. "The Evolution of Local Soviets in Petrograd, November 1917–June 1918: The Case of the First City District Soviet." *Slavic Review*, vol. 46, no. 1 (1987), pp. 20–37.

Rafilovich, V. E., ed. *Istoriia sovetskogo teatra*. Vol. 1, *Petrogradskie teatry na poroge Oktiabria i v epokhy voennogo kommunizma, 1917–1921*. Leningrad, 1933.

Raikhenstein, A. "1 maia i 7 noiabria 1918 goda v Moskve: Iz istorii oformleniia pervykh proletarskikh prazdnikov." In *Agitatsionno-massovoe iskusstvo pervykh let Oktiabria: Materialy i issledovaniia*, edited by E. A. Speranskaia. Moscow, 1971.

Rashin, A. G. *Formirovanie rabochego klassa Rossii*. 2d ed. Moscow, 1958.

Razumov, V. A. "Rol' rabochego klassa v stroitel'stve sotsialisticheskoi kul'tury v nachale revoliutsii i v gody grazhdanskoi voiny, 1917–1920." In *Rol' rabochego klassa v razvitii sotsialisticheskoi kul'tury*, edited by M. P. Kim and V. P. Naumov. Moscow, 1967.

Read, Christopher. *Religion, Revolution and the Russian Intelligentsia, 1900–1912*. New York, 1980.

Remington, Thomas. *Building Socialism in Bolshevik Russia: Ideology and Industrial Organization, 1917–1921*. Pittsburgh, 1984.

———. "Institution Building in Bolshevik Russia." *Slavic Review*, vol. 41, no. 1 (1982), pp. 91–103.

Remizova, T. A. *Kul'turno-prosvetitel'naia rabota v RSFSR, 1917–1925*. Moscow, 1968.

Riabkov, V. M. "Iz istorii razvitiia narodnykh universitetov v gody sotsialisticheskogo stroitel'stva v SSSR." In *Klub i problemy razvitiia sotsialisticheskoi kul'tury*. Cheliabinsk, 1974.

Rigby, T. H. *Communist Party Membership in the U.S.S.R.* Princeton, 1968.

———. *Lenin's Government: Sovnarkom, 1917–1922*. Cambridge, Eng., 1979.

Rodov, S. *Proletarskie pisateli*. Moscow, 1925.

Rogovin, V. Z. "Problema proletarskoi kul'tury v ideino-esteticheskikh sporakh 20-kh godov." In *Iz istorii sovetskoi esteticheskoi mysli*, edited by V. Z. Rogovin. Moscow, 1967.

Rosenberg, William G. "The Democratization of Russia's Railroads in 1917." In *Work, Community and Power*, edited by James E. Cronin. Philadelphia, 1983.

———. *Liberals in the Russian Revolution*. Princeton, 1974.

———. "Russian Labor and Bolshevik Power after October." *Slavic Review*, vol. 44, no. 2 (1985), pp. 213–38.

———. "Workers and Workers' Control in the Russian Revolution." *History Workshop*, no. 5 (1978), pp. 89–97.

Rosenstone, Robert A. *Romantic Revolutionary: A Biography of John Reed*. New York, 1975.

Rosenthal, Bernice Glatzer. "Theatre as Church: The Vision of the Mystical Anarchists." *Russian History*, vol. 4, no. 2 (1977), pp. 122–41.

Roslavets, Nikolai. "Sem' let Oktiabria v muzyke." *Muzykal'naia kul'tura*, no. 3 (1924), pp. 179–89.

Rostovtseva, I. "Uchastie khudozhnikov v organizatsii i provedenii prazdnikov 1 maia i 7 noiabria v Petrograde v 1918 godu." In *Agitatsionno-massovoe iskusstvo pervykh let Oktiabria: Materialy i issledovaniia*, edited by E. A. Speranskaia. Moscow, 1971.

Rothstein, Robert A. "The Quiet Rehabilitation of the Brick Factory: Early Soviet Popular Music." *Slavic Review*, vol. 39, no. 3 (1980), pp. 373–88.

Rougle, Charles. "The Intelligentsia in Russia, 1917–1918." In *Art, Society, Revolution: Russia 1917–1921*, edited by Nils A. Nilsson. Stockholm, 1979.

Sakwa, Richard. "The Commune State in Moscow in 1918." *Slavic Review*, vol. 46, no. 3/4 (1987), pp. 429–49.

Sass-Tissovskii, A. A. "Moi skitaniia." In *U istokov: Sbornik*, edited by I. P. Skachkov. Moscow, 1975.

Schapiro, Leonard. *The Communist Party of the Soviet Union*. 2d ed. New York, 1971.

Scheibert, Peter. "Lenin, Bogdanov and the Concept of Proletarian Culture." In *Lenin and Leninism*, edited by Bernard Eissenstat. Lexington, Mass., 1971.

Scherrer, Jutta. "Les écoles du parti de Capri et de Bologne: La formation de l'intelligentsia du parti." *Cahiers du monde russe et soviétique*, vol. 19 (1978), pp. 259–84.

———. " 'Ein gelber und ein blauer Teufel': Zur Entstehung der Begriffe 'bogostroitel'stvo' und 'bogoiskatel'stvo.' " *Forschungen zur osteuropäischen Geschichte*, vol. 25 (1978), pp. 319–29.

Schwarz, Boris. *Music and Musical Life in Soviet Russia*. Rev. ed. Bloomington, 1983.

Seemann, Klaus-Dieter. "Der Versuch einer proletarischen Kulturrevolution in Russland, 1917–1922." *Jahrbücher für Geschichte Osteuropas*, vol. 9 (1961), pp. 179–222.

Selunskaia, V. M., ed. *Izmeneniia sotsial'noi struktury sovetskogo obshchestva, Oktiabr' 1917–1929*. Moscow, 1976.

Semashko, N. "O dvukh zagranichnykh partiinykh shkolakh." *Proletarskaia revoliutsiia*, no. 3 (1923), pp. 142–51.

Seniushkin, F. M. *Kul'turno-prosvetitel'naia rabota professional'nykh soiuzov*. Moscow, 1924.

Service, Robert. *The Bolshevik Party in Revolution, 1917–1923: A Study in Organizational Change*. London, 1979.

Shakhov, G. A. *Maksim Maksimovich Shtraukh*. Moscow, 1964.

Shcheglov, A. V. *Bor'ba Lenina protiv bogdanovskoi revizii marksizma*. Moscow, 1937.

Shcheglov, D. "U istokov." In *U istokov: Sbornik*, edited by I. P. Skachkov. Moscow, 1960.

Sheshukov, S. *Neistovye revniteli: Iz istorii literaturnoi bor'by 20-kh godov*. Moscow, 1970.

Shklovskii, Viktor. *Khod konia: Sbornik statei*. Berlin, 1923.

Shtraukh, M. "Dva Sergeia Mikhailovicha." *Teatr*, no. 12 (1966), pp. 69–72.

Sirianni, Carmen. *Workers' Control and Socialist Democracy: The Soviet Experience*. London, 1982.

Slonim, Marc. *Russian Theater from the Empire to the Soviets*. Cleveland, 1961.

Smirnov, I. S. *Iz istorii stroitel'stva sotsialisticheskoi kul'tury v pervyi period sovetskoi vlasti*. 2d ed. Moscow, 1952.

———. *Lenin i sovetskaia kul'tura: Gosudarstvennaia deiatel'nost' V. I. Lenina v oblasti kul'turnogo stroitel'stva*. Moscow, 1960.

———. "Leninskaia kontseptsiia kul'turnoi revoliutsii i kritika Proletkul'ta." In *Istoricheskaia nauka i nekotorye problemy sovremennosti*, edited by M. Ia. Gefter. Moscow, 1969.

Smith, Canfield F. *Vladivostok under Red and White Rule*. Seattle, 1975.

Smith, S. A. "Craft Consciousness, Class Consciousness: Petrograd, 1917." *History Workshop*, no. 11 (1981), pp. 33–56.

———. *Red Petrograd: The Revolution in the Factories, 1917–1918*. Cambridge, Eng., 1983.

Smyshliaev, V. "Deiatel'nost' teatral'nogo otdela Moskovskogo Proletkul'ta." *Vestnik teatra*, no. 35 (1919), pp. 4–5.

Sochor, Zenovia A. *Revolution and Culture: The Bogdanov-Lenin Controversy*. Ithaca, 1988.

———. "Soviet Taylorism Revisited." *Soviet Studies*, vol. 33, no. 2 (1981), pp. 246–64.

———. "Was Bogdanov Russia's Answer to Gramsci?" *Studies in Soviet Thought*, vol. 22 (1981), pp. 59–81.

Sorenson, Jay B. *The Life and Death of Soviet Trade Unionism, 1917–1928*. New York, 1969.

Soskin, V. L. *Kul'turnaia zhizn' Sibiri v pervye gody novoi ekonomicheskoi politiki, 1921–1923 gg*. Novosibirsk, 1971.

———. *Ocherki istorii kul'tury Sibiri v gody revoliutsii i grazhdanskoi voiny*. Novosibirsk, 1965.

Soskin, V. L., and V. P. Butorin. "Proletkul't v Sibiri." In *Problemy istorii sovetskoi Sibiri: Sbornik nauchnykh trudov*, edited by A. S. Moskovskii. Novosibirsk, 1973.

Speranskaia, E. "Materialy k istorii oformleniia pervykh revoliutsionnykh prazdnestv v Saratove i Nizhnem Novgorode." In *Agitatsionno-massovoe iskusstvo pervykh let Oktiabria: Materialy i issledovaniia*, edited by E. A. Speranskaia. Moscow, 1971.

Spirtus, B. D. "Razoblachenie Kommunisticheskoi partii reaktsionnoi sushchnosti mekhanisticheskoi kontseptsii A. A. Bogdanova i ideologii 'Proletkul'tovtsev.'" *Izvestiia Krymskogo pedagogicheskogo instituta*, vol. 36 (1961), pp. 129–43.

Startsev, Abel. *Russkie bloknoty Dzhona Rida*. Moscow, 1968.

Stedman Jones, Gareth. *Languages of Class: Studies in English Working Class History, 1832–1982*. Cambridge, Eng., 1983.

Stites, Richard. "Iconoclastic Currents in the Russian Revolution: Destroying and Preserving the Past." In *Bolshevik Culture: Experiment and Order in the Russian Revolution*, edited by Abbott Gleason, Peter Kenez, and Richard Stites. Bloomington, 1985.

———. *Revolutionary Dreams: Utopian Visions and Experimental Life in the Russian Revolution*. New York, 1989.

———. "Utopias in the Air and on the Ground: Futuristic

Dreams in the Russian Revolution." *Russian History*, vol. 11, no. 2/3 (1984), pp. 236–57.

——— . *The Women's Liberation Movement in Russia: Feminism, Nihilism and Bolshevism, 1860–1930*. Princeton, 1978.

Struve, Gleb. *Russian Literature under Lenin and Stalin, 1917–1953*. Norman, Ok., 1971.

Sukhanov, N. N. *The Russian Revolution: A Personal Record.* Edited and translated by Joel Carmichael. Princeton, 1984.

Susiluoto, Ilmari. *The Origins and Development of Systems Thinking in the Soviet Union*. Helsinki, 1982.

Suvorov, L. N. "Iz istorii bor'by V. I. Lenina, partii bol'shevikov protiv bogdanovskoi 'organizatsionnoi nauki.' " *Filosofskie nauki*, no. 3 (1966), pp. 83–91.

Swain, Geoffrey. *Russian Social Democracy and the Legal Labour Movement*. London, 1983.

T., M. "V Moskovskom Proletkul'te." *Narodnoe prosveshchenie*, no. 32 (1919), pp. 19–21.

Tamashin, L. *Sovetskaia dramaturgiia v gody grazhdanskoi voiny*. Moscow, 1961.

Tandler, Frederika M. "The Workers' Faculty (Rabfak) System in the USSR." Ph.D. dissertation, Teachers College, Columbia University, 1955.

Tarabukin, N. "Proletarskii khudozhnik." *Rabochii zhurnal*, no. 3/4 (1924), pp. 135–38.

Tarasova, S. S. "Kul'turnoe stroitel'stvo v pervyi god sovetskoi vlasti." In *Pobeda Velikoi Oktiabr'skoi sotsialisticheskoi revoliutsii*, edited by G. N. Golikov. Moscow, 1957.

Teatral'naia entsiklopediia. Moscow, 1961–1967.

Thun, Nyota. *Das erste Jahrzehnt: Kulturpolitik und Kulturrevolution in der Sowjetunion*. Munich, 1974.

Thurston, Gary. "The Impact of Russian Popular Theatre, 1886–1915." *Journal of Modern History*, vol. 55, no. 2 (1983), pp. 237–67.

Tirado, Isabelle A. "The Socialist Youth Movement in Petrograd." *Russian Review*, vol. 46, no. 2 (1987), pp. 135–55.

Tolstoi, V. P. "Materialy k istorii agitatsionnogo iskusstva perioda grazhdanskoi voiny," *Soobshcheniia instituta isto-rii i iskusstv, Akademiia nauk SSSR*, no. 3 (1953), pp. 26–68.

Trifonov, N. A. *A. V. Lunacharskii i sovetskaia literatura*. Moscow, 1974.

Trotsky, Leon. *Literature and Revolution*. Ann Arbor, 1975.

Tumarkin, Nina. *Lenin Lives! The Lenin Cult in Soviet Russia*. Cambridge, Mass., 1983.

Utechin, S. V. "Philosophy and Society: Alexander Bogdanov." In *Revisionism: Essays on the History of Marxist Ideas*, edited by Leopold Labedz. London, 1962.

Valentinov, Nikolay. *Encounters with Lenin*. Translated by Paul Rosta and Brian Pearce. London, 1968.

Valkenier, Elizabeth. *Russian Realist Art*. Ann Arbor, 1977.

Vasil'ev-Buglai, Dmitrii. "Na fronte v 1918 godu." *Sovetskaia muzyka*, no. 2 (1940), pp. 12–15.

Vladimirov, Maksim. "Chudesa chelovecheskie." *Nedelia*, no. 32 (1974), pp. 6–7.

Vogeler, Heinrich. *Proletkunst: Kunst und Kultur in der kommunistischen Gesellschaft*. Hannover, 1920.

Voitinskii, N. "O gruppe 'Vpered,' 1907–1917 gg." *Proletarskaia revoliutsiia*, no. 12 (1929), pp. 59–119.

Volkov, V. S., ed. *Sovetskaia intelligentsiia: Kratkii ocherk istorii, 1917–1975 gg*. Moscow, 1977.

Volodin, A. I. "Iz istorii bor'by protiv makhizma." *Voprosy filosofii*, no. 6 (1959), pp. 132–36.

von Geldern, James R. *Festivals of the Revolution, 1917–1920: Art and Theater in the Formation of Soviet Culture*. Forthcoming.

von Hagen, Mark. *The Red Army and the Revolution: Soldiers' Politics and State-Building in Soviet Russia, 1917–1930*. Forthcoming.

Voprosy kul'tury pri diktature proletariata: Sbornik. Moscow and Leningrad, 1925.

Vucinich, Alexander S. *Science in Russian Culture, 1861–1917*. Stanford, 1970.

——— . *Social Thought in Tsarist Russia: The Quest for a General Science of Society, 1861–1917*. Chicago, 1976.

Wade, Rex A. *Red Guards and Workers' Militias in the Russian Revolution.* Stanford, 1984.

Weber, Richard. *Proletarisches Theater und revolutionäre Arbeiterbewegung, 1918–1925.* Cologne, 1978.

White, James D. "Bogdanov in Tula." *Studies in Soviet Thought,* vol. 22 (1981), pp. 33–58.

Wilbert, Gerd. " 'Linke' Kunst und Proletkul't in Sovetrussland, 1918–1919." In *Von der Revolution zum Schriftstellerkongress: Entwicklungsstrukturen und Funktionsbestimmungen der russischen Literatur und Kultur zwischen 1917 und 1934,* edited by G. Erler, R. Grübel, K. Mänicke-Gyöngyösi, and P. Scherber. Berlin, 1979.

Wildman, Allan K. *The Making of a Workers' Revolution: Russian Social Democracy, 1891–1903.* Chicago, 1967.

Willett, John. *Art and Politics in the Weimar Period, 1917–1933: The New Sobriety.* New York, 1978.

Williams, Robert C. *Artists in Revolution: Portraits of the Russian Avant-Garde, 1905–1925.* Bloomington, 1977.

———. "Collective Immortality: The Syndicalist Origins of Proletarian Culture, 1905–1910." *Slavic Review,* vol. 39, no. 3 (1980), pp. 389–402.

———. "The Nationalization of Early Soviet Culture." *Russian History,* vol. 9, no. 2/3 (1982), pp. 157–72.

———. *The Other Bolsheviks: Lenin and his Critics, 1904–1914.* Bloomington, 1985.

Wolfe, Bertram D. *The Bridge and the Abyss: The Troubled Friendship of Maxim Gorky and V. I. Lenin.* New York, 1967.

———. *Three Who Made a Revolution.* New York, 1964.

Wolkonsky, Serge. *My Reminiscences.* 2 vols. Translated by A. E. Chamot. London, 1924.

Yassour, Avraham. "Lenin and Bogdanov: Protagonists in the 'Bolshevik Center.' " *Studies in Soviet Thought,* vol. 22 (1981), pp. 1–32.

Zaichenko, N. S., ed. *Organizatsionnye kursy po kul'turno-prosvetitel'nomu delu na zheleznykh dorogakh.* Moscow, 1918.

Zaidman, A. D. "M. Gor'kii i Proletkul't," *Uchenye zapiski*

Gor'kovskogo gosudarstvennogo universiteta, istoriko-filologicheskaia seriia, vol. 65 (1964), pp. 138–69.

Zak, L. M. "Voprosy kul'turnogo stroitel'stva v sovetskoi istoricheskoi literature." In *Kul'turnaia revoliutsiia v SSSR, 1917–1965 gg.*, edited by M. P. Kim. Moscow, 1967.

Zakharchenko, N. V. "Kogda i kak obrazovalas' 'Kuznitsa.' " *Filologicheskie nauki*, no. 4 (1973), pp. 15–27.

———. " 'Kuznitsa' i Proletkul't." In *Pisatel' i literaturnyi protsess*, edited by I. M. Toibin. Vol. 2. Dushanbe, 1974.

Zavalishin, Viacheslav. *Early Soviet Writers*. New York, 1958.

Zelinskii, K. L. *Na rubezhe dvukh epokh*. Moscow, 1962.

Zelnik, Reginald E. *Labor and Society in Tsarist Russia: The Factory Workers of St. Petersburg, 1855–1870*. Stanford, 1971.

———. "Russian Bebels: An Introduction to the Memoirs of Semen Kanatchikov and Matvei Fisher." *Russian Review*, vol. 35, no. 2 (1976), pp. 249–89; vol. 35, no. 3 (1976), pp. 417–47.

Zolotnitskii, D. *Budni i prazdniki teatral'nogo Oktiabria*. Leningrad, 1978.

———. "Teatral'nye studii Proletkul'ta." *Teatr i dramaturgiia: Trudy Leningradskogo gosudarstvennogo instituta teatra, muzyki i kinematografii*, vol. 3 (1971), pp. 126–205.

———. *Zori teatral'nogo Oktiabria*. Leningrad, 1976.

Index

Compositor: Interactive Composition Corp.
Printer: Maple-Vail Book Mfg. Group
Binder: Maple-Vail Book Mfg. Group
Text: 10/13 Aster
Display: Helvetica Condensed, Aster